An Age of Progress?

An Age of Progress?

Clashing Twentieth-Century Global Forces

WALTER G. MOSS

ANTHEM PRESS
LONDON · NEW YORK · DELHI

Anthem Press
An imprint of Wimbledon Publishing Company
www.anthempress.com

This edition first published in UK and USA 2008
by ANTHEM PRESS
75-76 Blackfriars Road, London SE1 8HA, UK
or PO Box 9779, London SW19 7ZG, UK
and
244 Madison Ave. #116, New York, NY 10016, USA

British Library Cataloguing in Publication Data
A catalogue record for this book is available from the British Library.

Library of Congress Cataloging in Publication Data
Moss, Walter.
An age of progress? : clashing twentieth-century global forces /
Walter G. Moss.
p. cm.
ISBN 978-1-84331-301-4 (Hbk.)
1. History, Modern—20th century. I. Title.

D421.M626 2008
909.82—dc22
2007042449

ISBN-10: 1 84331 301 4 (Hbk)
ISBN-13: 978 1 84331 301 4 (Hbk)

1 3 5 7 9 10 8 6 4 2

Printed in India

To Nancy, our children, and grandchildren

Contents

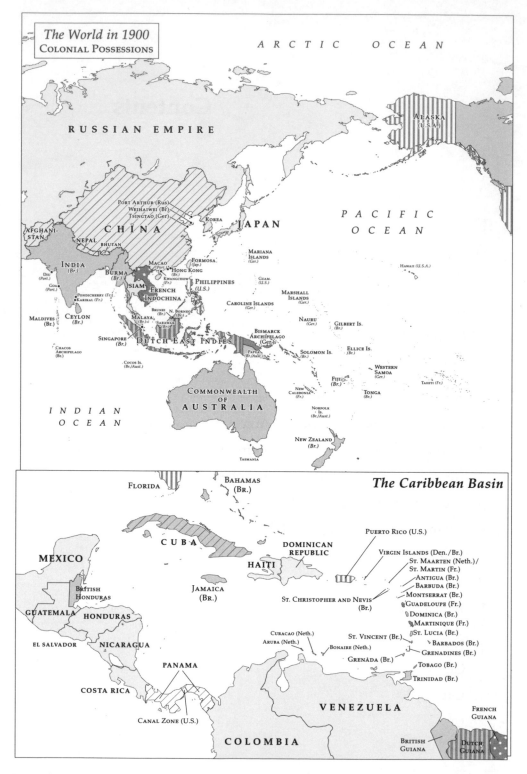

The World in 1900
Colonial Possessions

ARCTIC OCEAN

RUSSIAN EMPIRE

ALASKA (U.S.A.)

PACIFIC OCEAN

Port Arthur (Rus)
Weihaiwei (Br.)
Tsingtao (Ger.)

AFGHANI-STAN

NEPAL
BHUTAN

CHINA

KOREA

JAPAN

INDIA (Br.)

DIU (Port.)
GOA (Port.)

BURMA (Br.)

MACAO (Port.)
HONG KONG (Br.)
KWANGCHOW (Fr.)

FORMOSA (Jap.)

MARIANA ISLANDS (Ger.)

HAWAII (U.S.A.)

PONDICHERRY (Fr.)
KARIKAL (Fr.)

SIAM

FRENCH INDOCHINA

PHILIPPINES (U.S.)

GUAM (U.S.)

MALDIVES (Br.)

CEYLON (Br.)

CHAGOS ARCHIPELAGO (Br.)

MALAYA

SINGAPORE (Br.)

BRUNEI (Br.)
N. BORNEO (Br.)
SARAWAK (Br.)

DUTCH EAST INDIES

COCOS IS. (Br./Aust.)

MARSHALL ISLANDS (Ger.)

CAROLINE ISLANDS (Ger.)

NAURU (Ger.)

GILBERT IS. (Br.)

BISMARCK ARCHIPELAGO (Ger.)

PAPUA (Br./Aust.)

SOLOMON IS. (Br.)

ELLICE IS. (Br.)

WESTERN SAMOA (Ger.)

TAHITI (Fr.)

FIJI (Br.)

NEW CALEDONIA (Fr.)

TONGA (Br.)

INDIAN OCEAN

COMMONWEALTH OF AUSTRALIA

NORFOLK IS. (Br./Aust.)

NEW ZEALAND (Br.)

TASMANIA

The Caribbean Basin

FLORIDA

BAHAMAS (Br.)

PUERTO RICO (U.S.)

CUBA

DOMINICAN REPUBLIC

HAITI

VIRGIN ISLANDS (Den./Br.)
ST. MAARTEN (Neth.)/ ST. MARTIN (Fr.)
ANTIGUA (Br.)
BARBUDA (Br.)
MONTSERRAT (Br.)
GUADELOUPE (Fr.)
DOMINICA (Br.)
MARTINIQUE (Fr.)
ST. LUCIA (Br.)
BARBADOS (Br.)
GRENADINES (Br.)
TOBAGO (Br.)
TRINIDAD (Br.)

MEXICO

BRITISH HONDURAS

GUATEMALA
HONDURAS

EL SALVADOR
NICARAGUA

JAMAICA (Br.)

ST. CHRISTOPHER AND NEVIS (Br.)

CURACAO (Neth.)
ARUBA (Neth.)

BONAIRE (Neth.)

ST. VINCENT (Br.)

GRENADA (Br.)

PANAMA

COSTA RICA

CANAL ZONE (U.S.)

COLOMBIA

VENEZUELA

FRENCH GUIANA

BRITISH GUIANA

DUTCH GUIANA

Maps from: Richard Goff, Walter Moss, Janice Terry, Jiu-Hwa Upshur, and Michael Schroeder, *The Twentieth Century and Beyond: A Global History*, 7th ed. (McGraw Hill, 2008). Reproduced with permission of The McGraw-Hill Companies.

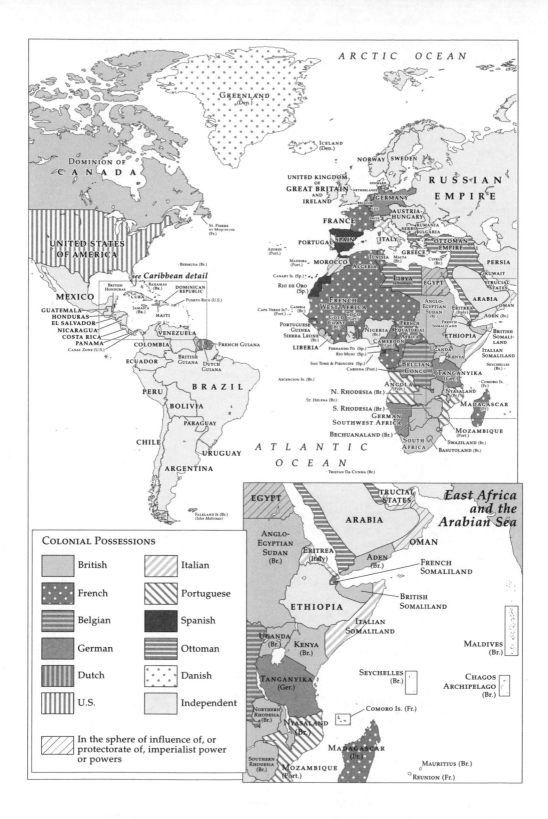

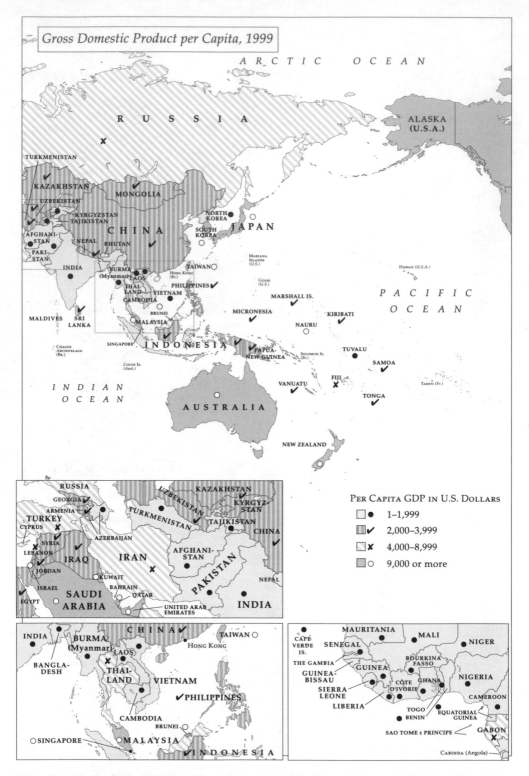

Maps from: Richard Goff, Walter Moss, Janice Terry, Jiu-Hwa Upshur, and Michael Schroeder,
The Twentieth Century and Beyond: A Global History, 7th ed. (McGraw Hill, 2008).
Reproduced with permission of The McGraw-Hill Companies.

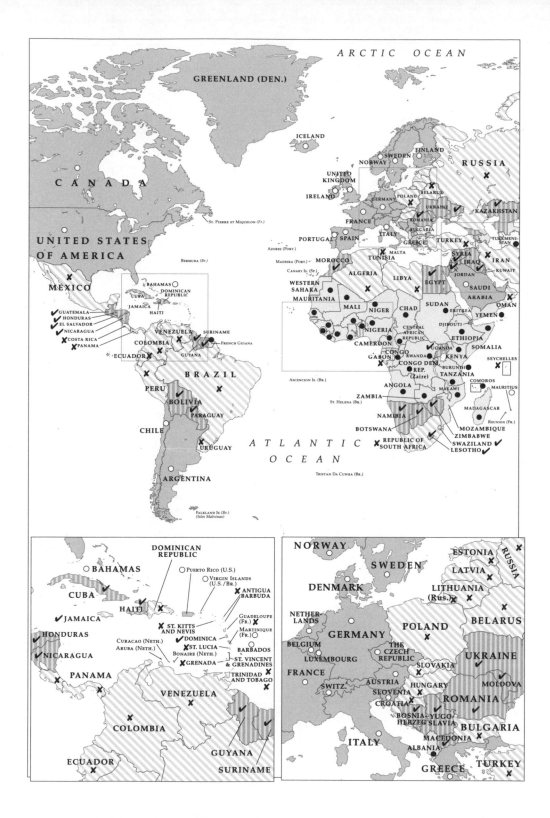

Chronology

1898–1902	Spanish-American War (1898) and major Filipino resistance to U.S. takeover
1899–1900	Famine in India
1899–1902	Boer War; War of a Thousand Days in Colombia
1900	Anarchist Gaetano Bresci assassinates King Humbert of Italy World population about 1.6 billion of whom more than five-sixths live in rural areas British Labour Party formed Boxer Rebellion in China Publication of Sigmund Freud's *The Interpretation of Dreams* Death of philosopher Friedrich Nietzsche
1901	Anarchist Leon Czolgosz shoots and kills U.S. President McKinley, who is replaced by Theodore Roosevelt First successful commercial tractor appears in Iowa
1903	Wright Brothers achieve first flight of a power-driven airplane heavier than air
1904–5	Russo-Japanese War
1907	Second international peace conference held at The Hague, Netherlands
1910	Death of Leo Tolstoy; Mexican Revolution begins

1912   Theodore Roosevelt runs for U.S. president on
              Progressive Party ticket but loses

1913   First moving assembly line produces Henry Ford's
              Model T cars
            Rabindranath Tagore receives Nobel Prize for
              Literature
            Igor Stravinsky's modernistic ballet *The Rite of Spring*
              creates uproar at its Paris premier

1914   WWI begins

1915–6   Armenian Genocide occurs in Ottoman Turkish Empire

1916   More than 1 million casualties result from the Battle of
              the Somme

1917   USA enters WWI
            At third battle of Ypres, British fire over 4 million
              artillery shells in 19 days
            Russian revolutions end Tsarist rule and later in the
              year bring communists to power under Lenin
            Mexican Constitution produced amidst years of
              revolution

1918   WWI ends; women over 30 vote for first time in British
              national election

1918–9   Worldwide influenza epidemic

1918–21   Civil War in Russia

1919   Paris Peace Conference; League of Nations created but
              USA never joins
            Woodrow Wilson's principal of self-determination
              limited to some European areas
            International Labor Organization (ILO) formed

1919–21   Irish nationalists' war for independence against Great
              Britain, followed by Irish civil war until 1923

1920   First licensed commercial radio station established in
              USA
            U.S. women vote for first time in national elections
            Soviet government legalizes abortion

1920s   Harlem Renaissance of U.S. black culture

1921   Soviet Russia institutes New Economic Policy (NEP)
              allowing small-scale private enterprise

1922   Benito Mussolini becomes prime minister in Italy

	Publication of James Joyce's novel *Ulysses*, T. S. Eliot's poem *The Waste Land*, and Herman Hesse's novel *Siddhartha*
1924	Death of Lenin; 1st British Labour government comes to power but lasts less than a year
1925	Scopes "Monkey Trial" in USA
1927	First sound movie, *The Jazz Singer* First tuberculosis vaccine
1928	Penicillin discovered
1928	Stalin ends NEP and begins First Five Year Plan
1929	Soviet forced collectivization begins U.S. stock market crash; Global Depression begins
1930	José Ortega y Gasset's *The Revolt of the Masses* published
1930–45	Rule of Getúlio Vargas in Brazil (ruled again 1951–4)
1931–3	Soviet famine kills millions, especially in Ukraine
1932	U.S. unemployment rate reaches 25 percent; Aldous Huxley's *Brave New World* published
1933	Hitler assumes power in Germany; Roosevelt's New Deal initiated
1935	Nuremburg Laws deprive German Jews of citizenship
1936–9	Spanish Civil War; Stalin has many Soviet political and military leaders executed
1937	Japan launches a full-scale attack on China Pablo Picasso paints *Guernica*, one of the greatest paintings of the century
1937–41	U.S. Supreme Court makes various decisions friendly to labor and greatly expands the role of the Federal government in the regulation of commerce and manufacturing
1939	WWII begins in Europe
1939–40	USSR takes over territories on its western border
1941	Franklin Roosevelt gives his Four Freedoms speech to U.S. Congress

	German invasion of the USSR Siege of Leningrad begins, by its end in 1944 one million Leningraders have perished USA enters WWII after Japanese bombing of Pearl Harbor
1942	Nazi leaders agree on "Final Solution" to kill Europe's Jews
1943	German forces surrender at Stalingrad Drug companies begin mass producing penicillin (the first antibiotic drug)
1944	D-Day landing of British and U.S. troops on French coast International Monetary Fund and the World Bank created
1945	Allied leaders of UK, USA, and USSR meet at Yalta and Potsdam conferences Atomic bombs dropped on Hiroshima and Nagasaki; WWII ends; UN comes into existence
1945–9	Civil War in China
1945–51	British Labour Party in power and inaugurates Welfare State, including British National Health Service Act of 1946, making everyone eligible for free medical services
1946	Winston Churchill first uses term "iron curtain" to describe separation of eastern and western Europe; Khrushchev later simplistically asserts that Churchill's speech marked the beginning of the Cold War
1947	India and Pakistan obtain independence First jet plane flown faster than the speed of sound Invention of the transistor makes possible great expansion of radio use
1948	Mahatma Gandhi assassinated; Israel becomes a state UN approves Universal Declaration of Human Rights World Council of Churches established
1949	1st Soviet atomic bomb tested; communists take over Chinese mainland Indonesia obtains independence

George Orwell's *1984* and Simone de Beauvoir's
The Second Sex published

1950   World population reaches 2.5 billion
                Indian Constitution of 1950 abolishes
                   "untouchability," but discrimination against
                   Dalits continues

1950–3   Korean War

1953   Death of Stalin; two British scientists demonstrate the
                   makeup of DNA

1954   French defeat in Indochina leads to independence
                   for Laos, Cambodia, and a divided Vietnam
                U.S. Supreme Court rules that segregated public
                   schools are unconstitutional

1954–62   Algerian Revolution against French control

1955   Polio vaccine licensed; McDonald's Corporation begins
                   opening franchises and by 1963 sells over
                   1 billion hamburgers

1956   UK Clean Air Act passed; Hungarian rebellion put
                   down by Soviet troops

1957   USSR launches Sputnik, the first manmade satellite,
                   into space
                U.S. government agency approves first pill (Enovid)
                   that can be used to prevent pregnancy
                Survey of young French adults lists Jean Paul Sartre as
                   the writer who most influenced their generation
                Albert Camus receives Nobel Prize for Literature
                Boris Pasternak's *Doctor Zhivago* smuggled out of
                   Russia and published abroad

1958–9   China launches Great Leap Forward triggering the
                   largest famine in Chinese history

1959   Invention of the silicon chip makes possible the
                   computer age; Fidel Castro comes to power in Cuba
                Sir Charles Snow delivers lecture "The Two Cultures"

1960   John Kennedy elected U.S. president

Early 1960s   Many African countries including Algeria, Kenya, and
                   Nigeria become independent
                "Green Revolution" begins in Asia increasing crop
                   production

1960–75   Second Indochina War

1961   Chairman of the U.S. Federal Communication
               Commission (FCC), refers to TV as a "vast
               wasteland"
               Frantz Fanon's *The Wretched of the Earth* and Michel
               Foucault's first major work, *The History of Madness in
               the Classical Age*, are published

1962   Cuban Missile Crisis
               Rachel Carson's *Silent Spring* and Milton Friedman's
               Capitalism and Freedom are published
               Second Vatican Council

1963   Britain, USA, USSR, and other countries sign Nuclear
               Test Ban Treaty
               Martin Luther King's "I Have a Dream" speech
               U.S. President John Kennedy assassinated
               Anthropologist Jules Henry's *Culture Against Man*
               criticizes U.S. culture

1964   Nikita Khrushchev ousted as head of Soviet
               Communist Party, replaced by Leonid Brezhnev
               Beatles appear on "The Ed Sullivan Show" and are
               viewed by one-third of the U.S. population
               Herbert Marcuse's *One-Dimensional Man* published

1965   U.S. President Lyndon Johnson institutes Affirmative
               Action
               First U.S. combat troops sent to Vietnam

1966   Mao Zedong begins Cultural Revolution in China

1967   Arab-Israeli Six-Day War leads to major Israeli
               territorial gains; first human heart transplant
               Gabriel García Márquez's *One Hundred Years of
               Solitude* appears and is translated into 32 languages by
               1981
               Three important deconstructionist books by Jacques
               Derrida, including *Of Grammatology*, are published

1968   U.S. reaches maximum troop strength in Vietnam
               Student rebellions in the United States and Europe
               reach their peak
               Czechoslovakian reform movement ended by Soviet
               troops

1969   U.S. astronauts land on the moon, moonwalk viewed
               by over a half a billion media viewers worldwide
            Nicaraguan Revolution led by Sandinistas
            Woodstock music festival in New York state

1970   1st Earth Day held; U.S. Environmental Protection
               Agency (EPA) created

1971   East Pakistan secessionist war against West Pakistan
            Microprocessors first appear and soon greatly expand
               power of computers

1972   First major international conference on the
               environment held in Stockholm

1973   U.S. Supreme Court (in Roe v. Wade) upholds woman's
               right to an abortion

1975   Helsinki Accords on human rights and other matters
            North and South Vietnam reunited under a
               communist government
            Andrei Sakharov awarded Nobel Peace Prize
            Alexander Solzhenitsyn receives Nobel Prize for
               Literature

1975–9   In Cambodia, Pol Pot and his Khmer Rouge
               responsible for over 1 million deaths

1976   Death of China's Mao Zedong; Jimmy Carter elected
               U.S. president
            Grameen Bank founded, made first micro-loan

1978   Polish cardinal becomes Pope John Paul II
               (until his death in 2005)

1979   Margaret Thatcher becomes British prime minister until
               1990
            Shah of Iran overthrown, Islamic fundamentalist
               government established
            Moral Majority, a conservative political lobbying
               group, founded in USA

1980   Ronald Reagan elected U.S. president
               (re-elected in 1984)

1980–8   Iran-Iraq War

1981   Polish government declares martial law and outlaws
               Solidarity trade union
            1st *World Values Survey* conducted

1984	India's Indira Gandhi assassinated; IRA attempt to kill Margaret Thatcher fails
1985	Mikhail Gorbachev becomes head of USSR Communist Party and begins reforms
1986	Nuclear accident at Chernobyl power station in Soviet Ukraine spews forth tons of radioactive particles
1987	By the Montreal Protocol, 46 nations agreed to reduce chlorofluorocarbon emissions Global military spending reaches $1.8 million per minute
1988	Harvard University granted a patent on genetically-engineered mouse
1989	Oil tanker Exxon Valdez spills 34,000 tons of oil into Prince William Sound on Alaska's Pacific Ocean coast
1989–90	Communist regimes fall in eastern Europe; Cold War ends
1990	Nelson Mandela freed from 27-years' imprisonment Reunification of Germany
1990–1	1st Persian Gulf War
1991	Wars break out in Yugoslavia leading to its eventual disintegration
1991	Soviet Union collapses
1992	UN Conference on Environment and Development held in Rio de Janeiro
1993	A truck bomb set off at the twin towers of NY's World Trade Center injures about 1,000 people and kills 6
1994	Nelson Mandela becomes president of South Africa Hutu–Tutsi clash in Rwanda and Burundi kills approximately 800,000 people, primarily Tutsis in a Rwandan genocide
1995	World Trade Organization (WTO) replaces GATT Russian life-expectancy estimate for males drops to age 58

Oklahoma City bombing of a U.S. federal building kills
168 people

1996   Sokal Hoax parodies postmodern deconstructionist
thought

1997   British Labour Party assumes power under Tony Blair
Hong Kong reverts to Chinese control
Asian Financial Crisis begins
General Motors, Proctor & Gamble, Phillip Morris, and
Chrysler spend more than $6.5 billion on advertising
Scottish scientists announce cloning of a lamb
Kyoto Protocol negotiated in attempt to deal with
global warming, but USA only major power not to
ratify it

1998   9 of 10 cities having earth's worst air pollution are in
China
Al-Qaeda responsible for bombings at U.S. embassies in
Nairobi, Kenya, and Dar es Salaam, Tanzania

1999   NATO bombing of Serbia; Russians launch major
offensive in Chechnia
Global population goes over 6 billion people,
almost half now live in urban areas but slum
inhabitants comprise about one-third of the
global urban population
Global life expectancy estimated at about 66 years
(as compared to 48 years in 1955)
More Africans die of AIDS than in the previous
10 years combined
Amartya Sen's *Development as Freedom* published

An Age of Progress?

Preface

As this book's subtitle indicates, it will examine many of the main twentieth-century global forces, which often clashed with one another. This work also attempts to present different, also often conflicting, viewpoints about these forces. And the question mark in the book's title (*An Age of Progress?*) suggests that contending judgments exist as to whether the century was one of overall progress. Thus, the following pages are more of an analysis and assessment of the century than an introduction to it, and are intended for students or general readers who already possess a basic knowledge of it. A rough draft of this manuscript was used in an advanced team-taught undergraduate seminar in the winter of 2007, and it stimulated much healthy debate.

As with any work dealing with twentieth-century global history, this work is limited and selective. It deals with some, but not all, of the important trends of the century. Within these trends, it concentrates more on developments within the more industrialized world of western Europe, the United States, and Russia/USSR than on those in the less industrially developed parts of the world.

There are two reasons for the relative neglect of areas outside of the industrialized West and Russia. First, except for Russian history, which I have taught and written about for many years, my knowledge of non-Western countries is simply too limited to do more than mention some ways that my main trends interacted with them. Secondly, the major developments of the century involved the industrialized West and Russia more than any other areas. In writing his *The Modern Mind: An Intellectual History of the 20th Century*, Peter Watson had intended to "delve into the major non-Western cultures to identify their important ideas and their important thinkers, be they philosophers, writers, scientists, or composers," but when he turned to specialists in non-Western cultures, he was told by all those he consulted that "the non-Western cultures have produced no body of work that can compare with the ideas of the West." He also concluded that the major innovations of the twentieth century were "almost entirely Western." Thus, his final 800-page plus book was primarily about Western cultural developments. A strong argument has also been made for the importance of Russia's global influence.[1]

In addition, as Chapter 7 emphasizes, we are all creatures of the cultures and sub-cultures we have belonged to, and however hard we attempt to overcome our provincialism, we are still shaped by them. Born as a white male in the United States and recipient of a Catholic liberal arts education that emphasized primarily the contributions of Western civilization, I will always be influenced by my upbringing and see the world from the viewpoint of a privileged U.S. citizen. Wide-reading, travel, and an effort to understand other cultures can only mitigate such provincialism, never completely overcome it.

Teaching twentieth-century civilization for almost three decades and co-authoring for a quarter of a century a twentieth-century text (now called *The Twentieth Century and Beyond: A Global History*) along with specialists in American, Middle Eastern, and Asian history has helped, however, to broaden my global understanding. Thus, I owe a debt to my longtime co-authors of that text, Richard Goff, Janice Terry, and Jiu-Hwa Upshur. I am also indebted to a new co-author of that work, Michael Schroeder, whose expertise is in Latin American history. In the team-taught seminar mentioned above, Michael co-directed it with me and read and commented on the entire manuscript, providing many valuable suggestions. Although our perspectives on the twentieth century continue to differ in a number of ways, he has helped broaden my outlook and knowledge of global developments. Responses from our students in this class also helped to improve the manuscript, with Ryan Cronkhite being especially helpful. In addition, my colleague Pamela Graves also read over the entire work, and I am indebted to her for her careful reading and suggestions.

At Eastern Michigan University, I am also grateful for the administrative support I received from Gersham Nelson, Philip Schmitz, Linda Schott, and Kate Mehuron, and for the help of two graduate assistants, Antonio Salinas and Paul Doran. At Anthem Press, Tej Sood oversaw the preparation of this manuscript in a manner that was both efficient and pleasant. My greatest debt, however, is to my wife, Nancy, who has once again proofread pages countless times and helped me in so many other ways. And our daughter, Jennifer, provided some useful environmental information.

In dealing with the issue of endnotes, I have tried to keep them limited primarily to citing the sources of most quotations and offering guidance for further reading. In that the Internet is increasingly becoming a source of reliable (and unreliable) information, I have also included many references to websites. In addition to the endnotes, readers will also find a Chronology and Glossary that will help them keep track of the major events of the century and indicate how I define some key terms, including disputed ones like terrorism. More information relating to modern Russia can be found in my *A History of Russia*, 2d ed., vol. 2 (also published by Anthem Press). Much general information on twentieth century global history can be found in the work mentioned above, *The Twentieth Century and Beyond: A Global History*, 7th ed. (McGraw-Hill, 2007). McGraw-Hill has also been kind enough to allow reproduction of two maps from that text.

1

A Century of Violence

Wars, assassinations, atrocities—these words appeared often in the twentieth century. No earlier century had witnessed as much killing. Population increases provided more people to kill; technological developments provided more efficient means to do so; and expanding media coverage informed more people about such killings and horrors as the century proceeded.

History books, however, are better at providing mind-numbing statistics regarding all this killing than they are at conveying much feeling for the millions of individual tragedies caused by it. The British novelist Ian McEwan hinted at this problem when he wrote about one of his characters:

> He was struck by the recently concluded war [World War II] not as a historical, geopolitical fact but as a multiplicity, a near-infinity of private sorrows, as a boundless grief minutely subdivided without diminishment among individuals who covered the continent like dust . . . For the first time he sensed the scale of the catastrophe in terms of feeling; all those unique and solitary deaths, all that consequent sorrow, unique and solitary too, which had no place in conferences, headlines, history, and which had quietly retired to houses, kitchens, unshared beds, and anguished memories.[1]

Some feeling for all these tragedies is also sometimes conveyed by first-hand accounts. A few early ones are provided here, and readers can only attempt to imagine some of the other millions of tragedies which lie behind the gruesome statistics of the remainder of the century.

Wars and Deaths at the Century's Beginning

The century began in bloodshed. In the Philippines, following the Spanish–American War (1898), tens of thousands of U.S. troops battled Filipino guerrilla forces resisting the U.S. takeover of this area won from Spain. From 1899–1902 both sides committed atrocities, and more than 4,000 U.S. troops died while the number of Filipino combatant and non-combatant deaths in the war is usually estimated at over 200,000. Here is what one participating U.S. officer had to say about the conflict:

> Our men have been relentless, have killed to exterminate men, women, and children, prisoners and captives, active insurgents and suspected people, from lads of ten up, an idea prevailing that the Filipino was little better than a dog, a noisome reptile in some instances, whose best disposition was the rubbish heap. Our soldiers have pumped salt water into men "to make them talk," have taken prisoners of people who had held up their hands and peacefully surrendered, and, an hour later, without an atom of evidence to show that they were even insurrectos, stood them up on a bridge, and shot them down one by one to drop into the water below and float down as examples to those who found their bullet-loaded corpses.[2]

Other soldiers who served in the Philippines made the following comments. One wrote:

> There is not a feature of the whole miserable business that a patriotic American citizen, one who loves to read of the brave deeds of the American colonists in the splendid struggle for American independence, can look upon with complacency, much less with pride. This war is reversing history. It places the American people and the government of the United States in the position occupied by Great Britain in 1776. It is an utterly causeless and defenseless war, and it should be abandoned by this government without delay. The longer it is continued, the greater crime it becomes—a crime against human liberty as well as against Christianity and civilization.

Another soldier described a specific attack as such:

> We burned hundreds of houses and looted hundreds more. Some of the boys made good hauls of jewelry and clothing. Nearly every man has at least two suits of clothing, and our quarters are furnished in style; fine beds with silken drapery, mirrors, chairs, rockers, cushions, pianos, hanging-lamps, rugs, pictures, etc. We have horses and carriages, and bull-carts galore, and enough furniture and other plunder to load a steamer.

Another soldier wrote:

> We bombarded a place called Malabon, and then we went in and killed every native we met, men, women, and children. It was a dreadful sight, the killing

of the poor creatures. The natives captured some of the Americans and literally hacked them to pieces, so we got orders to spare no one.[3]

In South Africa, British troops were engaged in the Boer War (1899–1902) against the Boers, who were primarily descendants of Dutch colonists. It was also a brutal conflict with atrocities on both sides before the British were finally victorious.

Besides the above conflicts, there were still others continuing or breaking out in 1900. In West Africa, tightening imperialist controls occasioned rebellion among the Ashanti people of the Gold Coast (modern-day Ghana). In northeastern Africa, Mohammed bin Abdullah Hassan, whom the British referred to as the Mad Mullah, had begun a military campaign to unite the Somalis and drive out the British infidels. With varying degrees of intensity, this warrior and self-proclaimed Mahdi (Islamic prophet/savior) continued his jihad (holy war) until British bombing and his death in 1920 ended the rebellion. In other parts of Africa, imperialist oppression and native resistance combined to produce numerous additional deaths during the first decade of the new century. In the Congo Free State, which was anything but "free," King Leopold of Belgium ruled as his personal possession a territory larger than the combined area of Germany, England, France, Italy, and Spain until finally foreign criticism of excessive colonial abuses pressured him to allow it to become a Belgian colony. During 1885–1908—the period of his personal control—millions of natives died prematurely due to the oppressive policies of the king and his Congo administrators. In German southwest Africa (today's Namibia) a rebellion by the Herero people between 1904 and 1907 led to fierce German retribution to quell the rebellion, and tens of thousands of native men, women, and children were killed.[4]

In Latin America the War of a Thousand Days, a Colombian civil war from 1899–1902, left approximately 100,000 dead. In China, an international force of eight countries combined in 1900 to end the anti-imperialist rampage of the Boxer Rebellion, which killed not only foreigners but also Chinese converts to Christianity. While Western papers highlighted the Boxer atrocities, the Russian writer Leo Tolstoy criticized both Nicholas II of Russia and Wilhelm II of Germany for participating in the armed international response which he labeled an unjust and cruel "slaughter."

Terrorism before World War I

On July 28, 1900 the anarchist Gaetano Bresci, a U.S. silk weaver, returned to his native Italy and assassinated King Humbert of Italy.

A year later, another anarchist, Leon Czolgosz, inspired by Bresci's deed, shot and killed U.S. President McKinley while he was attending the Pan-American Exposition in Buffalo. In the two decades before World War I began in 1914, anarchist assassins also killed a French president, two Spanish premiers, and an Austrian empress. In the Western world, such enemies of the very idea of centralized government were the era's most feared terrorists (a common term even then).

Terrorism is defined here as the non-governmental use of violence, or threat of its use, for political purposes, but on a lesser scale than a revolution or warfare, whether guerrilla or conventional, civil war or war between nations. From the late nineteenth century and throughout the twentieth century the term was used in different ways, but this essential core meaning remained. Most often the term "terrorists" was used by those critical of terrorist goals and/ or tactics. While terrorists generally defended their own actions, many of them preferred to think of themselves not as terrorists but as fighters against oppression or even "freedom fighters." I use "terrorism" and "terrorists" here only as descriptive terms, as my above definition indicates, and not as pejorative labels, much the same way as terms like "war" and "revolution" are used.

Perhaps no term in recent years has aroused as much controversy as terrorism, or has so eluded any general consensus on how it should be defined. Some argue that its definition should include "state terrorism" such as that practiced by Stalin, Hitler, and others. Although various governments certainly used terror and violence against their own people, it seems better to treat government terror differently from terrorism or what some might prefer to call "non-governmental terrorism." A second objection sometimes made is that the terms terrorism and terrorists are so intrinsically pejorative that they should be avoided by objective scholars. Such an approach, however, creates more problems than it avoids, and so I persist in using the terms as objectively as possible. During the twentieth century various governments, as well as guerrillas and terrorists, used violence to obtain their ends, and innocent civilians suffered far more from the actions of various governments' military forces than from that of all the century's terrorists combined. But regardless of how the varying types of violence are labeled, readers must decide for themselves—hopefully in a logically consistent manner—when, if ever, different types of violence are justified and why.[5]

In Paris in the early 1890s, as anarchist bombs exploded in places such as a railway-station cafe, a fashionable restaurant, and even in the French Chamber of Deputies, some Parisians feared to gather in public places, and fewer tourists visited the city. During the 1890s anarchist bombs exploded in other European cities like Barcelona, where a bomb at an opera house in 1893 killed and wounded over 70 people.

Besides anarchists, there were also others who were engaged in terrorism. Despite the existence of some Russian anarchists, the vast Russian Empire's chief advocates of terror were radical populists who believed terror was necessary in order to bring about a socialist order that would bring justice and equality to the masses, especially the vast majority of its people who were peasants. In 1881 such a group, the People's Will, assassinated Emperor Alexander II. In 1887 Alexander Ulianov, the older brother of future Soviet leader Vladimir Lenin, belonged to the self-proclaimed Terrorist Faction of the People's Will and was accused of plotting to kill Emperor Alexander III, son of the assassinated Alexander II. In his defense, Ulianov maintained that the use of terror was the only means available to bring about freedom in an oppressive state. But he did not deny advocating terror, and he was hanged. During the twentieth century many others who resorted to terror or violence for political purposes also claimed that it was justified in order to fight oppression.

In 1901, revolutionaries who thought of the People's Will as their "direct predecessors and spiritual fathers" formed the Party of Socialists-Revolutionaries (SRs), and during the next decade and a half their party was the leading, but not only, advocate of terrorist methods. According to one estimate, in the period 1905–16 revolutionary terrorists killed or wounded about 17,000 individuals, including high-ranking government officials. Lenin and his Bolshevik faction of the Russian Social Democratic Labor Party, who changed their name to Communist Party after coming to power in 1917, sometimes criticized the SRs for relying too heavily on terrorism. On other occasions, however, they defended terrorist methods, and individual Bolsheviks, including Stalin, sometimes carried out terrorist acts.[6]

Outside Russia, non-anarchistic terrorism was sometimes linked to nationalist causes. Although Serbia gained independence from the Ottoman Turkish Empire already in 1878, Serbian nationalists at the turn of the century were dissatisfied because many ethnic Serbs remained in neighboring territory outside their new state's boundaries. One such Serb was a young military officer named Dragutin Dimitrijevic, who in 1903 led a group of other young officers who stormed the royal palace and killed Serbian King Alexander and Queen Draga with gruesome excesses. Dimitrijevic believed they were failing the Serbian cause. In 1911, three years after Austria had further enflamed Serbian nationalism by annexing Bosnia and Herzegovina, where ethnic Serbians were the largest nationality, Dimitrijevic and some of his co-conspirators of 1903 formed a secret terrorist organization calling itself Unity or Death. It was also known as the Black Hand. According to its constitution, it would "carry out a revolutionary organization in all the territories where Serbians are living" and "fight with all means against all enemies" of Serb unity.[7]

In 1914, after Balkan wars in 1912–3 had expanded Serbian territories but not loosened Austria-Hungary's control over Bosnia and Herzegovina, the Black Hand recruited several young men to assassinate Austrian Archduke Franz Ferdinand when he visited Bosnia's capital, Sarajevo. Dimitrijevic was by this time not only the leading figure in the Black Hand, but also the head of Serbian Intelligence. The successful assassination of Ferdinand (and his wife Sophia) on June 28 led to a series of responses that by August 4 brought the major powers of Europe into World War I. Thus, the terrorist activities of Serbian nationalists were a major cause of a tragic war that caused deaths in unprecedented numbers.

Non-Violent and Violent Approaches: The Legacy of Leo Tolstoy and the Example of Theodore Roosevelt

Although some anarchists were terrorists, others were not. In the final decades of his life, the Great Russian writer Leo Tolstoy (1828–1910) was a non-violent anarchist. He shared the belief of all anarchists that existing governments were unjust, helping the rich exploit the poor, and therefore should cease to exist. But he also preached against all violence and instead encouraged people to bring about the downfall of governments by refusing to pay taxes or to serve as policemen or soldiers. After the assassination of Italy's King Humbert, Tolstoy wrote an essay, "Thou Shalt Not Kill," in which he criticized such killings, but even more he faulted monarchs for being responsible for far more "murders" in various wars and executions. As early as 1881 he had written to Alexander III trying to convince him to pardon his father's assassins. He wrote, "Your majesty, if you should do this . . . give them [the assassins] money and send them away somewhere to America, and write a manifesto starting with the words: 'but I say to you, love your enemies,' . . . from these words, like a flood, goodness and love would pour forth over Russia."[8]

During his long life, Tolstoy's views influenced many future pacifists. One such individual was the American Jane Addams, who visited him in Russia in the 1890s and during World War I chaired the Women's International Committee for Permanent Peace, which had branches in various countries including Australia, Austria, Belgium, Canada, Finland, Germany, Great Britain, Ireland, Hungary, British India, Italy, France, and Russia.[9] In the early twentieth century, Tolstoy corresponded with Mohandas Gandhi, then developing his non-violent resistance ideas among the Asian community in South Africa. Often later called Mahatma (meaning "great soul") Gandhi, he referred to himself as a "humble follower" of Tolstoy. Back in India between the two World Wars, Gandhi continued to develop non-violent resistance tactics in his struggle to bring about the independence of his native India, a goal finally achieved only in 1947.

The writings and example of Gandhi influenced others, including the American Martin Luther King, to reject violence as a means of struggle against evil, whether domestic or foreign. During the 1950s, others such as Nelson Mandela and his party, the African Nationalist Congress (ANC), attempted "over and over again" to use Gandhian non-violent resistance tactics in their battle against the racist apartheid system in South Africa. But Mandela eventually concluded that these tactics were "to no avail" and that the government had left them "no alternative to armed and violent resistance." As he later pointed out to two U.S. journalists, much of what worked for King in the USA could not successfully be employed in the more oppressive South African conditions. The Gandhian regard for life remained however, and Mandela consistently attempted to avoid or minimize the taking of human lives.[10]

The governments of the world and the vast majority of the century's inhabitants agreed less with Tolstoy and Gandhi's non-violent approach and more with the type of sentiments expressed by U.S. President Theodore Roosevelt. Successor to the assassinated President McKinley, he had no sympathy with the type of pardons Tolstoy had asked Alexander III to bestow on his father's assassins. In his autobiography Roosevelt wrote: "One of the painful duties of the chief executive in States like New York, as well as in the Nation, is the refusing of pardons. Yet I can imagine nothing more necessary from the standpoint of good citizenship than the ability to steel one's heart in this matter of granting pardons . . . I do not believe that life imprisonment for murder and rape is a proper substitute for the death penalty."[11]

He certainly did not pardon the assassin Czolgosz; he was electrocuted less than two months after he shot President McKinley. Furthermore, Roosevelt advocated deporting all anarchists. And at a time when about a million immigrants per year were arriving on U.S. shores, he wished to exclude anyone who believed in anarchistic ideas, an exclusion agreed to by Congress in 1903. Although awarded the Nobel Peace Prize for helping end the Russo-Japanese War in 1905, Roosevelt hated Tolstoy's "foolish theory that men should never make war." And he believed that the navy was an "infinitely more potent factor for peace than all the peace societies"—not surprising for a man who had been Assistant Secretary of the navy before resigning in 1898 in order to personally fight in Cuba during the Spanish–American War. [12]

Ironically, however, both Tolstoy and Roosevelt thought that the international peace conferences held at The Hague, Netherlands in 1899 and 1907 were not very useful. Although the conferences reflected the fact that Tolstoy was not alone in being concerned with the militarism of the time, the governments that participated in them displayed little enthusiasm or talent for restraining military growth. At the time of the first conference, Tolstoy wrote, "The Conference itself can be nothing but one of those hypocritical arrangements which aim not at peace, but, on the contrary, at hiding from men the one means of obtaining universal peace." During the second conference President Roosevelt, whose Secretary of State participated in it, admitted he paid little attention to it because he was "'utterly disgusted' with the nonsense chattered by professional peace advocates."[13] Despite, however, the contempt of Tolstoy and Roosevelt and the failure of the conferences to prevent World War I, the long-term significance of the two Hague conferences was greater than either man could then realize. Along with Geneva Conventions that occurred both before and after the two Hague conferences, the work of the conferences helped lay the groundwork for many later twentieth-century international agreements, including those regarding warfare and international law generally.[14]

From World War I to 1999

In his sweeping *The War of the World: Twentieth-Century Conflict and the Descent of the West*, historian Niall Ferguson states that he believes the "extreme violence" of the century resulted primarily from three causes: "ethnic conflict, economic volatility and empires in decline."[15] As we shall see in this and following chapters, these were certainly among its main reasons, but there were also others like nationalism and adherence to ideologies such as communism and Nazism.

Estimates vary widely on the total number of twentieth-century deaths due to violent conflicts and murderous government policies. Ferguson suggests the number was in the 167–88 million range. Another scholar, Rudolph Rummel, has estimated that over 300 million people were killed during the century as a result of warfare or murderous government policies such as those of Adolf Hitler, Joseph Stalin, Chinese communist leader Mao Zedong, and the Cambodian communist Pol Pot. Sometimes such murderous policies, referred to as democide by Rummel, occurred during wartime, but were not part of any effort to kill enemy soldiers or civilians who died because of military actions directed at military targets. Hitler's killing of 5 to 6 million Jews in World War II is an example of such wartime democide. More controversially, Rummel considers the bombing of such cities as Hamburg, Dresden, and Hiroshima during that same war as examples of democide. On his website, Rummel wrote the following: "Just to give perspective on this incredible murder by government, if all these bodies were laid head to toe, with the average height being 5', then they would circle the earth ten times. Also, this democide [which he estimates at 262 million] murdered 6 times more people than died in combat in all the foreign and internal wars of the century."[16]

Although some of Rummel's specific democide estimates seem high (thus inflating his total), there is little doubt that the overall number was of staggering proportions. Terrorist actions against government authorities, sometimes colonial rulers, or against innocent civilians killed far fewer people, but they also continued throughout the century.

Military and Civilian Wartime Deaths

Although the non-battlefield mass killings of the century greatly outnumbered those in battle, the number of deaths of soldiers was still unprecedented, especially in the century's two major wars. During the first one, called then the Great War, over 1 million soldiers lost their lives before the end of 1914 and over 8 million by the time an armistice was signed in November 1918. These sacrifices were difficult to justify in a war that was less clearly caused by one-sided aggression than was World War II. The Battle of the Somme was one battle that came to symbolize the tragic waste of human life. On July 1, 1916, the British launched an attack along the Somme River in France. As the British soldiers trudged across open fields, the Germans stood in their trenches and mowed them down, killing over 20,000 British troops in a single day. Before the Somme offensive ended in November, British, French, and German casualties (dead and wounded) numbered more than 1 million men. For all this loss and maiming of life, however, little territory changed hands. In fact, on the Western Front for more than three years, no offensive could advance the front line more than ten miles.

As a result of a little over four years of warfare, three out of every ten French men between the ages of 18 and 28, overwhelmingly soldiers, lost their lives. Although not as proportionally high as French losses, those of both Germany and Russia were numerically higher.

Yet the peace settlement at war's end brought no lasting peace, and in some ways contributed to German resentments that along with the Great Depression helped Hitler come to power in 1933.

During World War II battlefield deaths were even greater, at least twice the number of the earlier "Great War." It was, however, the non-battlefield deaths that seemed most shocking. In the two world wars combined civilian deaths outnumbered military deaths. During the first one, the Turks may have killed over 1 million Armenians in what is sometimes referred to as the Armenian Genocide.[17] The British naval blockade of Germany, which continued for months after the November 1918 armistice, caused anywhere from 424,000 to 800,000 civilian deaths, primarily due to malnutrition. Although a German Zeppelin initiated the bombing of civilians when it attacked London in 1915, relatively few people died as a result of such warfare in World War I. World War II was a different story, with Allied bombing causing most of the deaths from the skies, overwhelmingly to civilians. Although estimates for the overall loss of life because of Allied bombing vary, if post-war radiation deaths caused by the atomic bombs dropped on Hiroshima and Nagasaki are included, some estimates exceed 1 million deaths in Germany and Japan.

Although the bombing capability of the Axis Powers was not as great as that of the Allies, the German and Japanese governments still were responsible for far more civilian deaths. Against the Soviet Union, Hitler waged a "war of extermination." He killed off not only millions of Jews, but also millions of non-Jewish Soviet prisoners of war (POWs), political prisoners, Roma (Gypsies), homosexuals, handicapped people, and others. The 900-day German blockade of Leningrad killed approximately 1 million Leningraders, most of whom died of hunger and malnourishment—recent estimates for the total number of Soviet civilian and military World War II deaths hover around 25 million of the approximate 60 million total war deaths.[18] From the time Japan launched a full-scale attack on China in 1937 until 1945, the Japanese also took millions of civilian lives.

The most infamous example was the "Rape of Nanking" in 1937–8. Estimates of the number of Chinese, overwhelmingly civilians, killed in this bloodbath vary, with most recent estimates being between 200,000 and 400,000, in addition to 8,000–20,000 rapes.

Besides the two major wars of the century, other wars also killed numerous civilians. For example, in the Second Indochina War (1960–75), a portion of which included what Americans called the Vietnam War, several million people lost their lives, many of them civilians. The heavy U.S. bombing of North Vietnam and Cambodia brought about many of these deaths, and tapes of U.S. President Nixon released in 2002 reveal Nixon in 1972 telling his National Security Adviser Henry Kissinger: "The only place where you and I disagree . . . is with regard to the bombing." And Nixon added: "You're so goddamned concerned about the civilians and I don't give a damn. I don't care." Nixon also raised the idea of using a nuclear bomb, but Kissinger advised against it.[19] Partly because the nuclear bombing never occurred, however, other actions of both sides in the war combined to kill an even larger number of civilians than did bombs. Conflicts in wars between lesser powers also produced many civilian deaths. [20]

During the century, the moral distinction between killing enemy troops and enemy civilians was often blurred. World War I became a war of attrition in which exhausting the enemy's resources and morale became a major goal of both sides. German submarines and the British naval blockade were used to prevent not only weapons but food and other supplies from reaching the enemy's population, thus making the entire civilian population a target—the British Navy's greater success helped defeat Germany. The vital role that civilians played in the war effort also helped blur the line separating troops from civilians. The production of artillery shells, for example, was crucial. In less than three weeks during the Third Battle of Ypres (1917), the British fired as many shells as it took 55,000 workers a year to produce. And since many women went to work in defense factories—approximately 700,000 adult women were already employed in Germany's armament industry in 1917—such female armament workers and the factories they worked in could also be thought of as appropriate enemy targets. Although the limited bombing capacities of World War I prevented the mass targeting of factories, during World War II enemy armament plants (along with their workers) increasingly became targets, as did oil depots, transport lines, and other locations that contributed to the war effort.

Although the Germans bombed Warsaw and Rotterdam early in that latter war, in their bombing of Great Britain they at first stuck primarily to military targets, as did the British Air Force in bombing Germany. It did not take long, however, for such early restraints to dissipate. German bombing of British cities in late 1940 and early 1941 killed about 40,000 civilians. By the latter stages of the war massive Allied "area bombing" that struck major population centers was common. The Germans and Japanese by then, however, were incapable of causing the type of massive destruction that Allied bombing did to cities like Hamburg, Dresden, Tokyo, Hiroshima, and Nagasaki.

The Second Indochina War presented another example of how the distinction between killing military forces and civilians, especially in guerrilla warfare, became hazy. American troops often complained that it became all but impossible to distinguish enemy Vietcong, and those who assisted them, from other civilians. This reality helped lead to tragedies such as the U.S. killing of almost 400 men, women, and children in the Vietnamese village of My Lai. Lieutenant William Calley told his men that the village contained mainly Vietcong supporters. Frustrated by weeks of fighting the Vietcong and seeing their own unit sustain casualties; his men burnt down the village, raped girls and women, and engaged in an orgy of killing.

Although the other wars and conflicts of the century are too numerous to specify, they occurred all around the world. Sometimes they pitted nations against each other, as in the Iran–Iraq War (1980–8), or people seeking independence from a colonial power, as in the French–Algerian War (1954–62). Many were labeled civil wars such as in Russia (1918–21) or Spain (1936–9). Often these wars between different factions in a country were further complicated by foreign involvement, as occurred in Russia, Spain, or later in the Korean War (1950–3). Conflicts such as those occurring in Mexico (1910–20) and China (1917–37, 1945–9) defy any simple labels but took countless lives, especially in China, where many millions died. In Africa, where many conflicts occurred in the second half of the century, struggles for independence, ethnic and tribal rivalries, and Cold War influences all played a part. In Sudan between 1983 and 2000, ethnic conflict and civil war led to about 2 million deaths. Altogether, besides the two world wars, more than a dozen additional twentieth-century conflicts probably caused more than a million deaths each.[20]

In 1999, according to the Stockholm International Peace Research Institute, there were "27 major armed conflicts in 25 countries. The vast majority of the major armed conflicts in 1999 were in Africa and Asia; there were 11 in Africa, 9 in Asia, 3 in the Middle East, 2 in Europe and 2 in South America. All but two of the conflicts were internal. Most of the major armed conflicts registered for 1999 are protracted (17 have been active for at least eight years) or recurrent (4 conflicts)."[21]

Besides the major wars of the century, numerous other conflicts produced significant atrocities. For example, in Bosnia and Herzegovina in the early 1990s, "ethnic cleansing" occurred, mainly against Bosnian Muslims. One source estimates that by the end of 1995, "at least 200,000 civilians had been killed, and two million people made homeless," while another source suggests that tens of thousands of Bosnian Muslim women had been raped.[22] In a civil war in Guatemala that lasted for over three decades, ending only in the mid-1990s, the United States supported anti-communist government forces that tortured, raped, and killed many innocent civilians, especially many poor Maya peasants. One estimate suggests that around 200,000 lost their lives in this prolonged war.[23] A similar estimate was also earlier given for the number of lives lost in Colombia's *La Violencia* (The Violence), a chaotic period of civil war, government repression, and other types of violence, which was most intense from 1948 to 1958.

Non-democratic regimes were responsible for most of the century's deaths, both during war and "peacetime." None of the century's major conflicts pitted two democracies against each other, and the century's tyrants and non-democratic rulers perpetrated the century's mass government murders. Nevertheless, the world's democracies were not completely blameless. As long as democratic colonial powers such as France and Great Britain maintained their colonies, they were responsible for some violence—a great deal in cases like the French in Algeria. And the world's wealthier democracies also bore some responsibility for global poverty and the "structural violence" that often accompanied it (see below). During the Cold War, Western democracies sometimes supported repressive right-wing regimes, and in the late 1990s four of the five largest suppliers of conventional weapons on a global scale were found in Western democracies, with the United States supplying almost half of the global total.[24]

Deaths from Communist Governments

Despite Hitler's massive non-military killings, it was primarily communist leaders, especially Stalin, Mao Zedong, and Cambodia's Pol Pot, who killed the largest number of their own people. Overall, the most detailed study of communist atrocities, *The Black Book of Communism*, estimates that communism was responsible for 85–100 million deaths during the century. But it should be remembered that many communists did not share the penchant for killing evidenced by Stalin, Mao, and Pol Pot. Reforming communists like the Czech leader Alexander Dubček and Soviet leader Mikhail Gorbachev were much more humane, as were many communists opposing unjust governments in countries such as South Africa.[25]

It was Vladimir Lenin who set the stage for other blood-shedding communist leaders. He and his party came to power in 1917 without the support of a majority of the Russian Empire's people and while World War I was still in process. The war itself contributed to both economic volatility and the decline of empires, two of the three main causes listed by Ferguson for the twentieth-century's high levels of violence. The war brought about the collapse of the tsarist Russian Empire, as well as the Austro-Hungarian and Ottoman Turkish empires, and the economic volatility that contributed to the overthrow of the Russian tsar in March 1917 continued into the summer and fall of that year. Already by August, inflation had reduced the real wages of unskilled workers to about half of the January 1917 level, and workers' economic dissatisfaction helped Lenin and the Bolsheviks come to power in November 1917.

From the very beginning there was armed opposition to Lenin's government, and a full-scale civil war soon broke out. These circumstances and a Marxist ideology that preached class warfare helped imbue Leninism with a willingness to rely heavily on harsh, violent methods to remain in power and strengthen its hold over as much of the former Russian Empire as possible.

During its first two months in power, Lenin's government replaced the old courts with revolutionary tribunals and established the All-Russian Extraordinary Commission for Combating Counterrevolution and Sabotage, better known as the Cheka. It was the first of the names for the Soviet security police that continued to operate until the collapse of communism almost three quarters of a century later. Headed by Felix Dzerzhinsky, the Cheka's job was to ferret out opponents of the new regime ("enemies of the people"), who would then be tried in new revolutionary tribunals. But it almost immediately bypassed the tribunals and shot thousands of enemies without a trial. In December 1917 Dzershinsky stated: "Do not imagine, comrades, that I am simply looking for a revolutionary form of justice. We have no concern about justice at this hour! We are at war . . . and the fight is to the death."[26] In 1918 and the first half of 1919, according to one Cheka official, it alone sentenced and carried out over eight thousand executions in just 20 Russian provinces.

The Cheka's violent methods were generally in keeping with Lenin's own sentiments. In 1918 he wrote to Party leaders in Penza regarding peasant resistance:

1. You need to hang (hang without fail, so that the public sees) at least 100 notorious kulaks [supposedly rich peasants], the rich, and the bloodsuckers.
2. Publish their names.
3. Take away all of their grain.
4. Execute the hostages—in accordance with yesterday's telegram.
   This needs to be accomplished in such a way, that people for hundreds of miles around will see, tremble, know and scream out: let's choke and strangle those blood-sucking kulaks.
   Telegraph us acknowledging receipt and execution of this.
   Yours, Lenin
   P.S. Use your toughest people for this.[27]

Other Soviet leaders shared a similar attitude. Writing of the "bourgeoisie" in 1919, the head of the Red Army, Leon Trotsky, proclaimed: "We are forced to tear off this class and chop it away. The Red Terror is a weapon used against a class that, despite being doomed to destruction, does not wish to perish."[28] Such thinking sometimes led to people being killed not because of any specific crime but because of their social origin.

Although the Russian Civil War, along with the Allied Intervention in Russia that also occurred in the first few years of the new Soviet regime, contributed to the Soviet's "Red Terror," it by no means ended when opposing armies no longer threatened the communist hold over the country. Lenin still feared opposition from other parties and rebelling sailors, workers, and peasants. In 1921 he wrote, "If the Mensheviks or Socialist Revolutionaries [both leftist parties] so much as peek out again, they must all be shot without pity."[29] A little later he informed his justice commissar: "The courts must not ban terror . . . but must formulate the motives underlying it, legalize it as a principle, without any make-believe or embellishment. It must be formulated in the broadest possible manner, for only revolutionary law and revolutionary conscience can more or less widely determine the limits within which it should be applied."[30]

Lenin's thoughts were incorporated into the Criminal Code of 1922 and further expanded in the 14 sections of the infamous Article 58 of the Criminal Code of 1926. As Alexander Solzhenitsyn, who was sentenced under it in 1945, later noted: "There is no step, thought, action, or lack of action under the heavens which could not be punished by the heavy hand of Article 58. The article itself could not be worded in such broad terms, but it proved possible to interpret it this broadly."[31]

In early 1922 the Cheka was replaced by the State Security Administration (GPU and later OGPU). But its head remained the same, Felix Dzerzhinsky, as did its main headquarters, Moscow's infamous Lubianka. About it, Ilia Ehrenburg wrote in 1923, "Shake someone awake at night and say the word 'Lubianka' and he will stare at his bare feet, say goodbye to everybody, and even if he's young, and healthy as an ox, he'll break down and cry like a baby."[32]

Despite Lenin's responsibility for initiating a state that relied on institutions such as the Cheka, his successor, Stalin, soon outdid him in the taking of lives. In 1921 Lenin had instituted a New Economic Policy (NEP) that continued after his death in 1924 and lasted until Stalin brought it to an end in 1928. As compared to the policies of the civil war that preceded it and Stalin's actions that followed it, government actions in the NEP years were considerably less violent.

In 1929 Stalin insisted that the kulaks must be "liquidated as a class," and he began the mass collectivization of Soviet peasants, who constituted four-fifths of the population. Although the kulaks were theoretically rich peasants, the term was also applied to many other peasants who resisted Stalin's collectivization.

In the early 1930s, besides those killed for opposing Stalinist policies, over 2 million kulaks were sent to Siberia and other areas. Most of these peasants were exiled to remote areas but some were forced to work in labor camps, where many died early deaths. By 1940 about 8 million people had already been sent to the camps, although less than 2 million per year were there at any one time during the late 1930s.

Besides kulaks and hardened criminals, others exiled or sent to labor camps in the 1930s included various other "class enemies," members of minority nationalities, religious believers of various types, soldiers, and intellectuals. Stalin was also mainly responsible for the famine of 1931–3 that killed millions of additional people, especially in the Ukrainian area—some scholars believe that Stalin deliberately targeted Ukrainians, killing millions of them in the "famine-genocide."[33] Other Stalinist policies of the 1930s, including having people shot, led to many additional deaths. In the late 1930s, the abnormally suspicious Stalin had a large percentage of other Soviet political and military leaders killed. Territorial acquisitions in 1939 and 1940, when the Soviet Union was benevolently neutral as Nazi Germany attacked other European countries, led to still more deaths. After acquiring areas like Estonia, Latvia, most of Lithuania, and smaller segments of Poland, Finland, and Romania, Stalin and his authorities ordered the arrest, killing, internment, or deportation of many inhabitants, including suspected anti-Soviet nationalists and many clergy, upper-class families, and people with foreign contacts. Roughly 2 million people were so victimized prior to Hitler's troops arriving on the scene in the summer of 1941. Among those deported were many women, children, and the elderly, while some of the more feared opponents, or potential opponents, of the new communist order were shot.

From mid-1941 to his death in 1953, Stalin and his government were responsible for numerous other non-combat deaths of suspected individuals and Soviet nationalities, including Volga Germans. World War II turned many Soviet citizens into German-occupied peoples, POWs, or forced laborers in Germany. Other Soviet people came into contact with Western Allied Forces. Gains at the end of the war, in addition to those made in 1939–40, brought some additional peoples (for example, some West Ukrainians) into the USSR. Stalin tended to suspect all such people of being contaminated by foreign contacts, and many were arrested. Sometimes entire nationalities (for example, the Chechens and Crimean Tatars) were expelled from their homelands and sent off to Soviet Asia. Many others who were arrested found themselves in Soviet labor camps. The hardships suffered by those resettled or working in labor camps often led to premature death. To take just one example, by the end of December 1945 almost 27,000 Crimean Tatars sent to Uzbekistan had died. More than three-fourths of the dead were women and children. After the war, Stalin also displayed an increasing hostility and suspiciousness toward Soviet Jews, especially after the establishment of Israel in 1948. Some were arrested, and it is likely that if Stalin had not died in 1953 many Jews would have been deported to remote Soviet areas.

How many unnatural deaths in the USSR was Stalin responsible for in his quarter-century of power? Not counting the many millions killed by the enemy in World War II, perhaps 15–20 million would be a fair estimate, with many other calculations being both higher and lower than that figure. Stalin also bore considerable responsibility for killings and premature deaths in central and eastern European countries where Red Army troops helped bring communist governments to power after defeating Nazi Forces. Some of those included Germans expelled from countries like Poland and Czechoslovakia.

By the time Stalin died, Mao Zedong was the head of the Chinese Communist Party, which had ruled China since driving Kuomintang Forces under Chaing Kai-shek off the mainland in 1949. Having learned much from Stalin's example, Mao now became the era's chief agent of death until he died in 1976. Even before 1949 the Chinese communists had been responsible for millions of deaths in addition to those of the Kuomintang troops they killed in the civil war. In 1946, for example, they had begun a major land reallocation program in regions they controlled. By the end of 1949, millions of peasants and other opponents of the Chinese agricultural policies had been killed or sent to forced-labor camps. After 1949, millions more "counterrevolutionaries" were sent to prisons or camps, where many of them died. In 1958–9 Mao launched the Great Leap Forward, a poorly thought out plan to modernize Chinese industries, increase the size of collective-farming communes, and increase industrial and agricultural production. Its major result was famine, the worst in Chinese and probably world history. The number of deaths caused by it is far from certain, but foreign estimates for excess Chinese deaths from 1958 into the early 1960s range from about 15 to 30 million, with the overwhelming number being attributed to famine. Exactly what Mao thought about famine conditions is difficult to determine because many of his followers told him what he wanted to hear and not the truth. This fact could also help explain why China doubled its grain exports when millions were starving. In the late 1960s Wei Jingsheng (1950–), an ardent young follower of Mao, but later leading Chinese dissident and critic of its communist government, went into the countryside and discovered the appalling conditions brought about by the Great Leap Forward. In his *The Courage to Stand Alone: Letters from Prison and Other Writings* he describes details of the local famine and cannibalism as they were related to him.

After the failures of the Great Leap Forward became obvious, some of the other communist leaders limited Mao's powers, but by 1966 he was back on the offensive and launched the Cultural Revolution. Mao encouraged young Red Guards, who often cited sayings from *Quotations from Chairman Mao* in defense of their actions, to attack insufficiently radical Communist Party and government officials, as well as other authority figures like teachers and professors. Some were killed and others were sent into what one authority refers to as the "biggest penal system of all time."[34] The attacks wreaked havoc on the educational system and destroyed many religious temples and traditional art works and books. For a while in 1966–7 factions multiplied and chaos spread, as the Communist Party lost effective control over segments of what Mao had unleashed. Although he eventually used the army and loyal workers to reign in the Red Guards, and the turmoil eased by the end of the 1960s, the Cultural Revolution nevertheless continued to a lesser degree until Mao's death in 1976. Overall, it probably caused 500,000 to 1 million additional deaths.

Among those who suffered most under Mao were the people of Tibet, who fell under Chinese control after the communist troops first arrived there in 1950. One estimate is that "some 10 to 20 percent of the inhabitants . . . died as a result of Chinese occupation."[35]

Overall, it is likely that excluding famine victims, but including Tibetan deaths, at least 25 million people died as a result of Mao's policies. About 20 million of them were within the prison system. Mao's personal physician in his book *The Private Life of Chairman Mao* indicated that Mao possessed little human sympathy and thought that the loss of human life was a small price to pay to remake China according to his ideas. "Mercy to the enemy is cruelty to the people," was one of his sayings.[36] In 1958, considering the consequences of a nuclear war, he stated that if "900 million are left out of 2.9 billion, several Five Year Plans can be developed for the total elimination of capitalism and for permanent peace. It is not a bad thing."[37]

At the time of Mao's death in 1976 a Mao admirer in Cambodia, Pol Pot, was attempting to apply many of Mao's ideas in his own country. This Marxist and leader of the Khmer Rouge came to power in 1975. He did so partly because the heavy U.S. bombing of Cambodia—more than three times the amount of bombing inflicted on Japan in World War II—had destabilized the country and inadvertently increased support for this extreme anti-Western communist group.

In the next several years, the Khmer Rouge brought about a more radical transformation of the country in a shorter period of time than their fellow communists in the Soviet Union or China had succeeded in doing. But rather than creating a state "overflowing with harmony and happiness" as the Party's 1976 Four Year Plan had envisioned, the policies of Pol Pot and his followers brought about sufferings of hellish proportions. From 1975 to 1979, when they were overthrown, they were responsible for the deaths of over 1 million people out of a population of 7–8 million. Their policies involved driving people out of the cities, and most of those not imprisoned in camps or other locations, or killed or dying from mistreatment or famine, were assigned to collective farms. The Khmer Rouge also forbade the circulation of money and the practice of religion. They waged fierce class warfare and attacked family life and traditional classes and culture. And they attempted to seal the country off from any corrupting foreign influences. Besides the upper classes, the main victims were ethnic minorities such as the Chinese and Vietnamese, the sick (many in hospitals were killed or driven into the streets), and Catholics and Muslims. Gruesome tortures often preceded death, and the Khmer Rouge often not only displayed an indifference to individual human life, but also engaged in sadistic behavior. The former ruler of Cambodia, Prince Sihanouk, while held prisoner by the Khmer Rouge, often observed them torturing animals and believed many of them were "addicted to torture."[38] They also prepared human body parts of some of their victims for food.

What Pol Pot had in common with Mao and Stalin, and to a lesser extent some other communist leaders, was a belief that the restructuring of society and human life, as well as safeguarding his own power, justified the taking of human lives. Further, many communist leaders argued that the class-based societies they wished to replace were responsible for all sorts of evils, including many that caused countless suffering and early deaths from such causes as poverty and malnutrition. Confident that their Marxist vision presented the key to a better future, the most extreme communist leaders mentioned above encouraged their followers to be ruthless toward the "enemies of the people." Stalin, Mao, and Pol Pot equated pity and human compassion with squeamish weakness and instead encouraged the more martial virtues of hardness and toughness. The very name "Stalin," adopted by the young Joseph Djugashvilli to suggest he was a man of steel, indicates this mindset, and Stalin's supporters were fond of the saying "you can't make an omelet without breaking eggs," often ignoring the obvious difference between eggs and human beings. All three leaders believed in class warfare and that they had to be alert and prepared constantly to "purge" their enemies or "enemies of the people." None of the three appreciated the importance of freedom and self-respect to the human psyche, but instead insisted on remolding or reeducating human beings, by force if necessary. ("Thought Reform" was one of the slogans under Mao.) Besides, as one of Mao's victims during the Cultural Revolution wrote about a character in a novel, "The Party needed to make a target of people like him to arouse the will and spirit of the people, to whip up the masses into displays of righteous indignation."[39] Stalin and Pol Pot, as well as Hitler and other dictators, also made such use of "enemies of the people."

Hitler and Right-Wing Authoritarian Movements

Adolf Hitler and his Nazi followers in Germany combined ideas of racial supremacy, anti-communism, German nationalism, and selected borrowings from the ideas of Darwin and Nietzsche to concoct a powerful mixture that justified the taking of millions of lives. Hitler's main target of hate and scapegoating for German problems was the

Jewish people. He blamed them for the beginning of World War I, for Germany losing it, for German economic miseries afterwards, and for giving birth to and sustaining communism. Such sweeping charges were, of course, ludicrous. But the national humiliation that resulted from the war and the imposed peace terms afterward, the economic volatility of inflation (in the early 1920s) later followed by a depression worse than that in the USA, and the fear of communist gains as people became more desperate were all real enough.

Within months of Hitler's coming to power in January 1933, amidst the Great Depression, he began persecuting Germany's Jews, who numbered about 500,000, or less than 1 percent of the population. First, he removed them from the civil service and important cultural positions. Then, in 1935, the Nuremburg Laws took away Jewish citizenship rights and forbade them to marry anyone defined as German. The late 1930s witnessed various other types of persecutions and brutalities including numerous pogroms. Because of such treatment and because the Nazis wanted to rid Germany of its Jews, many of them left the country before World War II—by 1939 only about 164,000 Jews remained. Most of the millions of unarmed Jews the Nazis murdered by shooting, gassing, and other methods during the war were from occupied territories, especially Poland and the Soviet Union.

Like the communist tactic of dehumanizing the capitalists, the kulaks, and other "enemies of the people," Nazi propaganda portrayed the Jews as less than human, comparing them with rats, lice, vermin, and the plague. As a pamphlet of Hitler's elite SS (*Schutzstaffel*) phased it, the Jew's "spirit is lower than that of an animal ... a monster, subhuman."[40] Jews were humiliated by all means possible in order to make them act in subhuman ways and thus confirm the perception that they were not, as one wife of a camp commander put it, "human beings, but animals."[41]

Like the communists, the Nazis emphasized the necessity of hard-heartedness. The Nazi governor of Poland said, "Gentleman, I must ask you to arm yourself against all feelings of sympathy. We have to annihilate the Jews wherever we find them." The SS especially prided itself on its hardness. One camp commander later noted as an example that in training for toughness and overcoming sympathetic feelings, the SS ordered a man to kill his own dog, preferably with a knife. Such exhortations and training help explain why some Jewish children were "thrown on the floor" and had "their heads trampled with boots."[42]

Nazi racist ideas also contributed to killing of millions of Slavic peoples, Roma (Gypsies), and physically and mentally handicapped people, as well as the forced sterilization of hundreds of thousands. In the Nazi ranking of races, the Roma were almost as low as the Jews, and the Slavs were also considered grossly inferior. As Germany expanded, Hitler planned to kill or remove many of these peoples he considered inferior in order to make more room for German colonists.

Although no other non-democratic anti-communist movement ever came close to the Nazi regime in the taking of innocent lives, such governments as those of Benito Mussolini in Italy (1922–45), Francisco Franco in Spain (1939–75), General Suharto in Indonesia (1965–98), and military governments in such Latin American countries as Argentina (1976–83), Brazil (1964–85), and Chile (1973–89) were all responsible for large numbers of deaths due to oppressive government actions.

Terrorist Activities, 1919–99

From 1919 to 1921, Irish nationalists, including their Irish Republican Army (IRA), fought a war of independence against Great Britain that ended with a treaty recognizing the Irish Free State as a self-governing dominion comprising most of Ireland. But much of Ulster in the north, where Protestants were dominant, remained a part of Great Britain. Dissatisfied with the situation in Northern Ireland and with not gaining full independence on the rest of the island, which did not occur until after World War II, the IRA and many other Irish nationalists rejected the treaty and fought an unsuccessful civil war against the Irish Free State government that lasted until 1923. Having lost that struggle, the IRA continued sporadic attacks in subsequent decades in both the Irish Free State and Northern Ireland. In 1939, for example, it oversaw a campaign of bomb detonations in various British cities including London, Birmingham, Manchester, and Coventry. Most of the explosions destroyed property but took no lives. One in Coventry, however, killed five people.

In the 1950s the IRA was responsible for more bombings. In the 1960s, to counter the IRA in Northern Ireland, an opposing force that also used terrorist methods came into being, the Ulster Volunteer Force (UVF). As a result of increasing tensions between Catholics and Protestants in Northern Ireland, British soldiers arrived to better maintain order. In 1972, however, 13 unarmed Catholics were killed during a clash with British troops during a banned civil rights demonstration in the city of Derry (Londonderry). Subsequent resentment of the killings increased support for the IRA. Despite a split over the question of violence in the IRA in 1969, its terrorist activities now increased, reaching a high point between 1972 and 1976, but also continuing thereafter. Besides killing some prominent individuals, most notably (in 1979) Lord Mountbatten, former Viceroy of India, the IRA also tried but failed to kill British Prime Minister Margaret Thatcher and others attending a Conservative Party conference in 1984. IRA terrorist actions continued sporadically in the late 1980s and 1990s until a shaky settlement on Northern Ireland was finally reached in 1998. In 2002, the IRA apologized for deaths of 650 civilians killed by them since the late 1960s—the Council on Foreign Relations, an independent U.S. organization, estimated that in that same time period the IRA killed a total of about 1,800 people. "The IRA's primary targets were British troops, police officers, prison guards, and judges— many of them unarmed or off-duty—as well as rival paramilitary militants, drug dealers, and informers in Ulster." Another reliable source gives a roughly similar estimate and also calculates that the opposing UVF and other rival militants were also responsible for more than 1,000 deaths.[43]

In other parts of Europe in the interwar years, terrorism "certainly stemmed more from the extreme right than the left."[44] In Germany and Italy, some terrorists were veterans who eventually joined the Nazi and Fascist parties respectively. In 1922 right-wing terrorists killed Germany's Jewish foreign minister, Walter Rathenau. Mussolini, the head of the Fascists who came to power in Italy that same year, supported the Croatian right-wing Ustasha group. The latter pushed for Croatian independence from Yugoslavia and in 1934 was implicated in the murder of Yugoslavian King Alexander, as well as French Foreign Minister Louis Barthou, with whom Alexander was having a meeting. In general, however, not only in Europe but beyond, terrorism—if one excludes what is sometimes referred to as "state terrorism" (e.g. that of Hitler or Stalin), which does fit our definition of terrorism—was less prominent in the interwar period than it had been earlier.

After World War II terrorism took many forms. In the first few decades after the war it was most prevalent in Asia, the Middle East, and Africa, and was often linked with religious causes or, more frequently, nationalist aspirations against imperialism. In India, Hindu, Muslim, and Sikh differences often led to bloodshed. A Hindu terrorist upset with Gandhi's tolerant attitude toward Muslims assassinated him in 1948. In 1970 left-wing Naxalite terrorists killed policemen and teachers, burned buses, and attacked Gandhi centers and U.S. agencies in Calcutta (Kolkata). In 1984 Prime Minister

Indira Gandhi (no relation to Mohandas Gandhi) was assassinated because of her crackdown on Sikh radicals. In 1985, 329 people, most of them Canadians, were killed when their Air India flight went down over the Atlantic Ocean, south of Ireland. The Canadian government accused three Sikhs of being implicated in planting explosives on the plane—only in the twenty-first century was one man found guilty, and two not so, for involvement in the crime. In 1991 Rajiv Gandhi, son of Indira who had served as prime minister (1984–9), was assassinated. The suicide assassin, a young woman, was part of one of the most effective terrorist and guerrilla groups in Asia, the Tamil Tigers. This group had opposed Gandhi's policies in the island country of Sri Lanka, just off the southern coast of India, and their ultimate goal was to gain independence from Sri Lanka and create a Tamil state of their own on the island—the Tamils constituted almost 20 percent of Sri Lanka's population. Known for their intense dedication to their cause, their frequent resort to suicide missions, their effective use of propaganda (including on the Internet), and their fund-raising abilities, the Tigers were still waging their struggle at century's end. In Japan a poison gas attack in the Tokyo subway system in 1995 killed 12 and injured 5,500 people. Over 100 members of Aum Shinrikyo, a religious sect who believed they were persecuted, were indicted for this and other crimes.

In post-war Palestine, two future Israeli prime ministers, Menacham Begin and Yitzhak Shamir, were leaders of terrorist groups working to drive the British occupiers out of Palestine. In 1946, two years before the British left and Israel was created, Begin's terrorist group, Irgun, blew up the south wing of Jerusalem's King David Hotel, killing over 90 people including British officials, Jews, and Arabs. Palestinian Arab terrorism directed against Israel became most prominent after the Israelis occupied Palestinian Arab territory in the "Six-Day War" of 1967. For the remainder of the century the ultimate goal of such terrorism was to drive the Israelis out of occupied Palestinian territories and create an independent Palestinian Arab state, which a 1947 UN Partition Plan had envisaged but conflict in the region had prevented from occurring. One of the most infamous acts of Palestinian terrorism was the killing of 11 Israeli athletes and one German policeman in 1972 at the Munich Olympics.

In December 1988 Pam Am Flight 103 went down over Lockerbie, Scotland. Only in the early twenty-first century were two Libyans brought to trial and one of them convicted of planting a bomb on the plane. Although the motive for the crime remained unclear, two suspected reasons were the 1986 U.S. bombing of Libya's capital,

Tripoli, and seaport of Benghazi and the 1988 downing of an Iranian passenger jet by a U.S. Navy warship in the Persian Gulf. The first U.S. act resulted from retaliation for suspected Libyan involvement in a Berlin nightclub bombing that killed some U.S. military people, and the second from a case of mistaking the Iranian plane for a fighter jet.

In Africa during the 1950s terrorism overlapped with guerrilla warfare against imperialist powers in various areas especially in Algeria and Kenya. It took Algerians from 1954 to 1962 before they gained independence from France, at the cost of hundreds of thousands, perhaps close to a million, Algerian lives. Frantz Fanon (1925–61), a psychiatrist born in Martinique, worked in an Algerian hospital and sympathized with the Algerian cause. After the French government kicked him out of Algeria, he wrote *The Wretched of the Earth*, which argued that to overcome colonialism all means had to be used, including violence. For the next few decades Fanon's ideas had a strong influence on Third World anti-colonial rebels, who used a variety of tactics including terrorism. In Kenya, the leading terrorists acting against British officials and colonists, as well as their Kenyan collaborators, were labeled the Mau Mau. Although the British killed thousands of Kikuyu (the chief Kenyan ethnic opposition group) in an effort to crush the Mau Mau, Kenya finally received its independence in 1963.

Terrorism and guerrilla warfare also overlapped in Latin America. The leading Latin American theorist of terrorism in the 1960s was the Brazilian Marxist Carlos Marighella. His books *For the Liberation of Brazil* and *The Minimanual of the Urban Guerrilla* provided practical, though not always effective, suggestions for terrorists, especially in urban areas.[45] He believed that even decentralized and at times almost random terrorism could create panic and destabilize the government. He foresaw that a government's reaction to such terror might be increased repression, but he thought that this would gain more sympathy for the terrorists. Another prominent theoretician of revolutionary violence, but more of larger-scale guerrilla warfare than terrorism, was another Marxist, Che Guevara. He fought alongside Fidel Castro and helped him come to power in Cuba in 1959. Castro and Guevara subsequently encouraged guerrilla warfare in other countries, with Guevera being captured and killed in Bolivia in 1967. The following year Cuba hosted revolutionaries from other countries, including Yasser Arafat, leader of the Palestinian Liberation Organization (PLO). Arafat thought that Marighella's thinking on urban guerrilla war was "a theme uniting international revolution."[46] Despite the influence of Marighella's ideas, however, he was no more successful in Brazil than Guevera was in Bolivia.

In the late 1960s the leading terrorist movement in Latin America was that of Uruguay's Tupamaros, who adopted some of Marighella's ideas. Their terrorism included killings, kidnappings, and bank robberies. Among those killed was a U.S. police adviser to the Uruguayan government (1970); among those kidnapped was the British ambassador (1971). The Tupamaros advocated socialist principles, especially greater economic equality. But the Uruguayan public sided more with the government than with Tupmaros terrorism, and the government crushed the terrorists during the early 1970s. In neighboring Argentina in the mid-1970s, leftist opponents of the government and military committed hundreds of political murders and assaulted military installations, but, as in Uruguay, a repressive military government soon crushed the movement. In the 1980s and 1990s Latin American terrorist activity was most prominent in impoverished Peru, where two leftist groups, the Shining Path and the Tupac Amaru Revolutionary Movement, were most prominent. As often occurred in Latin America, the terrorism of the Shining Path sometimes reached the proportions of guerrilla warfare. In the decade and a half after its founding the organization killed "at least 2,500 soldiers and policeman" and many more civilians.[47] But by the mid-1990s it had splintered and declined in significance. From December 1996 to April 1997 the Tupac Amaru held hostages they had seized at the Japanese embassy in Lima, but the Peruvian government finally attacked the hostage takers and freed the hostages. By the end of the century, terrorism in Peru had been defeated, at least temporarily, but great poverty and inequalities continued into the new century, providing fertile ground for new terrorist outbreaks.

In Europe, besides the nationalist and separatist terrorism of the IRA and the Basque Nation and Liberty (ETA) terrorists in Spain, other leading terrorists in the late 1960s and 1970s were members of the German "Red Army Faction" (RAF) and Italian Red Brigades. The German group emerged out of German student radicalism in the late 1960s and engaged in bombings, bank robberies, and assassinations. Although many of the original leaders were arrested in the early 1970s, the RAF continued sporadic terrorist acts until it disbanded in 1998. The Italian Red Brigades were more active, engaging in about 14,000 terrorist attacks in the decade after their founding in 1970. By the mid-1980s, however, their popularity and activities had waned considerably, and they soon disintegrated.

As in Europe, so in the United States, the late 1960s witnessed an outbreak of terrorism. One significant group of terrorists was the Weathermen (later Weather Underground), which emerged out of the Students for a Democratic Society (SDS). Another far left group was M19CO, which was most active in the early 1980s. It was a mixed racial group, containing about as many women as men. In its most noted attack it robbed an armored car and killed a guard and two policemen in the process. U.S. leftist terrorism declined thereafter, but did not completely disappear.[48]

During the late 1980s and 1990s U.S. right-wing terrorism became more significant. Its practitioners bombed abortion clinics, committed racist crimes, and by 1997 formed hundreds of self-proclaimed militias, which, according to one expert, "all emphasized preparation for an apocalyptic showdown with a tyrannical government and a race war that would begin in the year 2000."[49] Several confrontations between federal law officials and right-wing extremists fueled this terrorism. At Ruby Ridge, Idaho in 1992 several people were killed in a shootout; and in 1993 a two-month federal siege of a religious sect (Branch Davidians) who were stockpiling arms near Waco, Texas brought about the deaths of almost 80 sect members, plus several federal agents. Two years later, on the anniversary of the destruction of the sect's compound, two men influenced by the militia movement and in revenge for the siege near Waco blew up the Federal Building in Oklahoma City, killing 168 people.

A U.S. terrorist who criticized both leftists and rightists was Theodore Kaczynski. He was arrested in 1996, and was guilty of mailing out bombs to scientists and businessmen as part of his effort to help overthrow "the economic and technological basis" of society. He began his "Manifesto" with the following words: "The Industrial Revolution and its consequences have been a disaster for the human race . . . They have destabilized society, have made life unfulfilling, have subjected human beings to indignities, have led to widespread psychological suffering (in the Third World to physical suffering as well) and have inflicted severe damage on the natural world. The continued development of technology will worsen the situation."[50]

During the 1990s internationalist terrorist threats became more serious for U.S. citizens as well as many others around the world. After defeating Iraq in the 1991 Gulf War, the United States set up military bases in several Muslim countries. In 1992 the Saudi-born Osama Bin Laden, who had fought in Afghanistan against Soviet troops and been chiefly responsible for forming the terrorist organization al-Qaeda, called for a jihad (holy war) against Western "occupation" of Islamic lands. In 1996 he addressed the United States as follows: "Terrorising you, while you are carrying arms on our land, is a legitimate and morally demanded duty. It is a legitimate right well known to all humans and other creatures . . . The coward is the one who lets you walk, while carrying arms, freely on his land and provides you with peace and security . . . Our youths knew that the humiliation suffered by the Muslims as a result of the occupation of their sanctities can not be kicked and removed except by explosions and Jihad."[51]

During the 1990s Bin Laden and his followers and sympathizers carried out or at least attempted explosions within the USA and at U.S. embassies and other targets abroad. In February 1993 a truck bomb beneath the twin towers of New York's World Trade Center injured about one thousand people and killed six, many less than the terrorists had hoped—but, of course, in the new century, on September 11, 2001, these same towers were destroyed by Bin Laden's followers who slammed hijacked commercial airplanes into them, killing nearly 3,000 people. In 1998, al-Qaeda was responsible for bombings at U.S. embassies in Nairobi, Kenya, and Dar es Salaam, Tanzania. Some other earlier plots, such as a 1995 plan to blow up about a dozen in-flight U.S. trans-Pacific jetliners, were never realized.

Overall, one reliable estimate states that 7,152 people of all nationalities, including 666 Americans, were killed as a result of international terrorist occurrences (those involving two or more nationalities) in the 1980s and 1990s. When cases of domestic terrorism, such as the Oklahoma City bombing, are added from the various nations of the world, the total is much higher.[52]

In his overview of terrorism as of 1998, Walter Laqueur stated that by the use of terrorist methods "in the near future it will be technologically possible to kill thousands, perhaps hundreds of thousands."[53] Many other experts believed that by then it was already possible.

Structural Violence

In addition to the types of violence already dealt with, there remains one more kind to mention—structural violence. It is different than the previously discussed violence in that it is less direct. It is the "physical and psychological harm that results from exploitive and unjust social, political and economic systems."[54] In the twentieth century and beyond, this type of violence continued to deny many of the world's poorest people access to sufficient food, proper sanitation, and health care, thus greatly reducing their life expectancy. About global poverty the World Health Organization (WHO) observed in the mid-1990s, "[It] wields its destructive influence at every stage of human life, from the moment of conception to the grave. It conspires with the most deadly and painful diseases to bring a wretched existence to all those who suffer from it." Dr. Paul Farmer, who has worked hard to mitigate the consequences of structural violence in Haiti, summarized WHO's conclusion in the following words, "Poverty is the world's greatest killer."[55] Poor people were also more likely than wealthier ones to be victimized by more direct types of violence such as war, government repression, crime, and family and ethnic violence. Finally, the unjust systems that gave birth to structural violence also inadvertently helped foster opposition movements that in turn resorted to violence. One thinks, for example, of the unjust Russian tsarist order against which Lenin, Trotsky, Stalin and others rebelled.[56]

The Public Response

Although the responsibility of leaders like Hitler and Stalin for twentieth-century violence was considerable,[57] the massive deaths of the century also occurred because millions of people supported or acquiesced in their policies or those of other leaders who gave the orders for large-scale killings. This was especially true in wartime. In the first six months of World War I, for example, there were almost 2 million British volunteers for military service. During World War II, a combined total of more than 1 million Koreans and Taiwanese offered to fight for Japan. As minorities such as Turkish Armenians and European Jews discovered in two world wars, war also often permitted or encouraged atrocities beyond those allowed in peacetime. After attacking eastern Europe, the Nazis often encouraged ethnic hatred not only against Jews, but also, for example, inciting Ukrainians against Poles.

The Nobel-Prize winning economist Amartya Sen has insisted that a good deal of twentieth-century violence flowed from "the illusion of a unique and choiceless identity," for example, that of nationality, race, or class. He added that "the art of constructing hatred takes the form of invoking the magical power of some allegedly predominant identity that drowns other affiliations and in a conveniently bellicose form can also overpower any human sympathy or natural kindness that we may normally have."[58]

Except for absolute pacifists, most people justified some killing but condemned the taking of other lives. Such judgments were seldom based on any logically consistent principles such as those enunciated in the Christian Theory of a Just War.[59] For example, most U.S. citizens condemned any form of communist or terrorist activity that led to deaths, especially that of "innocent civilians," but were inclined to ignore or justify the massive taking of civilian lives that resulted from Allied bombing, both conventional and nuclear, during World War II. Even before the U.S. nuclear bombing of Hiroshima and Nagasaki, which immediately or in the aftermath killed a few hundred thousand individuals, massive Allied fire bombing and other non-nuclear bombing had killed a higher total number of people in other cities like Dresden, Hamburg, Darmstadt, and Tokyo.

Contemporary or later arguments by those who maintained that such large-scale killing was unnecessary, that the war could still have been won without such massive deaths, remained largely unexplored by the average American.[60] Part of the reason for this was that deaths of foreigners mattered much less to most people than the deaths of their own citizens. In the United States, the Gulf War of 1991 against Iraq and Saddam Hussein was considered a great success partly because less than 200 American lives were lost. It is difficult to believe that most Americans would have thought the war worth the cost if the price had been thousands or tens of thousands of American lives. Charges that the U.S.-led sanctions against Iraq in the decade after the war led to hundreds of thousands of Iraqi civilian deaths, whether true or not, seemed to matter little to most Americans, partly because many of them never heard about such charges.

There are many reasons why the deaths of foreigners or those considered fundamentally different seemed to matter much less to people than the deaths of those more similar. And there are additional reasons that help to explain how individuals from almost all nations at various times in the century were able to justify killing enemies, whether from other nations, classes, religions, or some other criteria of "otherness." It is natural for people to feel more compassion for those closer to them—for family members, neighbors, or members of a group or nation with whom they identify. In addition, in the case of a nation or state, patriotism and nationalism were often reinforced by education, by media, and by social and cultural rituals such as the singing of national anthems, and, especially in wartime, by government propaganda.

In Nazi Germany and the communist societies of Lenin, Stalin, and the Asian Marxists, control over education and media resources enabled the government to convince many in their societies that "enemies of the people" were deserving of death. In democratic countries that espoused respect for human life and dignity, military training had to overcome resistance to killing; for as Gwynne Dyer has written, "The most important single factor that makes it possible for civilized men to fight the wars of civilization is that all armies everywhere have exploited and manipulated the ingrained warrior ethic that is the heritage of every young human male."[61] And in a chapter on military training, especially U.S. Marine training, Dyer indicates how an emphasis on toughness, compliance with orders, peer pressure, and concern for one's fellow soldiers, can turn a young man (or at least a boy being made into a "man") into someone who will kill when told to do so. As one U.S. Marine drill instructor stated it about a typical recruit, "I can train that guy; I can get him to do anything I want him to."[62]

Observers as astute as the psychologist William James recognized that military training and wars appealed to positive as well as negative human traits. Well before World War I, he called for the creation of a "moral equivalent of war," for opportunities for people to perform more of the heroic type of actions of war without all the accompanying tragedies of it. To many young men, however, life on the eve of the Great War was still too humdrum, too unheroic; and because we know of the horror that followed, we read with sadness lines such as those written by the poet Rupert Brooke upon the outbreak of the war:

> Now, God be thanked Who has matched us with His hour,
> And caught our youth, and wakened us from sleeping . . .

The carnage of World War I, however, punctured such romanticism. English poets like Siegfried Sasson and Wilfred Owen and the German novelist Erich Maria Remarque, all of whom served in the war, captured some of the disillusionment brought by the war in their writings. In one of Owen's finest poems, "Dulce et Decorum Est," he ends it this way:

> Gas! Gas! Quick, boys!—An ecstasy of fumbling,
> Fitting the clumsy helmets just in time;
> But someone still was yelling out and stumbling
> And flound'ring like a man in fire or lime . . .
> Dim, through the misty panes and thick green light,
> As under a green sea, I saw him drowning.
>
> In all my dreams, before my helpless sight,
> He plunges at me, guttering, choking, drowning.
>
> If in some smothering dreams you too could pace
> Behind the wagon that we flung him in,
> And watch the white eyes writhing in his face,

His hanging face, like a devil's sick of sin;
If you could hear, at every jolt, the blood
Come gargling from the froth-corrupted lungs,
Obscene as cancer, bitter as the cud
Of vile, incurable sores on innocent tongues,—
My friend, you would not tell with such high zest
To children ardent for some desperate glory,
The old lie: *Dulce et decorum est*
Pro patria mori. [It is sweet and honorable to die for one's country]

The Latin words he ended his poem with were from the poet Horace and were taught to many British schoolboys. Captain Owen was machine-gunned to death a week before the war ended on the eleventh hour, of the eleventh day, of the eleventh month of 1918. One hour later, with bells still ringing in celebration, his parents received the telegram informing them of their son's death.

Like some pre-war poetry, however, many later films again romanticized war. In 1977 Philip Caputo recalled how as a young college student in 1960 he enrolled in a Marine Officer Training Program partly as a result of the romantic heroism of such war movies as *Guadalcanal Diary* (1943), *Sands of Iwo Jima* (1949), and *Retreat, Hell!* (1952). He explained his motivation as such: "The heroic experience I sought was war; war, the ultimate adventure; war, the ordinary man's most convenient means of escaping from the ordinary ... Already I saw myself charging up some distant beachhead like John Wayne in *Sands of Iwo Jima*, and then coming home a suntanned warrior with medals on my chest ... I needed to prove something—my courage, my toughness, my manhood."[63] After being sent to Vietnam and soon realizing that "both we and the Viet Cong began to make a habit of atrocities," he no longer saw combat in such romantic terms.[64]

Other Vietnam veterans also recalled the impact of films about World War II, especially the very popular *To Hell and Back* (1955), starring Audie Murphy and based on the autobiography of this war hero turned actor. Both Ron Kovic, in his *Born on the Fourth of July* (1976), and Lieutenant William Calley, court-martialed for the Vietnam atrocity My Lai, mentioned Murphy's influence on their desire to fight in Vietnam. During the 1991 Gulf War, decorated combat veteran Colonel David Hackworth observed of Western troops, "Hollywood completely colors their way of seeing war."[65]

In almost all cases of wars and atrocities, the enemy was depicted as less human by the use of derogatory terms. We have already mentioned the Nazis' equating the Jews with all sorts of subhuman creatures from rats to lice, and some Japanese publications depicted the British and Americans as beasts. One Japanese officer during the "Rape of Nanking," was quoted as saying: "I regard them [the Chinese] as swine. We can do anything to such creatures."[66] But racist images also were common among the Allied powers during World War II. In the United States and Great Britain, some people referred to the Japanese as little or yellow monkeys. The U.S. War Correspondent Ernie Pyle, who covered the war in the Pacific wrote, "Out here I soon gathered that the Japanese were looked upon as something subhuman and repulsive; the way some people feel about cockroaches or mice."[67] During the Vietnam War, Americans commonly referred to the Viet Cong as "gooks." As one sergeant testified: "[Our] colonels called them gooks, the staff all called them gooks. They were dinks, you know, subhuman."[68]

Even when the enemy was not of a different race but of a different class or religion, the same type of dehumanization made it easier to kill. In early 1918 a communist was mistakenly killed in the Soviet city of Saratov because he was wearing a fashionable suit and mistaken for a *burzhui* (a term of abuse for the bourgeoisie). Glasses also made a person suspect. And clean fingernails and uncalloused hands got some people shot by the Reds during the civil war. Sergei Kirov, a future communist leader whom Stalin perceived as a challenger to his own power, called the leaders of the civil war's White Forces "lice"; and in the 1930s Soviet Prosecutor Andrei Vyshinsky spewed forth the following during Moscow trials of some of the most important accused enemies of Stalin: "Shoot these rabid dogs ... Down with that vulture Trotsky ... Down with these abject animals! Let us put an end once and for all to these miserable hybrids of foxes and pigs, these stinking corpses! Let their horrible squeals finally come to an end! Let's exterminate the mad dogs of capitalism."[69]

Among those dehumanized by Lenin and his successors were any labeled bourgeoisie, capitalists, counterrevolutionaries, kulaks, or enemies of the people. Such labeling made easier Stalin's demand in 1929 that the kulaks be "liquidated as a class." Writer Vasily Grossman described how Communist Party activists in Ukraine "looked on the so-called 'kulaks' as cattle, swine, loathsome, repulsive: they had no souls; they stank; they all had venereal diseases; they were enemies of the people ... What torture was meted out to them! In order to massacre them, it was necessary to proclaim that kulaks are not human beings." But Grossman also indicated other factors that helped cause the killings, for example Party people's anxiety to please their superiors or gain personally from confiscating kulak property.[70]

Overwhelmingly, killings and terrorist acts were committed by people who thought their beliefs justified what they were doing.

The ideas of nineteenth-century thinkers like Marx (1818–83), Darwin (1809–82), and Friedrich Nietzsche (1844–1900), as well as racist, nationalist, and imperialist ideas, were often used, properly or improperly, to justify such killings. So too, but to a lesser extent, were religious ideas. In the Western press in the final decades of the century, there was much talk of "militant Islam" or "Islamic terrorists," but most Muslims did not advocate terrorism, and individuals from other religions also advocated or practiced terrorism. They included (among many others) Catholics who worked within the IRA, Protestants who bombed abortion clinics in the United States, Hindus in India who attacked Muslims, and the Jewish student of religious law who thought he was acting "on God's orders" when he assassinated Israeli Prime Minister Yitzhak Rabin in 1995 because of Rabin's peace plans. Yet the communist leaders, who were responsible for the greatest number of mass killings in the century, were all committed atheists who persecuted religion. Although the Nazis did not preach atheism, Hitler "was passionately hostile to Christianity" and, like Nietzsche, thought it was begun by Jews in an attempt to aid slaves to overthrow their Roman rulers.[71] Jonathan Glover, who identified himself as one who does "not believe in a religious moral law" (i.e., any moral law dictated by traditional religion), nevertheless recognized that many of the century's protests against atrocities came from religious people.[72]

Glover began his book *Humanity*, which is essentially an analysis of twentieth century wars and atrocities from an ethical perspective, with a section on Nietzsche. The latter predicted that morality based on traditional religious beliefs would gradually disappear. Glover stated that the century has generally moved in that direction and that the challenge for people at the end of the century was to create a humanized ethics. He added that when "there is no external moral law, morality needs to be humanized: to be rooted in human needs and human values."[73]

Besides beliefs and ideas mattering, technology also played a role in making killing easier. The dropping of bombs, for example, not only made it possible to kill more people, but also depersonalized the killing. Those dropping the bombs did not have to view the blood their bombs spilled or the limbs they tore asunder. Furthermore the bureaucracy and complexity of modern states and warfare helped dilute feelings of personal responsibility for the deaths of those considered "enemies of the people" or government.

A similar lack of responsibility was felt by many people in regard to the structural violence inflicted on the world's impoverished people. One humanitarian who observed first-hand the consequences of such violence believed there were at least three reasons for this relative indifference: 1) the suffering of its victims was too psychologically and culturally remote from the experiences of many people in wealthier parts of the world; 2) the vastness of the problem, often conveyed in facts and statistics, made it difficult to appreciate the individual suffering it entailed; and 3) "the dynamics and distribution of suffering [caused by structural violence] are still poorly understood." This same observer believed that much of this suffering resulted from denying poor people the fruits of scientific and technological progress, a subject which we examine in our next chapter.[74]

2

Science, Technology, and the Acceleration of Change

The long-term impact of scientific-technological developments on twentieth-century life was enormous. These developments were crucial, for example, in greatly increasing people's life expectancy (see below) and the global population from 1.6 billion in 1900 to 6 billion in 1999, an increase that would have major environmental consequences (see Chapter 6).

The line between technology and science, especially applied sciences such as aeronautics, agronomy, electronics, engineering, medicine, and metallurgy, is sometimes difficult to discern. For understanding twentieth-century history, however, what is most essential is to comprehend the areas of human life that were most affected by their combined impact. In general, science deals more with principles and theories, whereas technology is concerned with techniques, tools, instruments, machines, and other products that help humans to accomplish various tasks. Science itself was often poorly understood and took on significance for most people only when it led to technological developments like advancements in medical treatment or sending men to the moon. In the early twentieth century physicists like Max Planck, Albert Einstein, Niels Bohr, Ernest Rutherford, James Chadwick, Werner Heisenberg, Hans Bethe, and Enrico Fermi participated in a golden age for their science. And people heard of some of their new terms such as Quantum Mechanics, the Theory of Relativity, and the Uncertainty

Principal, but few non-scientists really understood their meaning. It was only after leading physicists, including Bohr, Bethe, and Fermi, had come together on the Manhattan Project during World War II and demonstrated one of the practical applications of the new discoveries in physics that most people came to appreciate the importance of their work. That fruit of their project was, of course, the atomic bomb, and its use against Hiroshima and Nagasaki testified more than any words could to the significance of applied physics.

In modern times, scientific and technological innovations proliferated first in Europe and the United States and were interconnected with various economic, social, political, and cultural factors that stimulated such innovations.[1] The profit motive, for example, was one, but so too were wartime needs in circumstances where governments assumed greater control over economic and scientific life. Wars stimulated research into technical areas such as computers (see below), but also into many other fields like medicine. A UN-sponsored book dealing with the twentieth century up to the 1960s proclaimed that "the major wars of the period accelerated the development of medical techniques and their application in many fields," including "extensive immunization" and "the use of new drugs such as penicillin."[2] The belief that humans should control nature and use it for their own benefit was also stronger in the Western tradition than, for example, in parts of the world where Buddhism, Hinduism, or Islam greatly affected people's thinking.

In 1899 the head of the U.S. Patent Office declared that "everything that can be invented has been invented." Of course, he was wrong, but much of the technology significant for the twentieth century had indeed already been invented in the nineteenth century. Nevertheless, its application was still in its childhood even in the most industrialized countries in the world. In 1900 less than 5 percent of U.S. homes possessed telephones, and on U.S. roads, there were only about 8,000 automobiles.

Electricity

Well before 1900 America's most famous inventor, Thomas Edison (1847–1931), contributed to the invention and development of the phonograph, the generation of electricity, the light bulb, and motion pictures. By 1904, however, only about 5 percent of U.S. homes possessed a phonograph, and by 1907 only about 8 percent of residences were wired for electricity. It is true that by 1900 there were over 3,000 U.S. electric power stations, some owned privately and some publicly, generating electricity from a variety of power sources including Niagara Falls. But at first electricity, both in the United States and abroad, was used primarily for lighting streets, operating public transit, and by stores, restaurants, and other commercial and industrial enterprises. In 1900, for example, the H. J. Heinz Company erected in New York a six-story advertising sign using 1,200 bulbs, featuring a gigantic pickle and the company slogan "57 Varieties."[3]

Although the first paid theater showing of motion pictures (one-minute ones) occurred in Paris in 1895, it took a while for movies to become popular. The first nickelodeons (movie theaters) did not open in the United States until 1905, but by 1908 the estimated daily attendance at New York City's 600 nickelodeons was over 300,000 people. In Russia by 1913 there were an estimated 1,500 film houses, often labeled electric theaters. The label was appropriate not just because of the projectors reliance on electricity, but also because it was often a power source for other theater features like lighting and electric pianos.

During the twentieth century, perhaps no other technological advancement, even the automobile, affected the people of the world more than electricity. Many of the other technological achievements of the century for both homes and businesses, including automobile factories and most radios, televisions, and computers, depended on it. This flexible and convenient form of energy revolutionized both factory production and household chores and enjoyments.[4] Throughout the century, the United States utilized the most electricity. In the interwar years, major European countries such as Germany were still far behind. In the Soviet Union, Vladimir Lenin and Joseph Stalin placed great hopes on electricity. In 1920 Lenin said that "communism is Soviet Power plus the electrification of the whole country" and that for the peasants electricity would replace God. But it was Stalin who presided over the greater increase in the production of Soviet electricity, for example, about a sevenfold increase from 1927 to 1937.

By mid-century, the USSR, North America, Europe, and Japan, were using the overwhelming percentage of the world's electricity, whereas about 60 percent of the world's population was only using about 2 percent of it. In the second half of the century, however, many less affluent countries accelerated the electrification of their countries. As in the United States, the Soviet Union, and many other more industrialized countries, less developed countries sometimes constructed large hydroelectric facilities. During the 1960s in Egypt, for example, the Aswan High Dam was built, which doubled Egypt's electrical power. Other countries like Congo (Zaire) and Brazil also emphasized hydroelectric power. As the century ended, China was in the midst of a multi-year, multi-billion dollar Three Gorges Dam Project on the Yangzi River. Worldwide, however, by century's end, other sources of electricity, including coal-burning installations and nuclear power plants, collectively generated more electricity. Between 1987 and 1996 China more than doubled its electrical consumption, and India and Indonesia almost doubled theirs. By 1996, however, with a combined population about nine times that of the United States, these three countries were still only collectively consuming a little over two-fifths as much electricity. And by then all of Africa was only consuming about one-tenth that of the United States. Overall, in the early 1990s more than one-third of the world's people were still without household electricity.

Electricity came especially slowly, if at all, to rural areas. Many western European countries, however, moved more quickly in this regard than did the United States, where only about 11 percent of the farms were electrified in 1935. That was the year that President Franklin Roosevelt established the Rural Electrification Administration, and by 1950 almost nine-tenths of U.S. farms were electrified. By that date in the Soviet Union, a little less than one-sixth of the country's collective farms (the most prominent type of Soviet farm, still containing almost one-third of the Soviet Union's population in 1959) were electrified. By the mid-1960s almost all Soviet farms had electricity. By 1971, however, electricity was enjoyed by only 4 percent of African, 15 percent of Asian, and 23 percent of Latin American villages. What electricity means to peasants in such areas has been indicated by Paul Harrison, who traveled extensively in the Third World: "Electricity frees the peasant from the tyranny of early bedtime. It is the essential precondition ... to a fan, a fridge [refrigerator] or a record player. But it can also help a village to develop small-scale industry."[5] Although the percentage of urban people in these regions who had access to electricity was much higher, some urban poor who lived in slums and shantytowns did not have household electricity, though the number declined as the century neared its end.

Health and Science

As with electricity, medical knowledge and techniques had advanced considerably before 1900. The impact of these advances had only begun, however, even in the Western world, where most advances first appeared. Especially important were late nineteenth-century discoveries about the origins of diseases, such as the findings by the Frenchman Louis Pasteur and the German Robert Koch regarding germs, bacteria, and immunology (including the use of vaccines). Even though the death rate by 1900 had dropped in the Western world, average life expectancy for men at birth in 1900 was still under 50 years of age in the United States, the United Kingdom (Great Britain and Ireland), Germany, and France. Women's life expectancy was a few year's longer. In India, average male life expectancy was only about 25 years. These averages were so low primarily because of the high death rates for children. In the combined European countries mentioned above, more than 15 percent of infants died before reaching their first birthday. In European Russia the figure was around 25 percent. In Mexico, it was close to 30 percent. In 1895, X-rays were discovered and at New York's Pan-American Exhibition of 1901 an X-ray machine was on display, but was not yet considered reliable enough to locate the bullet that was buried inside President McKinley, who was shot while attending the exhibition and died eight days later.

By 1930 in the major countries of the Western world, life expectancy had increased by roughly 10 years as compared to 30 years earlier. In other less technologically developed parts of the world the gain was not as significant. In India, for example, it increased no more than a few years.

The major reason a person in developed Western countries could expect to live longer had to do more with improved sanitation, nutrition, and public health practices than with scientific advances in creating new medicines. Illustrating this was a poll conducted by the *British Medical Journal*, as reported on in early 2007, in which the journal's readers selected developments in sanitation as the greatest medical advance since the mid-nineteenth century, although the discovery of antibiotics and the development of vaccines were also highly ranked.[6]

In 1900 the three diseases that killed most people in the United States were pneumonia, tuberculosis, and the related illnesses of diarrhea and enteritis (an inflammation of the intestines). By 1930 the death rate for diarrhea and enteritis had declined the most (by about 80 percent), primarily because of improvements in providing purer water and milk and better disposal of sewage and other waste. Tuberculosis rates fell by more than 60 percent mainly because of earlier detection and better preventive methods that greatly reduced the spreading of this contagious disease. A tuberculosis vaccine was developed in France in the 1920s but was not widely used before World War II. Better public health measures also reduced

pneumonia rates. As with tuberculosis, further drops occurred after
the development of a series of drugs, primarily in the 1930s and
1940s, such as penicillin (the first antibiotic drug), streptomycin, and
various sulfa compounds. Such drugs were also effective in curing
other illnesses like typhoid, typhus, and venereal diseases.

Another way of dealing with diseases was to immunize against
them. Although a smallpox vaccine had been developed in the late
eighteenth century, and a few other vaccines a century later, most
vaccines were not discovered until the twentieth century. By 1950
vaccines helped avert such earlier widespread diseases as
diphtheria, tetanus, typhoid, typhus, cholera, and whooping cough.
In the 1950s an effective polio vaccine was developed against the
poliomyelitis virus, which earlier in the century had left countless
individuals permanently crippled including U.S. President Franklin
Roosevelt. Other vaccines became common in the second half of the
century including those for measles, mumps, and hepatitis.

In 1918 and 1919 a worldwide influenza epidemic killed over 20
million people, more than World War I. Other epidemics followed in
subsequent years but were less severe, partly because of better health
practices. In the 1940s vaccines against several influenza strains were
developed, but immunization was difficult because so many different
types of influenza viruses existed. Even in the United States only a
very small portion of the population received flu shots before the
1980s, at which time such shots became more readily available.

During the second half of the twentieth century, death rates
continued to drop and life expectancy rose for many of the same
reasons as had occurred earlier in the century. Continuing new
scientific advances were one factor, but so too was the more
widespread global adoption of basic health and sanitation principles
discovered long before 1950. Whereas life expectancy worldwide
was estimated at about 48 years in 1955, by 1999 it was about 66 years.
In the more technologically advanced countries, heart/circulatory
diseases and cancer, more common in older people, replaced
infectious and parasitic diseases as the leading killers. As compared
to those living in 1900, people in these countries in 1999 were also
taller, heavier, and suffered less disabilities at comparable ages.[7]

The most important advances in medical technology made possible
all sorts of new surgical procedures by the end of the century including
transplanting of the heart, liver, kidney, bone marrow, pancreas, and
cornea. The first successful kidney transplant occurred in the 1950s,
but for years afterwards transplant rejection by a body remained a
problem, and most kidney recipients did not survive beyond one year
after surgery. The first heart transplant was performed in South Africa

in 1967, but the recipient lived only a few weeks. The following year, there were over 100 such transplants in numerous countries, but only about one-fourth of the patients lived for more than six months. Gradually, however, immunologists discovered ways to reduce the body's rejection of transplants, and the survival rate for all transplants increased. By 1999 there were a total of over 21,000 transplants in the United States alone, with kidney recipients comprising more than half the total and having a better survival rate than those who received a liver or heart, the two next most common transplant recipients. Other patients received artificial replacements such as hips made of steel and plastic or benefited from developments in microscopic surgery that made new delicate procedures available for the first time. In general smaller instruments and the use of laser and ultrasonic devices made surgery less intrusive and reduced recovery time.

Another important development was the invention of new imaging techniques and equipment, for example the CAT scanner (Computerized Axial Tomography) and MRI (Magnetic Resonance Imaging). In the last few decades of the century, they provided doctors with much more comprehensive views of the human body than traditional X-rays.

Medical technology also produced many new drugs for fighting various diseases and their side effects such as those of the heart and the many varieties of cancer. None of them, however, produced as dramatic an impact as penicillin and the sulfa drugs had earlier. Perhaps just as importantly, new scientific findings broadened people's knowledge of what caused diseases (for example, linking smoking and lung cancer) and how to take better preventive measures to reduce one's chances of getting sick. By quitting smoking, watching their diet more closely, and exercising more, many people increased their life expectancy. Perhaps the most influential drug developed in the 1950s did not fight disease but prevented pregnancy—many people simply referred to it as "the pill." (See Chapter 5 for its significance in women's struggle for reproductive self-determination.)

Of some concern at the end of the century was the fact that some drugs were losing their effectiveness against certain diseases. Many scientists and public health experts blamed the overuse of antibiotics, from doctors over-prescribing them to their use in products such as animal feed. This overuse in turn stimulated the evolution of germs (super-bugs) that developed immunities against many existing antibiotics. Because of low profit margins on antibiotic drugs, which were generally used only for a short time (as opposed to more long-term used drugs such as statins), many pharmaceutical companies resisted investing in the development of new antibiotic drugs that might prove more effective against super-bugs.

A still greater problem was the continuing spread of the HIV/AIDS (Acquired Immune Deficiency Syndrome) epidemic. At the end of 1999 the United Nations estimated that about 34 million people were infected with HIV, more than two-thirds of them in sub-Saharan Africa. In that area, AIDS had become by far the leading cause of death. Many of the infected women transmitted HIV to the infants born to them, and during the 1990s life expectancy decreased in that part of Africa by several years, much more in some of the hardest hit countries. In 1999 far more Africans died of AIDS than in the previous 10 years combined. Altogether worldwide, almost 19 million people died of AIDS from the time the epidemic began spreading at the end of the 1970s until the end of the century.[8]

In colonial and less developed areas of the world, the application of scientific medical principles came slower than in the more industrialized areas. Climate, sanitary conditions, greater poverty and malnutrition, and lack of access to adequate medical care and medicines also prevented death rates from falling as much as in more developed regions. By the end of the century, as compared to the United States, the infant death rate in Mexico was 4 times greater; in India, 10 times greater; and in Niger, 27 times greater. And the chances of an infant surviving until his first birthday were even better in much of western Europe and Japan than in the United States.[9]

In 1997, 97 percent of the deaths of young children (those under five years old) occurred in the "developing world." The great majority of these deaths were medically preventable. According to the World Health Organization (WHO), which has done much to improve global health conditions, 43 percent of the deaths of all ages in the "developing world" in 1997 were due to infectious and parasitic diseases as compared to only 1 percent in the "developed world." While diseases like malaria had all but been eliminated in rich countries, such diseases still plagued poorer nations—about a million deaths a year were caused by malaria at the end of the century. One journalist noted that "virtually everyone in the West African interior has some form of malaria . . . It is malaria that is most responsible for the disease wall that threatens to separate Africa and other parts of the Third World from more developed regions of the planet in the twenty-first century. Carried by mosquitoes, malaria, unlike AIDS, is easy to catch. Most people in sub-Saharan Africa have recurring bouts of the disease throughout their entire lives, and it is mutating into increasingly deadly forms."[10]

In addition, many of the same diseases that struck Europe and the United States in the early 1900s, like pneumonia and germ-related diarrhea, were still killing large numbers of people in poorer parts of the world in the 1990s. (As late as 2004, pneumonia was killing more than 2 million children per year in the combined regions of Africa, Asia, Latin America, and the Caribbean.)[11] It is such phenomena that led Dr. Paul Farmer (see above, Chapter 1), based largely on his experiences in Haiti, to charge that the world's poor were being denied the fruits of technological and medical progress that long had been enjoyed by more prosperous people. A UN Report in 2003 made a similar point when it declared that "water-related diseases are among the most common causes of illness and death, affecting mainly the poor in developing countries ... In 2000, the estimated mortality rate due to water sanitation hygiene-associated diarrhoeas and some other water/sanitation associated diseases ... was 2,213,000 ... The majority of those affected by water-related mortality and morbidity are children under five. The tragedy is that this disease burden is largely preventable."[12]

Nevertheless, some progress also occurred in the less developed parts of the world. In 1974 only 5 percent of the world's children had been immunized against diphtheria, tetanus, tuberculosis, whooping cough, measles, and poliomyelitis; by 1995, 80 percent were immunized. Between 1955 and 1995 the death rate for children under five throughout the world was cut by more than 60 percent.

Yet in at least one part of the world, Russia, there was regression in health care in the late 1980s and 1990s, partly due to the confusion and turmoil resulting from the transition of the Soviet Union to Russia and 14 other countries, all proceeding by trial and error to construct new political and economic systems. By the end of 1995 Russian life-expectancy estimates for males had dropped to about 58 years of age (a decade later it remained about the same). This figure was about eight years lower than in 1964–5 and four years lower than in 1980–1. It was also much below the average for all Latin American and Asian countries. Some of the causes were alcoholism; heavy smoking; a polluted environment; stress; inadequate diets; and poor sanitation, medical care, and supplies. This period witnessed an increase in infectious diseases like cholera, diphtheria, dysentery, tuberculosis, and sexually transmitted diseases. In the late 1980s close to half the rural hospitals and polyclinics were without sewer connections and four-fifths of them were without hot water. Such sanitation problems were worsened by shortages such as lack of disposable syringes. Other medical equipment was also in short supply; for example, only half of the country's hospitals and polyclinics possessed X-ray machines. As one indication of Russia's poor health-care system, Russian officials confirmed in 1995 that 10 times as many Russian women were dying in childbirth as were women in the advanced Western countries.

Russia's health woes served as a reminder that basic public health practices and equipment (like disposable syringes and X-ray machines), as well as people's environment and life-styles, still affected the average person's health far more than the latest publicized and expensive developments in medical research and technology.

At the end of the century, many of these notable advances were coming about as a result of genetic research and engineering (the modification of an organism by transferring into it a piece of another organism's genetic material). Again, however, the first to benefit were the people in the most scientifically advanced and affluent parts of the world.

After 1953, when two British scientists demonstrated the makeup of DNA (Deoxyribonucleic Acid), the key to heredity, steady advances were made in the discovery and manipulation of genetic functions. Beginning in the 1970s and 1980s genetic engineering was applied to plants and animals, and in the 1990s to some humans suffering from such diseases as genetic immune deficiencies and cancer. Plants were genetically altered to improve crop production by enabling them, for example, to better survive herbicides intended to kill only weeds or by making them more immune to certain crop diseases. In 1988 Harvard University was granted a U.S. patent on a type of mouse genetically engineered for use in cancer experiments. The following year DuPont, one of the world's major corporations, began selling such mice for experiments. In the 1990s, millions of doses of a genetically engineered hormone were injected into cows to enable them to produce more milk. By then not only plants, mice, and cows but sheep, pigs, chickens and other animals were sometime subjects of genetic alterations, often by a medical industry searching for new medicines or cheaper ways of making old medicines. As scientists learned more about genes, they also learned more about cloning (reproducing genetically identical genes, cells, or organisms), and often used cloning techniques in connection with genetic engineering. In 1997 Scottish scientists announced that they had cloned a lamb called Dolly from the udder cells of a sheep.

By the end of the century, the scientists' increasing knowledge of genes had brought about an explosion of genetic testing and counseling. In criminal cases DNA samples of the hair, blood, semen, or other bodily fluids of a suspect were matched with those found at a crime scene. Some companies began DNA testing of prospective employees, and lawmakers wrestled with the question of whether to ban mandatory tests or the use of such results by companies or insurance providers. Genetic counseling on the other hand was willingly sought by many individuals. Couples, for example, could discover whether they carried the gene that caused cystic fibrosis. Those who were struck by the disease had to inherit the gene from both parents. Embryos could also be tested to see if they contained the gene, sometimes leaving unfortunate prospective parents with a painful decision regarding abortion. In general, new genetic developments raised many new ethical issues.

At century's end scientists were still unsure about the genetic origins, if any, of some diseases. But scientists spurred on by the Human Genome Project, begun in the 1980s under the auspices of the U.S. government, were close to completing the mapping and sequencing of the tens of thousands of genes contained in human DNA—the project was completed by the U.S. company Celera Genomics in 2000. This successful research offered great future promise for helping scientists and medical personnel in their fight against various diseases.

Meanwhile, genetic therapy that provided altered genes or obstructed defective genes in people lacking certain healthy genes continued. So too did the engineering and cloning of cells to provide medicines such as engineered insulin for diabetics and interferon for certain viral diseases and cancers. Similar procedures provided new vaccines, and some scientists believed that the best hope in the fight against AIDS would be a genetically engineered vaccine that scientists were still working on developing at century's end.

Science, Technology, and Agricultural Developments

Just as the application of science and technology to health and medicine was vital to increasing world population, so too their application to agriculture was the main reason for increased agricultural yields. And this increase in turn enabled far fewer people to produce far more food by the end of the century than had been produced in 1900. In the United States, about 38 percent of the working population was engaged in agriculture in 1900; by the end of the century, 2 percent of the population was producing a great deal more than the 38 percent had at the century's beginning. In Japan in 1947, a little over half of the people were still farmers, but by the mid-1980s, less than one-tenth were. In these post-war years, many other countries like Mexico, Algeria, and South Korea, to name just a few, also significantly decreased their farming population. Yet, overall global food production almost tripled between 1950 and 1985, before various environmental factors began slowing growth for the rest of the century.

In 1901 the first successful commercial tractor appeared in Iowa. Thereafter the increased use of tractors and other farm machinery, as well as irrigation, chemical fertilizers, and pesticides, accounted for some of the increased productivity, but so too did the discovery and application of various scientific principles regarding soils and crops. In Asia, for example, a "green revolution" occurred beginning in the 1960s that introduced new strains of rice, wheat, and other crops, helping India triple its wheat harvest in less than two decades. As growth rates slowed by the century's end, the expanded application of genetic engineering offered hope for increased productivity through production of heartier crops that better resisted herbicides, crop diseases, and significant climatic changes.

As with other applications of genetic engineering, however, crop applications increased the danger that humans could tamper with nature in ways that might have adverse consequences. Western Europeans were especially wary of genetically engineered food and took stronger measures than were taken in North America to insist on strong labeling laws, making it easier to avoid such food. As with health, so too with agriculture, enormous differences existed between nations and between the rich and poor within nations regarding the extent to which scientific and technological changes affected individual lives.

Transportation, Communications, and Consumer Products

Well before the beginning of the century, railways had revolutionized the way people and goods traveled between towns and cities. After World War I electrification and diesel power helped modernize railway lines and, although increasingly challenged by newer modes of transportation, railways continued to be significant.

Within cities before World War I electricity had had more of an impact on urban transport than had the automobile, even in the Unites States. In the 1880s and 1890s, many U.S. and major European cities replaced horse-drawn urban trams with electric streetcars (or tramcars) and greatly expanded their rail lines. These steps often expanded into rural areas and helped create new suburbs.

In the United States, it even became possible for people to travel from one state to another by transferring from one interurban line to another. By the time the Pan-American Exhibition of 1901 was held in Buffalo, people could reach it by interurban transfers all the way from Indiana and Illinois. In 1902 the people of the United States took 4.8 million trips on streetcars. Urban electric transport was not limited to the trams that ran in the streets, but in some cities also extended to underground systems or elevated tracks. New York, for example, had both by 1904.

Although the gasoline-powered automobile began to replace electric urban transportation for many people in the interwar years in the United States, in many other countries electric urban transportation remained more important. In Moscow, for example, far more people traveled by subway lines (opened in the 1930s) and electric trams and buses than by automobile, and this remained true throughout the century. The mix between public and private transport in various countries reflected many factors; in the United States, for example, the political clout of the oil, steel, and auto industries helped increase pressures to facilitate the expansion of the auto industry, partly at the expense of public transport.

By 1913 Henry Ford's new assembly line was turning out automobiles in rapidly increasing numbers. In 1920 there were 8 million automobiles registered in the United States; by 1940, 27 million; by 1980, 122 million; and by the end of the century, 132 million. Between 1908 and 1925 the price of Ford's Model T decreased from $850 to $260. Outside the United States during the interwar years, automobile ownership was more limited. In 1938 there were more than five times as many registered motor vehicles in the United States than in Great Britain, France, and Germany combined. In 1950 the United States still produced about three-fourths of the world's motor vehicles. In the latter half of the century, however, their production and ownership increased rapidly in other parts of the world, and by 1999 the United States was only producing about one-fourth of the world's total. The development of roads, highways, and places to eat and sleep accompanied this tremendous increase of automobiles and trucks.

In 1903 one of the century's great technological developments, powered air and space travel, began when the Wright Brothers first flew an airplane heavier than air. In 1927 Charles Lindbergh became the first man to fly solo nonstop from the United States to Europe, where he landed in Paris, later returning to the most tumultuous welcome in the United States that any individual had ever received. A decade later Frank Whittle of England built the first jet engine, and the British produced a small number of jet planes during World War II, as did the Germans. But more conventional Allied fighter planes and bombers, including the two that dropped atomic bombs on Japan, proved much more decisive in the war effort. In 1947 a pilot first flew a jet plane faster than the speed of sound; and eventually jet airliners became common, greatly increasing business and leisure travel. In 1957 the Soviet Union was able to launch Sputnik, the first manmade satellite into space. In 1969, U.S. astronauts landed on the moon. At the end of 1989, two Russian astronauts returned to earth after spending a year on Mir, a Russian space station. In late 1997 the USA, in cooperation with the European Space Agency, launched the Cassini-Huygens spacecraft to explore Saturn and its moons— the seven-year journey of over 2 billion miles was completed in 2004 and the spacecraft's cameras began a multi-year project of sending images back to earth. In 1998 the failure of a single U.S. commercial satellite led to the temporary loss of service of some radio programming, most U.S. pagers, and some other commercial and financial services. The failure was a reminder of how dependent many people had become on space satellites, as well as on modern technology generally. By 1998 it was estimated that more than 600 commercial, civil, and military satellites were in orbit, and that they were being used not only by the mass media, but also by a wide range of financial and other institutions and, less directly, by millions of individuals.

The first licensed commercial radio station was established in the United States in 1920. A decade later more than half the homes in the United States possessed radios. The 1920s was a period of rapid expansion in the production of many types of consumer products, thanks in part to the proliferation of mass production techniques that Henry Ford had popularized by introducing his assembly line shortly before the outbreak of World War I. By 1929, on the eve of the Great Depression, many U.S. middle-class urban families owned not only a radio but also an automobile, telephone, phonograph, sewing machine, washing machine, and vacuum cleaner. Following the onset of the Great Depression, worldwide consumption slowed considerably, and it was not until after World War II that another great outburst of consumer spending occurred.

Both in the 1920s and after World War II, consumption was greatest in the United States with western Europe and Japan lagging behind, and the rest of the world even more so. In the Soviet Union, for example, the production of consumer goods was a low priority and remained so throughout the communist period, although improving somewhat in the decades following Stalin's death in 1953.

In 1965 only about one-fifth of all Soviet families possessed a washing machine, and one-tenth a refrigerator. In China it took several more decades for just urban consumers to reach such levels, and the much larger rural population of China lagged even further behind.

After World War II the consumer product that received the most attention was television. Although the first televisions were developed already before that war, in 1946 only 8,000 U.S. homes possessed them. By 1960 they were in about 45 million U.S. homes or about nine-tenths of all households. By the late 1980s the U.S.-based Cable News Network (CNN) was transmitting to about 150 nations, and popular U.S. programs like *Dallas* were also being viewed around the world. By the early 1990s there was 1 television for every 9 people in Thailand, and 1 for every 32 people in India. Yet many people still did not have access to television, often because they were without electricity (see also below, Ch 7, for the effects of radio and television on culture).

The invention of the transistor in 1947, however, eventually brought radio communication even to many without household electricity, an especially important consideration in less technologically developed countries. Audio tape cassettes, introduced in the 1960s, could also be used with batteries. In the 1980s the use of portable Walkmans, combining a radio and tape player, spread throughout the world.

Along with televisions and transistors, computers also revolutionized communications after World War II. Like some other important twentieth century inventions, the computer's development was stimulated by wartime research. Toward the end of the war, scientists at the University of Pennsylvania created a computer (weighing 27 tons) used by the U.S. military for such purposes as target calculations. This and subsequent early computers were very large, used thousands of vacuum tubes, and were primarily machines for rapid and complex calculations. U.S. military and government departments and agencies, such as the Department of Defense and the Census Bureau, and defense contractors were among the first purchasers of these huge machines. In 1955 businesses bought a total of about 150 computers and by the end of the 1950s IBM was the leading seller of them. By then transistors were replacing vacuum tubes inside the computers, making it possible for them to be smaller and yet more powerful. By 1970 there were about 75,000 computers being used in the United States, with businesses and universities being major users.

The invention and development of the microprocessor during the 1970s made possible the advent and increasing sales of Personal Computers (PCs). In the decades following their first appearance in

1971, microprocessors became steadily more powerful, enabling small personal computers to accomplish more than had roomfuls of huge early computers. Built on a small silicon chip no larger than a postage stamp, a microprocessor could contain millions of transistors. Another vital element in expanding the sale of PCs was the rapid increase in software that allowed PCs to perform an ever expanding number of functions. In 1983 about 7 percent of U.S. homes contained computers; by 2000 about half of the households did, and by then the United States possessed about 30 percent of the world's computers, followed by Japan, Germany, the United Kingdom, France, and China, who altogether possessed less computers than the USA.

In the 1980s and 1990s a growing number of people at their work and in their homes began communicating with other individuals and institutions via the Internet, the global network of computer networks. Sending and receiving email, gathering information by the use of search engines, making airline and other reservations, banking, buying books and other products, viewing artistic works, listening to music, and reading newspaper articles all became more common by means of the computer. At century's end delivery systems for information via computers, cable television, and telephone systems were becoming increasingly interconnected.

Besides being placed in computers, microprocessors soon also helped control various other pieces of machinery from automobiles to microwave ovens. Their widespread use was evidence of the increasing technological trend toward smaller and lighter products. Even before transistors and microprocessors made their appearance, the creation of synthetic products in laboratories had begun to propel twentieth century technology in this direction. In 1909 chemist Leo Baekeland patented bakelite, the first completely synthetic plastic. But it was not until the second half of the twentieth century that plastics assumed such a dominant role in the production of such a wide array of products.

Still another important development intertwined with the computers was digitization, the process of using various combinations of the numbers 0 and 1 to represent all sorts of symbols, sounds, and visual materials including the letters of the alphabet. By doing this not only computers, but also televisions, telephones, radios, compact disks, cameras, and other devises could store and transmit enormous amounts of data and do it more accurately than previously. Digitization was a major reason why at the century's end, all means of communication were becoming more interconnected and overlapping.

Computers were also either essential or at least instrumental in making possible the widespread use of credit cards, ATMs, and barcodes that revolutionized banking and business practices as the second half of the century progressed. Along with other electronic equipment including Xerox machines, already widely used by 1970, and fax machines, the use of which did not expand much until the late 1980s, computers propelled the world into the Information Age.

As with many technological products, computers sometimes caused unforeseen difficulties. During the late 1990s governments, businesses, non-profit institutions, and individuals around the world spent hundreds of billions of dollars just to rectify what at first seemed like a simple problem: To save money and computer memory, computer and software manufacturers had installed programs using two digits instead of four to represent the year. Thus, for example, 98 instead of 1998. As the year 2000 approached the fear was great that if costly steps were not taken—an easy and cheap solution was never discovered—computers and other electronic devices so programed would mistake 00 for 1900, not 2000. Largely because of great expenditures, however, the year 2000 was not accompanied by the massive disruptions many people feared.

Science, Technology, and the Military

In warfare, technological advancement meant primarily the ability to kill more people, but by the end of the twentieth century advanced military technology was also being used to hit military targets while minimizing civilian casualties. As compared to a century earlier, by 1914 there was more than 100 times as much metal available. In 1917 at the Third Battle of Ypres, the British fired over 4 million artillery shells in just 19 days. Such shells, along with machine guns that could fire more than 600 bullets per minute, poison gas, torpedoes, and other instruments of death, accounted for the unprecedented wartime losses. Belligerents also used airplanes and, to a more limited extent, tanks, but they did not yet account for great losses. In World War II their destructive power would be much greater. In that war not only bombs, but mass-produced bullets and shells from tanks, artillery, and naval ships were expended in record numbers. This led to civilian and military deaths being at least several times higher than in World War I.

By 1944 the Soviet Union alone was producing more war materials than Hitlerite Germany, and during the entire war the United States (the Great Arsenal of Democracy according to Roosevelt) produced about twice as much as its Soviet ally and much more than Germany, Japan, and Italy combined. In addition, Great Britain produced almost as much as the USSR. According to one account, "Total Soviet production alone amounted to 100,000 tanks, 130,000 aircrafts, 800,000 field guns and mortars and up to half a billion artillery shells, 1.4 million machine guns, 6 million machine pistols and 12 million rifles."[13] Facing such odds, it is hardly surprising that the Axis Powers lost the war, especially after the policies of Germany and Japan brought the USSR and the USA into the war.

During World War II many scientists in the participating countries became involved in military research, most significantly the Manhattan Project (see above). Following the war, many of these individuals continued working on military research and development. Some scientists from defeated Germany continued such research in the United States or Soviet Union, which became antagonists in the Cold War that lasted over four decades. As it developed, scientific and technological expenditures devoted to developing and producing weapons increased. In 1954, two years after testing its first hydrogen bomb (H-bomb), the United States tested one with a destructive power equaling 15 million tons of TNT. During the 1950s the Soviet Union also tested H-bombs, and both countries began developing intercontinental ballistic missiles (ICBMs).

By the mid-1970s, the two chief antagonists possessed well over a million times the destructive power of the Hiroshima bomb and much more than enough to destroy the earth's population. By this time perhaps as many as 40 percent of the world's scientists and engineers were engaged in one way or another with Research and Development (R&D) commissioned or used by the military. In the 1980s, spending on military R&D continued to escalate as ventures like the U.S. Strategic Defense Initiative (SDI), intended to create an Anti-Missile Defense System in space, soaked up expenditures. By 1987 the nations worldwide were spending about $1.8 million a minute for military reasons, with the United States and Soviet Union accounting for about 60 percent of the total from 1975 to 1987. Only the cessation of the Cold War at the end of the 1980s finally brought a halt to the escalating growth of such spending. Yet even after the Cold War and collapse of the Soviet Union in 1991, the Brookings Institute estimated in 1998 that the United States was still spending $35 billion a year on nuclear weapons and affiliated programs. This same reputable institute estimated that from 1940 to 1996 the U.S. government spent 11 percent of its total budget expenditures and 29 percent of its military spending on researching, developing, and producing such weapons and programs.

One of the ironies of the expenditure of such vast sums was that never before in history had so much money been spent for technological instruments (nuclear weapons) that even its developers hoped they would never have to use. The development of less lethal military technology, however, also continued—and it was used. The Vietnam War and Persian Gulf War of 1990–1 are good examples. As Stanley Karnow has noted, "With the exception of nuclear weapons, nearly every piece of equipment in America's mighty arsenal was sooner or later used in Vietnam," including all sorts of electronic detection devises and chemical agents to destroy jungles and crops. And "by 1967, a million tons of supplies a month were pouring into Vietnam to sustain the U.S. force."[14] During this war the United States used more different types of bombs, including laser-guided ones, and a greater quantity of them than it had in World War II.

Yet, despite its superior technology, the United States was unable to win the Vietnam War. It lost this war not only because it was unable to overcome the fierce determination of its North Vietnamese and Viet Cong enemies, but also because the U.S. government lost the backing of many Americans. One reason for the erosion of support was the impact of another piece of technology—television. It strengthened a tendency that had been building since the horrors of World War I, a reluctance to sacrifice human lives, primarily those of one's own nation, in the absence of compelling reasons to do so. Never before had the media had such an impact, and as correspondents and pictures captured some of the brutal realities of war and as U.S. casualties increased, many Americans decided they no longer wished to sacrifice U.S. lives in Vietnam. In the final years of the Vietnam War, not wishing either to admit defeat or continue suffering high casualties, the United States gradually withdrew troops while escalating the bombing. For the remainder of the century, the United States would place increasing emphasis on relying on technology to achieve military aims while minimizing U.S. casualties.

The 1990–1 Persian Gulf War was an example. In January and February of 1991 the U.S.-led UN coalition force used a vast array of weapons, including laser-guided missiles and bombs from ships and planes, to attack Iraqi command centers, troops, communication facilities, bridges, and supply depots. Less than 200 U.S. lives were lost in combat, and the war Americans watched on their televisions in January and February of 1991 was more akin to some exotic high-tech video game or futuristic film than to the gruesome scenes many remembered from the Vietnam conflict. Although Iraqi soldiers and civilians suffered more from the UN forces' inflicted damage than the victors' restricted television coverage allowed to be shown, the

U.S.-led forces claimed that "smart weapons," with great accuracy had enabled them to minimize civilian casualties. Although this was only partly true, the claim did reflect a growing awareness that the killing of civilians, even "enemy" civilians, was becoming less acceptable.[15] Although continued post-war UN sanctions against Iraq led to many more Iraqi civilian deaths than had occurred during the war itself, they were less dramatic and visible than wartime casualties.

During the Gulf War Iraq had launched Scud Missiles at Saudi Arabia and Israel, and a major U.S. concern was that Iraq was continuing to develop lethal weapons of war, including missiles and chemical and biological agents. After a dispute about UN weapons inspectors' access to certain Iraqi sites in December 1998, the United States and Great Britain launched another air attack on Iraq in order to set back Iraq's weapons development and overall military capacity and to weaken ruler Saddam Hussein's government. For four days bombers, fighters, and sea- and air-launched Cruise Missiles attacked about 100 military and industrial targets.

The campaign was designed to accomplish military and political objectives while at the same minimizing U.S. and British casualties. And guidance systems even more refined than those used in the Gulf War made it possible to minimize the loss of Iraqi civilian lives as well. In fact, no U.S. or British lives were lost, and Iraqi civilian and military deaths from the attacks apparently amounted to no more than a few hundred. Although advanced technology was enabling military planners to reduce the human cost of war, the financial cost remained high. Each of the more than 400 Cruise Missiles launched cost on average about $1 million.

In the spring of 1999 the United States and Great Britain, as part of a NATO attack against Serbia to prevent its further mistreatment of ethnic Albanians in Kosovo, launched another massive bombing campaign. This NATO operation was again designed to minimize the attackers' casualties, which it did, and NATO and the U.S. portrayed it as a "clean war." They claimed that almost all its many thousands of bombs and missiles had hit precise targets, thereby also minimizing Serbian civilian losses. Of course, some unintended deaths, both of Serbian and ethnic Albanian civilians, occurred as a result of the bombing, but the exact number, whether in the hundreds or thousands, was disputed.

In the final decades of the twentieth century, however, most of the killing occurring in wars was being done among nations and peoples without the type of advanced military technology possessed by the major powers. After the Cold War ended, the major security concern of the world's leading nations was over the type of threat posed by

Saddam Hussein and terrorist groups, that they might obtain or develop nuclear, chemical, or biological means to threaten large population centers. Connected with this fear was a general worry about nuclear proliferation and the fate of all the nuclear materials and know-how once possessed by a Soviet Union that after 1991 had ceased to exist.

Rationalization, Efficiency, and the Organization of Technological Research

The dizzying array of twentieth century technological developments depended on certain concepts and organizations. The German thinker Max Weber (1864–1920) recognized an increasing emphasis on rationalization as a characteristic of modern Western societies. This rationalizing approach emphasized efficiency, control, predictability, and quantification. In the United States, the engineer Frederic Taylor (1856–1915) advocated scientific management and advised companies how most efficiently to organize their workforce in order to maximize production and profits. Henry Ford applied such techniques to his assembly line. And the ideas of Taylor and Ford spread far beyond the United States, even to communist Russia, where many of the efficiency ideas of these two men were advocated in the 1920s.[16] By the end of the twentieth century, such "rationalization" of production (and services) had spread to almost all branches of modern economies from fast food restaurants to the entertainment industry.[17] The development of the computer, itself a reflection of the rationalization drive, further accelerated the rapid application of efficiency, control, predictability, and quantification.

Weber believed that bureaucracy reflected the rationalizing tendencies of the modern age, and as the century progressed science and technology were increasingly controlled by bureaucratic structures. As one expert stated it, "During the twentieth century the main locus of inventive activity shifted away from the individual inventor to the professional Research and Development (R&D) laboratory, whether in industry, government, or academia."[18] Weber's own Germany, as well as the United States, had been leaders in developing such laboratories. Edison and Kodak had established such industries before 1900, and General Electric and DuPont followed soon afterward.

During the twentieth century these companies and others like Bell, Westinghouse, IBM, and newer electronic, pharmaceutical, and genetic engineering companies were in the forefront of technological developments. In the United States, some of these companies not only developed consumer goods, but also worked on government contracts to research and develop military technology. In the Soviet Union, the government and Communist Party organized and oversaw virtually all research and development. But either way, especially from 1941 to 1991, a great deal of R&D expenditures of the superpowers went for military purposes and was controlled by bureaucratic structures.

As the century came to an end, the R&D dominance of the rich countries of the world was one of the keys to their continuing prosperity; and, conversely, the R&D deficiencies of the poorer countries of the world was one of the reasons for their continuing poverty. As one indication of the rich countries technological dominance, the number of patents for inventions and research developments granted to less affluent nations was miniscule as compared to that of wealthier nations. The R&D spending of such companies as Monsanto, Merck, and Microsoft was greater than that of the entire amount of such expenditures of many poorer countries of the world. And the dominant concern of such companies for profits meant that they performed most of their R&D to produce products that would be bought by those who could afford them. This left out many of the poorer peoples of the world. Pharmaceutical research concerned itself primarily with the medical problems typical in the richer countries of the world and paid relatively little attention to those more common in less affluent nations. And agricultural research (such as that of Monsanto) was primarily oriented toward the agricultural concerns of the rich countries, which often differed in substantial ways from those in poorer nations.

Thus, twentieth-century scientific and technological research was often motivated by military or financial considerations and, like science and technology generally, was used for varying purposes, some nobler than others. By the end of the century, however, there was little doubt that the impact of science and technology had greatly accelerated during the century, leaving humans with the increasing challenge of coping wisely with all of their discoveries and developments.

3

Capitalism, Socialism, and Communism

The scientific and technological developments of the twentieth century occurred within economic or social systems such as capitalism and communism. Of the two, capitalism generated by far the most such developments. As the economist Joseph Schumpeter noted, in its search for new products, new consumers, and new markets, capitalism constantly revolutionized "the economic structure *from within*, incessantly destroying the old one, incessantly creating a new one." He even wrote that "this process of Creative Destruction is the essential fact about capitalism."[1] The system itself can be defined as an economic one in which means of production such as land, labor, and machinery are privately owned by individuals and businesses that produce and exchange goods and services primarily to earn a profit—in contrast, under communism the government usually owned the means of production. By 1900, countries with capitalist economies dominated the globe. Among them the United States, Germany, Great Britain, and France were the leading powers, and to a lesser extent Austria-Hungary and Russia, in both of which capitalism was at a less advanced stage of development. Although socialism/communism was advocated by the German-born Karl Marx (1818–83), no communist party was able to come to power until the communist revolution of 1917 in Russia.

Although Marx recognized the tremendous productive capability of capitalism, he also believed that it was flawed by "growing inequalities, bitter class conflict, worsening cycles of economic expansion and recession, [and] competitive and individualistic values."[2] He was confident, however, that capitalism would eventually give way to socialism/communism—for Marx communism was a more advanced form of socialism in which a centralized government would cease to exist. The new Marxian order would do away with economic and social injustice, "degrading poverty, conflicting classes, contending nations, and human alienation."[3] Such was the Marxist dream that proved powerfully attractive in the twentieth century to many of the earth's downtrodden people and their sympathizers.

From 1917 until the end of the Cold War in the late 1980s, proponents of capitalism and communism waged an ideological and propagandistic struggle that sometimes spilled over into armed conflict. The intertwined issues of the economic organization of society, poverty, economic and social justice, access to consumer goods, and which system—capitalism, communism, or something in between—could best address these issues were central to much of the political and military conflict of the twentieth century. Even after the end of the Cold War and the collapse of many communist regimes, the question of how much or how little government economic involvement there should be remained one of the central political questions within and between nations. And right-wing and left-wing political groups continued to debate the extent to which government involvement and state aid should be used to help those in need.

Because of its dynamic nature, capitalism evolved so that many aspects of it looked different in 1900 than in 1850, or in 1999 as compared to 1900. The essence of capitalism, however, did not change; its primary purpose remained the earning of profit. By 1999 capitalism also displayed many different varieties depending on the culture within which it developed. U.S. and Japanese capitalist institutions and methods, for example, differed in various ways, and the capitalist practices that evolved in Russia after the collapse of communism there in 1991 reflected Russia's own unique national features. In addition, by the end of the century, partly in response to the challenges of communist and socialist systems (see below), most of the world's economies were "mixed economies," neither purely capitalistic nor socialistic.

Even the U.S. State Department in 2001 declared that though "the United States is often described as a 'capitalist' economy," it "is perhaps better described as a 'mixed' economy, with government playing an important role along with private enterprise."[4]

Socialism, Communism, and Post-Communism

To earn the greatest profit, most nineteenth century capitalists paid workers as little as possible. But workers, including some influenced by Marxian ideas, began to organize and demand better pay and conditions. By 1900 a strong trade union movement was developing in countries such as Great Britain and Germany—trade unionism remained weaker in the United States, and only in the 1930s did it begin expanding rapidly. Some union members and leaders advocated a moderate socialism which was strongly influenced by a revisionist Marxism that advocated democratic, reformist means of obtaining power. The goal of such socialism was primarily greater economic equality through such steps as government ownership of at least the chief means of production. In general, democratic socialists wished to control and regulate the economy in behalf of the entire population. Thus, democratic socialists began using the term socialism differently than it was used in communist countries, starting with Russia in 1917, where it continued for more than six decades to be perceived as a transitional stage to communism. As an indication that they perceived their country still in this transitional condition, the communist leaders in Russia from 1922 onwards proclaimed their new state the "Union of Soviet Socialist [not Communist] Republics" (USSR). And although the terms communist systems and communism are usually used, and will be here, when referring to twentieth-century Marxist states, the term "Marxist socialist states" would probably be more accurate.

In the years before World War I democratic socialist movements and parties such as the German Social Democratic Party and British Labour Party gained strength. In the German parliamentary election of 1912, the Social Democrats received more votes than any other party—the main problem for them, however, was that compared to Kaiser Wilhelm II the legislature had little power. Although socialists had advocated the international solidarity of workers and preached against war, most socialists supported their own nation's war effort once World War I began in July–August 1914. The war weakened international socialists' efforts in numerous ways, especially after the communists came to power in 1917 in Russia.

Although the communists in Russia remained the only communists able to gain and retain power until World War II, communist parties were formed in most countries, often by radical socialists who split with more moderate and democratic socialists. From 1921 until 1928 the Russian communists allowed some small-scale private enterprise. In 1928–9, however, the government under Stalin took over the remaining private means of production and began establishing a command economy, as opposed to the "market economy" characteristic of capitalism. The command economy continued in the Soviet Union for the next six decades. Under it the state determined the types, amounts, and prices of almost all goods produced, including most agricultural produce. The only significant exception was what was produced on the peasant's small household plot. Although the productivity on these plots was much higher than on the state and collective farms controlled by the government, all of these private plots together only comprised a small percentage of the total agricultural land.

The institution of a command economy enabled economic growth to move more rapidly in the direction desired by the state. By such means as determining salaries, taxes, and prices the state was able to increase revenues. It could then invest in whichever sectors it wished, such as heavy industry and defense, largely ignoring the type of consumer demand that existed in market economies.

In the decades following World War II communist governments sprung up in many countries, especially in east-central Europe, where they were aided by Soviet power, and in China in 1949, where the Chinese communists won out after a long civil war. These new governments also established command economies. Although the Soviet experience throughout most of the 1920s and the Chinese communists' economic policies after the death of Mao Zedong (1976) indicated that communist regimes have at times allowed considerable private enterprise, the command economies became identified with communist systems and for a long time characteristic of them. Like the Soviet economy earlier, the new command economies were more successful in increasing industrial growth than in pleasing consumers. Consumer goods were inferior in both number and quality as compared to those produced by market economies. Although communist governments engaged in some tinkering to make their economic systems more efficient and less resented by consumers, communist leaders hesitated to retreat too much from command-economy principles. Greater economic freedom might fuel demands for greater political freedom.

Some communist leaders such as Nikita Khrushchev, head of the Soviet Communist Party from 1953 to 1964, strongly believed in the superiority of the communist economic system. As a youth he had worked for foreign-owned mining concerns in the southern part of the Russian Empire, and came to believe that much of what Marx had written about the evils of capitalism was true. In 1959, for example, Khrushchev stated that "the lion's share of all produced wealth goes in the capitalist countries to the exploiters and their hangers-on, whereas under socialism greater per capita production means an actual improvement of living conditions for the working man ... Under it [socialism/communism] production is subordinated not to profit-making but to the maximum satisfaction of the requirements of all members of society."[5] And under Khrushchev the standard of living of most Soviet citizens did noticeably increase.

Yet Khrushchev realized that the command-economy system placed certain roadblocks in the way of greater improvements. As Khrushchev's son Sergei later wrote: "The very logic of that system demanded bureaucratic interference in the production process at all levels and in all areas, as well as detailed supervision not just of every factory and collective farm, but of every shop, brigade, and worker's bench, of every individual worker ... What the command approach meant, in essence, was that party leaders at every level had to analyze the most trivial details."[6]

In his forced retirement, Khrushchev himself stated: "A man labors and lives in order to satisfy his material and spiritual needs. If capitalism satisfies these requirements better than socialism, it will become increasingly difficult for us to propagate our point of view and consolidate our way of life. Eventually, we will run the danger of losing everything."[7]

Two decades after Khrushchev spoke these words into a tape recorder (the tape was subsequently smuggled out of Russia), the Soviet communist system was close to "losing everything," just as Khrushchev had predicted. From 1978 to 1985 the performance of the Soviet economy was dismal, partly because of all of the accumulated inefficiencies of the command economy. Overall, the Soviet economy remained the most backward of the major industrial nations, the quantity and quality of its consumer goods and services being especially poor. It was largely because of such economic inadequacies that Mikhail Gorbachev began his *perestroika* (restructuring) reforms after coming to power in 1985.

Gorbachev did not originally intend to dismantle the command economy, but rather to give it a major overhaul that would go beyond the minor tinkering attempted by previous leaders. *Perestroika* and other reforms that accompanied it, however, soon took on a life of their own, helping lead to the collapse of the communist regime and, in 1991, to the Soviet Union itself, which dissolved into 15 sovereign nations. A few years before, mainly as a result of Gorbachev's policies, the iron fist of Soviet control over eastern Europe had been relaxed, and the countries in that region preceded the Soviet Union in jettisoning communism. In all of these cases, the failure of communist economies to successfully compete with capitalist (or mixed economic) ones contributed to the collapse of communist regimes.

During the 1990s the movement of these former communist countries to establish market economies displayed mixed results, with countries such as Poland, Hungary, the Czech Republic, and Estonia being more successful than others like the larger states of Russia and Ukraine. In Russia there emerged what was sometimes referred to as "crony capitalism." It enabled some individuals with appropriate political connections to amass great fortunes, partly by taking over previously state-owned assets, but by 1999 the average Russian was worse off financially than he/she had been under communism. Public opinion polls indicated that Russians believed their country was worse off than under Lenin, Stalin, and other earlier communist leaders.

With about one-fifth of the world's population at the century's end, China still maintained a communist government, but had abandoned many aspects of its earlier command economy and created what it called a "socialist market economy" that gradually became more capitalistic and less socialistic during the 1980s and 1990s. Although state ownership and control continued in areas the government considered vital—for example, the oil, electricity, and metal industries—the new economy was characterized by increasing private enterprise and significant foreign investment, including that from Chinese abroad in places such as Taiwan and Hong Kong, the latter of which finally reverted to Chinese control in 1997. During these two decades, the Chinese mixed economy expanded at a rapid pace, as did the purchase of consumer goods by the many Chinese who became more prosperous. As in other parts of the communist world, so too in China, the realization had spread that the older command economy was deficient in producing consumer goods. In the 1980s and 1990s, the so-called "eight bigs"—television sets, refrigerators, stereos, cameras, motorcycles, furniture suites, washing machines, and electric fans—became especially prized consumer items.

As communism was expanding and then declining around the world, democratic socialism enjoyed its own successes and failures. In Great Britain the Labour Party came to power for most of 1924 and then again from 1929 to 1931, 1945 to 1951, 1964 to 1970, and 1974 to 1979. In 1997 the Labour Party again assumed power, but under its leader, Tony Blair, it had already renounced some of its earlier socialist ideas. By the end of the century the differences between European moderate conservative parties and socialist parties had narrowed considerably and European socialists felt less indebted to Marxist ideas, whether revisionist or not, than ever. As in Great

Britain, so in France, Germany, and numerous other European countries, especially Scandinavian ones, democratic socialists were in power or shared it for varying periods of time from the 1920s until the end of the century. Outside of Europe, but never in the United States, socialists of various types also ruled on many occasions, especially after World War II as independent nations proliferated in Asia and Africa.

Capitalism, Consumption, and Marketing

Among the most significant factors influencing capitalist developments in the twentieth century were changing technology, the two world wars, the Great Depression, which began in 1929, and the challenges of communism and socialism.

From 1873 to 1896 the world suffered from a global depression. One of the reasons for it was that technological developments had increased productive capacity more rapidly than market demand; and insufficient demand, partly because of the low incomes of many people, hindered economic growth. Marx had thought that the desire of the capitalists to keep wages low would help undermine capitalism because such low wages would hamper consumption and contribute to overproduction/underconsumption. But it was not just low incomes that prevented greater demand. It was also attitudes toward consumption—a word in the mid-nineteenth century still primarily thought of as a synonym for tuberculosis.

In the early twenty-first century, it is difficult for many people to comprehend how different back then were attitudes toward the consumption of goods. In the United States, for example, before the Civil War (1861–5), most people valued frugality and spent money on little beyond necessities such as food, shelter, and clothing. Household appliances were still relatively simple, and about half of the American people in the 1870s still lived on farms. If significantly more goods were to be sold, consumers had to desire much more than just basic goods. In the late nineteenth century they began to do so, and as the new century progressed, so too did consumer appetites. By the end of the twentieth century, consumer demand and its stimulation by businesses and governments, primarily in the more affluent countries of the world, was a central force influencing not only economics but also many other aspects of life. Even China's communist government took great pains to increase consumer demand when its growth rate slowed after an Asian Financial Crisis near the end of the twentieth century.

In the late nineteenth and early twentieth centuries western Europe and the United States were in the forefront of stimulating consumption.[8] No doubt, the dizzying array of new inventions, for example, the automobile and those connected with electricity, helped increase demand and would continue to do so throughout the century, but so too did a wide range of new marketing techniques. There were, however, setbacks along the way, especially two world wars and, between them, a Great Depression that temporarily decreased consumer purchases. In the 1920s such purchases shot up along with the productive capacity to produce goods. One scholar has written, "Ten years after the war [World War I], conspicuous consumption had become a [U.S.] national mania."[9] But the low wages of many and an uneven distribution of income finally helped slow consumer demand and contributed to the outbreak of the Depression in 1929. It impoverished many people (the U.S. unemployment rate by early 1933 was 25 percent), increased frugality, and, along with World War II, dampened consumer demand until after the war. Consumption expenditure, however, then, re-emerged stronger than ever, and for the rest of the century it continued, with only minor setbacks, to climb. Many Americans, including U.S. presidents, perceived that ever-increasing consumption was necessary for the nation's prosperity, though few would state the case as bluntly as one marketing consultant of the mid-1950s, who said: "Our enormously productive economy . . . demands that we make consumption our way of life, that we convert the buying and use of goods into rituals, that we seek our spiritual satisfactions, our ego satisfactions, in consumption . . . We need things consumed, burned up, worn out, replaced, and discarded at an ever increasing rate."[10]

By the 1990s users of computers and many other products had personally experienced the replacing and discarding spoken of by this consultant. The obsolescence of older products resulted partly from new technological developments but also because companies could increase their profits by insuring that goods would not last too long (planned obsolescence) and could soon be replaced by newer ones. A British film of 1951, *The Man in the White Suit*, humorously depicted how displeased both management and labor might be with anyone who could invent a fabric that never wore out. But even if such an invention occurred, the clothing industry had some protection because in the twentieth century it emphasized ever-changing fashions, and many people wished to be "fashionable."

To increase consumer demand, companies also developed a vast array of other marketing techniques, designed to persuade consumers to purchase more products and services—by the end of the century more U.S. citizens were employed in providing services than in manufacturing products. Twentieth-century marketing stressed not only advertising but market research, increased emphasis on displaying and packaging products, and new ways of selling them. By the late 1990s the marketing of various products ranging from leading brands of cereals to Nike athletic shoes (made primarily by foreign laborers) cost more than did producing them.

Toward the end of the nineteenth century, new ways of selling goods involved the development of department stores and their display windows, and the use of catalogues such as those of Sears, Roebuck and Company and Montgomery Ward. The first Sears catalogue appeared in 1891, and its 1900 catalogue contained over one thousand pages of illustrated goods. As the century progressed, so too did new outlets for sales including supermarkets, discount and convenience stores, shopping malls, and vending machines. Also vital to increasing demand was the development of installment buying and credit cards, which enabled consumers to buy products before they had the cash to pay for them.

One of the most successful U.S. companies in selling products directly to consumers through its own sales representatives was Avon Products, founded in 1886. By early 1999 it sold products to women in 135 countries and employed almost 2.6 million independent sales representatives. Sales in areas such as Brazil and the former communist countries of Europe increased notably in the 1990s, and Avon had begun to penetrate the enormous Chinese market.

By the end of the twentieth century, the explosion of cable TV channels and the growth of the Internet led to new methods of selling products such as directly to the consumer via Home-Shopping Networks and electronic commerce. In 1999 *Time* magazine, which earlier in the century had named such individuals as Mahatma Gandhi and Mikhail Gorbachev its person of the year, bestowed that honor on Amazon.com's CEO Jeff Bezoz.

From 1865 to 1900 U.S. advertising expenditures increased at least tenfold and in the new century, they continued to skyrocket. Already by 1910 electric outdoor advertisements saturated more than 20 blocks on New York's Broadway Avenue. As the mass media developed, advertising became an integral part of it, increasing first in newspapers and magazines, then on radio, television, and, at the end of the century, on the Internet.

In the 1920s radio advertising was still in its infancy. Although it increased tenfold in the United States from 1927 to 1929, companies still only expended one-twentieth as much as for radio advertising as for that in newspapers. Yet the mere titles of programs such as the

Palmolive Hour and the *Maxwell House Hour* indicated that advertisers were already significant, and debate already existed as to how extensive radio advertising should be. In 1926 *The New York Sun* reflected fears that it might get out of hand in the following fictional satire of a radio broadcast:

> This, ladies and gentlemen, is the annual Yale-Harvard game being held under the auspices of the Wiggins Vegetable Soup Company, makers of fine vegetable soups. The great bowl is crowded and the scene, by the courtesy of the R. & J. H. Schwartz Salad Company, is a most impressive one.
>
> The Yale boys have just marched onto the field, headed by the Majestic Pancake Flour Band, and is followed by the Harvard rooters, led by the Red Rose Pastry Corporation Harmonists, makers of cookies and ginger snaps.
>
> The officials are conferring with the two team captains in midfield under the auspices of the Ypsilanti Garter Company of North America. They are ready for the kickoff. There it goes! Captain Boggs kicked off for Yale by courtesy of the Waddingham Player Piano Company, which invites you to inspect its wonderful showrooms.
>
> The ball is recovered by "Tex" Schmidt by arrangement with the Minneapolis Oil Furnace Company, Inc., and is run back 23 yards by courtesy of Grodz, Grodz & Grodz, manufacturers of the famous Grodz Linoleums.
>
> On the next play the Harvard runner is thrown hard by McGluck one of Mahatma Cigarette Company entertainers, and is completely knocked out by two Yale guards, Filler and Winch, by courtesy of the Hazzenback Delicatessen Products Corporation, makers of exquisite potato salads, cheeses, smoked ham and salads. Yale is penalized 15 yards through the kind cooperation of the National Roofing and Copper Gutters Company.
>
> The teams are lining up again. It is a forward pass . . . a long forward pass under the direction of the Great Western Soap Powder Company, makers of the world's finest soap powders and cleaning fluids. The pass was caught by Schnapps, the Harvard back, who slipped on the wet ground under the auspices of the Hector M. Milligatawney Chocolate Works, the world's leading manufacturers of bon bons and almonds . . . [11]

By the end of the century, U.S. TV sports broadcasting had gradually moved closer to this 1920s parody.

By 1999 television advertising had become increasingly pervasive and expensive. During prime time in the United States, an average of almost 16 minutes out of every hour was devoted to ads and promotions, and in daytime, about 20 minutes of every hour. To place an ad during the 1999 Super Bowl cost companies $1.6 million for a half minute—a year later it increased to $2 million a half minute.

Newspaper, magazine, and radio advertising also continued to increase. Other means of advertising included direct mail, outdoor billboards, buses and other means of transit, before and sometimes subtly (or not subtly) within movies, inside sports arenas, on chair-lift poles at ski resorts, window displays, calendars, skywriting airplanes, prominently placed brand names or logos on apparel and other goods, on shopping bags, shopping carts, and, increasingly as the century closed, on the Internet.

The April 11, 1998 issue of *The Economist* reported the increasing enthusiasm of European advertisers for placing ads in places such as bus shelters and public toilets. In 1999 a company called Free-PC gave away portable computers to individuals who were willing to provide all sorts of personal information and agree to have a portion of their monitor constantly displaying advertising. In the United States even many schools accepted advertising of various sorts, including television ads that came with certain types of educational programing. Overall, from 1950 to 1990 global advertising spending, adjusted for inflation, increased almost sevenfold and continued increasing in the 1990s. In 1997 General Motors, Proctor & Gamble, Phillip Morris, and Chrysler collectively spent more than $6.5 billion on advertising, or about the equivalent of what the U.S. Environmental Protection Agency spent. In 1999 global spending for advertising was over $400 billion, with U.S. advertisers spending almost half the total, or a little over 2 percent of the U.S. GDP. By this time, it was estimated that the average person in the USA was bombarded by 1 million commercials by the age of 20, and U.S. ads for a wide variety of products were seen increasingly around the globe.

As the century progressed advertisers used all the tools of psychology and other appropriate disciplines in order to increase consumer demands. Zelda Fitzgerald, wife of the famous writer of *The Great Gatsby* (1925), grew up early in the century but recalled that even in that period, "We grew up founding our dreams on the infinite promises of American advertising."[12] A more modern economics textbook stated that some advertising is "to bring new products to our attention." But that much of it "is also designed to exploit our senses and lack of knowledge ... One of the favorite targets of advertisers is our sense of insecurity ... Those who fear rejection can find solace and confidence in the right mouth freshener or deodorant ... Eternal youth can be preserved with a proper mix of vitamin supplements, face lotions, and laxatives [and the author might have added hair products for gray hair and baldness].[13] A classic example of the 1920s involved Listerine antiseptic. In order to increase its sales an advertising agency suggested it be advertised as a way of combating bad breath, something most Americans had not thought much about before then. After the new Listerine ads began to appear, however, more people did begin to think about their breath, and Listerine sales rose dramatically.

Another technique used throughout the century was celebrity endorsements. Advertisers apparently thought that people would buy products endorsed by celebrities even if the product had nothing to do with a celebrity's expertise or claim to fame.

In the 1920s U.S. baseball's leading slugger, Babe Ruth, lent his name to various non-sports products. After retiring, baseball's Joe DiMaggio became identified in the minds of millions not only for his past baseball heroics (and having briefly been married to film actress Marilyn Monroe), but also as a spokesman for Mr. Coffee. In the 1980s and 1990s basketball star Michael Jordan became the leading celebrity advertiser of all time. He not only advertised Wilson sporting goods, Gatorade, and Nike athletic shoes, products an athlete might have some insights about, but he also endorsed a wide variety of other products including those of McDonald's, Coke, Wheaties cereal, MCI telecommunications, Ball Park Franks, Hanes underwear, Chevrolet vehicles, Rayovac batteries, Oakley sunglasses, and Bijan, which featured a Michael Jordan cologne. His relationship with Nike went far beyond simple endorsements and included his own Jordan brand of Nike shoes and apparel, for women as well as men. A business newsletter in mid-1998 estimated that Jordan would earn about $42 million from his sponsors for a year's efforts. In its June 22, 1998 issue *Fortune* magazine estimated that during his career Jordan had been responsible for generating at least $10 billion as a result of his economic impact on everything from increased basketball ticket sales to the promotion of various goods and services.

Realizing that women made most consumer purchases and did most of the shopping, advertisers paid special attention to them. Already by 1926 *Ladies Home Journal* featured advertisements on more than half of its pages. About four out of every five pages of a 1990 issue of *Bride's* magazine were devoted to advertising. From the beginning, women were also the main target of afternoon radio soap operas, which got their name because of the advertisement of soap and other products on them. One of the most successful ad campaigns of the early 1920s was developed for General Electric by an ad agency executive named Bruce Barton, who developed a series of ads entitled "Any Woman." Their theme was that electric appliances such as washing machines could liberate women from many hours of household chores. Advertisers also paid special attention to, and often fostered, women's insecurities about their appearance. An Avon ad of the 1990s, for example, began "Gee, wouldn't it be nice if you could wave a magic wand and take ten years off your skin?" Avon's website declared its vision "to be the company that best **understands and satisfies** the product, service and self-fulfillment needs of women—globally."[14]

As the century progressed, businesses and advertisers also increasingly targeted children and young adults, and the commercialization of holidays such as Christmas was part of the process. By the early 1990s the U.S. population was spending more for Christmas gifts than the people of most nations spent on all purchases during an entire year. Children's toys received early emphasis. From 1905 until 1920 toy production in the United States increased well over tenfold. In 1999 Mattel, a U.S. worldwide leader in the manufacturing and marketing of children's toys, put on a celebrity-attended "All-Star Salute to the Barbie Doll's 40th Anniversary." In its first 40 years more than 1 billion Barbie and Barbie companion dolls were sold throughout the world; by 1999 two Barbie dolls were being sold every second. It was also appropriate that a Barbie doll fashion show displaying changing fashions over the years was part of the "salute," for Barbie profits over the years have come not only from Barbie but also her many clothes and other accessories as well as fees from companies such as Reebok and Benetton that paid to have Barbie wear their products. In 1997 Mattel spent $246 million on advertising, but also attempted to bolster sales by a variety of other means. For example, at the 1999 "salute" it acknowledged "Ambassadors of Dreams," who were women of achievement. As a Mattel marketing spokesperson indicated, these women, like the Barbie doll, could teach little girls that they could be anything they wish.

In the Middle East, the popularity of Barbie dolls was great enough by 1999 that the 22-nation Arab League and the Iranian government each had announced plans to counter its popularity—and the Western, secular values they believed Barbie encouraged—by sponsoring the production of a more appropriate doll for the children of their countries.

As with advertising generally, advertising aimed at the children's market increased sharply along with media growth. Television proved to be an ideal medium for beaming advertisements to children as they watched cartoons and other entertainment day after day. One estimate of the early 1990s indicated that U.S. children and teenagers were exposed to about three hours of television commercials a week. From its beginnings in the 1920s making animated cartoons until the end of the century, the Disney Company specialized in children's entertainment. In 1997 it ranked eighth in advertising spending among U.S. companies. The Disney Company's impact on children extended through almost all types of media and beyond and throughout most of the world, including France and Japan, where, as in the United States, the company established gigantic Disneyland parks.

In the United States and many other countries governments were reluctant to regulate advertising, but a few exceptions were made such as the prohibition in 1972 of cigarette advertising on U.S. television. Nevertheless, such advertising continued in print, on billboards, and through other means. In the late 1990s, when state governments negotiated with major cigarette companies over cigarette makers' liability for sicknesses, one of the central charges against the companies was that they deliberately targeted youth in their advertising campaigns.

Although the concept of a consumer culture will be explored in more detail later (see Chapter 7), this section can end with two quotes from ad people. In the early 1990s the American Advertising Federation wrote an open letter appearing in *Time* magazine to the U.S. president reminding him "of advertising's role as an engine of economic growth. It raises capital, creates jobs, and spurs production ... It increases revenues since jobs produce taxable income, and greater sales increase sales taxes ... Incentives to advertise are incentives for growth."[15] In the second quote an ad executive responded in *Business Week* to criticism of advertising directed at youth: "No one's really worrying about what it's teaching impressionable youth. Hey, I'm in the business of convincing people to buy things they don't need."[16]

Capitalism, Progressivism, and the Decline of *Laissez Faire*

The two quotes ending the last section lead to some consideration of the moral position of capitalism. In 1976 Daniel Bell's *The Cultural Contradictions of Capitalism* appeared. In it he stressed that the rise of mass consumption led to the abandonment of capitalism's earlier emphasis on hard work, savings, and frugality, that "in its products and in its advertisements, the corporation promotes pleasure, instant joy, relaxing, and letting go," and that this situation left "capitalism with no moral or transcendental ethic."[17] A modern historian writes "capitalism's main benefits are so clear: a steady increase in incomes and a broadening of opportunity. The negative side is equally obvious: capitalism exalts material values over spiritual ones, and its market forces can have harsh consequences."[18] More than a century before Daniel Bell (and almost a century before Schumpeter's words on capitalism quoted at the beginning of this chapter), Marx and Engels noted that capitalism's constant application of new technology in the quest for profits made it a revolutionizing force that would undermine traditional values. They wrote:

> The bourgeoisie cannot exist without constantly revolutionizing the instruments of production, and thereby the relations of production, and with them the whole relations of society ... Constant revolutionizing of production, uninterrupted disturbance of all social conditions, everlasting uncertainty and agitation distinguish the bourgeois epoch from all earlier ones. All fixed, fast frozen relations, with their train of ancient and venerable prejudices and opinions, are swept away, all new-formed ones become antiquated before they can ossify. All that is solid melts into air, all that is holy is profaned, and man is at last compelled to face with sober senses his real condition of life and his relations with his kind.[19]

Other writers have stressed other effects of capitalism, both positive and negative, with a good deal of the evaluation depending on the definition of capitalism.[20] If, however, it is defined strictly as an economic system, as it is at the beginning of this chapter, then some confusion can be avoided. Such a definition leads to an emphasis on the core of capitalism—the seeking of profits in a market economy. As the conservative economist Milton Friedman once wrote, "The social responsibility of business is to increase its profits."[21] Such profits came from the sale of great books, reproducing beautiful music, generating valuable computer programs, and providing medical care and various types of instruction; but profits also came from cigarettes harmful to people's health and guns and other weapons that killed people—at the end of the twentieth century global arms sales and weapons transfers amounted to almost $34 billion dollars, with U.S. corporations being the leading arms producers. Profits were also gained from selling entertainment programs that harmed young, and perhaps older, minds—conservatives tended to stress pornographic materials, liberals were more inclined to point to excessive depictions of violence.

Individuals in capitalist or market economies exhibited both noble and ignoble behavior. In making fortunes, some individuals worked hard, displayed great creativity, and built up companies with a reputation for dependability and good service, but others earned their wealth more through deception, corruption, graft, and other methods. Some hoarded their fortunes, but others became great philanthropists and aided noble causes. Some capitalists were great supporters of democracy; but others supported authoritarian non-democratic regimes, including that of Nazi Germany. And it was not just many German capitalists who directly or indirectly supported Hitler's regime. From 1934 to 1938 U.S. exports to Germany of lubricating oil and motor fuel almost tripled. "Half of all German imports of iron and scrap metal came from the United States. U.S. corporations including Standard Oil, General Motors, DuPont and even IBM all expanded their German operations."[22] In essence, twentieth-century capitalism was morally ambiguous, without "a moral or transcendental ethic" except the selling of goods and services and the making of profit.

The apparent amoral position of capitalism does not mean that the seeking of profits in a market economy has not had effects with moral consequences. It has had certain implications, for example, regarding freedom (see below, Chapter 5). And historically capitalism has often been linked to imperialism, but not all capitalist countries have engaged in imperialism (Switzerland, for example, did not have the military force to do so), and communist regimes have also been imperialistic. Contrary to Lenin's view, imperialism is not part of the essence of capitalism.

The moral ambiguity of capitalism led in the twentieth century to government efforts to supplement it by providing an overall philosophy of the public good. The belief that people should be able to earn profits in a market system, that the availability of an ever expanding number of goods and services was good, and that capitalism was the best means to insure this end was not in itself a comprehensive social philosophy. Capitalism itself provided no adequate answers for how to deal with such problems as unsafe working conditions, unfair business practices, pollution, public health, slum housing, or the abuse of child labor (quoting official reports, Karl Marx in *Das Kapital* provided many instances of such abuse, for example: "That boy of mine when he was 7 years old I used to carry him on my back to and fro through the snow, and he used to have 16 hours [of work] a day . . . I have often knelt down to feed him as he stood by the machine, for he could not leave it or stop."[23]) And capitalism left unaddressed the main concern (at least in theory) of socialists and communists, the problem of the distribution of income, and whether great poverty should exist along with great wealth.

A central principle for many capitalists, especially in Great Britain and the United States was that of *laissez faire*, which was hostile to almost any government regulation of business or private property, especially any that would curtail employers' rights. During the nineteenth century, slave owners and factory owners sometimes trotted out this principle to defend their "right" to own human property (slaves) or to pay low wages, hire young children, or maintain unsafe working conditions. Although the British abolished slavery three decades before the United States did and the British government mitigated *laissez faire* in some respects, the principle still exercised considerable influence at the time of the Irish famine of the late 1840s, contributing to the death of approximately 1 million people between 1846 and 1851, and the emigration of about twice that number from 1845 to 1855.[24] As one economist wrote, "Ship after ship sailed down the river Shannon laden with rich food, carrying it from starving Ireland to well-fed England, which had greater purchasing power."[25] The British government refused to allow the Irish peasants to eat this exported food themselves, partly because it was considered the private property of absentee English landlords.

To address the type of problems that capitalism made worse, or at least failed to address, there arose in the final decades of the nineteenth century a diverse movement "to limit the socially destructive effects of morally unhindered capitalism, to extract from those [capitalist] markets the tasks they had demonstrably bungled, to counterbalance the markets' atomizing social effects with a counter calculus of the public weal [well-being]."[26] This movement did not attempt to overthrow or replace capitalism but to constrain and supplement it in order to insure that it served the public good. The early leaders of this reform movement first appeared in western Europe, but their influence also spread to the United States and became especially evident during the so-called Progressive Era from 1890 to 1914. Although this cross-fertilizing trans-Atlantic movement had no common name and was quite heterogeneous, many of its proponents thought of themselves as "progressives."

Strangely enough, one of the early influences on this movement was the undemocratic German politician and statesman Otto von Bismarck. In the 1880s, in order to strengthen his government's appeal and weaken that of the German socialists, he approved three measures providing nationally backed insurance for sickness, accidents, and old age. A combination of workers, employers and, to a lesser extent, the government funded them. By 1914 almost all German wage earners had coverage for sickness and accidents, but to be eligible for an old age pension, a worker had to have contributed payments for 30 years.

Between 1906 and 1912 Great Britain's Liberal Party took similar steps, in some cases recognizing a debt to Bismarck. In 1908 the government enacted an Old-Age Pension Law for those over 70 who were poor and "deserving." A National Insurance Act of 1911 provided some workers national insurance for sickness and unemployment to be funded by employee and employer contributions, as well as by the state. Other measures dealt with other social concerns such as medical assistance for school children, the regulation of advertising, "workingman's compensation," and minimum wages for some sweatshop workers. To help the state contribute to these programs, it raised taxes, especially on the wealthy, some of whom protested that the government was enacting socialism. Indeed, Bismarck's policies have sometimes been referred to as "state socialism," but such "socialism" lacked many of the elements desired by those who generally called themselves socialists, and one of the leading forces behind the British reforms, besides Chancellor of the Exchequer David Lloyd George, was Winston Churchill, then a member of the Liberal Party but never a socialist. Son of aristocrat Lord Randolph Churchill and his American wife, heiress Jennie Jerome, Churchill began and ended his career as a member of the Conservative Party and while a Conservative, twice (1940–5, 1951–5) served as prime minister. Before World War I, many other countries in western Europe, as well as Australia and New Zealand, enacted social legislation to aid poor old people, the sick, or unemployed. In Europe, France did the most to help poor mothers. On the local level, European municipal governments also took steps to ameliorate some of the harsh social conditions of the day and to take control of some previously owned private enterprises.

Up until the 1870s, most utilities, sanitation operations, and urban transportation were privately owned, but by 1909 the great majority of large cities in western Europe's two strongest countries, Great Britain and Germany, had taken over most of these operations. By then most of the largest cities of each country owned their own water, gas, and electric operations, as well as streetcars, public baths, slaughterhouses, and markets. Some people spoke of these developments as examples of "municipal socialism," but one of the leaders in this movement toward municipal ownership was the retired capitalist millionaire Joseph Chamberlain, who became mayor of Birmingham, England in 1873 and later attained national political prominence. In addition, the early leadership in other English cities was also often provided by businessmen.

The British socialist Sidney Webb declared ironically in 1889 that

the practical man, oblivious or contemptuous of any theory of the social organism or general principles of social organization, has been forced, by the necessities of the time, into an ever-deepening collectivist channel. Socialism, of course, he still rejects and despises. The individualist town counsillor will walk along the municipal pavement, lit by municipal light and cleansed by municipal brooms with municipal water, and seeing, by the municipal clock in the municipal market, that he is too early to meet his children coming from the municipal school, hard by the lunatic asylum and the municipal hospital, will use the national telegraph system to tell them not to walk through the municipal park, but to come by the municipal tramway, to meet him in the municipal reading-room, by the municipal museum, art-gallery, and library, where he intends to consult some of the national publications in order to prepare his next speech in the municipal town hall in favour of the nationalization of canals and the increase of Government control over the railway system. "Socialism, sir," he will say, "don't waste the time of a practical man by your fantastic absurdities. Self-help, Sir, individual self-help, that's what has made our city what it is."[27]

In the United States, many leading urban reformers were influenced by what was being accomplished in British and German cities. By the mid-1920s, 60 out of the nation's 69 largest cities had city-owned waterworks, but only a small percentage of the large cities had succeeded in purchasing other utilities, and only 4 of them ran their own public transit. As opposed to most western European urban reformers, those in the United States were "hemmed in . . . in ways no progressives elsewhere experienced."[28] This was primarily because the courts generally interpreted the Constitution in ways sympathetic to unfettered capitalist interests, and this was true on the national as well as local level. By 1900 the Supreme Court was attempting "to protect business from the states" and from the Federal Government, and "against these two bulwarks the doctrine of public interest made slow progress." In 1895, after the Supreme Court ruled that a 2 percent Federal Income Tax on high-income individuals and businesses was unconstitutional, the *St. Louis Post-Dispatch* wrote, "Today's decision shows that the corporations and plutocrats are as securely entrenched in the Supreme Court as in the lower courts which they take such pains to control."[29]

A Graduated Income Tax was one of the planks of the Populist Party platform in the 1892 U.S. presidential election, in which the party carried four states. Among other desires, the party also wanted the government to take over ownership of railroads, steamship lines, telegraph and telephone systems. The Populists were primarily farmers, laborers, and small businessmen resentful of the dominant power of wealthy capitalists. In 1896 the Democratic candidate, William Jennings Bryan, also won the Populist nomination but was narrowly defeated in the presidential election of that year.

In the next few decades, the more urban based U.S. Progressive Movement attempted to insure that capitalism served the greater well-being of the general public. Muckraking journalists who exposed social ills, some of which were connected with unregulated businesses, helped the Progressives get national and state legislation passed. In 1906, for example, Congress passed a Meat Inspection Act, a Pure Food and Drug Act, and an Employer's Liability Act; in 1908, however, the Supreme Court declared the last act unconstitutional.

The states, however, took up the battle, and 22 states enacted workmen's compensation laws by 1913, which also had the effect of stimulating employers to improve safety conditions. That same year, the Sixteenth Amendment was added to the Constitution, enabling Congress to introduce an income tax on high-income citizens and corporations.

The year before, in the presidential election of 1912, former Republican President Theodore Roosevelt ran against the man who had replaced him, fellow Republican William Howard Taft. Roosevelt ran on the Progressive Party ticket, charging that Taft was too much beholden to big business. The Progressives advocated social legislation such as the prohibition of child labor, improvements of women's working conditions, and comprehensive social insurance (for such occurrences as sickness, unemployment, and old-age poverty). Although the Progressives obtained more votes than the Republicans, the Democrats won the election.

Nevertheless, the Progressive Movement did contribute to additional gains in the years that followed including limiting the work hours of women and children. By early 1917, 39 states had enacted such legislation affecting women, and many states had also limited children's hours—in 1900 about one-fifth of U.S. children aged 10 to 16 were working. Federal laws to restrict child labor were passed in 1916 and 1918, but both were declared unconstitutional by the Supreme Court. In 1924 Congress passed an amendment to the Constitution that would have allowed Congress to determine work rules for those under the age of 18, but not enough states ratified the amendment, so it died. Further substantial Federal legislation restricting child labor came only in the 1930s, following the Great Depression.

In most of Latin America around 1900, *laissez-faire* support was weaker than in the United States. Many governments had already been active promoting capitalist enterprises and the expansion of infrastructure—roads, railroads, telegraphs, and port facilities—mainly in export sectors and in concert with U.S. and European capital. These policies benefited mainly elites. As capitalist businesses grew, social tensions mounted; and workers, both rural and urban, demanded more for themselves. Like European and U.S. Progressives, they attempted to at least ameliorate some of the harmful effects of capitalism—some, of course, wished to go further and overthrow capitalism. In Mexico, dissatisfaction with the status quo helped fuel the Mexican Revolution that stretched out throughout the 1910s. In the south of Mexico many poor landless rural workers (*campesinos*), led by Emiliano Zapata, rallied around his slogan of "Land and Liberty," while a host of other radical ideologies attracted others. Some of the progressive elements of Mexico's 1917 Constitution—such as the right of workers to bargain collectively, minimum wages and benefits, and universal public education—can be traced to these popular and working-class impulses.

Argentina, Brazil, and Chile, in the last decades of the nineteenth century, experienced massive European immigration, the rapid growth of cities and export businesses, and mounting demands by workers for political rights and a bigger piece of the economic pie. In Latin America generally, "the years between 1914 and 1927 saw a surge of labor mobilization. It was the high point of anarchist, anarcho-syndicalist, and syndicalist influence, when the capital cities of every major Latin American nation were rocked by general strikes."[30] (See Chapter 1 for anarchism; syndicalism advocated a trade union-led general strike that would paralyze society, destroy its government, and bring about a new organization of society based on unions.)

World War I increased government controls over national economies. In the United States, for example, the Federal Government temporarily controlled the nation's railway, telephone, and telegraph systems. Although the war's end led to relinquishing many government controls, an important precedent for dealing with national emergencies had been set.

The agonies of the Great Depression, which reached their apex in the early 1930s, led many governments again to impose more regulations on business and economies. In countries and regions as different as the United States, Nazi Germany, and Latin America, government economic controls greatly increased.

Although some opponents of U.S. President Franklin Roosevelt claimed that he was imposing socialism in the United States and Hitler's party was officially called the National Socialist German Workers' Party, both economies in the 1930s remained essentially capitalistic, with most capital remaining in private hands and the profit motive still fully operative.[31] No doubt, however, the capitalism that remained in both countries was far from any type of *laissez-faire* capitalism, and closer to what was later referred to as a mixed economy, although the latter term is sometimes limited to economies that are hybrids of capitalism and left-wing socialism.

Roosevelt's New Deal introduced Social Security, a national system of unemployment compensation, and aid to poor women with dependent children; and it provided government jobs that employed all sorts of people from artists to workers on construction projects. It also brought about greater government regulation of agriculture, industry, labor relations, money supply, and the financial transactions of banks and stock markets. In general, the government, including a changed Supreme Court, increased the rights of workers and consumers in their dealings with employers and businesses.

In Germany, where the unemployment effects of the Depression were even more devastating than in the United States, the government also instituted massive public works projects in order to employ workers—many others were hired by a revived German armaments industry. Even more than Roosevelt, Hitler increased government control over businesses, but he also privatized some previously government-run enterprises and enabled large conglomerates such as that of the Krupp family and I. G. Farben to reap great profits. But rather than increasing workers' rights, he abolished trade unions and prohibited collective bargaining and strikes.

In Latin America the Depression prompted even greater levels of state intervention. Militaries often seized power to keep radicalized workers in check, and to reinforce existing relations of power and privilege, with landowners, the military, and business owners toward the top of the social hierarchy, and poorer people toward the bottom. Such right-wing regimes bore some resemblance not only to Nazism, but even more so to the earlier Italian Fascism created by Benito Mussolini, who was admired by such rulers as Brazil's Getúlio Vargas and Chile's Arturo Alessandri. In Mussolini's "corporate state," which gradually emerged in the late 1920s and 1930s, big businesses helped run the economy, but by 1937 the government possessed the controlling interest in steel, heavy machinery, shipping, electricity, and telephones.

The Welfare State

During World War II governments again regulated their economies more than in peacetime, and immediately after the war Great Britain introduced what came to be called (initially by its opponents) a "welfare state." In Europe, "welfare" meant much more than its usual narrow use in the United States. One definition of the welfare state perceives it "as a capitalist *society* in which the state has intervened in the form of social policies, programs, standards, and regulations in order to mitigate class conflict *and* to provide for, answer, or accommodate certain social needs for which the capitalist mode of production in itself has no solution or makes no provision."[32] Such a state took a much more systematic and comprehensive approach than any state before the war to insure that all its citizens could count on basic subsistence when needed during sickness, unemployment, and old age. Especially notable was the British National Health Service Act of 1946, which made everyone eligible for free medical services.

The government in power at the time (1945–51) was a Labour government, which thought of itself as socialist, but the other major parties in Great Britain, which considered themselves capitalist oriented, supported many of Labour's welfare-state proposals. And in the post-war years welfare-state policies were enacted and expanded in most western European countries even when the party in power considered itself pro-capitalist. In her memoirs, British Prime Minister (1979–90) Margaret Thatcher criticized the behavior of her own Conservative Party before she assumed its leadership: "The welfare state? We boasted of spending more money than Labour, not of restoring people to independence and self-reliance."[33]

Thus, the welfare state became the characteristic form of government in western European countries. Most of them, however, still considered their economic system to be essentially capitalist, though the term "mixed economy" was also increasingly used. It indicated the mix of private market and government initiatives that increasingly characterized not only their economies but also those of other major industrial nations such as the United States and Japan.

During the half century after World War II, government expenditures for social programs assisting the poor, old, and sick steadily increased in the major industrialized nations of the world. Since all people who lived long enough got old and everyone was apt to get sick at some point, many of these measures affected all social classes and not just the poor. By the late 1990s public spending for social programs made up about half of all the combined government expenditures in western and central Europe, the United States, Japan, Australia, and Canada. To pay for these increases, governments levied higher taxes. Many governments also passed measures that insured or encouraged employers to provide certain benefits to their workers. By 1993, for example, the number of annual vacation days received by most west European industrial workers was two to three times as high as that of their counterparts in the United States. In general, U.S. provisions for the sick, aged, and unemployed were also less sweeping than in most of the other industrialized democracies.

Up until the 1980s the countries of western Europe also brought more of their economies under government control in a variety of other ways, sometimes by taking over direct or indirect control of certain industries. From 1945 to 1948, for example, the British government took over the Bank of England, public transport (including civil air and railways), and the coal, steel, gas, electricity, and public communications industries. Altogether, more than one-fifth of Britain's economy was transferred from the private to the public sector. In France during this same period, the government took similar steps in regard to major banks, coal mines, gas, and electricity. During the early 1980s France initiated another wave of nationalization of industries, bringing the total of public owned industry to almost one-third of all French industry. Government ownership was also extensive in Italy.

In the 1980s, however, new economic winds began blowing over Europe and the United States. Margaret Thatcher and Ronald Reagan provided much of the force behind them, and they aimed at dismantling at least portions of the welfare state and what Thatcher referred to as "a centralizing, managerial, bureaucratic, interventionist government" that "jammed a finger in every pie."[34]

In Great Britain, the Thatcher government privatized publicly owned industries in transportation, communications, and utilities, such as British Telecom, British Airways, and British Gas. Although it did not privatize England's National Health Service, it did promote more private health care. In her memoirs Thatcher claimed that under her leadership Britain "was the first country to reverse the onward march of socialism" and that under her "the state-owned sector of industry had been reduced by some 60 percent ... [and] over six hundred thousand jobs had passed from the public to the private sector." She also asserted, with considerable justification, that Britain "set a worldwide trend in privatization in countries as different as Czechoslovakia and New Zealand."[35] Although it is true that the collapse of communism in eastern Europe and its retreat in China naturally led to considerable privatization, the trend was also clear in many other parts of the world. France, for example, in the late 1980s reprivatized state banks and some other industries that had been nationalized earlier in the decade. And the tendency continued into the 1990s. *The Economist*, a periodical supportive of privatization, estimated that between 1994 and 1997 $152 billion worth of assets had been privatized in western Europe alone.

In the United States, where the government never owned many enterprises, there was more emphasis on "deregulation." Even before President Reagan came to office, there had been some of it in the airline and trucking industries, but Reagan appointed cabinet officers who were much more zealous about deregulation, and various agencies such as the Environmental Protection Agency cut back significantly their regulation efforts. Reagan critics charged him with failure to protect the environment, and also especially faulted him for the deregulation of the savings and loan industry, which they claimed led to an increase of risky loans and other abuses that eventually cost U.S. taxpayers hundreds of billions of dollars.

In Latin America during the 1980s and into the 1990s, Thatcher–Reagan type policies were also influential under the guise of the doctrine known as neoliberalism. Because of large debts, many Latin American countries were required to accept "austerity measures" imposed by organizations such as the International Monetary Fund (IMF), which was dominated by the USA and other major Western powers. These measures often led to government budget cuts in areas such as education and health care.

In general, both Thatcher and Reagan claimed that their policies were increasing individual, social, and entrepreneurial initiatives and freedoms and decreasing dependency and bureaucracy, as well as taxes. And while it is true that taxes were decreased in both Great Britain and the United States, the tax cuts benefited the rich more than the poor, and the gap between rich and poor widened in both countries—the gap was wider in the United States than in other major countries and continued to widen in the 1990s as the earnings of the wealthy, most notably CEOs, financiers, athletes, and entertainers, reached unprecedented heights. By late 1999 the gap was the widest since the Great Depression of the early 1930s. Although Reagan began by cutting spending in such social programs as food stamps, welfare payments, school lunches, and student loans, government budget deficits nevertheless increased significantly. This was partly because of huge increases in military spending, but also because of significant opposition to any efforts to diminish "entitlements" (government benefits).

The growth of these benefits paradoxically contributed both to the staying power of the welfare state and for demands that it be scaled back. Those who received entitlements—about half of all U.S. families in 1992 received one or more such entitlement, with Social Security recipients being the largest group—were reluctant to see them reduced. Yet their continuing escalation fueled taxpayer resistance to increasing taxes to pay for them. In the United States, Social Security and health care in 1955 (before Medicare and Medicaid) accounted for 7 percent of Federal Expenditures; by 1995 it escalated to 40 percent. In Britain, despite all Thatcher's privatization efforts, there was only a 3 percent decline between 1979 and 1996, in the proportion of public versus private funding for social security and protection, education, and housing. Despite all the efforts of Reagan, Thatcher, and others, the government entitlements gained in the post-war decades generally remained intact.

As the century came to an end, however, it was clear that attempts to at least slow the growth of welfare-state spending would continue even among politicians from parties traditionally favorable to the welfare state. In the United States, President Clinton signed a Welfare Reform Bill in 1996, and by early 1999 less than three-fifths as many families were on welfare as in 1995. In Great Britain, the Labour government's chief financial minister, Gordon Brown, was (according to *The Economist*) "obsessed with getting people off welfare and into work." [36] In Germany the government of Gerhard Schroder, whose Social Democratic Party came to power in 1998 for the first time in 16 years, indicated he was more willing to limit welfare-state growth than previous Social Democratic governments had been.

Corporations: National and Multinational

A major reason for the rise of Progressive Reform Movements at the end of the nineteenth century was the rising power of large corporations in the major capitalist countries. Sometimes, through mergers, the creation of trusts, or other means, they directed a large number of companies. In 1880 John D. Rockefeller's Standard Oil Company controlled at least 90 percent of U.S. refined oil. In 1901 American financier J. P. Morgan formed the world's largest corporation, United States Steel, which oversaw more than 60 percent of the U.S. steel output. Large banking operations such as that of Morgan's and that of the European Rothschilds also had extensive holdings, which extended into many countries. From 1897 to 1904 more than 4,000 U.S. companies merged into less than 300 combinations, and by the end of this period a little over 300 businesses were said to control about 40 percent of U.S. manufacturing assets. It was a similar story in most of the other leading industrial countries. In Germany, the Krupp firm, in which the German Emperor William II was a major shareholder, produced coal, iron, steel, and various products from them, especially armaments. By 1913 it employed almost 70,000 people. In Japan, the economy was dominated by the *zaibatsu* (financial cliques), a small number of family firms that emerged as great holding companies such as Mitsui and Mitsubishi. At first, they were engaged primarily in mining, banking, shipping, and foreign trade, but later also branched out into other areas. According to one estimate, by 1933 Mitsui had some control over at least 130 different companies.

In the United States the great increase in the power of corporations, as we have seen, was often aided by judicial interpretations of the Constitution. In 1886, the Supreme Court ruled that state efforts to regulate railroad rates were unconstitutional. That same year the Court conferred upon the corporation the legal rights of a person, yet unlike a person it retained only "limited liability." This ruling was based on an extension of the Fourteenth Amendment, originally designed to protect the rights of freed slaves. In the next half century more than 50 percent of the Court's decisions applying this amendment were in behalf of corporations. Yet by the time of the birth of the Populist Party in 1891, resentment had already clearly shown itself against railway corporations and other big businesses such as Rockefeller's Standard Oil Trust. Feeling this pressure, and mindful of the voting power of farmers, industrial workers, and small- business owners, in 1887 Congress created the first Federal regulatory agency, the Interstate Commerce Commission, which initially was primarily concerned with insuring fair railway rates. Three years later, Congress passed the Sherman Anti Trust Act—as one senator stated, "Something must be flung out to appease the restive masses."[37]

The legislation declared that combinations that restrained trade were illegal, and this law remained significant in future government anti-trust actions. Moreover, the United States government went further than the governments of most other industrialized nations in attempting to curb business monopolies. Exactly how the law was to be interpreted, however, was determined primarily by court decisions and subsequent legislation. A Supreme Court decision of 1895, for example, found that a sugar trust controlling 98 percent of domestically refined sugar did not violate the law. In 1911, however, the law was applied to break up the Standard Oil and American Tobacco Company trusts. In hearing these two cases, the Court arrived at what became known as the "rule of reason," interpreting the Sherman Anti Trust Act to apply only to "unreasonable" efforts to reduce competition. In 1914, in an attempt to further restrict monopolies and unfair trade practices, Congress established a Federal Trade Commission and passed the Clayton Anti-Trust Act, amended in 1950 to further strengthen anti-monopoly legislation.

Despite these efforts, U.S. businesses continued to grow larger and mergers continued, and even some of the fragments of former trusts remained formidable—for example, the largest piece of the divided Standard Oil Trust, Standard Oil of New Jersey (eventually known as Exxon), remained large enough to supply one-fourth of all Allied oil in World War I. In the interwar years (and afterwards) larger chain stores increasingly put smaller operations out of business. By 1924, for example, A & P already operated more than 11,000 stores, and by 1931 J. C. Penney had almost 1,500 stores. The introduction of anti-chain-store legislation in many states during the 1920s did little to curtail such growth. Despite the fact that chain stores put smaller stores out of business, they usually provided more convenient shopping and lower prices. By 1926 almost 4,000 public utility companies had gone out of business; and by 1930 six business groups including a General Electric holding company (Electric Bond and Share Company) controlled over half of the nation's electrical power. By 1933 the country's three largest automobile manufactures produced 90 percent of its automobiles, and four of its tobacco companies (including the American Tobacco Company), 90 percent of its cigarettes. Overall, less than 600 corporations owned more than half of all the assets of the nation's almost 400,000 corporations. Later in the century, fast food chains such as McDonald's, which began franchising in 1955 and by the end of the century had stores in over half the countries of the world, became large corporations. So too did discount stores such as Wal-Mart, which emerged in the 1960s and by early 1999 had over 900,000 employees worldwide, including those in stores in Argentina, Brazil, Canada, China, Germany, Mexico, Puerto Rico, and South Korea.

Although the continuing role of small companies should not be ignored—in the early 1990s in both the United States and Germany about half of all exports were created by companies with less than 20 employees—the tendency toward bigness and mergers continued throughout the century. In Japan, U.S. occupation forces after World War II began to break up the large *zaibatsu*, but slowed the process as the Cold War intensified, and by 1991 Mitsui, Mitsubishi, and Sumitomo each produced goods and services worth more than the gross national products (GNPs) of all but 20 countries in the world. Other companies that produced more than at least seven-tenths of all the nations of the world included General Motors, Royal Dutch/Shell, Exxon, Ford Motor, Toyota Motor, IBM, AT&T, General Electric, British Petroleum, Daimler-Benz, Phillip Morris, Fiat, Wal-Mart, and DuPont, as well as about 30 other companies.

As the decade progressed, the big got bigger as year after year from 1992 to 1998 the total value of merging companies increased. In 1998, one-fourth of all mergers involved "cross-border" deals, including the largest industrial merger in history, that of Germany's Daimler-Benz and U.S. carmaker Chrysler. Also notable were the mergers in the field of communications and entertainment. Time Warner (created by a merger in 1989 of Time Inc. and Warner

Communications) merged in 1995 with Turner Broadcasting Systems to create the largest world media network. Its revenues came from TV and film production, broadcast, cable, and satellite TV, music and publishing, the Internet, theme parks, and shops. In 1995 the Walt Disney Company took over Capital Cities/ABC, thereby adding to Disney's already extensive holdings a major broadcast network, cable TV networks (such as ESPN and A&E), numerous TV and radio stations, publishing and international media companies, and newspapers. In 1995 Westinghouse Electric Corporation bought CBS Inc. and in 1996 purchased the Infinity Broadcasting Corporation, which added more radio stations to the company; the following year Westinghouse changed its name to CBS. In 1999 CBS and media conglomerate Viacom announced their intended merger. Besides the three merged media giants mentioned above, several others joined with them to dominate the world of media. The smallest of these elite by late 1998 was the Australian Rupert Murdoch's News Corporation, but even it listed about 800 subsidiaries in Australia, the United States, Great Britain and numerous other countries. General Electric, a company with 1998 revenues just about equaling the combined total of the five largest media companies, also had an important media stake, owning NBC and NBC Cable Services, which operated some cable networks including the Consumer News and Business Channel (CNBC).

Although in 1998–9 the U.S. government brought software giant Microsoft to trial for anti-trust violations, overall it did not seem especially worried about the growing number of mergers and acquisitions. When in late 1998 Exxon and Mobil announced their planned merger, subject to Federal Trade Commission review, there was little government opposition even though the two companies had evolved out of the two largest divisions of the breakup of Standard Oil in 1911. One of the few Congressman who questioned the deal thought that so few others did so because of the financial-political influence of the two oil giants. In late 1998 and early 1999 British Petroleum acquired two other former pieces of the old Standard Oil group with the purchases of Amoco and Atlantic Richfield.

By the end of the century, just as at the beginning of it, some journalists and other authors were expressing concerns over the growing power of corporations, especially the multinational ones (from 1970 to 1995 the number of such corporations increased from 7,000 to 40,000). The main concern of these authors was that the corporations' powers were not matched by their responsibilities, their rights not balanced by their duties, and that they subverted the democratic process. A few quotes will suffice to indicate their concerns. "Corporations exist to pursue their own profit maximization, not the collective aspirations of the society. They are commanded by a hierarchy of managers, not by democratic deliberation ... Hundreds of these large corporate political organizations are now astride the democratic landscape, organizing the ideas and agendas, financing electoral politics and overwhelming the competing voices of other, less-well endowed organizations and citizens."[38] "The real 'logic' of the borderless world is that nobody is in control—except, perhaps, the managers of multinational corporations."[39] "The transnational corporations carry on inexorably. Increasingly flagless and stateless, they weave global webs of production, commerce, culture and finance virtually unopposed."[40] "Public accountability is the essence of democracy. But the institutions for assuring corporate accountability at the local, national, and international levels are extremely weak."[41]

Large corporations were so powerful primarily because of the resources at their disposal. The corporate giants that owned much of the media were of course in a very special position, but even those without media holdings were able to afford the best lawyers and the most capable lobbyists. Big corporations were also able to influence legislators through political contributions, and the media and general public through advertising, company press releases, and by contributing money to various causes. By the end of the century, U.S. corporate public relations employees outnumbered news journalists by more than four to one, and in many newspapers corporate press releases provided considerable content.[42] As we have seen, companies such as Mattel and Avon attempted to assure women how devoted they were to their interests. Phillip Morris long encouraged women to smoke its Virginia Slims brand by associating the cigarette with the noble cause of women's liberation. General Electric (GE) stated that "Progress" was its "most important product," and oil companies have attempted to improve their image by assurances of their concern for the environment.

Corporations also had tremendous power because they created jobs and paid taxes. Nations and states or regions within nations competed with each other to attract major corporations because of their financial impact. In the United States, members of Congress usually attempted to protect the major corporations in their districts or states. Representative Barney Frank of Massachusetts, one of Congress's most liberal and outspoken members by the end of the century, once admitted that he wouldn't have voted to build the F-18 Airplane if the GE plant constructing it had been in Ohio rather than Massachusetts.

Because of the eagerness of communities to attract big corporations, they were often given tax incentives, and their political clout also enabled them to influence national tax legislation so that they were treated favorably. In 1981 corporations lobbied heavily for a tax cut bill supported by President Reagan, who in his days as an actor had been a spokesman for General Electric. They argued that if corporate taxes were not reduced jobs would be lost. After the bill was passed, the taxes of GE and other corporations were cut, and from 1981 to 1983 GE rather than paying Federal taxes actually received a rebate. Public indignation over such favorable treatment led, however, to tax reform in 1986. Nevertheless from 1986 to 1997, a period in which GE cut 123,000 U.S. jobs, it was able to reduce its global tax rate from 34 percent to 24 percent, while increasing its profits 228 percent. For most individual tax payers, of course, it was the opposite—the more they made, the higher percentage tax they had to pay. One reason for such a low corporate tax rate, at least on its U.S. payments, was what has been called "corporate welfare," which includes various types of government tax breaks, subsidies, and bailouts—what *Time* magazine, certainly no opponent of corporate America, called "the U.S. government's cafeteria of corporate welfare." In 1998 *Time* estimated that this corporate welfare was costing taxpayers more than $125 billion a year.[43] By fiscal 1998 corporate income taxes were contributing a smaller proportion of the Federal revenues (about 11 percent of the total) than they had in 1980. Other governments also treated major corporations favorably, although like GE, some corporations were more effective than others at reducing their tax rates. In 1999 *The Economist* estimated that the Australian Rupert Murdoch's News Corporation paid an "effective tax" of only about 6 percent on its pre-tax profits from mid-1994 to mid-1998.

Major corporations also frequently violated the law. In his *Who Will Tell the People*, William Greider noted that from 1975 to 1984, more than 60 percent of the 500 leading U.S. corporations committed one or more "significant illegalities." He also cited some of the offenses of one of the major corporations of the world, General Electric. In the years 1977 to 1991, they included (among others) "criminal fraud for cheating the Army," "making false claims to the Air Force," perjury, bribery, "discriminating against low-income consumers," "conspiracy to fix prices," and numerous pollution offenses. And Greider states that GE "is certainly not the worst" of U.S. corporations, that "its behavior is not unusual" and that "the story of corporate crime or cover-ups is so routine, it is losing its shock value."[44] *The Economist* of September 18, 1999 even declared that most polls listed GE as the world's most-admired corporation.

Even when major corporations were brought to trial, they often had the legal expertise to minimize damages or recover financially by passing the costs of adjudication on to the consumer. Ten years after the Exxon Valdez 1989 oil spill in Alaska, and five years after a Federal court ordered Exxon to pay $5.2 billion in punitive damages to fishermen and others in a class-action civil case, none of the money had been paid because Exxon was still appealing it. In 1998 tobacco companies agreed to pay $246 billion over 25 years to the states in the United States to assist them to recover Medicaid money spent for dealing with smoking-related illnesses. In addition, they had to pay other court settlements as a result of individual suits, yet they expressed confidence that they could continue to be profitable, partly as a result of increasing prices but also because of increased foreign sales.

Despite the many problems with large corporations, defenders of them believed their benefits far outweighed their defects. They delivered, at what seemed reasonable prices, an ever increasing number of goods and services, and, despite cutbacks, they provided many jobs. When in April 1999 the U.S. high-tech company Compuware and the city of Detroit announced an agreement in principle to move Compuware's corporate headquarters (along with thousands of employees) to downtown Detroit, the *Detroit Free Press* announced the news with an oversized headline, devoted several pages to the story, and featured an editorial celebrating the announcement as a cause of great joy. Although western European unemployment was over 10 percent for most of the decade, in the United States it reached a 29-year low in 1999. Although corporations benefited from "corporate welfare," they did pay taxes and contribute to community and philanthropic causes. Many of them wanted to be "good neighbors," or at least be perceived as such. Moreover, in a period such as the 1990s, when more people than ever owned stocks (whether individually, in mutual funds, or within or outside of retirement plans), and the stock value of major corporations increased dramatically, many people benefited. Certainly the CEOs and other major executives with lucrative stock option plans benefited the most, but to a lesser extent so too did millions of smaller shareholders. For example, by early 1999 the value of GE shares had increased more than sixfold since the beginning of the decade. Of course, the capitalist developments discussed in this chapter affected people primarily in the wealthier countries of the world. We will examine capitalism's impact on the poorer countries of the world in our next chapter.

4

Imperialism, Nationalism, and Globalization

Imperialism

Imperialism has existed for many centuries and is defined in different ways. Some scholars have related it directly to their definition of empire.[1] For our consideration here, however, which lies mainly with the twentieth century, it seems best to define it as a country's extension of rule or authority by force or the threat of its use over a foreign territory. Such a simple definition sidesteps the very complex arguments among scholars about formal and informal empires and what constitutes an empire. Such debates need not bog us down here.

The imperialism of the late nineteenth and early twentieth centuries had many unique features.[2] The desire for new markets to absorb the increasing capitalist productive capacity and to help overcome the global depression of 1873 to 1896, along with technological advances in shipping, communications, and military capacities, stimulated a new outburst of imperialism. British Prime Minister Lord Salisbury said in 1895, "We must be prepared to take the requisite measures to open new markets for ourselves among the half-civilized or uncivilized nations of the globe."[3] In 1898, the year of the U.S. annexation of Hawaii and of the Spanish–American War, political orator and soon-to-be senator from Indiana, Albert Beveridge, expressed a similar sentiment:

American factories are making more than the American people can use; American soil is producing more than they can consume. Fate has written our policy for us; the trade of the world must and shall be ours . . . We will establish trading-posts throughout the world as distributing points for American products. We will cover the ocean with our merchant marine. We will build a navy to the measure of our greatness. Great colonies governing themselves, flying our flag and trading with us, will grow about our posts of trade. Our institutions will follow our flag on the wings of commerce . . . The Philippines are logically our first target.[4]

As we have seen in Chapter 1, however, many Filipinos did not agree and desired independence rather than passing from Spanish to American control. Their struggle for independence cost them dearly, and only in 1946, after having agreed to conditions that still favored U.S. interests, did they become independent.

By the early twentieth century, nine western European countries controlled over four-fifths of the earth's lands. From 1876 to 1915, Britain, France, Germany, Belgium, and Italy took over, or less often redistributed, about one-fourth of the world's lands, including most of Africa, which were added to already substantial overseas colonies such as India and the Dutch East Indies. In addition, the United States, Russia, and Japan made lesser gains. Furthermore, imperialist interference extended to other areas from Latin America to China. Besides seeking new markets, capitalist governments, companies, and individuals such as the British entrepreneur Cecil Rhodes also sought raw materials, new investment opportunities, and cheap labor. The desire for economic gains intertwined with strategic concerns, national rivalries, and feelings of religious/cultural superiority on the part of the imperialist powers.

This sense of superiority was based chiefly on the idea that the imperialist powers were Christian and civilized whereas those being subjugated were thought to be neither. Ignoring the fact that many Filipinos were already Christians, U.S. President McKinley said about them: "There was nothing left for us to do but to take them all, and to educate the Filipinos, and uplift and civilize and Christianize them."[5] One of the chief characteristics of the "civilized" powers was their scientific-technological superiority. Thus, civilizing colonial peoples fitted in nicely with the goal of expanding markets. One British local official declared, "If they [Africans] wanted to follow more or less civilized methods of living they would want these items of European manufacture." *Native Mirror*, a Rhodesian newspaper, was more specific when it stated in 1934 that "Africans should aim at better homes, better furniture, better utensils, better dress, better wagon carts and ploughs, better stock and better gardens." Soap was another commodity that different soap manufacturers touted as "one of civilization's greatest gifts."[6] The Polish-English writer Joseph Conrad, a critic of imperialism, wrote about European imperialists competing "for the privilege of improving" the African "as a buying machine."[7]

Two other early twentieth century critics of imperialism, Russian writer Leo Tolstoy and India's Mohandas Gandhi, who was influenced by Tolstoy, noted the identification of "civilization" with material goods. Tolstoy wrote, "This faith is a belief that those inventions and improvements for increasing the comforts of the wealthy classes and for fighting ... are something very important and almost holy, called, in the language of those who uphold such a mode of life, 'culture,' or even more grandly 'civilization.'"[8] And Gandhi observed that "if people of a certain country, who have hitherto not been in the habit of wearing much clothing, boots, etc., adopt European clothing, they are supposed to have become civilised out of savagery ... Formerly, men travelled in wagons; now they fly through the air in trains at the rate of four hundred [sic] and more miles per day. This is considered the height of civilisation."[9]

When Gandhi wrote of "wearing clothing" he realized the great importance to Britain of cotton textile exports to India, for textiles were its main export and India was the chief recipient of them. Gandhi pointed out how India possessed sufficient cotton and once produced enough homespun material to clothe itself. In the 1920s he launched a major campaign encouraging people to discard their English-made clothing, to spin and weave for themselves, and wear homespun clothes. And, of course, he did so himself and permanently adopted the loincloth attire that all the later pictures of Gandhi show him wearing. This campaign and personal practice reflected many of his values and goals including his belief in the nobility of human labor, simplicity, bridging the gap between classes, and promoting Indian independence.

Although Westerners' idealistic words about civilizing the "uncivilized" often masked more concrete economic or military objectives, this does not mean that all who claimed to support imperialism for the sake of the "uncivilized" were insincere. After Rudyard Kipling's famous poem, "The White Man's Burden," appeared in a U.S. magazine in 1899, it increased public support of the U.S. takeover in the Philippines, for the British writer's poem helped many Americans to believe, or at least half-believe, they were pursuing a noble task. He began his poem:

> Take up the White Man's burden—
> Send forth the best ye breed—
> Go bind your sons to exile
> To serve your captives' need;
> To wait in heavy harness,

On fluttered folk and wild—
Your new-caught, sullen peoples,
Half-devil and half-child.
Take up the White Man's burden—
In patience to abide,
To veil the threat of terror
And check the show of pride;
By open speech and simple,
An hundred times made plain
To seek another's profit,
And work another's gain.[10]

Although most readers of Kipling's poem today realize how full of false assumptions and stereotypes it is, readers of a century ago were still living at a time when many, including soon-to-be-U.S.-president Theodore Roosevelt, believed imperialism to be a noble activity.[11]

Imperialist rivalries helped lead to World War I, and as a result of the war Germany lost its overseas colonies, primarily to Britain and France. The Austro-Hungarian and Turkish Empires were also broken up, although most former Arab subjects of the Turks soon fell under British or French control. The pre-war Russian Empire also disintegrated, with most of its territories soon joined together in a smaller Soviet Union. In general, however, imperialist controls were almost as extensive in 1939 as they had been in 1900. And Germany, Japan, and Italy all intended to create new empires, but ultimately failed in that quest during World War II. Conversely, as a result of the war, the Soviet Union was able to expand its own borders and create a new sort of empire in eastern Europe, where it set up satellite states under communist control. At the end of the 1980s, decades after the collapse of the British and French Empires, the Soviet empire also collapsed.[12]

Racism

About the concept of race there has been much debate and many mistaken ideas—Anglo-Saxons, Aryans, and Jews, for example, are not "races." Toward the end of the twentieth century, the Executive Board of the American Anthropological Association (AAA) issued a statement that it declared "does not reflect a consensus of all members of the AAA, as individuals vary in their approaches to the study of 'race.'" The board's statement then went on to state the following:

In the United States both scholars and the general public have been conditioned to viewing human races as natural and separate divisions within the human species based on visible physical differences. With the vast expansion of scientific knowledge in this century, however, it has become clear that human populations are not unambiguous, clearly demarcated, biologically distinct groups ... There is greater variation within "racial" groups than between them ... Any attempt to establish lines of division among biological populations [is] both arbitrary and subjective ... "Race" thus evolved as a worldview, a body of prejudgments that distorts our ideas about human differences and group behavior.[13]

An AAA website also recommended an essay that declared that "race is not a scientifically valid biological category."[14] The AAA statement on race also noted that the concept of race "became a strategy for dividing, ranking, and controlling colonized people used by colonial powers everywhere."

Thus, racism was closely linked with colonialism and other forms of imperialism, and it became more prevalent in the last half of the nineteenth century, partly due to faulty interpretations of Darwin's ideas. U.S. Senator Beveridge, for example, referred to the Filipinos as a "barbarous race." He opposed any self-government for them partly on racist grounds, referring to their "savage blood, oriental blood, Malay blood."[15] During the struggle against Filipino rebels, U.S. soldiers sometimes referred to Filipinos as "niggers" or used other racial slurs. Some historians believe that the term "gooks" or some variant of it, a word some U.S. soldiers later applied to other Asians during the Korean and Vietnam wars, was one of these slurs.[16] Even some of the opponents of U.S. imperialism in 1898, such as *Nation*'s editor E. L. Godkin, reflected racist attitudes. He argued that taking over "dependencies inhabited by ignorant and inferior races" would be more trouble than it was worth.[17] In 1934, the Indonesian nationalist Sutan Sjahrir wrote that "the most extraordinary and sharpest form of race distinction and racial opposition is possible only in a colonial society."[18] Jawaharlal Nehru, who in 1947 became the first prime minister of an independent India, earlier wrote while reflecting on British imperialism in India that "the idea of a master race is inherent in imperialism."[19]

In the United States at the beginning of the twentieth century, racism was evident in many forms, most dramatically as it affected African Americans. At that time more than 90 percent of them lived in the South, where their conditions had worsened in the 1880s and 1890s. Lynchings escalated, and by 1910 most Southern blacks were unable to vote and had become increasingly segregated—in 1896 the Supreme Court approved of the principle. In 1913 government officials in Washington, D.C. began the official segregation of their employees, and in the South many black Federal workers were fired. The Collector of Internal Revenue in Georgia defended such actions, saying that "a Negro's place is in the cornfield."[20] Segregated schools, churches, housing, restaurants, bars, hospitals, barber shops, public transportation and restrooms became commonplace throughout the South, and for the most part remained so until after a Supreme Court decision of 1954 ruled that segregated public schools were unconstitutional. Even after that, compliance was slow and most forms of segregation continued into the 1960s, when the Civil Rights Campaign of Martin Luther King and others finally began to achieve major results. (See below, Chapter 5.)

Other forms of early twentieth-century American racism or bigotry included antisemitism and racial hostility toward native Americans and immigrants coming from southern and eastern Europe. Hostility towards Jews, as that toward other ethnic groups, was sometimes influenced by mistaken racial ideas, but religious, cultural, and economic factors also played their part.

Whatever the source(s) of the prejudice, antisemitism was also widespread in other areas at the beginning of the twentieth century. In the Russian Empire discrimination against Jews was especially notable, and pogroms against them sometimes erupted.[21] By 1914 almost one-third of the empire's more than 5 million Jews had emigrated, mainly to the United States. In Austria, where Hitler was born and spent his youth, and in France—where the Dreyfus Affair occurred, beginning in 1893 and involving a Jewish army officer charged with treason—strong antisemitic tendencies were also evident. The antisemitism that emerged during the Dreyfus Affair helped convince Theodore Herzl, a young Austro-Hungarian journalist then reporting from France, that Jews could obtain justice only by obtaining their own state. His conviction helped give birth to Zionism, which in turn helped bring about (in 1948) the new state of Israel.

During and shortly after World War I, attacks frequently occurred on Jews in eastern Europe (including Russia's western borderlands), an area containing most of Europe's Jews. During the interwar years discrimination against Jews was notable in both Poland and Romania. The most virulent form of antisemitism, however, was that practiced by the Nazis, which led to the Holocaust and the death of approximately 6 million Jews during World War II.[22]

Throughout the century, antisemitic and racist attitudes continued to exist in many parts of the world. One of the most institutionalized extreme forms of racism was the apartheid system that characterized South Africa for most of the latter half of the century. In his autobiography Nelson Mandela, who became the first black president of South Africa in 1994, wrote that by mid-century "if it had not already been so, race became the *sin qua non* of South African society ... Where one was allowed to live and work could rest on such absurd distinctions as the curl of one's hair or the size of one's lips." South African apartheid became even more discriminatory than U.S. segregation. As Mandela noted, "If whites wanted the land or houses of the other [racial] groups, they could simply declare the land a white area and take them." As opposed to such racism, Mandela consistently worked for a "nonracial, united and democratic South Africa." [23]

Racism often led to ethnic conflicts, but ethnic identification, like national identification, was a more complex phenomenon than race. Nevertheless, the observation by the Indian-born economist Amartya Sen was correct in noting that twentieth-century violence was often encouraged by rigidly classifying people according to a single classification, such as race, ethnicity, nationality, or religion, and forgetting that all humans have multiple identities and share common numerous human qualities. Reminding his readers of such common qualities, Sen quoted Shakespeare's lines from *The Merchant of Venice* (Act III, Scene 1): "Hath not a Jew eyes? hath not a Jew hands, organs, dimensions, senses, affections, passions? fed with the same food, hurt with the same weapons, subject to the same diseases, healed by the same means, warmed and cooled by the same winter and summer, as a Christian is?"[24]

Nationalism, Self-Determination, Ethnicity, and Conflict

Nations and Nationalism

Many definitions of "nation" exist. A Random House dictionary, for example, gives as its first two the following:

1. A body of people associated with a particular territory, that is sufficiently conscious of its unity to seek or possess a government peculiarly its own.
2. The territory or country itself.[25]

The first definition is most useful because it emphasizes the importance of people thinking that they make up a single nation, and it recognizes that they need not yet form an independent state. In the nineteenth century the Polish people, without an independent country of their own, were an example of a people that qualified as a nation by this definition; and from 1910 to the end of World War II, Korea could also be thought of as a nation even though it was not an independent country but controlled by Japan. The Soviet Union, however, was never a nation, but rather a union of many different nationalities such as Russians, Ukrainians, Estonians, and Georgians. The reasons why people think they form a nation can vary greatly, and may include one or more of the following which they believe they have in common: culture, ethnicity, language, religion, historical experiences.

Very few of the countries of the world in 1999 existed as independent states in 1800, whether in Europe, the Americas, Asia, or Africa. In Europe in 1800 Germany, Italy, Ireland, Finland, Poland, Greece, and many more areas were not independent countries. In eastern and southeastern Europe the Austrian, Russian, and Ottoman Turkish Empires existed in place of the many independent countries that subsequently occupied the European lands of these empires. In 1914, these three empires still existed, although the Turks by then had lost almost all their European territory, partly because of the growth of nationalism in the Balkan area.

Although nationalism has been defined many ways, it certainly involves an emotional loyalty toward one's nation. Isaiah Berlin once stated that it "is an inflamed condition of national consciousness which can be, and has on occasion been, tolerant and peaceful."[26] Nationalism as we understand it today first arose in the late eighteenth and early nineteenth centuries. Its spread in the nineteenth and twentieth centuries often helped give birth to independent nations as one group after another (for example, Germans or Italians) became "sufficiently conscious of its unity to seek or possess a government peculiarly its own."

Nationalism often encouraged imperialism by providing the basis for the belief in a nation's greatness and mission abroad. But imperialism, in turn, inadvertently stimulated nationalism in new places, such as colonial territories, as part of an anti-imperialist reaction on the part of the subjugated, or at least the elites who spoke on their behalf. This was true both in Europe, especially at the beginning of the nineteenth century in reaction to Napoleonic conquests, and later in the rest of the world in reaction to European colonial rule and imperialist activities. It was also true in some Latin American countries such as Nicaragua in response to early twentieth-century U.S. imperialism.

Upon obtaining (or regaining) independence and sovereignty, some countries, such as Poland after World War I, already possessed a strong sense of nationhood, but others did not—in Poland's case, the memory of its existence as an independent country before it was divided by its neighbors in the late eighteenth century helped keep alive its nationalism.

The development of nationalism and a sense of nationhood, whether before or after statehood was achieved, was often a gradual process that was stimulated not only by foreign interventions and invasions, but also by other factors. The existence of a strong enemy was one such stimulant. In a vicious cycle, nationalism often both fostered enmity and was fostered by it, as we see, for example, in the case of German–French hostility before and during World War I. Other conditions that helped spur nationalism included advances in communication and transportation (roads, railroads, telegraphs, newspapers, etc.); formal and informal education, including propaganda put out or supported by national government agencies; and emphasis on national history, culture, holidays, symbols, traditions, official language(s), and heroes. In much of this there was a certain amount of myth making or what Eric Hobsbawm and Terence Ranger have referred to as "invented tradition."[27] The creation of national laws and institutions, including a military and civilian bureaucracy, and a national economy also helped to strengthen a sense of nationhood. In some cases it was at first only a small number of urban intellectuals who attempted to arouse others to recognize that they were part of a unique nation. Peasants, for example, often possessed little sense of national identification until education and other modernizing forces helped to instill it.[28]

Self-Determination, Achieving Independence, and Ethnicity

The breakup of European empires resulting from World War I and subsequent birth or rebirth of nations was facilitated by the principle of self-determination. In November 1917, the new Soviet government in Russia proclaimed, in a Declaration of the Rights of the Peoples of Russia, "the right of the peoples of Russia to free self-determination, even to the point of separation and the formation of an independent state." Several months later U.S. President Woodrow Wilson in a speech to the U.S. Congress stated: "National aspirations must be respected; peoples must be dominated or governed only by their own consent. 'Self-determination' is not a mere phrase. It is an imperative principle of action, which statesmen will ignore at their peril ... Every territorial settlement involved in this war must be made in the interest and for the benefit of the populations concerned and not as a part of any mere adjustment or compromise of claims amongst rival states."[29]

The Soviet proclamation, however, was partly propaganda and was never intended to be as sweeping as it sounded. Although the

Soviet government supported self-determination for the colonies of Western empires, in the former Russian Empire it generally prevented the principle from being exercised except where it could not be thwarted due to the civil war and Allied intervention in Russia, both of which followed World War I.

The application of Wilson's proclamation was also very limited, primarily to European portions of the former German, Austria-Hungarian, and Russian Empires. From that area, independent countries such as Poland, Czechoslovakia, Estonia, Latvia, and Lithuania emerged, partly from the national aspirations of these formerly subjected peoples and partly from Western diplomatic considerations like the desire to create non-communist states on Russia's western borders. At the Paris Peace Conference of 1919 non-Europeans, including Arabs from the former Ottoman Turkish Empire, discovered that the Western colonial powers did not intend to apply the principle beyond Europe. And for several years after the war, British troops even fought against the Irish who sought the right to self-determination.

One of the difficulties of the principle was that it was more complex than it first appeared. Although it suggested that each nationality should have the right to live under its own government and that boundaries—at least eastern European ones—should reflect this principle, seldom did territories contain just one nationality. Ireland, for example, contained both Irish Catholics and in the north many descendants of earlier Protestant immigrants from Scotland and other parts of Great Britain. In such a situation could one speak of a single Irish nationality, and what precisely did nationality and self-determination mean? Yugoslavia, created in 1918 as the Kingdom of Serbs, Croats, and Slovenes, contained numerous nationalities intermingled in such a way as to make any division into separate ethnic territories extremely difficult.

Despite such difficulties, nationalities invoked the principle countless times during the remainder of the century as various peoples, including those in Asia, Africa, and the former USSR, struggled for their independence. Moreover, the United Nations Charter stated that one of the purposes of the UN was to "develop friendly relations among nations based on respect for the principle of equal rights and self-determination."

Although self-determination in the interwar period occurred mainly in eastern Europe, some nationalities of the region, like the Ukrainians and Belorussians, did not achieve it until much later. Instead, they remained sizable minorities in other countries, chiefly Soviet Russia and Poland. Large minorities also remained in some of the other countries of the area such as the Hungarian (Magyar) minority in Romania.

In Africa, on the eve of World War II, there were only two independent counties, Egypt and Liberia. After the war, opposition to colonial rule was often led by political movements that fostered a sense of nationalism within individual African countries—a weaker Pan-African Movement, which sought a wider unity among African peoples, also existed. Nevertheless, when independence finally came, mainly in the 1960s, a sense of nationhood was still weak in many countries, partly because their boundaries generally depended on the original carving up of Africa by the colonial powers, which paid little attention to ethnographic, religious, or cultural considerations. In some countries such as Nigeria, the most populated country in Africa, many different ethnic groups existed without a great deal in common. In northeast Africa under colonial rule, the Somali people resided in five different areas: British Somaliland, French Somaliland, Italian Somaliland, Ethiopia, and Kenya. With independence, the British and Italian Somalilands became Somalia, and French Somaliland eventually became Djibouti; but Ethiopia and Kenya also continued to number Somalis among their numerous ethnic groups.

In Asia, independence came earlier than in Africa, with most Asian colonial territories receiving independence in the late 1940s and 1950s. As in Africa, anti-colonial movements had stimulated nationalism. Once independence was achieved, other forces helped bolster nationalism. Just as German–French enmity before and during World War I had fostered nationalism in both countries, so the continuing hostility between India (mainly Hindu) and Pakistan (mainly Muslim), after Britain divided British India into these two states in 1947, encouraged nationalism in both these Asian countries.

In both Asia and Africa, national political parties and new governments also attempted to nurture a sense of national identity by many of the same methods earlier used by Western countries and Japan. Education, propaganda, and creating national laws, institutions, and a national economy helped to strengthen a sense of nationhood, as did the effective use of communication media—in Africa, some states went even further than instituting government radio stations and newspapers by placing loudspeakers in villages.

Such steps attempted to supersede regional or ethnic loyalties. In Africa and Asia, as in many other parts of the world, most countries contained many ethnic groups. As with other definitions such as race, nation, or nation state, differences exist as to how ethnicity should be defined, and the term sometimes overlaps with nation and nationalism. In the 1990s, for example, Serbian nationalism was often cited as an example of "ethnic nationalism," as opposed to the type of nationalism that existed in a multinational country such as the United States. The *Harvard Encyclopedia of American Ethnic Groups* classified ethnic groups based primarily on regional and religious grounds and listed 106 of them including not only American Indians, Afro-Americans, German-Americans, and Irish-Americans, but also Burmese-Americans, Copts, Kalmyks, Appalachians, and Mormons. As this list makes clear, ethnic groups were generally thought of as smaller units than nations.

National and Ethnic Conflicts

As we have seen in Chapter 1, much of the conflict and warfare of the twentieth century involved anti-imperial, racial, national, or ethnic hostilities, and quite often these types of conflicts overlapped.

Early in the twentieth century imperialist activities by the major European countries, the United States, and Japan in China inadvertently stimulated the emergence of the nationalist Kuomintang Party led by Sun Yat-Sen. After World War I, the Chinese Communist Party also came into being and was encouraged by the Soviet Union to cooperate with the Kuomintang to overthrow Western imperialist influences in China.

In the Russo–Japanese War of 1904–5, racist and nationalist feelings, as well as imperialist rivalry in Manchuria and Korea, played a part. S. Witte, one of the chief ministers of Tsar Nicholas II of Russia, noted the tsar's "attitude of hostility toward and contempt for Japan and the Japanese, as can be seen from official reports in which he refers to the Japanese as 'macacques' [monkeys]. If not for his belief that the Japanese are an unpleasant, contemptible, and powerless people who could be destroyed at one blow from the Russian giant, we would not have adopted a policy in the Far East that led us into the unfortunate war with Japan."[30] Japanese success in the war occurred partly because of the strong nationalism that had characterized Japan and fed its modernization and militarization in the previous half century and would continue to do so until Japan was finally defeated in World War II.

In Europe nationalistic forces helped lead to World War I. Historian Bernadotte Schmitt went so far as to write: "The primary cause of the war was a conflict between political frontiers and the distribution of peoples, the denial of . . . the right of self-determination."[31] This was especially true in regard to Serbia, which believed that Bosnia and Herzegovina, in which ethnic Serbs formed the largest nationality, should be part of a greater Serbia. The assassination of the Austrian Archduke Franz Ferdinand by a Bosnian Serb was the match that ignited the war. During the war, what some historians consider the first genocide of the twentieth century occurred when the Turks deported and killed large numbers of Armenian civilians. The numbers so killed are disputed, but Armenians claim that it was well over 1 million.

In interwar Europe the problem of national minorities continued to cause problems and the right to self-determination continued to be invoked. In Czechoslovakia one out of every five persons was ethnically German. In September 1938 Hitler referred to Woodrow Wilson's earlier statements regarding self-determination and claimed that it must now be obtained by these Germans in Czechoslovakia. Germany soon afterward annexed most of them, the so-called Sudeten Germans. In the Baltic city of Danzig (later the Polish Gdansk) the population was overwhelmingly German, but interwar Danzig was under the League of Nations' jurisdiction. Hitler insisted on Danzig's right to self-determination and to reunite with Germany, an insistence that helped lead to the outbreak of World War II in Europe.

The war itself exacerbated racism and nationalism and led to the Nazi's mass executions of Jews and other peoples who according to Nazi racist ideas were "inferior." In the United States, the media often depicted the Japanese in racist ways and the government removed more than 100,000 Japanese–Americans from their homes and placed them in detention camps.

With the emergence of the Cold War following World War II until its end in the late 1980s, ideological conflict seemed to take precedence over national and ethnic strife.[32] Yet many anti-colonial battles of this period were struggles fueled by nationalism and against the racism that was so often entwined with imperialism. Ethnic conflicts also frequently occurred. The Algerians' war against French colonialism from 1954 to 1962 was a good example. The length and bitterness of the war came about to a great extent because of the fear of French and other European colonists and their descendents (about 10 percent of the population) that they would lose their privileged positions in an independent Algeria in which they would be greatly outnumbered by native Algerians, whom some colonists referred to as "dirty little rats." After the overthrow of Japanese World War II control in southeast Asia, the Vietnamese led the fight against the restoration of French rule in Indochina, finally defeating the French, after hundreds of thousands of lost lives, in 1954. The United States perceived its struggle in Vietnam in the 1960s and early 1970s as a battle against communist expansion, but many people in Vietnam looked upon the war as a continuation of the nationalist struggle against Western imperialism.

Between 1946 and 1948, as the British pulled out of British India (India and Pakistan) and Palestine, conflicts erupted among the different peoples in each territory. About 800,000 people died in a Hindu–Muslim conflict in the first area, and the first Arab–Israeli War broke out in the second region. These conflicts also created millions of refugees, as wars often do. Like the differences that sometimes led to bloodshed between Catholics and Protestants in Northern Ireland, the Hindu–Muslim and Jewish–Muslim violence in British India and Palestine resulted not only from religious differences but also from economic, social, and cultural ones.

Other major conflicts between nationalities or ethnic groups in the Cold War era and beyond included a secessionist war in Nigeria (1967–70) resulting in about 2 million deaths; religious-ethnic strife which ebbed and flowed in Sudan from the 1960s through the 1990s and led directly or indirectly to the loss of millions of lives; a Hutu–Tutsi clash in Central Africa, primarily in Rwanda and Burundi, that in 1994 caused the deaths of about 800,000 people, overwhelmingly civilians; a Bengali or East Pakistan secessionist war (aided by India) against West Pakistan in 1971 that brought about the deaths of more than another million people; an Iran–Iraq War from 1980 to 1988, which caused about another half a million deaths; and during the 1990s, conflicts among Serbs, Croats, Bosnian and Kosovar Muslims and other ethnic groups in the former Yugoslavia that led to the deaths of hundreds of thousands and created millions of refugees. Besides all these casualties, many others were caused by numerous other national or ethnic differences.

Conflicts in the northeast part of Africa known as the Horn of Africa between Somalis and Ethiopians, as well as between Eritreans and Ethiopians, continued on and off for decades with the latter conflict still occurring in 1999. In South Africa, the apartheid system of severe segregation and discrimination against the majority black population and other non-whites, which was implemented following World War II, continued in force until the beginning of the 1990s; and despite Nelson Mandela's skillful leadership in the mid and late 1990s, decades of discrimination left many lingering problems and resentments that would continue into the twenty-first century.

In Indonesia the ethnic Chinese minority, often resented because of their financial prominence, were sometimes victimized, as were the people of East Timor, which Indonesia annexed in 1976, and where opposition continued to some degree or other for the rest of the century. In Malaysia, differences between Malays and ethnic Chinese also led to sporadic violence and to the withdrawal of Singapore, a majority of whose people are Chinese, from the Malaysian Federation in 1965. In India, where there were 35 languages spoken by 1 million or more people each, ethnic or religious strife often occurred and led to the assassination of Prime Minister Indira Gandhi in 1984—no relation of Mohandas Gandhi, who was also assassinated (in 1948) because of similar strife. Her son Rajiv Gandhi—who became prime minister of India after his mother's brutal assassination in 1984—was also assassinated (in 1991) because of India's involvement in a religious-ethnic conflict in neighboring Sri Lanka between the Buddhist Sinhalese majority and the Hindu Tamil minority.

In one of his novels, Indian-born writer Salman Rushdie captured well the conflicts that so often troubled the land of his childhood, both internally and with neighboring Pakistan: "In Punjab, Assam, Kashmir, Meerut—in Delhi, in Calcutta—from time to time they slit their neighbor's throats . . . They killed you for being circumcised and they killed you because your foreskins had been left on. Long hair got you murdered and haircuts too; light skin flayed dark skin and if you spoke the wrong language you could lose your twisted tongue."[33] Other parts of Asia where self-determination movements or ethnic strife existed included Tibet (under Chinese control) and Kashmir (divided between India and Pakistan).

As the Soviet Union began collapsing in the late 1980s and finally expired in 1991, national and ethnic strife increased, for example between Armenians and Azerbaijanis over the territory of Nagorno-Karabakh. In the mid-1990s the Chechens fought to secede from Russia and the war led to tens of thousands of deaths. Further south the Kurds remained throughout the century one of the most significant nationalities without a country of their own. Instead, their homeland of Kurdistan was divided between Turkey, Iran, Iraq, Armenia, and Syria, and their fight for greater autonomy often led to bloodshed and greater repression especially in Iraq and Turkey. In the Middle East, the clash between Jews and Arabs was not the only case of ethnic-religious strife; in Lebanon, for example, differences between Muslims and Christians remained a major source of conflict. In the Mediterranean Sea on the island of Cyprus, antagonism between Greek and Turkish Cypriots was ongoing.

Ethnic dissension was also evident in most other parts of the world. The collapse of communist authority from 1989 to 1991 not only released pent up ethnic nationalist forces in the Soviet Union and Yugoslavia but also made possible the division (in 1993) of Czechoslovakia into two nation states, the Czech Republic and

Slovakia. In western Europe during the final decades of the century ethnic or national dissension existed not only in Northern Ireland and Spain (where movements for Basque and Catalonian autonomy existed), but also in such major countries as Great Britain, France, and Germany. In Great Britain white hostility to several million Asian, African, and Caribbean ethnic minorities sometimes occurred, and separatist movements existed in Scotland and Wales, where national parliaments with considerable autonomy from London were elected in 1999. In France, where by 1991 over one-tenth of the population was foreign born, extreme right-wing elements often blamed many of France's problems such as crime and unemployment on ethnic minorities like the Algerians. In Germany, where about one-fifth of the people in some of its major cities were foreigners, Turkish workers and their families were sometimes abused.

In the United States, despite considerable progress, racial and ethnic divisions and tensions continued throughout the century. At century's end the policy of affirmative action, earlier designed to increase opportunities for ethnic minorities and women, remained a contentious issue. Racially motivated hate crimes occurred on occasion. A considerable number of African Americans continued to live in urban ghettos, and unemployment and imprisonment rates among young African Americans were much higher than for white youth. As the number of Hispanic Americans increased so too did calls for reducing U.S. immigration, especially that of illegal immigrants via Mexico. In Canada, the separatist movement among French Canadians in Quebec was strong. In Latin America, incidents of ethnic conflict also occurred, most noticeably in Guatemala. In 1999 a Truth Commission Report concluded that the Guatemalan military (aided in part by U.S. financial support and training) had committed "acts of genocide" against the Mayan Indian people in a civil war that lasted from 1960 to 1996 and killed more than 200,000 Guatemalans. As often happened during the Cold War, ethnic conflict was intermingled with ideological and economic-social causes: the Guatemalan military, for example, depicted the war as an attempt to wipe out a communist guerilla movement.

Westernization and Its Opponents

The concept of Westernization has often been used to indicate the adoption of Western techniques, ideas, or customs by non-Western nations or peoples. The term, however, represents a very complex phenomenon. To begin with, the West (meaning primarily western

Europe and the United States) is far from being homogeneous. The cultures of Spain, Germany, and the United States, for example, vary considerably. And within any one country, there are quite often many subcultures, often at variance with one another. Moreover, non-Western nations never completely Westernize nor completely reject their traditional cultures.[34] Despite these complexities, however, the term Westernization remains useful.

In mid-nineteenth-century Russia there were two groups of thinkers who were referred to as Westernizers and Slavophiles. One of the first group's thinkers, Peter Chaadaev, declared that Russia was a wasteland that had contributed nothing of value to civilization. The group believed that Peter the Great (d. 1725) had performed a great service by attempting to "Westernize" Russia, and they rejected the Slavophiles' belief in the superiority of Russian Orthodoxy and pre-Petrine Russia. Like Peter the Great earlier, the Westernizers tended to look upon the Russian peasants as backwards and in need of Westernization. The Slavophiles looked at Russia and the West from a "We-They" perspective. From their point of view, the West overemphasized materialism, rationalism, individualism, and legalism, while Russia (at least before Peter the Great) had properly emphasized spiritual values, faith, intuition, the community, and social and political relations based more on moral bonds than on impersonal laws.

The novels of Dostoevsky later reflected some of these same ideas, and his contemporary the botanist Nikolai Danilevsky claimed in his book *Russia and Europe* (1869) that European civilization was not the only type of civilization and that there were no universal values, but that different historical-cultural types existed and that Europe and Russia belonged to two very different types. (In an article in *Foreign Affairs* in the summer of 1993 and later in his 1996 book *The Clash of Civilizations and the Remaking of World Order*, Samuel P. Huntington of Harvard expressed ideas similar to some of those of Danilievsky, stating, for example, that Western and Slavic-Orthodox civilizations were quite different and sometimes antagonistic.)[35]

Although not a Slavophile, Leo Tolstoy also rejected the idea that Russia should follow the path of the West. In 1906, he wrote: "For the Russian people to enter on the path along which the Westerners went, would mean consciously to commit the same acts of violence that the Government demands ... More than that, they would be deprived, like the Western nations, of their chief blessing—their accustomed, beloved, agricultural life."[36]

The Russian people, however, followed not Tolstoy's ideas but those of Lenin, whom Theodore Von Laue called "the designer of the most successful global model of a Westernizing anti-Western counter-revolution."[37] Lenin and Stalin attempted to technologically modernize and partially "Westernize" Russia in order to successfully compete with the West and eventually have the Soviet Union become the dominant power in the world. Despite the ideological differences between Marxism-Leninism and Danilevsky's ideas, the communist empire established by Stalin was fairly close in size to the Russian-dominated federation that Danilevsky envisioned coming into existence from the Adriatic Sea to the Pacific Ocean. But the communist partial Westernization rejected the freedom, democracy, rule of law, and market economies that generally characterized the West, especially after Hitler's defeat in World War II. And such post-war phenomena as Zhdanovism, a Soviet campaign against Western cultural influences, also reflected Soviet opposition to too much Western influence.

Critical of the West in the tradition of the Slavophiles, Dostoevsky, and Tolstoy, the Russian novelist Alexander Solzhenitsyn (b. 1918) looked at communism as a Western import into Russia that was contrary to its best traditions. Critical of both communism and contemporary Western life, which he believed was too materialistic and irreligious, he advised Russians not to follow Western materialistic and individualistic ways. And after the collapse of the Soviet Union in 1991, he was deeply disappointed that, despite his advice, many of these ways became more common in Russia during the 1990s. Yet by 1999, Russian dissatisfaction with the West had also increased because Russian-style capitalism and democracy had not yet proven as successful as many had hoped they would. Furthermore, NATO's bombing of Serbia (Slavic and Orthodox like Russia) intensified hostility to that predominantly Western military organization, of which Russia was already suspicious because of its decision to include Poland, Hungary, and the Czech Republic as members.[38]

Russia's ambivalence about Westernization was matched just about everywhere else in the non-Westernized world during the nineteenth and twentieth centuries. Like Japan in the late nineteenth century and the Soviet Union later, many non-Western countries, or at least their elites, believed that they had to adopt at least some Western technology and practices in order to strengthen themselves so as not to be victimized by outside powers. Mustafa Kemal (Ataturk), the father of modern Turkey, espoused this view. By 1981 Paul Harrison, an astute observer of the Third World, made these observations about Westernization: "Every capital city in the world is getting to look like every other ... but the style is exclusively western. And not just in consumer fashions: the mimicry extends to architecture, industrial technology, approaches to health care, education and housing ...

The Third World's obsession with the western way of life has perverted development and is rapidly destroying good and bad in traditional cultures."[39] Harrison attributed this Westernization to 1) the policies of Third World elites who copied too many of the ways of the dominant colonialists, 2) youth rebelling against their own indigenous traditions, and 3) the overwhelming influence of Western media, advertising, products, and tourists.

In the remaining years of the twentieth century, Westernization continued its relentless advance. In the 1990s, American journalist Robert D. Kaplan noted Westernized shopping malls in Bangkok, Thailand and people there reflecting the "style of glossy magazine advertisements, no matter how inconvenient the result."[40] With its satellite dishes, ATM machines, and stores, the Thai city of Nong Khai reminded him of a California suburb. In a shop advertising quick service to obtain a travel visa he observed a young girl watching the TNT cartoon channel. Like most other travelers in the final decades of the century, Kaplan could not escape contemporary Western music blaring from radios and audio and video cassettes. On buses, in hotels, in restaurants, and even in less expected places it often reverberated, whether or not one wished to hear it. In the National Museum of Accra, the capital of the West African nation of Ghana, while he was observing native drums and other artifacts, his ears were assaulted with a rock video blaring from the television set of the Museum's duty guard.

Other travel writers and journalists observed similar phenomena.[41] Paul Theroux visited many remote islands in the Pacific Ocean and found that videos of the gun-touting Rambo of U.S. movie fame were popular and that Rambo was one of the folk heroes of the islands. Writing about the same time as Theroux (the early 1990s), Frank Viviano commented on buses in the Philippines blaring out American music from their tape decks. The collapse of communism in many countries at the end of the 1980s and beginning of the 1990s also sped up some aspects of Westernization such as the increased use of Western marketing techniques and media in place of communist propaganda. In 1990 in Ulam Bator, capital of Mongolia, Vivano observed that Marxist–Leninist symbols and artifacts were being removed and that young people were eagerly watching MTV tapes of Madonna and Prince, and that Western music from boomboxes rang out over one of the city's central squares. Writing about the mid-1990s in Moscow, David Remnick noted how much Moscow had changed in a decade, observing among other changes that hundreds of women had left their poorly-paid jobs as doctors, engineers, and teachers in order to sell cosmetics for Avon and Mary Kay.

Yet throughout the century there were always some individuals and groups, like the earlier Slavophiles in Russia, who protested against too much Westernization and insisted on the superiority of many traditional values and ways. One modern scholar has written: "Whether it was the Philippines, or any number of African territories, or the Indian subcontinent, the Arab world, or the Caribbean and much of Latin America, China or Japan, natives banded together in independence and nationalist groupings that were based on a sense of identity which was ethnic, religious or communal, and was opposed to further Western encroachment."[42]

Gandhi in India, though tolerant religiously, opposed to his country's traditional caste system, and in favor of what he considered appropriate technology, was a traditionalist in many ways and did not want his country to imitate the West in establishing a modernized, industrialized, and urbanized existence. In a work of 1909, Gandhi proclaimed that "this [Indian] civilization is unquestionably the best" and that those in India who had become "affected by Western civilization have become enslaved."[43] Commenting on Gandhi shortly before his death, one of his biographers declared that "he abhorred Westernization as much as ever."[44] Similar comments could be made about the Japanese writer Yukio Mishima (1925–70), who believed that Westernization was corrupting Japan's purer traditions and spirit.

As with the Slavophiles, Solzhenitsyn, and Gandhi, the anti-Western reaction was sometimes connected with an anti-secularist impulse and a desire to maintain a culture more religiously oriented than modern Western culture. In the late 1920s such motivation helped give birth in Egypt to the Muslim Brotherhood, branches of which later arose in other parts of the Middle East and northern Africa including Sudan. Although outlawed in some places, the Brotherhood remained significant at different times in many Islamic countries, whether legal or not, throughout the rest of the century.

The establishment of Israel in 1948, which many Arabs considered a representative of the West, and subsequent Arab–Israeli Wars helped strengthen Arab anti-Western sentiments. And the victory of Iranian Islamic fundamentalists in 1979, who replaced the more Westernizing shah of Iran, also strengthened anti-Western feelings and Islamic fundamentalism in other parts of the Islamic world. This "world" included about one-fourth of the earth's nations, including Indonesia, the world's fourth most populous state. At the end of the century in Islamic countries such as Algeria, Afghanistan, Iran, and Turkey, serious differences continued to exist between Islamic fundamentalists and less religiously-oriented, more modernizing elite elements.[45]

In sub-Saharan Africa, where Islam was not as strong as in north Africa, some African intellectuals developed cultural movements stressing Africa's uniqueness. The Senegalese statesman and poet Leopold Senghor championed the principle of negritude, a concept he developed along with the Caribbean poet Aimé Césaire. For Senghor, though he at times stressed the importance of common human traits, negritude highlighted Africa's cultural uniqueness and differentiated Africans from Europeans. Senghor's fellow countryman the historian Cheikh Anta Diop (1923–86) also emphasized African uniqueness and claimed that its true roots went back to ancient Egypt, which he claimed was "a Negro civilization" and superior to the Greco-Latin civilization out of which Europe developed. Although the ideas of Senghor and Diop differed in some important ways, they both contributed to the belief that Africans were more community oriented, spontaneous, intuitive, creative, spiritual, and in harmony with nature than Europeans, who emphasized individualism, logic, and the scientific-technological mastering of nature. Such a position resembled that of nineteenth-century Russian Slavophiles and many other later defenders of traditional cultures from various parts of the world.[46]

In Latin America thinkers often criticized the United States, but were more sympathetic to Europe. At the very beginning of the twentieth century, Uruguayan José Enrique Rodó's wrote the influential essay *Ariel* (1900), which pictured the United States as cold, materialistic, and soulless, and encouraged Latin Americans to reject U.S. influence and remain true to their national personalities, which valued beauty and truth more. Unlike Diop, however, Rodó valued highly Greco-Roman aesthetic ideals and believed Latin American culture, at its best, was heavily indebted to them. Toward the end of the century, the Mexican writer Carlos Fuentes, who also served as Mexico's ambassador to France in the mid-1970s, expressed similar attitudes toward the United States and Europe.[47] In Latin America, as in other parts of the world, hostility towards U.S. government policies in the late twentieth century, often coexisted with extensive U.S. cultural influence. In Nicaragua in the 1980s, for example, the battle hymn of the Sandanista National Liberation Front included the phrase "We fight/Against the Yankees/The enemy of humanity," but U.S. television shows and music were very popular.

Often more critical of Europe was the Latin American *indigenismo* movement, which sometimes contrasted unfavorably European culture, or at least certain aspects of it, with traditional indigenous Indian culture. One advocate of the movement, the Peruvian José Carlos Mariátegui (1894–1930), like the Chilean poet Pablo Neruda

(1904–73), combined a Marxist critique of modern Western societies with an appreciation of many traditional Indian values.

The relation of non-Western countries to Westernization was further shaded by the presence of many different cultural strains in any one country. In Iran, for example, before an Islamic government replaced the shah in 1979, the capital Teheran was much more Westernized and secularized than the rural areas, where fundamentalist Islam remained strong. By the mid-1990s, after a decade and a half of Islamic rule, the public contrast had narrowed. Yet in the capital, despite signs reading "Death to America," journalist Robert Kaplan observed that "Western consumerism assaults you everywhere with signs"[48] for various consumer products, and he was told that one of the most popular television programs in Teheran was *Baywatch*, whose actresses' bikinis offered a sharp contrast to the formless black chador worn publicly by many Iranian women.

Despite the continuing impact of the West in various parts of the world, by the end of the twentieth century it was much less dominant than it once had been. The massive European killing in World War I had led some thinkers to accept the view proposed by Oswald Spengler in his *Decline of the West* (1918–22) that the West had indeed declined. The collapse of European empires in the decades following World War II led others to speak of Western decline. And most recently (in 2006), Niall Ferguson has argued that "it seems justifiable to interpret the twentieth century not as the triumph but as the descent of the West, with the Second World War as the decisive turning point." Further emphasizing his point, he notes that by the end of the century the gap between European and East Asian wealth had closed considerably, that China had one of the world's most dynamic economies, that radical anti-Western Islam was on the rise, that Muslim populations were increasing much faster than European populations, and that Europe's Muslim population, some of whom were illegal immigrants, was increasing rapidly.[49]

Globalization and International Finance

Globalization can be defined as the process of increasing inter-connectedness between the world's peoples and their societies that accelerated rapidly in the final decades of the twentieth century.[50] Some historians, however, have argued that increasing economic interconnectedness was already occurring prior to World War I. Between 1850 and 1913 world trade increased tenfold. Improvements in communication and transportation methods, along with the imperialism that these methods helped make possible, brought many of the world's peoples into more contact with each other. So too did foreign investment, especially by the British, who in the decade from 1885 to 1894 invested more than half of their total investments abroad. The migration of peoples, especially out of Europe, where about 1 million people a year were leaving in the early twentieth century, also mixed peoples together more than previously. Both because of imperialism and the appeal of European ideas and customs, intellectuals, and social elites in other regions of the world, including the United States, were often influenced by European culture.

Throughout the twentieth century, however, nationalism acted as an impediment to even closer connections between different peoples and nations and helped produce two world wars. During the period of these wars and the Great Depression which occurred between them, economic barriers and restrictions such as tariffs and blockades impeded further interconnectedness, as did the Cold War and the conflicts that often accompanied decolonialization. Even wars, however, both hot and cold, increased some cross-border contacts. During the two world wars, for example, many Americans first saw Europe or Pacific areas. The post-World War II occupation of Japan, Korea, and portions of Europe introduced more Americans and other victors, including Soviet troops in Europe and North Korea, to foreign countries. The Cold War led to the deployment of U.S. forces around the globe and to the retention of Soviet troops in eastern Europe.

Meanwhile, technology, especially airplanes, rockets, radios, movies, television, space satellites, computers, and the Internet, continued to make the world a smaller place and bring more people into contact with one another even before the end of the Cold War. Its end, however, about a decade before the close of the twentieth century, further reduced barriers to globalization. By 1999 global spending on travel and tourism had more than doubled as compared to that of 1989 and included many more people from ex-communist countries, whose right to foreign travel had been earlier restricted.

Capitalist forces, including multinational corporations, and decreasing national barriers to trade, financing, and investments also propelled globalization onward. During and shortly after World War II, the Western allies agreed to encourage international economic growth and free trade by forming the International Monetary Fund (IMF), the International Bank for Reconstruction and Development (World Bank), and the General Agreement on Tariffs and Trade (GATT). In 1995, the World Trade Organization (WTO) replaced GATT. In the decades following the war, trade barriers diminished, especially among non-communist nations, and world trade climbed steadily. By 1999 it was about 16 times higher than in 1950.[51] Decade by decade, more countries became integrated into the global trading system, as GATT/WTO increased from 23 original members to 134 by July 1999. Also furthering trade between nations were various regional trade arrangements. Examples included those that formed and sustained the European Common Market (begun in the late 1950s and since 1993 known as the European Union) and various groupings in the Western Hemisphere that came into existence in the latter part of the century such as the Andean Common Market, the Caribbean Community and Common Market (CARICOM), Mercosur, and the North American Free Trade Agreement (NAFTA).

During the last few decades of the twentieth century the IMF, in return for loans and economic assistance to areas such as Latin America began insisting on austerity measures that would cut government spending. This sometimes meant reduced public funding for such areas as food subsidies, education, health care, and public transport. These so-called neoliberal policies reflected the economic approaches of U.S. President Reagan and British Prime Minister Thatcher (see Chapter 3), who favored privatizing many state-owned enterprises, shrinking the economic role of governments, and fostering "free markets."

Even before the collapse of the Soviet Bloc in eastern Europe, Communist China had begun moving closer to a market economy and had become more integrated into the world economy. Between 1978 and 1995 its foreign trade increased more than 13 times, and foreign investment in the country went from a negligible amount to about one-quarter of a million different foreign-financed projects. McDonald's, Kentucky Fried Chicken, Marlboros, and many other foreign businesses and products came to China. Despite this, however, and despite U.S. attempts to get China to reduce barriers to U.S. exports, by 1998 the United States had run up a record-high trade deficit with China. In the late 1990s China attempted to join the WTO, but had not yet sufficiently met the group's criteria for membership. Nevertheless, in 1999, China's prime minister declared that China would continue to open itself wider to international contacts, and in 2001 China became a WTO member.

After the collapse of communism in the Soviet Bloc from 1989 to 1991, capitalism spread rapidly in the region, which became more intertwined in the globalized world economy. For example, in Poland, Hungary, and the Czech Republic foreign investment doubled in 1995. These three countries, which also became part of NATO by the end of the decade, adopted capitalist practices more successfully than some others such as Russia and Ukraine. As the century came to an end, however, even those two countries that had been reluctant or less successful in the transition from command to market economies offered no clear-cut viable alternative to participating in free-market globalization. The Russian economic system of the late 1990s, for example, was often referred to as "crony capitalism." And critics of it emphasized the extent to which it was marked by corruption, favoritism, and organized crime, and how little it had helped the average Russian—much of the money earned by the new rich was not reinvested in Russia but stashed in foreign banks. Yet, like many other countries that had not yet developed a mature capitalism, Russia remained dependent on the IMF for huge loans, and the IMF and the major economic powers that dominated it continued to demand signs of free-market progress as a condition for further loans.

Nevertheless, protectionist impulses never completely died out, and some individuals, groups, and countries continued to resent and resist various aspects of economic globalization.

One of the causes of an Asian Financial Crisis that began in 1997 and then affected other regions of the world—"the most serious financial crisis in half a century," declared U.S. President Clinton[52]— was the unprecedented growth of global money movements. In the early 1970s, after decades in which countries kept strict controls over monetary exchange rates and the flow of capital across borders, capitalist countries began to loosen up such controls. This meant an increased trading of currencies at whatever rates the market dictated and a steep climb in foreign investments. By 1999, eight times more money per day was being exchanged in foreign exchange markets than in 1986, and the value of such exchanges exceeded by over 100 times the value of an average day's world trade. From 1970 to 1997, investors in industrialized countries increased their spending on foreign stocks almost 200-fold; and from 1980 to 1997, the percentage of U.S. pension-fund assets invested abroad went from 1 percent to 17 percent. Many Americans through their pension and mutual funds became investors in foreign companies and properties. Banks in the United States, Europe, and Japan also invested heavily abroad.[53]

With such vast amounts of money available and the technological capacity to quickly invest or withdraw large sums, the economies of various countries, especially in emerging markets became highly susceptible to the sentiments of foreign investors. In 1997 international investors lost confidence in Thailand's currency and began selling it in massive amounts. Soon afterward, they also began selling the currencies of other emerging markets such as Indonesia, Malaysia,

the Philippines, South Korea, and Taiwan. By 1998–9, the currencies of
Russia and Brazil had also come under extreme pressure. The currency
crisis in all these countries adversely affected their economies. In a
mid-1999 report the World Bank estimated that Indonesians earning
less than $1 a day had increased by 30 million people as compared to
before the financial collapse, and the Asian Development Bank
estimated that millions of children had dropped out of Indonesian
schools because of their family's increased poverty.

The financial crisis beginning in 1997 led some leaders such as
Malaysian Prime Minister Mahathir Mohamad to enact stricter
controls on money flows in and out of his country. It also led to some
demonstrations, for example in South Korea, against IMF demands
for what it considered economic reforms. In addition, the crisis
generated increased criticism from those who believed that
international finance needed greater regulation. But this crisis did not
prevent persistent globalization and the continued dominance of free-
market financial principles advocated by the United States, other
major capitalist powers, and the IMF. It also created opportunities for
major foreign corporations to buy devalued businesses in emerging
markets cheaply, and it renewed charges that globalization primarily
served the interests of the more advanced industrialized countries,
along with some elites in emerging markets.

Although economic and technological developments were central to
globalization, other aspects of the process were also increasingly
evident in other spheres in the final decades of the century. Amartya
Sen noted that "globalization has, over thousands, of years, contributed
to the progress of the world, through travel, trade, migration, the
spread of cultural influences, and the dissemination of knowledge
and understanding (including science and technology)." He also
insisted that "the active agents of globalization have sometimes been
located quite far from the West." Nevertheless, he agreed that this
process sped up in the final decades of the twentieth century.[54]

A major facilitating agency for late twentieth-century globalization
was the United Nations system. It included the UN central organs (six
of them) plus various programs, funds, and intergovernmental
agencies such as the UN Development Program, the IMF, the World
Bank, the International Atomic Energy Agency (IAEA), the World
Health Organization, and the UN Educational, Scientific, and
Cultural Organization (UNESCO). Prior to the UN's formation in
1945, there had been some attempts to deal with international
problems on a global level, but these efforts took place when
there were far fewer independent nations in the world and were not
as comprehensive, sustained, or successful as the overall UN efforts.

In 1907, for example, most (44) of the then independent nations of the world met at a Second Peace Conference at The Hague, Netherlands (the first had been in 1899), and between World War I and World War II a League of Nations existed. The League, however, was hampered because the United States refused to become a part of it, and other major nations such as Germany, the USSR, and Japan participated for only a portion of the interwar years.

UN contributions to globalization spanned the spectrum from environmental causes to furthering human rights and led to a broadening of international values, standards, and laws. Just a few examples will illustrate the range. It sponsored the first major international conference on the environment at Stockholm in 1972. This conference led to agreement on certain principles and the establishment of new international agencies and programs including the UN Environment Program. In 1992, the UN sponsored another major conference, the UN Conference on Environment and Development, which was held in Rio de Janeiro. In attendance were representatives of over 150 countries, including, for at least a brief time, most heads of states. Also present were representatives of about 1,500 non-governmental organizations (NGOs). Although serious differences existed on various points, the conference did agree to certain principles, an agenda for future action, and over 150 countries signed important agreements on such concerns as biological diversity and climate change.

Related to environmental causes was the problem of nuclear proliferation. By the beginning of the 1990s, 141 countries had agreed to adhere to a 1968 Non-Proliferation Treaty. The International Atomic Energy Agency (IAEA) oversaw compliance, and when Iraq was suspected of non-compliance in the 1990s a United Nations Special Commission responsible for disarming Iraq was established to work with the IAEA.

In 1948 the UN formulated a Universal Declaration of Human Rights and followed it up in subsequent years with conferences and agreements on a variety of rights, including the rights of women and children. The UN also authorized certain types of intervention in behalf of peoples' rights, for example in behalf of Kurds and Shiite Muslims in Iraq, after earlier approving a UN Persian Gulf intervention (led by the United States) to restore an independent Kuwait after it was invaded by Iraq in 1990. In the 1990s, the UN was also heavily involved in attempting to safeguard human rights in Bosnia and Kosovo. It took charge of administering the latter area with the help of NATO and other forces after NATO bombing ended in 1999 (see Chapter 5 for more on the UN and human rights).

Although UN operations were only partially successful, they did reflect an increasingly global approach to world problems.

Another reflection of this approach in the 1990s was the increasing importance of international non-governmental organizations (INGOs) such as Amnesty International, CARE, Greenpeace, the International Red Cross, Oxfam, and the World Medical Association. In the successive crises in the Balkans in the 1990s, for example, many INGOs offered substantial aid to refugees and other victims of Balkan violence and turmoil. UN offices such as that of the High Commissioner for Refugees often worked closely with and depended heavily on relief-aiding INGOs. By 1997 one source estimated that approximately 5,000 INGOs existed.

The growth of INGOs reflected a growing global awareness and concern that was heightened by the Information Age's ability to bring us almost instant analysis and images of suffering and problems anywhere in the world. The NATO campaign in 1999 against Serbia after the Serbs had killed or, more frequently, made refugees out of about 1 million Albanians in Serbia's Kosovo province, was an unprecedented multinational intervention in the name of humanitarian principles.

By this time the debate about globalization, especially its economic dimensions, had spilled out into the streets of dozens of cities. In June and again in November 1999, so-called "anti-globalization" protesters timed their demonstrations to coincide with meetings of the leading economic countries (the G8) and the World Trade Organization (WTO). The protesters in cities such as London and Seattle blamed the world's major powers, the international organizations they dominated, and multinational corporations (for example, Nike and Starbucks) for taking unfair advantage of Third World countries, damaging the environment, and weakening labor rights. Although economist Amartya Sen agreed with many of their criticisms, he thought that "anti-globalization" was not a good term for their discontent and that their critique was "perhaps the most globalized moral movement in the world today."[55] Meanwhile, on the pages of newspapers, magazines, and books, authors debated globalization's merits and defects.

One of the most enthusiastic and widely-read writers trumpeting its plusses was Thomas L. Friedman, Pulitzer Prize-winning *New York Times* foreign affairs columnist and author of *The Lexus and the Olive Tree* (1999)—he later extended his praise of globalization in *The World Is Flat: A Brief History of the 21st Century* (2005). In the first of these two books dealing with globalization, he stated that it replaced the Cold War system and "became the dominant international system at the end of the twentieth century."[56] He referred to globalization as a "dynamic ongoing process" that "involves the inexorable integration of markets, nation-states, and technologies to a degree never witnessed before—in a way that is enabling individuals, corporations, and nation-states to reach around the world farther, faster, deeper, and cheaper than ever before." He cited the example of his mother, who told him in 1998 that she was playing bridge on the Internet with three Frenchmen one day and someone from Siberia on a previous occasion. He noted that "globalization has its own defining technologies: computerization, miniaturization, digitization, satellite communications, fiber optics and the Internet." He saw globalization as an extension of free-market capitalism, with its emphasis on free trade, competition, deregulation, and privatization; its dream of spreading such capitalism worldwide; and its promise that such methods would lead to improved global economic conditions. Friedman also stated that "globalization has its own dominant culture, which is why it tends to be homogenizing," and that this culture is primarily influenced by U.S. culture "from Big Macs to iMacs to Mickey Mouse." Although he recognized some objections to globalization, including legitimate environmental and national cultural concerns, he asserted that "the 'wretched of the earth' want to go to Disney World—not to the barricades." Finally, Friedman wrote: "Those countries that are most willing to let capitalism quickly destroy inefficient companies, so that money can be freed up and directed to more innovative ones, will thrive in the era of globalization. Those which rely on their governments to protect them from such creative destruction will fall behind in this era."[57]

Perhaps the most distinguished economist to criticize many aspects of the globalization process of the 1990s was Joseph Stiglitz. In the late 1990s, he served first as chair of U.S. President Bill Clinton's Council of Economic Advisors and then as chief economist of the World Bank. In 2001, he received the Nobel Prize in Economics, and in 2002 his *Globalization and Its Discontents* appeared. In an article in the *New Republic* (April 17, 2000), he wrote:

> Next week's meeting of the International Monetary Fund will bring to Washington, D.C., many of the same demonstrators who trashed the World Trade Organization in Seattle last fall. They'll say the IMF is arrogant. They'll say the IMF doesn't really listen to the developing countries it is supposed to help. They'll say the IMF is secretive and insulated from democratic accountability. They'll say the IMF's economic "remedies" often make things worse—turning slowdowns into recessions and recessions into depressions.
>   And they'll have a point.[58]

While he was still chief economist at the World Bank, it issued a mid-1999 report estimating that the number of people earning less than $1 a day had increased by 200 million since 1993. The 1999 UN Development Report claimed that globalization was furthering U.S. economic and cultural preeminence, increasing the gap between rich and poor countries, and that "global inequalities in income and living standards have reached grotesque proportions." It insisted that conditions in 60 countries were worse than they had been in 1980. According to the author of the report, the wealthiest 200 people on earth possessed more money than the total income of the poorest 40 percent of the population, and the gap between the richest 20 percent of the earth's population and the poorest 20 percent—those most liable to be undernourished, in ill health, illiterate, and without adequate housing and sanitary conditions—more than doubled since 1960. The report attributed the growing gap partly to widening disparities in technological abilities, especially as related to computers and telecommunications. It noted that it would cost the average person from Bangladesh eight years' wages to buy a computer.[59]

Like another Nobel-Prize winning economist, Amartya Sen, Stiglitz agreed with many of these criticisms but insisted that he was not against globalization, just the way it had been carried out. In an interview in January 2002, he acknowledged that it "could be a force for the good of the poor," and he stated "the problem is not globalization itself but the international economic institutions, particularly the IMF that pushed a set of ideas, like market fundamentalism, a particular view of capitalism seen as the best possible economic system, the only economic system."[60] He thought the IMF approach represented "a curious blend of ideology and bad economics, dogma that sometimes seemed to be thinly veiling special interests." He believed this approach reflected a "colonial mentality—the certainty of knowing better than developing countries what is best for them." He added that "globalization today is not working for many of the world's poor. It is not working for much of the environment. It is not working for the stability of the global economy." He admitted that China and some other countries benefited from globalization—partly because it ignored much IMF advice–but that in other countries, such as many in Latin America, IMF-style globalization created instability and benefited primarily the rich. He also believed "new technologies can support cultural diversity by making it easier for communities to express themselves. But globalization has sometimes been pushed too fast and in an inappropriate way, threatening the stability of existing cultures."[61]

In a more recent book, *Making Globalization Work* (2006), Stiglitz contends that governments should be allowed to subsidize domestic cultural efforts in order to safeguard cultural diversity. In general, he supports government interventions and regulations for ecological reasons and in order to improve people's quality of life. His approach to unfettered capitalist principles on a global scale is akin to the position championed by early twentieth century European and American progressives, including Franklin Roosevelt, on a national level. Unlike the Reagan-Thatcher economic philosophy, this progressive approach wanted to increase, not decrease, government interventions for the public good. Stiglitz believes that government oversight is especially important in countries in the early stages of capitalist development, such as Russia in the 1990s, where regulatory mechanisms and business law were poorly developed. Stiglitz also points out that advocates of the dominant IMF approach of the late twentieth century ignored the fact that the major economic powerhouses who dominated the IMF often themselves failed to practice "free trade." The best example of this was probably the denial of fair competition to foreign farmers as a result of the massive agricultural subsidies provided to their own farmers by the United States, the European Union, and Japan.

The Indian physicist, philosopher, and activist Vandana Shiva has been even more critical of economic globalization. She has declared that "economic globalization has become a war against nature and the poor ... The globalization of non-sustainable industrial agriculture is evaporating the incomes of Third World farmers through a combination of devaluation of currencies, increase in costs of production and a collapse in commodity prices." Shiva also has stated that "patents and intellectual property rights are supposed to prevent piracy. Instead they are becoming the instruments of pirating the common traditional knowledge from the poor of the Third World and making it the exclusive 'property' of Western scientists and corporations."[62] We have already seen how membership in GATT/WTO increased from its original 23 members to 134 by July 1999. As new countries joined the world's chief trading organization they had to agree to respect such "property" rights and pay royalties on such goods, which channeled billions of dollars per year from poorer countries to Western corporations such as those of the pharmaceutical industry.

The debate on globalization reinforces a point made by Friedman in 1999 that new technologies and capitalist influences seemed to make some sort of continued globalization inevitable. He wrote that "the defining economists of the globalization system are

Joseph Schumpeter and former Intel CEO Andy Grove, who prefer to unleash capitalism. Schumpeter [thought] . . . that the essence of capitalism is the process of 'creative destruction'—the perpetual cycle of destroying the old and less efficient product or service and replacing it with new, more efficient ones." Friedman quoted James Surowiecki of *Slate* magazine who commented on the insight shared by Schumpeter and Grove: "Innovation replaces tradition. The present—or perhaps the future—replaces the past. Nothing matters so much as what will come next, and what will come next can only arrive if what is here now gets overturned. While this makes the system a terrific place for innovation, it makes it a difficult place to live, since most people prefer some measure of security about the future to a life lived in almost constant uncertainty . . . [Friedman's ellipses] We are not forced to re-create our relationships with those closest to us on a regular basis. And yet that's precisely what Schumpeter, and Grove after him, suggest is necessary to prosper [today]."[63] One of Stiglitz's main concerns has been that in "destroying the old" we don't also destroy many people's lives, valuable cultural traditions, and the earth itself. He also emphasized that global capitalist practices had to be moderated by various global governance systems that look beyond just the profit motive.

5

Freedom and Human Rights

As the nineteenth century was coming to an end, some U.S. citizens thought their country was betraying the freedom-loving dream of its Founding Fathers. The occasion for the dismay was the annexation of the Philippines, despite considerable Philippine resistance, following in the wake of the Spanish–American War of 1898. Early the following year, the philosopher William James wrote, "We are now openly engaged in crushing out the sacredest thing in this great human world—the attempt of a people long enslaved . . . to be free."[1]

Although people strongly disagreed on the exact meaning of freedom during the new century (see below, "Debates on Freedom"), it nevertheless remained a cherished goal of individuals, groups, and nations around the globe. *Liberty* was the name of a leading U.S. anarchist publication at the start of the century. When the future first prime minister of India, Jawaharlal Nehru, was imprisoned by British authorities in his homeland in 1934, he wrote an autobiographical work entitled *Toward Freedom*. In 1941 U.S. President Franklin Roosevelt gave his "Four Freedoms" speech, in which he proclaimed to Congress that "we look forward to a world founded upon four essential human freedoms."[2] That same year his wife, Eleanor, and others founded Freedom House, which continued to exist into the twenty-first century, when its website described it as "an independent non-governmental organization that supports the expansion of freedom in the world . . . [and is] a vigorous proponent of democratic values and a steadfast opponent of dictatorships of the far left and the far right."[3] From the late 1940s through the

1960s, when many former colonial territories struggled for their independence, freedom was often their rallying cry.[4] Anti-communists during the Cold War often contrasted the communist camp to the "free world" led by the United States. "Freedom Now" became the chief rallying cry of the U.S. Civil Rights Movement of the 1960s. And when Nelson Mandela completed his autobiography in 1994, begun in the midst of his decades in a South African prison, he entitled it *Long Walk to Freedom* and indicated in it how he consistently struggled for freedom.

Freedom and Politics: Some Major Developments

By the end of the twentieth century nationalism and self-determination had helped lead to the collapse of colonial empires. Most of the earth's independent countries in 1999 had obtained their independence after World War II, primarily in the first three decades after the war. This gaining of national independence increased political freedom globally. Gains for freedom also came as a result of the collapse of such freedom-denying regimes as that of the Nazis in Germany and the communists in the USSR. The denial of freedom under such despots as Hitler, Stalin, and Mao Zedong was so extensive and had such terrible consequences that the restrictions on freedom under less repressive regimes often paled in comparison to the horrid sufferings of the millions of innocent people imprisoned in such camps as those of Auschwitz, Dachau, and the Soviet Gulag.

From the death of Stalin in 1953 until Mikhail Gorbachev became head of the Soviet Communist Party in 1985, people in the Soviet Bloc were less oppressed than during Stalin's time. But they were still denied many basic freedoms such as freedom of the press or other media. Gorbachev, however, greatly increased Soviet freedoms and allowed eastern European countries to assert their pent-up desires for liberty. The destruction of the Berlin Wall and the reuniting of East and West Germany under a democratic government in 1989–90 dramatically demonstrated the gains for freedom in this region.

The collapse of the Soviet Union (and Gorbachev's powers) in 1991 meant that 15 former republics that had been part of the USSR became independent countries. For some, like the three Baltic republics of Estonia, Latvia, and Lithuania, the increasing freedoms were substantial, though some of the large numbers of Russians who remained in these Baltic countries complained of discrimination. But other newly independent states of the former USSR continued to be ruled by oppressive governments. Under President Boris Yeltsin

(1991–9), Russia itself became freer politically, but Yeltsin's decreasing popularity indicated that more political freedom was not necessarily the chief concern of Russians. In the minds of most Russians, economic hard times, more glaring economic disparities, less government aid, increased street crime and pornography, and other difficulties were more significant than the increased freedoms to elect a government of their choosing or to read, speak, or write whatever they chose without fear of retribution from authorities. In several polls taken around the end of the century, Russian opinion regarding both Gorbachev and Yeltsin was far more negative than toward any Soviet leader including Stalin.[5]

By the end of the century the earth's people in general were freer, at least in a political sense, than they had been a decade before. According to Freedom House in 1989–90 there were 105 free or partly free countries and 62 unfree ones. In 1999–2000 there were 145 free or partly free countries and 47 unfree ones. Free societies were most prominent in the Americas and western and east-central Europe (primarily parts of the former Soviet Bloc), less so in Asia, and least so in Africa and the Arab countries.[6]

Two Non-Western Philosophical Approaches to Freedom: Tagore and Berdyaev

Differences about freedom between politicians on the left and on the right revolved mainly over the role of government, but various individuals emphasized other aspects of freedom besides the political. Two interesting non-Western thinkers who did so were the Indian poet and philosopher Rabindranath Tagore and the Russian philosopher Nikolai Berdyaev.

Tagore was the Nobel Prize recipient for Literature in 1913, and he continues today to be widely read in Bangladesh and India—both of whose national anthems are taken from Tagore's songs. Early in the century Tagore wrote in one of his poetic pieces, "Freedom is all I want."[7] His concept of freedom was influenced, however, not only by Western ideas of it, but also by the Asian religious traditions of Hinduism and Buddhism. Whereas Western concepts of freedom placed great emphasis on the autonomous self, Tagore believed that "our self-will is only the appearance of freedom," and recognized a "negative form of freedom, which is licence . . . [and a] positive freedom, which is love." To him freedom was primarily about freeing ourselves from the "boundaries of our personal self," from the ignorance of self absorption and by uniting with the eternal.

For Tagore, however, freedom was not just a mental exercise; he also stressed the importance of action, saying that "the soul of man is ever freeing itself from its own folds by its activity."[8] After traveling to Europe and the United States, he wrote in the 1920s that freedom had become "feeble and ineffectual" in the West, sapped by industrialization and the "immense power of money."[9]

But Tagore was by no means hostile to all Western culture. He valued the West's contributions to science, rationality, and religious and cultural diversity. He was critical of imperialism and colonialism, but also of any traditionalism, nationalism, or fanaticism that led to a close-mindedness that narrowed rather than liberated the mind. He valued English poetry and gave credit to English thinkers for developing the idea of political liberty, but thought the English were violating this idea in their rule over India. Although he admired late nineteenth-century Japan for breaking Western imperialistic controls over it, he criticized later twentieth-century Japanese nationalism and imperialism. And although he admired Soviet accomplishments in increasing literacy, he asked of Soviet Russia in 1930: "Are you doing your ideal a service by arousing in the minds of those under your training anger, class-hatred, and revengefulness against those whom you consider to be your enemies? . . . Freedom of mind is needed for the reception of truth; terror hopelessly kills it."[10]

In 1939, the *émigré* Russian philosopher Nikolai Berdyaev completed his book *Slavery and Freedom*. In it he devoted chapters to various phenomena that could limit human freedom: false religious ideas, nature, society, technological civilization, individualism, government, war, nationalism, aristocracy, the bourgeois spirit, revolution, collectivism, sex, aesthetics, history, and the fear of death. He stressed first the human personality and believed that only by exercising our unique creative powers could we overcome potentially enslaving forces such as nature, family, society, and government. He was a religious man who believed that Christianity could be liberating if understood correctly, but he opposed all dogmas and orthodoxies.

Although critical of the communist regime that had exiled him from Russia and of Fascism, Berdyaev was, like Tagore, also critical of the bourgeois democratic West and what he thought was its limited concept of freedom. He believed that "democratic culture also is of no high quality, it has been vulgarized." Like Marx, he criticized the West's "fetishism of goods," and noted how "man . . . has fallen into the power of his own tools," how the "overgrowth of the multiplicity of things in his everyday life embarrasses and enslaves a man." To Berdyaev "the bourgeois is always a slave. He is the slave of his property and of his money, he is a slave of the will to enrichment, a slave of bourgeois public opinion, a slave of social position . . . The bourgeois creates a realm of things, and things take control of him." Although also critical of the Western socialist movements of his day for being too materialist and collectivist, he believed that "a class society is based upon falsehood and wrong" and was "a denial of the dignity of personality." What he desired was "personalist socialism." He thought only it could lead to "the liberation of man."[11]

Technology, Freedom, and the Counter Culture of the 1960s

Just as Berdyaev had written that man had "fallen into the power of his own tools," Aldous Huxley and George Orwell had written the anti-utopian novels *Brave New World* (1932) and *1984* (1949) depicting how technology could help dominate people. And Charlie Chaplin, reacting in part to the influence of Frederic Taylor and Henry Ford (see above, Chapter 2's section on "Rationalization . . ."), visualized such a fear in his last silent film, *Modern Times* (1936). But it was left to later critics, primarily of the 1950s and 1960s, to explore in more depth the relationship between technology and freedom and to suggest some new approaches to freedom in an increasingly technocratic world. Perhaps the most comprehensive criticism of technological society and its reliance on "technique" came from the Frenchman Jacques Ellul. In his *The Technological Society*, first appearing in France in the mid-1950s, he criticized modern societies for sacrificing all other goals, including moral and aesthetic ones, to that of efficiency. He wrote that technique "brings mechanics to bear on all that is spontaneous . . . technique is opposed to nature." He added that "technique requires predictability and, no less, exactness of prediction. It is necessary, then, that technique prevail over the human being. For technique, this is a matter of life or death. Technique must reduce man to a technical animal, the king of the slaves of technique. Human caprice crumbles before this necessity; there can be no human autonomy in the face of technical autonomy. The individual must be fashioned by techniques."[12]

In his Foreword to the revised American edition of his book in 1964, Ellul admitted that he thought it probable that technological society would continue eating away at people's freedom, but added that "if an increasing number of people become fully aware of the threat the technological world poses to man's personal and spiritual life, and if they determine to assert their freedom by upsetting the course of this evolution, my forecast will be invalidated."[13]

A more influential thinker among radicals of the 1960s was the German Jewish *émigré* to the United States Herbert Marcuse (1898–1979). Strongly influenced by both Marx and Freud, he was critical of both Soviet communism and Western capitalism. He agreed with Ellul that humans had become less free in the twentieth century as technology had progressed. He started the first chapter of his 1964 book *One-Dimensional Man* with the sentence "A comfortable, smooth, reasonable, democratic unfreedom prevails in advanced industrial civilization, a token of technical progress."[14] To Marcuse the development of mass media and its propagandizing, whether for reasons of ideology, political control, or commercial gain, was just one symptom of growing unfreedom. He believed that by increasing the consumption of goods and services, the elite who ran technological society in the West had conditioned people to accept the increasing loss of their freedoms. "If the individuals are satisfied to the point of happiness with the goods and services handed down to them by the administration, why should they insist on different institutions for a different production of different goods and services? And if the individuals are preconditioned so that the satisfying goods also include thoughts, feelings, aspirations, why should they wish to think, feel, and imagine for themselves? True, the material and mental commodities offered may be bad, wasteful, rubbish—but *Geist* [spirit or mind] and knowledge are no telling arguments against satisfaction of needs."[15]

Marcuse thought that "freedom from the rule of merchandise over man is a precondition of freedom."[16] He insisted, however, that science and technology could be "great vehicles of liberation," and that it was "not technology, not technique, not the machine [that] are the engines of repression, but the presence, in them, of the masters who determine their number, their life span, their power, their place in life, and the need for them."[17] Like Marx, Marcuse believed that technology was developing to the extent that if it was used correctly humans could abolish poverty and live much fuller lives. Like Freud in his *Civilization and Its Discontents*, he realized the part psychological repression of one's instincts had played in past civilizations, but went beyond Freud in believing that technology could help create a culture that eliminated *surplus* repression and emphasized such values as beauty, cooperation, and joy more than working "harder in order to get more of the merchandise that has to be sold" (as in the West) or the drab "gray-on-gray culture of the socialist societies of Eastern Europe."[18]

Marcuse wrote these words shortly before the most tumultuous events of 1968, the year in which New Left student rebellions in the United States and Europe reached their peak. And the book in which he published them (*Essay on Liberation*) was published the next year, the year of the Woodstock Music Festival in New York state. There, in muddy fields, hundreds of thousands of young people reflected a youth counter culture that desired a freer lifestyle than that of their parents. Advocates of such a lifestyle wished to discard the more self-disciplined, self-denying, time-regulated, competitive, technocratic world of adults and embrace a more spontaneous, less-regulated existence. Folk and rock music, drugs such as marijuana, communal living arrangements, unconventional dress and hair (often long hair and beards for men), casual sex, occasional nudity, and protests and demonstrations were all part of the counter culture.

It is not difficult to see why Marcuse and a few others such as Norman O. Brown, who went further than Marcuse in encouraging youth to throw off Freudian repression and create a society of "erotic exuberance," appealed to some of these youths. As Theodore Roszak, an advocate of the youthful counter culture who wrote a 1969 book, *The Making of a Counter Culture*, that began with a chapter on "technocracy's children," wrote, "The emergence of Herbert Marcuse and Norman Brown as major social theorists among the disaffiliated young of Western Europe and America must be taken as one of the defining features of the counter culture."[19] Marcuse believed that only a "revolution which makes technology and technique subservient to the needs and goals of free men" could end repression.[20]

In 1970 Charles A. Reich's best-selling *The Greening of America* appeared. Reich acknowledged his debt to Marcuse and wrote of an American crisis of which two elements were 1) "uncontrolled technology and the destruction of environment" and 2) the "decline of democracy and liberty." But he indicated that "there is a revolution coming . . . It will not require violence . . . It promises a higher reason, a more human community, and a new and liberated individual."[21] And he began the last chapter of his book thus:

> Today we are witnesses to a great moment in history . . . the rebirth of people in a sterile land. If that process had to be summed up in a single word, that word would be freedom. Freedom from outmoded economic and political doctrines, freedom from oppressive institutions, freedom from the San Quentin [a prison] consciousness by which we lock the doors of our minds. Freedom that is expressed in every metaphor of the new consciousness, long hair, a new way of walking, the ocean and the open road.[22]

By the end of the century, it was clear that Reich was too optimistic. Historian Walter Laqueur later indicated some of the reasons why.

Although he was writing mainly about the European youth movement, his insights also apply to that in the United States.

> Some of the more farsighted leaders of the movement realized that the power in the advanced countries was so solid, the means of repression at its disposal so manifold, that the attempt to wrest power from its hands was hopeless . . . The central dilemma confronting the revolutionary youth movement was that their demand for absolute freedom collided with complex political-economic realities limiting freedom and democracy . . . It was romantic in inspiration and romantic movements are always based on a mood rather than a programme . . . It had no alternative to offer.[23]

For more perspective on the student rebels in western Europe and the United States in 1968, it is also appropriate to note what the English poet Stephen Spender wrote that same year about young Czechoslovaks and other youths in the Soviet Bloc. After visiting Prague and talking to students months before Soviet tanks crushed hopes for accelerating freedoms, Spender stated that "those who are struggling for freedom in Russia and the People's Democracies [eastern European states] mean by freedom very much the freedom that we have."[24] Although sympathetic to the rebellious Western youth of that time, Spender thought that they undervalued the considerable freedoms they already enjoyed.

Technology, Freedom, and Privacy

Despite the fears of the 1960s, by the end of the twentieth century technological advances had broadened freedoms in many ways. Who could doubt, for example that computers, the Internet, satellite TV, and mobile phones had done just that? To sit at a computer and be able to access some of the world's great literature, art, or music broadened one's freedom. Historians or other researchers could hardly doubt that they were less restricted in finding information than they had been decades earlier, especially with the development of rapid search engines such as Google. Thanks to the Internet, people had increasing alternatives to viewpoints voiced on mainstream media. Although some governments such as that on mainland China continued to control much of the information their peoples received, including from the Internet, continuing technological developments made it increasingly difficult. Among other obstacles, oppressive governments found it harder than ever to prevent their citizens from finding out and being influenced by what was occurring in other countries.

Yet, as always, technology also had a darker side. One of the most pressing concerns was its relationship to privacy. As more people used computers for emailing, buying goods, and doing electronic searches, they provided more electronic data about themselves that might be accessible to others or stored permanently in government and corporate data banks. (See below on "Human Rights" for the expression of an earlier concern with privacy rights.) A 1997 European Union report on the technologies of political control noted that "much of this technology is used to track the activities of dissidents, human rights activists, journalists, student leaders, minorities, trade union leaders, and political opponents." The report concluded that such tracking could exert a "chilling effect" on those who "might wish to take a dissenting view and few will risk exercising their right to democratic protest."[25]

As data gathering accelerated to new heights and concerns rose, governments enacted new laws attempting to deal with privacy concerns that by 1999 were more acute than ever. Companies engaged in electronic commerce also had to address their customers' fears about compromising their privacy or risk losing business. Also reflecting privacy concerns were annual conferences, beginning in 1991, held on "Computers, Freedom, and Privacy." These multi-day conferences brought together a wide range of panelists including educators, government officials, and representatives of major corporations and other businesses, as well as of non-governmental organizations like the American Civil Liberties Union. Some of these conferences, such as the 1999 conference that focused on "the Global Internet," included many international panelists from areas such as Asia, Latin America, and Europe, as well as the United States, where the first nine conferences were held. Panelists discussed numerous and far-ranging issues including the relationship between computers and censorship, content monitoring, hacking, international and national privacy laws and other protections, oversight and enforcement, privacy protection technology, and the use of data banks. Some speakers reflected fears of oppressive surveillance, as foreshadowed by Big Brother's actions in Orwell's novel *1984*.

Although fears of the use of computer-generated data perhaps attracted most attention, other technologies, sometimes in cooperation with computers, also caused alarms. One example was the use of surveillance video cameras. In Chaplin's *Modern Times* (1936), a factory boss used such a device to spot Chaplin's hero taking a smoking break in a restroom, but it was not until later in the century that the use of such cameras became widespread. For example, between the late 1980s and 1990s, over 300,000 cameras were placed "throughout the

United Kingdom, transmitting round-the-clock images to a hundred constabularies, all of them reporting decreases in public misconduct."[26] Although most citizens approved of such surveillance and one might argue that the cameras increased people's freedom by lessening fears of crime, some civil libertarians worried about the loss of privacy and the misuse of such a technology.

Freedom and Other Values

The fact that freedom has not always been valued more than anything else, as the Russian unhappiness with Gorbachev and Yeltsin demonstrated, should come as no surprise. Throughout history other values, for example power, security, and religious faith have often been placed first. In the nineteenth century, Dostoevsky dealt with the issue in a famous passage in his novel *The Brothers Karamazov*. In a chapter entitled "The Grand Inquisitor" Dostoevsky depicted a fictional head of the sixteenth-century Spanish Catholic Inquisition criticizing Jesus, who miraculously had come back to earth, for giving people freedom and for not realizing they wanted happiness not freedom. The Inquisitor insists that "men in their simplicity and their natural unruliness cannot even understand [freedom], which they fear and dread—for nothing has ever been more insupportable for a man and a human society than freedom." The Inquisitor "claims it as a merit for himself and his Church that at last they have vanquished freedom and have done so to make men happy."[27]

During World War II Erich Fromm (1900–80), a German Jewish immigrant to the United States who had once worked with Marcuse, tried to explain the appeal of Nazism and other totalitarian beliefs in his book *Escape from Freedom*. In a new preface to a 1965 printing he wrote that "modern man still is anxious and tempted to surrender his freedom to dictators of all kinds, or to lose it by transforming himself into a small cog in the machine, well fed, and well clothed, yet not a free man but an automaton."[28] What both Dostoevsky and Fromm realized is that freedom can create anxiety and be experienced by some as a burden that they are willing to exchange for greater security.

Besides security, another value that sometimes conflicted with freedom was equality. The historian Clinton Rossiter once noted that "the preference for liberty over equality lies at the root of the Conservative tradition, and men who subscribe to this tradition never tire of warning against the 'rage for equality.'"[29] And at the end of the twentieth century, a conservative historian echoed that sentiment when he wrote "the main threat to freedom today comes not from tyranny but equality—equality defined as identity of reward."[30] A related concern has been "the tyranny of the majority," which was already a serious fear expressed by Alexis de Toucqueville in his nineteenth-century classic study *Democracy in America*. He also expressed his concern that under certain conditions "democracy would extinguish . . . liberty of the mind."[31] Similarly, in a more recent book, *The Future of Freedom* (2003), Fareed Zakaria, the editor of the prestigious journal *Foreign Affairs*, wrote at length of the dangers of "illiberal democracy" to freedom. As he and others before him observed, majority rule does not necessarily protect the freedoms of minorities, whether they are ethnic, religious, or simply behaviorally non-conforming minorities.

In the final decades of the twentieth century, the preference of another value over at least one type of freedom was dramatically illustrated in the struggle over abortion rights between pro-choice and pro-life factions. The very choice of labels indicated that one side believed a woman's freedom to decide for herself on this question was paramount, while the other side was willing to deny that freedom because it believed the right to life of a fetus was a greater value.

Debates on Freedom

Besides a consensus about gains for freedom with the demise of colonialism and oppressive regimes, there has also been general agreement that there must be some limits on individual freedoms for the sake of the public good. Few would argue, for example, that they should be free to drive their cars as fast as they wish and ignore traffic lights within a city. Other freedom issues, however, have been more contentious.

At the beginning of the twentieth century an increasing number of voices in the United States and Great Britain were challenging the more prominent *laissez-faire* ideology that counseled against government intervention on behalf of the disadvantaged. Typical of the older prominent ideology was U.S. President Cleveland's declaration upon vetoing a bill in 1887 to assist drought sufferers. He said, "though the people support the Government the Government should not support the people." But by the 1890s the "essence of liberty to a large number of Americans was the freedom to escape poverty," and some, such as the Populist Party, thought that people's freedom would be increased, not lessened, if the government took control of railroads and telephone and telegraph systems.[32]

In the decades before World War I, however, the U.S. Supreme Court consistently believed it was defending the freedom of employers when it declared unconstitutional government attempts to limit child labor or maximum hours that could be worked or to establish minimum wages. With very few exceptions, it was not until after the Great Depression had struck and Franklin Roosevelt had become president that the Court, with some new members, began to cease interpreting such legislation as violations of basic constitutional freedoms.

In the United States, Franklin Roosevelt played a leading role in broadening the definition of freedom in ways anathema to many conservatives. In his State of the Union speech to the Congress in 1941, he said, "We look forward to a world founded upon four essential freedoms." He identified them as "freedom of speech and expression," freedom to worship God in one's own way, "freedom from want," and "freedom from fear." Three years later, he told the Congress that "freedom cannot exist without economic security and independence. 'Necessitous men are not free men.'" And he called for a "second Bill of Rights" that would include the following:

- The right to a useful and remunerative job in the industries or shops or farms or mines of the Nation;
- The right to earn enough to provide adequate food and clothing and recreation;
- The right of every farmer to raise and sell his products at a return which will give him and his family a decent living;
- The right of every businessman, large and small, to trade in an atmosphere of freedom from unfair competition and domination by monopolies at home or abroad;
- The right of every family to a decent home;
- The right to adequate medical care and the opportunity to achieve and enjoy good health;
- The right to adequate protection from the economic fears of old age, sickness, accident, and unemployment;
- The right to a good education.[33]

Although there were some attempts by subsequent presidents to make some of these rights a reality—for example, Lyndon Johnson's "War on Poverty" program, in the 1960s—such "rights" as adequate health care were still not fully realized in the United States or many other countries by the end of the century.

During the 1980s the administrations of two Western heads of state, Margaret Thatcher and Ronald Reagan, presented a major challenge to Roosevelt's way of thinking. Both leaders believed domestic freedoms were best promoted by decreasing government's role, not by increasing it to the extent proposed by Roosevelt's "second Bill of Rights." (For more on Thatcher and Reagan, see above, Chapter 3's section "The Welfare State.")

In his well-regarded essay "Two Concepts of Liberty" (1958), the historian Isaiah Berlin emphasized that the most important type of liberty (or freedom) was freedom from various types of coercion, especially by governments. To him having money, intelligence, or other means to help one exercise one's freedoms might be important, but such assets did not enter into the definition of freedom. "Everything is what it is: liberty is liberty, not equality or fairness or justice or culture, or human happiness or a quiet conscience."[34]

A good deal of the debate over freedom hinged on whether or not one defined it narrowly as Berlin did or more broadly as Roosevelt had. Many conservatives followed Berlin in defining freedom narrowly, but they drew different conclusions than he did from their narrow definition. Berlin himself thought highly of Roosevelt's New Deal, although he believed it entailed some sacrifice of liberty because he did not agree with Roosevelt that "necessitous men are not free men." But he viewed the New Deal as "certainly the most constructive compromise between individual liberty and economic security which our own time has witnessed,"[35] and, according to a friend, "he was passionately against Thatcherism: he knew that 'free' markets destroy people's lives."[36]

Writing of U.S. disputes over freedom in the 1950s, historian James MacGregor Burns compared them to the story of blind men feeling various parts of an elephant and all insisting that the animal part they felt truly described the elephant as a whole. Burns then added: "For over two centuries Americans had debated and squabbled and even warred over the definition of freedom. During the 1950s the quarrel turned into a cacophony."[37] In subsequent decades the differences continued.

The main reasons for contention and confusion over whether or not freedom had been increased or decreased by various actions were because of fuzzy thinking and the complexity of liberty and freedom. Even these two terms, as the American historian David Hackett Fischer indicated in his book *Liberty and Freedom*, have sometimes had different shades of meaning. Since there are so many different types of freedom and it affected different people in varying ways, what different individuals stressed varied greatly according to their own experiences and values. In his 1993 book *Out of Control: Global Turmoil on the Eve of the Twenty-first Century*, Zbigniew Brzezinski touched on one such difference. He stated that traditionally freedom was perceived within a context of civic rights and responsibilities, but that lately it was increasingly "defined as the accumulation of rights and entitlements as well as license for any form of self-expression and gratification." Greatly contributing to this growing trend, he believed, was the media, especially television, which extolled self-gratification.[38]

As the powers of governments generally increased in the twentieth century, one of the biggest disagreements about freedom was between those who stressed that "big government" was a major threat, perhaps *the* major threat, to people's freedom and those who insisted that a strong and active government was necessary to maximize people's freedoms. Besides the differing positions of political leaders on this issue, differences can also be seen between prominent commentators on freedom.

Two prominent economists who influenced many late twentieth-century conservatives were the Austrian-born Friedrich von Hayek (1899–1992) and the American Milton Friedman (1912–2006). Hayek, a professor for long periods in both London and Chicago, wrote books such as *Road to Serfdom* (1944) and *The Constitution of Liberty* (1960) in which he emphasized the importance of property rights for freedom and criticized socialism and any attempt by governments to redistribute wealth, for example to aid the poor. Hayek believed that to maintain freedom, free-market capitalism had to be allowed to operate unfettered. Government officials who disrupted the spontaneous economic order in the name of "social justice" (which Hayek labeled a myth) were to him a great threat to freedom.

Friedman was already on the faculty at the University of Chicago when Hayek arrived there and like him won a Nobel Prize in Economics during the 1970s. One of his most influential books was *Capitalism and Freedom*, first published in 1962. After many other books and promotions of his ideas, including a regular column in *Newsweek* and a PBS television series, Friedman noted that the central theme of his efforts was the "promotion of human freedom." Like Hayek, he advocated a strong free-market economy with little government interference and was critical of the twentieth-century trend toward big government, centralized planning, and the welfare state. And like Hayek, he indicated in his *Capitalism and Freedom* that free markets would do more to aid people than many laws designed to overcome social injustice. Although not completely opposed to government efforts to aid poverty—he favored, for example, a negative income tax that would actually put money in the pockets of impoverished people—he did criticize many government agencies and programs that he believed threatened freedom. For example, he called for the abolition of the U.S. Food and Drug Administration (FDA), believing that it was in the self-interest of pharmaceutical and other companies to oversee adequately the safety of their own products. He also criticized U.S. Fair Employment Practices legislation designed to overcome discrimination as an infringement on an employer's freedom. When asked at the end of the century whether he would keep or eliminate fourteen U.S. cabinet departments, he responded he would eliminate most of them, including those overseeing commerce, education, energy, and labor, but keep the State Department and those overseeing defense, justice, and the treasury.[39]

Friedman was a long-time exponent of some ideas that later became popular U.S. conservative aspirations such as a flat tax and school vouchers. But he was more consistent than many conservatives later influenced by him. He criticized, for example, the U.S. "War on Drugs," which he thought interfered with individual rights. Not only did he influence the economic policies of the Reagan and Thatcher administrations, but also those of U.S. Federal Reserve Chairman (1987–2006) Alan Greenspan and the leaders of a number of other countries such as Chile under General Pinochet in the late 1970s and 1980s and Estonia in the 1990s.[40]

Other U.S conservatives like Richard Pipes saw programs such as affirmative action and school busing as impinging upon freedom and believed that "the entire concept of the welfare state . . . is incompatible with individual liberty."[41]

In opposition to such thinking, the British historian and social critic R. H. Tawney insisted during World War I that true economic freedom demanded that workers have a voice in running the industries in which they labored. And whereas Hayek saw government social planning as a threat to freedom, the U.S. philosopher John Dewey had already argued in the 1930s that such planning was necessary to broaden freedom for the masses.

In the 1950s the French writer Albert Camus stated that "there is no possible freedom for the man tied to his lathe all day long who, when evening comes, crowds into a single room with his family." For Camus true freedom meant not only freedom from political oppression, but also freedom from grinding poverty and economic injustice. Such an enlarged freedom he believed was "for societies and for individuals, for labor and for culture, the supreme good that governs all others."[42] Similarly, the historian Herbert J. Muller, writing in his *Freedom in the Modern World* (1966), thought that "real freedom" for many necessitated social reforms on behalf of workers, poor people, and the "underprivileged."[43]

At the end of the century, Amartya Sen wrote in his *Development as Freedom* (1999) that true freedom required not just political and civil rights, but also "substantive freedom," which meant economic and social opportunities that might include such things as jobs and subsidies, unemployment benefits, and inexpensive health care. Poor, uneducated people without land, jobs, or access to health care, might be free to associate with whomever they please and to vote and exercise other personal and civic rights, but Sen argued that they were not as free as those who possessed many more opportunities due to their greater resources.[44] A contemporary of Sen, Martha Nussbaum, made a similar point when she declared "liberty is not just a matter of having rights on paper, it requires being in a position to exercise those rights. And this requires material and institutional resources."[45]

Human Rights

Although Franklin Roosevelt's second Bill of Rights was not translated into the type of legislation he had hoped for, it did influence the Universal Declaration of Human Rights, which was produced by his widow, Eleanor, and others. The United Nations approved this declaration in 1948, and it became the basis for numerous future international, regional, and national declarations, conventions, and other agreements. It contained 30 articles which stipulated that people should enjoy not only basic civil and political rights, but also economic, social, and cultural rights. Article 2 states that "everyone is entitled to all the rights and freedoms set forth in this Declaration, without distinction of any kind, such as race, colour, sex, language, religion, political or other opinion, national or social origin, property, birth or other status." Article 12 deals with privacy: "No one shall be subjected to arbitrary interference with his privacy, family, home or correspondence, nor to attacks upon his honour and reputation. Everyone has the right to the protection of the law against such interferences or attacks." Article 25 (1) indicates some of the more important economic rights, "Everyone has the right to a standard of living adequate for the health and well-being of himself and of his family, including food, clothing, housing and medical care and necessary social services, and the right to security in the event of unemployment, sickness, disability, widowhood, old age or other lack of livelihood in circumstances beyond his control."

Among social/cultural rights were the opportunity to form or join a union and the right to education, which it was stipulated should "be free, at least in the elementary and fundamental stages."[46]

For the remainder of the century this Universal Declaration influenced many causes, declarations, nations, and leading freedom fighters. In 1968 the "Manifesto of Prague Youth" called for socialism to be based on the declaration. At the 1993 World Conference on Human Rights, over 150 countries (over three-fourths of all existing countries) declared their commitment to it, partly because its wording was general enough to allow for varying interpretations of its articles. Among the many tireless freedom fighters, two who were especially prominent and reflected the Universal Declaration's influence were Nelson Mandela in South Africa and Andrei Sakharov in the Soviet Union.

In South Africa Mandela battled against the government-imposed apartheid, a system of severe segregation. In 1953, in a speech he was prevented from personally delivering to the African National Congress (ANC), the freedom-fighting party which he helped to lead, he stated that "we declare our firm belief in the principles enunciated in the Universal Declaration of Human Rights that everyone has the right to education," and he then quoted several lines from Article 26 regarding education. He also declared that every ANC member should fight for the realization of the principle that "everyone has the right to form and to join trade unions for the protection of his interests"—this was the exact wording of Article 23 (4) of the declaration.[47] In 1955, thousands of delegates from the ANC and other groups adopted a Freedom Charter that reflected some of the principles of the Universal Declaration. Seven years later Mandela was sentenced to prison and spent the next 27 years there. Finally freed from prison, Mandela became the president of a new post-apartheid South Africa in 1994. In 1998, on the fiftieth anniversary of the Universal Declaration, he addressed the UN General Assembly and told them: "For those who had to fight for their emancipation, such as ourselves who, with your help, had to free ourselves from the criminal apartheid system, the Universal Declaration of Human Rights served as the vindication of the justice of our cause. At the same time, it constituted a challenge to us that our freedom, once achieved, should be dedicated to the implementation of the perspectives contained in the Declaration."[48]

In the Soviet Union from the late 1960s until his death in 1989, nuclear physicist Andrei Sakharov consistently battled for greater freedom for the citizens of his own country as well as for all those oppressed by other governments. He frequently mentioned the obligation of the USSR to observe the Universal Declaration of Human Rights and to honor such rights as freedom of expression, the rights of ethnic minorities, and the right to emigrate. Working for freedom alongside Sakharov in the late 1960s and early 1970s was the *Chronicle of Current Events,* an underground journal that carried its motto on its first page. It was the text of Article 19 of the Universal Declaration:

> Everyone has the right to freedom of opinion and expression; this right includes freedom to hold opinions without interference and to seek, receive and impart information and ideas through any media and regardless of frontiers.[49]

Because of his defense of human rights Sakharov was exiled from 1980 to 1986 to the city of Gorky, and various editors and contributors to the *Chronicle* suffered harsher punishments. But their courage and that of dissidents in other communist countries, such as playwright Vaclav Havel in Czechoslovakia, was crucial in eventually leading to the collapse of communist regimes throughout eastern Europe and the Soviet Union from 1989 to 1991.

In other countries individuals such as Chinese dissident Wei Jingsheng, South Korean dissident and later president Kim Dae Jung, and Aung San Suu Kyi, general secretary of the National League for Democracy in Burma (Myanmar), were also influenced by the Universal Declaration and persecuted for their human rights activities.

The Cold War and Human Rights

During the Cold War the U.S. government and its allies referred to their countries as part of the "free world" and criticized the lack of freedom in communist countries. Critics of U.S. foreign policy, however, charged it with often supporting right-wing authoritarian regimes that denied basic human rights, especially in Latin America.

The dramatic suppression of freedom in places such as Hungary in 1956 and Czechoslovakia in 1968 underlined the lack of freedom in the communist world. In negotiations in Helsinki in 1975, the United States and its allies successfully bargained to have the USSR and other European Soviet Bloc countries agree to recognize various human rights, including those of their own subjects. This agreement led to the formation of Helsinki Watch groups in Moscow and then other Soviet cities, as well as similar groups in some other European communist countries. Sakharov's wife, Elena Bonner, was one of the charter members of the Moscow group. The Helsinki Watch organizations performed a valuable service in calling attention to human rights abuses, and communist governments (inadvertently proving the justice of the groups' criticisms) often responded by repressing these critics.[50]

Meanwhile, the United States was often propping up or helping to install non-democratic, anti-communist governments. Two especially notorious cases were in Guatemala and Chile. After a left-wing Guatemalan government launched an agrarian reform program that nationalized (with compensation) some of the United Fruit Company's land, the U.S. government quickly acted in behalf of this U.S. company: in 1954 it used the CIA to orchestrate a military coup against Guatemala's elected government. The coup brought to power a repressive right-wing regime that remained in power for decades and was responsible for countless human rights violations. In 1973 in Chile the CIA again aided the overthrow of a democratically elected left-wing government which was replaced by a repressive right-wing regime, that of General Augusto Pinochet, who ruled until 1989.[51] The Pinochet government was responsible for constant violations of human rights and the arrest and killings of thousands of innocent people.

In the late 1970s President Jimmy Carter often spoke of human rights and indicated his desire to make it a cornerstone of U.S. foreign policy. Like Franklin and Eleanor Roosevelt, he included among these rights the right to food, shelter, health care, and education. But unlike most of his Cold War U.S. predecessors, he leveled strong criticisms against authoritarian right-wing, as well as communist, regimes. His government eventually denied economic credits and/or military aid to right-wing regimes such as those of Argentina, Chile, Nicaragua, and Uruguay because of their abuses. He also pushed the U.S. Senate to ratify two United Nations conventions, The International Covenant on Economic, Social and Cultural Rights and the International Covenant on Civil and Political Rights, both of which reflected principles of the Universal Declaration. (By 2007 the U.S. Senate had still not ratified the first covenant, and it ratified the second declaration only in 1992.) In addition, Carter's human rights commitment led him, among other measures, to support a UN arms embargo against South Africa, to push for the release of South Korean political prisoners, and to criticize certain policies of the shah of Iran.

If Carter attempted, with mixed successes, to refashion U.S. foreign policy so that it took measures against non-democratic right-wing regimes, as well as communist ones, that violated human rights, his successor, Ronald Reagan, was not so even-handed. Under him, the more usual U.S. Cold War pattern was resumed of criticizing communist violations of human rights and downplaying authoritarian right-wing abuses.

Women, Youth, and Sexual Rights

During the extended struggles for more freedoms of various kinds women often played a prominent part, but they also struggled to extend their own specific rights. Among the many criteria Freedom House (see above) used to measure freedom was the extent to which gender equality and the rights of minorities existed. With the notable exception of New Zealand, which granted female suffrage in 1893, women did not vote in national elections, or in most countries in local elections, until sometime in the twentieth century. In two of the countries that considered themselves most democratic, the United Kingdom and the United States, it was not until World War I ended that women got to vote in national elections—women over 30 in the December 1918 British election and women aged 21 or over in the 1920 USA election. Some other European countries granted the vote during the interwar years, but in many other countries, such as France, Italy, and many Latin American countries, women were not able to vote until after World War II. By the end of that war, of course, outside of Europe and the Americas, most areas were still colonial possessions, where female suffrage was not yet a major issue.

In addition to not being able to vote, women's rights were curtailed in various other ways during at least part of the century. A tsarist Russian law code stated that "the woman must obey her husband, reside with him in love, respect, and unlimited obedience, and offer him every pleasantness and affection as the ruler of the household."[52] Not until 1914 were Russian married women able to travel around the country without the permission of their husbands. In most of Europe around 1900 women were treated as minors and were not able to open a bank account, sue, or dispose of property without their husbands' consent. In the 1930s Nazi propaganda insisted that women's emancipation ideas were fueled by Jewish influences and that the main task of "pure" German women was to have many children. In the Nazi wartime death camps such as Auschwitz, more Jewish women than men were executed. In many parts of Latin America, patriarchal law codes that discriminated against women were slow to change. Not until 1999, for example, did Guatemala change a statute that forbade married women from working outside the home without spousal permission.

In numerous other ways women had less freedom than men, partly because they had much greater child-care responsibilities, received less education, and were more economically dependent. In Britain at the beginning of the century a worker's wife averaged about six pregnancies, though one or two of these might not result in a live birth.

At the other end of Europe, the average Russian woman, who would be a peasant, was pregnant even more often—she also saw more of her children suffer from sickness and death. In the United States, the average number of live births per woman was about four.

Not surprisingly, the issue of birth control assumed more prominence as the twentieth century advanced. By 1900 it was permissible to write about birth control or advocate it in Britain, and condoms were even sold in some urban pharmacies in Russia. In the United States, however, the Comstock Act of 1873 made the importing or transporting of birth control information or devices illegal. Among others, Emma Goldman and Margaret Sanger were arrested early in the twentieth century for violating the law, but Sanger and her cause eventually prevailed. After numerous earlier victories that greatly increased contraceptive use, Sanger witnessed in 1965, a year before her death, a Supreme Court ruling (in Griswold v. Connecticut) that struck down a Connecticut law prohibiting the use of contraceptive devices. By then Sanger had helped fund research to develop a contraceptive pill that had come into use. In parts of western Europe as well as the United States, many woman took the pill, and feminists perceived it as a symbol of woman's liberation. By 1975, for example, about two-thirds of British woman aged 15 to 44 were on it.[53]

In the Soviet Union, the primary method of birth control by the late 1970s was abortion. By then, most urban woman in the European part of the country had six or more abortions during their lifetime. The Soviet government had first legalized abortion in 1920, but in 1936 Stalin had banned it (except when the mother's health was endangered). Only in 1955 was it again legalized.

The right to an abortion came later in the West. In 1973 the U.S. Supreme Court (in Roe v. Wade) upheld a lower Texan court ruling based in part on Griswold v. Connecticut, upholding a woman's right to have an abortion. By that time abortions were already legal in Britain, but in prominent Catholic European countries such as France, Italy, and Spain woman gained abortion rights only later in the 1970s and 1980s. By century's end only Ireland, Malta, Poland, and Portugal, all with large Catholic populations, still had very restrictive abortion laws. Poland passed the law only in the early 1990s. Prior to the collapse of its communist government, abortions there, as in the communist world generally, were unrestricted. Outside of Europe by 1999, abortion was still illegal in much of Latin America, Africa, and the Middle East, as well as many other Muslim areas like Indonesia.

Partly as a result of greater birth control measures, the number of children woman gave birth to and raised decreased significantly as the century advanced. The trend began first in the most advanced industrialized countries and accelerated later in countries that adopted communism, and with it greater access to abortions. Already by 1930, the birthrate for northern and western European women was only about half of what it had been in 1890. In the 1950s, women in the more developed countries averaged only 2.8 children, and by 2001, the fertility rate in these countries was 2.1 (the U.S. rate) or below, and well under that rate in some European countries and Japan—for example, it was 1.2 or less in Russia, the Czech Republic, Italy, and Spain.

In the 1950s, the average fertility rate in less developed countries was about 6.2 children, slightly higher in Africa and slightly lower in Asia, Latin America, and the Caribbean. A half century later the fertility rate in Asia and Latin America was less than half of what it had been in the 1950s. The African fertility rate (the world's highest) also declined but not as sharply. In Asia, China's reduction was especially significant, partly as a result of a strict family limitation policy.

As family size decreased, women's educational opportunities increased, and it is difficult to overestimate the liberating effects of education. As Nelson Mandela commented, "Education is the great engine of personal development. It is through education that the daughter of a peasant can become a doctor."[54] At the beginning of the century far more women than men were illiterate, but the situation was beginning to improve. In Russia where most peasants were still illiterate, the fraction of girls in primary schools shot up from one-tenth to one-third between 1850 and 1911. Before World War I, however, Russian women were still not permitted to enroll as regular students in the universities. In England, the situation for women at universities was somewhat better, but at Cambridge and Oxford women could not receive degrees until after the war— opportunities for women at U.S. universities, though not equal to that of men, were generally better than in Europe.

In various countries, the situation for women improved after the war in regard to education as well as other opportunities. By the 1920s, one in four British university students was a woman. In Russia, the establishment of a communist regime in 1917 was followed in the next few years by a whole host of measures that proclaimed the political and legal equality of women. Improved female educational opportunities were one dimension of the new order. By 1939 about four-fifths of Soviet females aged 9 to 49 could read, as compared to 1926 when only about two-fifths of them could. The number of women completing secondary and higher education also rose sharply, with women making up 43 percent of all higher education students by 1937.

After World War II outside of the USSR and the more advanced Western countries, educational opportunities for women were still inferior but gradually improving. The percentage of girls in primary schools in India went from 14 to 27 percent between 1937 and 1950 and in Egypt from 24 to 35 percent in these same years. Nevertheless, in certain areas, such as Africa, the Middle East, and South and Southeast Asia, the gap still remained great by the end of the century. In Africa and Asia, illiteracy rates for women were still much higher than for men. It was estimated that worldwide at least two-thirds of all those lacking literacy were women.

In higher education, although remaining a minority globally, women gradually surpassed the number of men in some countries. In the USSR, women still comprised only 43 percent of all higher education students in 1960, but by 1988 their percentage had increased to 54 percent. In the United States women's percentages went from 41 percent in 1970 to 57 percent in 1999.

As the century advanced more women went to work outside of their homes, thereby generally decreasing their economic dependence. This general trend was not, however, without its ups and downs and geographic peculiarities. Before World War I about 10 percent of British women worked outside their homes after marriage. During that war almost 1.5 million women were added to the employment roles, but then after the war most of them were replaced by men, many returning veterans. By 1921, despite a large number of single and widowed women, men outnumbered women by more than two to one in the workforce. By 1990, however, there were almost as many women as men employed, though more women than men worked part-time. In the Soviet Union from 1928 to 1940, as Stalin attempted to accelerate industrialization, women went from about 28 percent of the non-agricultural work force to about 40 percent of it. In the United States the fraction of married women who resided with their husbands and worked outside the home went from about one-fourth to about two-thirds between 1960 and 1991. In Africa during the latter decades of the century, many women remained in rural areas, where they were more tradition bound, and did the bulk of the farming while their husbands went to the cities to work.

By the end of the century women still earned much less than men and women comprised about 70 percent of the world's poor. In the Soviet Union, where women had supposedly been equal to men for seven decades, a 1989 survey of the percentage of women in the top managerial positions revealed that they held less than 1 percent of such positions in transport and construction, and between 6 and 10 percent of those in agriculture, communications, and industry.

A 1991 UN report noted that in the United States only 2 of the top 1,000 corporations were headed by women, but another UN report of 2000 indicated that real gains had been made by U.S. women, with 47 percent of all managerial and administrative positions being filled by women as compared to 33 percent in the United Kingdom and 11 percent in Japan. In general, by the end of the century the greatest income inequalities existed in many parts of Africa and South and Southeast Asia.

Besides lesser political, educational, and economic opportunities, women continued throughout the century to be disadvantaged in other ways. In 1997, UN Secretary General Kofi Annan stated "Violence against women has become the most pervasive human rights violation, respecting no distinction of geography, culture or wealth."[55] A major concern to international women's rights groups was female genital mutilation. Amnesty International estimated that by the early twenty-first century 135 million women and girls had been subjected to the practice, primarily in Africa and in some Muslim areas outside of Africa. One reason given for the custom was the belief that it lessened a woman's desire for sex, thus reducing the likelihood that she would engage in sex outside of marriage.

As in freedom struggles generally, the winning of greater women's rights came only after their leaders battled for decades to obtain more freedoms. And after less stormy methods failed, these battles sometimes involved breaking the law. British female suffragists, for example, in 1912 engaged in a campaign of breaking glass windows at the prime minister's residence and in business sections of London. After they were imprisoned, some of the suffragists engaged in hunger strikes.

As the century advanced more women entered politics. In Britain, Margaret Thatcher served as prime minister (1979–90) longer than any of her twentieth century male predecessors. By the end of the century, the Scandinavian countries had the greatest percentage of women legislators with Sweden topping the list with 43 percent of parliamentary members. The United Kingdom had 18 percent in its House of Commons, and the United States 13 percent in the House of Representatives and 9 percent in the Senate. This placed the USA tied for 41st among 178 countries. In a reversal of the general twentieth century trend, fewer women in the former communist countries of eastern Europe and the Soviet Union were in parliamentary bodies in the 1990s than in the early 1980s. In the early 1980s, however, it was still the communist parties and not the parliaments that held the real power, and women were not very powerful in those parties.[56] In the Soviet Union, for example, during the early 1980s, the percentage of women on the party's Central Committee (the most powerful group of its size in the party) never climbed over 5 percent. Thus, the political weakness of women in most former communist countries in the 1990s was really not new.

After World War II women's political participation and women's rights also concerned the United Nations. In 1946 a UN Commission on the Status of Women was established. The Universal Declaration of 1948, upon insistence by the female members of the commission which drew it up, demanded that the first article start, "All human beings are born free and equal" rather than "All men are created equal," as was initially proposed.

Article 16 of that same declaration dealt with women's equal rights in marriage. Part of the article read: "Men and women of full age, without any limitation due to race, nationality or religion, have the right to marry and to found a family. They are entitled to equal rights as to marriage, during marriage and at its dissolution." In 1979 the UN adopted the Convention on the Elimination of all Forms of Discrimination against Women, which entered into force in 1981. The Convention obliged signatory governments to ensure the equal treatment of women and was quite specific in its details. And a permanent UN monitoring committee was established to ensure compliance. Working through the UN, women continued to push for greater recognition of women's rights through such mechanisms as UN world conferences on women held every five years beginning in Mexico City in 1975.[57]

The UN was also important in advocating children's rights. It adopted the Convention on the Rights of the Child, which went into effect in 1990. By the end of the century more countries had ratified it than any of the UN's other human rights conventions. The convention spelled out various rights of children (individuals under age 18) and was monitored by the Committee on the Rights of the Child.

Throughout the century children were especially vulnerable to the effects of war and other disruptions. In Russia, for example, by 1922 war, revolution, and famine had produced about 7 million homeless children. Many of them lived in unsanitary conditions and engaged in unhealthy practices such as stealing, drinking, and prostitution. Although the homeless problem gradually improved, future major disruptions, including Stalin's collectivization, the 1932–3 famine, and World War II, once again exacerbated the problem.[58]

A report at century's end by the Children's Rights Division of Human Rights Watch indicated that despite UN efforts many of the world's children still suffered from homelessness and various types of exploitation. The report found that "some 300,000 children are serving as soldiers in current armed conflicts," that "more than half of the world's refugee population are children," and that "130 million children of school age in the developing world—21 percent of all school age children in the world—had no access to basic education in 1998."[59]

In general, however, many youth, especially in the world's most prosperous countries, had greater freedom and more rights in 1999 than in 1900. A larger percentage of young people were in schools and a smaller percentage worked at full time jobs. In the latter half of the century, advances in communication and transportation and the expansion of consumer cultures which specifically targeted youth, helped create a youth culture of music, films, TV programming and more. By 1999 this culture had partially supplanted the parental and adult influences that were more prominent in 1900.

Related to the rights of women and youth were the sexual rights of all people including homosexuals. In 1895, at the height of his career as an English playwright, Oscar Wilde was sentenced to two year's hard labor for committing homosexual acts. And this was in Great Britain, a country that prided itself on emphasizing individual rights. In the first half of the twentieth century, thousands of additional British citizens were prosecuted for homosexual activities. Private homosexual acts by adults were not legalized until 1967 in England and Wales; 1980 in Scotland, and 1982 in Northern Ireland.

In the United States, homosexual acts were prohibited by sodomy laws, most of which prohibited sexual acts such as oral and anal sex for all people. In the 1950s, the notorious Senator Joseph McCarthy attacked homosexuals as well as communists, and he headed a committee that wrote a report entitled "Employment of Homosexuals and Other Sex Perverts in Government." Not until 1961, did the first U.S. state, Illinois, throw out a sodomy law. By the end of the 1970s, about 20 states had jettisoned such laws. In the 1980s, some other states also got rid of their sodomy laws, but a 1986 Supreme Court ruling (Bowers v. Hardwick) upheld a Georgia law outlawing sodomy and declared that the Constitution did not give homosexuals the right to engage in sodomy. This 1986 ruling slowed the repeal momentum, and by century's end more than a dozen states still had some type of sodomy law in effect.

By 2000, all the countries of the European Union had decriminalized private adult consensual homosexual behavior, and the UN Commission on Human Rights had interceded on behalf of homosexual rights. On the other hand, about 70 countries still prohibited same-sex sexual relations, with Afghanistan, Arab Emirates, Iran, Mauritania, Pakistan, Saudi Arabia, Sudan, and Yemen still allowing the death penalty for violations of such laws.

Nevertheless, in the Western world, and to a lesser extent worldwide, homosexuals were freer in 2000 than in 1900 to engage in homosexual behavior. Not only were laws less restrictive, but public opinion in most countries had become more accepting of homosexuals. As in other struggles for rights, these gains did not come easily and involved many campaigns by those who believed they were unjustly persecuted.

Minority Rights

The largest group of twentieth-century minorities globally—if one does not consider women a minority—was ethnic and religious minorities. Most countries had significant minorities, and many of them believed they were not treated fairly. As we have seen, wartime conditions heightened fears of minority disloyalties and provided excuses for rampant discrimination. In addition to attacks on Armenians in World War I and Jews in World War II, there was also Stalin's arrest and deportation of various Muslim and Turkish peoples of the Caucasus and Black Sea areas during the latter war. Even in the United States, which trumpeted itself as "the land of the free," there was one blatant example of minority mistreatment during World War II—the deportation and interment behind barbed wire of more than 100,000 Pacific Coast Japanese- Americans for no other reason than their loyalty was suspect simply because of the war then being waged against Japan.

Of course, despite its respect for most of its citizens' rights, the United States had also been remiss in other cases, especially in regard to the rights of its African-American people. And this had been true before, during, and after World War II. Despite the Supreme Court ruling of 1954 (see Chapter 4), many southern states resisted desegregation in the name of "states' rights." Finally, real progress was made, largely as a result of civil rights actions by leaders such as Martin Luther King. Influenced by Gandhi's non-violent civil disobedience ideas and gifted with a spell-binding voice, he helped awaken the conscience of political leaders, both by his actions and words. Before a crowd of hundreds of thousands spread out between the U.S. capital's Lincoln Memorial and Washington Monument and a television audience of millions, he gave his most famous speech ("I Have a Dream") in 1963. He began:

> Five score years ago, a great American [Lincoln], in whose symbolic shadow we stand today, signed the Emancipation Proclamation . . . But 100 years later, the Negro still is not free. One hundred years later, the life of the Negro is still sadly crippled by the manacles of segregation and the chains of discrimination.

And he ended with his resounding call for freedom:

> Let freedom ring. And when this happens, when we allow freedom to ring, when we let it ring from every village and every hamlet, from every state and every city, we will be able to speed up that day when all of God's children, black men and white men, Jews and Gentiles, Protestants and Catholics, will be able to join hands and sing in the words of the old Negro spiritual, "Free at last! Free at last! Thank God Almighty, we are free at last!"[60]

The next year President Lyndon Johnson, a strong supporter of civil rights, signed the Civil Rights Act, which prohibited discrimination of all kinds on the basis of race, color, religion, or national origin. The following year, the Voting Rights Act of 1965 gave the Federal Government powers to see that blacks could register to vote without discrimination. Largely as result of this pressure, the percentage of black registered voters increased almost tenfold in Mississippi and more than threefold in Alabama between 1964 and 1969.

In 1965, Johnson initiated "affirmative action" by signing an executive order requiring government contractors to "take affirmative action" to ensure equality in hiring—in 1967, this order was amended in an effort to overcome gender as well as racial discrimination. In the decades that followed, additional affirmative action policies were developed and the whole effort was controversial and produced some backlash, but in a speech several months before his executive order Johnson outlined his rationale for it: "This is the next and more profound stage of the battle for civil rights. We seek not just freedom but opportunity, not just legal equity but human ability, not just equality as a right and a theory, but equality as a fact and equality as a result."

By the end of the century, U.S. blacks were without doubt freer than they had been at the beginning of the century, but a higher percentage of them than the U.S. population as a whole still had their "substantive freedoms" (to use Sen's term mentioned above) limited in various ways by poverty and other factors. Those most literally limited were young black men imprisoned for various crimes, often drug related. By 1999 among black men in their early thirties, many more had been imprisoned for some period than had graduated from college. The U.S. Justice Department stated that about 1 of 11 black males in their late twenties was incarcerated for a year or more in a state or federal prison.

A special case of repression was the treatment of India's Dalits (sometimes referred to as untouchables), numbering about 160 million people in 1999. Although Gandhi, Tagore, and the

Congress Party that fought for Indian independence had all spoken out against such discrimination, it had long been part of India's caste system. Many people justified this system because their Hindu beliefs led them to conclude that one's caste was earned by one's behavior in a previous existence. Although the Indian Constitution of 1950 abolished "untouchability," and affirmative-action type laws benefited some Dalits, discrimination and oppression against most Dalits continued, especially in rural areas, where more than four-fifths of the Dalits lived. Laws aimed at protecting them were often not enforced. A Human Rights Watch report of 1999 indicated that the centuries-long oppression of Dalits was far from over.

> Dalits are discriminated against, denied access to land, forced to work in degrading conditions, and routinely abused at the hands of the police and of higher-caste groups that enjoy the state's protection. In what has been called India's "hidden apartheid," entire villages in many Indian states remain completely segregated by caste . . .
> . . . "Untouchables" may not cross the line dividing their part of the village from that occupied by higher castes. They may not use the same wells, visit the same temples, drink from the same cups in tea stalls, or lay claim to land that is legally theirs . . . Most Dalits continue to live in extreme poverty, without land or opportunities for better employment or education . . . Dalits are relegated to the most menial of tasks, as manual scavengers, removers of human waste and dead animals, leather workers, street sweepers, and cobblers. Dalit children make up the majority of those sold into bondage to pay off debts to upper-caste creditors.[61]

As with human rights generally, the rights of minorities were addressed by the UN and various non-governmental organizations (NGOs). From 1947 until it changed its name in 1999, a UN Sub-Commission on Prevention of Discrimination and Protection of Minorities existed. It was subsequently labeled the Sub-Commission on the Promotion and Protection of Human Rights. The UN also helped bring about several international covenants and declarations that affirmed the rights of minorities, including the right, if so wished, to their own culture, religion, and language.[62]

As an example of UN efforts, in 1996 the UN Committee on the Elimination of Racial Discrimination condemned the Indian government for not preventing acts of discrimination against "untouchables" and failing to punish those responsible. For its part, the Indian government denied that the Convention on the Elimination of All Forms of Racial Discrimination applied to "untouchables." As the Indian government's response indicated, UN attempts to further human rights were not always successful.

Workers and Unions

An impressive twentieth century history prepared under the auspices of the United Nations Educational, Scientific, and Cultural Organization (UNESCO) and published in 1966 stated, "In virtually every country labour had to struggle long and often bitterly in order to establish the right freely to form and join unions without interference by employers or governments."[63] In Great Britain, much of this struggle had already occurred before the beginning of the century and further gains were made in the Trade Disputes Act of 1906. But in much of the rest of the world, including the United States, workers' rights such as the right to join a union and strike had yet to be gained.

The Mexican Constitution of 1917 recognized various workers' rights including the right to bargain collectively and to earn a minimum wage. Although such rights were not always enforced, Mexico officially recognized more workers' rights than did the United States in the 1920s. Not until Franklin Roosevelt became president in 1933 did new legislation and new Supreme Court decisions increase workers' rights to form or join unions, to picket and strike, and to appeal if subjected to unfair labor practices. To aid workers in this process and to oversee fair treatment, the government established a National Labor Relations Board, and by 1945 had dealt with 36,000 cases of "unfair labor practices."

While workers in the United States were gaining new rights in the mid and late 1930s, laborers in countries with extremist governments such as the Soviet Union, Nazi Germany, Fascist Italy, and militaristic Japan had already lost some of the rights they once had. Although the defeat of the Axis powers in World War II allowed for more labor gains in the defeated nations, communist countries continued to limit workers' rights. Trade unions existed, but almost always were controlled by the communist parties of their respective countries. Only on rare occasions did genuine independent union movements or actions occur. Workers seldom dared to engage in militant actions such as work stoppages and demonstrations. When they did, as in the Soviet city of Novocherkassk in 1962, they were often met with lethal force. More than two dozen people there were killed or died soon after as a result of government force, and seven "ringleaders" of the "uprising" received death sentences.

Not until 1980 did a genuine independent and powerful trade union develop in the communist world when Solidarity emerged in Poland as a result of worker dissatisfaction and strikes. In the late summer of that year the government signed an agreement with the head of Solidarity, Lech Walesa, agreeing to salary increases, the workers' right to form independent unions and strike, and numerous other far-reaching concessions. During the next 16 months workers, including many peasants, joined Solidarity, and it, in cooperation with a powerful Catholic Church headed by the Polish pope John Paul II, came to rival the ruling Communist Party as a political force. Finally, in December 1981, the government established martial law, outlawed Solidarity, and arrested many of its leaders.

The union, however, survived as an underground force and reemerged in the late 1980s to once again become a legal force after Soviet leader Gorbachev signaled his desire for reform in communist eastern Europe. The transformation in this period that occurred in the Soviet Union and the European countries that it had earlier dominated was accompanied by the rise of other independent workers' movements. And the collapse of communist governments from 1989 to 1991, culminating in the Soviet Union, meant that this time independent labor organizations were to remain as legally recognized entities.

Thus, by the end of the century the world's workers were certainly freer than in 1900 to exercise such rights as the freedom to organize and have union representation. One indication of this was that more than nine-tenths of the world's governments agreed at a 1995 UN-sponsored Social Summit in Copenhagen to declare their support for workers' rights including the right to form unions and engage in collective bargaining. Yet in 1999, the International Labor Association (ILO), formed in 1919 and later affiliated with the UN, found that the right to strike was still not recognized in a number of countries including Liberia, Myanmar, and Saudi Arabia, and that "major gaps in the exercise of freedom of association and the right to collective bargaining persist." And its report added that "workers in many parts of the world are either denied the right to form and join a trade union, or are working in situations where these rights are significantly curtailed."[64]

Even when workers' rights were recognized in theory, they were not always granted. China, for example, in 1998 signed the International Covenant on Civil and Political Rights (see above), which recognized workers' rights "to form and join trade unions." The Chinese government, however, continued to repress workers who opposed its restrictions upon labor.

In the last several decades of the twentieth century, another problem became more pressing for labor, that of globalization (see Chapter Four's section on "Globalization and International Finance"). Although it offered new opportunities for many workers, it weakened the power of many national unions, which were forced to make concessions or see jobs shipped abroad. The ILO report mentioned above analyzed the impact of globalization and other developments of the late twentieth century on labor. To what extent many of these developments threatened labors' freedoms, as the ILO often contended, was dependent on how that complex term "freedom" was defined.

6

Changing Environments

Closely connected to the twentieth century's changes in science, technology, economics, and politics have been those to the environment. One historian wrote that "the human race, without intending anything of the sort, has undertaken a gigantic uncontrolled experiment on the earth. In time, I think, this will appear as the most important aspect of twentieth-century history, more so than World War II, the communist enterprise, the rise of mass literacy, the spread of democracy, or the growing emancipation of women."[1]

In his book *The Coming Anarchy* (2000), Robert Kaplan declared that "it is time to understand 'the environment' for what it is: *the national-security issue of the early twenty-first century*. The political and strategic impact of surging populations, spreading disease, deforestation and soil erosion, water depletion, air pollution, and, possibly, rising sea levels in critical, overcrowded regions like the Nile Delta and Bangladesh—developments that will prompt mass migrations and, in turn, incite group conflicts—will be the core foreign-policy challenge from which most others will ultimately emanate."[2]

Two major and interconnected factors, both fuelled by scientific and technological developments, were responsible for the twentieth century's unprecedented environmental changes and their importance by century's end: population growth and economic activities, especially industrialization and increased consumption. The explosion of twentieth century consumption (see Chapter 3) not only placed increasing demands on scare resources to produce more goods, but also increased pollution in the process of producing and disposing of worn out or obsolescent products.[3] In the final decades of the century, environmentalists increasingly spoke of the need for sustainable development, for adapting economic, social, cultural, and political policies that would help protect the environment so that it could adequately continue to sustain future generations.

Population and Resources

The eminent global historian William McNeill stated that a visitor from outer space would think that the "most remarkable change of the [twentieth] century" would be the "increase in human numbers and urbanization."[4] From 1900 to 1950, world population increased from 1.6 billion to 2.5 billion, and then reached 6 billion in 1999. The annual growth rate in the 1990s, however, was lower than in the three previous decades. This unprecedented population increase was primarily due to the sharp decrease in the death rate that had begun already in the nineteenth century and left more people alive to procreate. But this escalating population, plus new technologies adapted partly to provide for them, put increasing pressure on limited resources such as cropland, food, water, forests, and energy sources (including the wood from forests).

By the 1990s the world was using twice as much cropland, 9 times as much freshwater, and 16 times as much energy as in the 1890s.[5] One reason for availability of more land for crops was due to a major increase in irrigation. In the 1970s, for example, Saudi Arabia began using some of its oil revenues to exploit underground water supplies. By the mid-1980s this desert state had increased irrigation enough to export some of the wheat it grew. But from Saudi Arabia to the Ogallala Aquifer, which provided a vast U.S. irrigation supply from Texas to South Dakota, most underground water supplies were considerably lower by the end of the century than they had been at the beginning, and water rationing had become more common in various parts of the world. The increasing depletion of water was especially difficult for poorer parts of the world such as the Indian subcontinent and sub-Saharan Africa, where more than a combined 2 billion people lived by the end of the century. In India by century's end about twice the amount of water was being pumped from the ground as rainfall was able to replenish. Partly because of diminishing water supplies, the amount of cropland available per person was decreasing noticeably by century's end, creating great hardships for many poorer peoples in the world.[6]

Water was also a source of power used by dams to generate electricity. Overall, the world used about one-third more energy during the twentieth century than it had in the previous 100 centuries *combined*. The most industrialized countries used the most, especially the United States, where by the end of the century the average person used twice as much energy as a European did and more than 26 times as much as someone from India.

During the century the world's forests, much of it tropical forest lands, also decreased by about one-fifth, mainly due to increased demand for timber and conversion of forest lands to farmlands. A similar story of declining resources occurred regarding certain types of animal life, as some species ceased to exist and others, for example whales, greatly decreased. Although the number of fish available in 1900 and 1999 cannot be calculated, J. R. McNeill states that "by the 1980s, fishermen landed as much in two years as their ancestors had in the entire nineteenth century," and that humans probably took more fish from the world's waters in the twentieth century than in the combined total of all previous history.[7]

A surprisingly significant contributor to diminished resources, as well as to global warming (see below), was the sharp increase in global meat production. In the last half of the twentieth century, it increased about fivefold, thus roughly doubling on a per capita basis. Although people in the wealthier countries of the world, especially in the United States, ate more meat per capita than people in poorer nations, the latter about doubled their per person meat consumption in the century's final decade. A 1998 report noted that "if the 670 million tons of the world's grain used for feed were reduced by just 10 percent, this would free up 67 million tons of grain, enough to sustain 225 million people . . . If each American reduced his or her meat consumption by only 5 percent, roughly equivalent to eating one less dish of meat each week, 7.5 million tons of grain would be saved, enough to feed 25 million people."[8] A later UN publication summarized the environmental impact as follows: "The livestock sector emerges as one of the top two or three most significant contributors to the most serious environmental problems, at every scale from local to global. The findings of this report suggest that it should be a major policy focus when dealing with problems of land degradation, climate change and air pollution, water shortage and water pollution and loss of biodiversity." Specifically, the report stated that if the land needed for the direct care and grazing of animals was added to that required to produce food for them it would account for 70 percent of all farm land. It added that "the livestock sector is a key player in increasing water use, accounting for over 8 percent of global human water use, mostly for the irrigation of feedcrops," and that the "expansion of livestock production is a key factor in deforestation, especially in Latin America where the greatest amount of deforestation is occurring."[9]

From the Countryside to the City

An important part of the environmental story of the twentieth century was the everyday living condition of people. As the century began, most people, slightly more than five-sixths of the world's population, lived in rural areas. Most of these people were poor peasants.

In fiction and in anthropological studies we can get some idea of how these poor people lived. In Anton Chekhov's short story "The Peasants" (1897), he depicted a three-generational Russian peasant family of 13 living in a dark, dirty, filled-with-flies, one-room peasant hut. "Bottle labels and newspaper cuttings were stuck on the walls instead of pictures. The poverty . . . In the course of the summer and the winter there had been hours and days when it seemed as though these people lived worse than the beasts." The hut sat on a street of other such huts, with the last one being the village tavern. Although this family was larger than average, the story captures well the type of existence faced by most Russian peasants at the beginning of the century.[10]

A mid-century portrayal of a rural Mexican family by anthropologist Oscar Lewis in his classic *Five Families* is also realistic. The book portrays a family of seven, including three adult sons, living in a windowless adobe hut of one room, plus a kitchen made of cane stalks. The floor of the hut is dirt, and the walls were "papered here and there with old newspapers, religious posters, and calendars." The hut is without electricity or indoor plumbing. Between 8 and 20 trips per day, depending on the season, had to be made to the village fountain for water. Matches to light a fire or a candle were a luxury. To feed the family throughout the year, its members worked at various jobs, for example farming in communal fields, making rope, or working as farmhands for a landowner. When the men left early (5:30 AM) to work in the fields, the 54-year-old mother of the family got up around 4:00 AM to prepare tortillas for the men to eat during the day. Although Mexican peasant life had improved somewhat since the Mexican revolution had produced a new constitution in 1917, the father of this family "believed that he did not live much better than he had under the pre-Revolutionary government."[11]

By the end of the century, the percentage of people living in rural areas was almost down to half of the world's population, but most of these rural inhabitants were still poor peasants or farmers. Many of them resided in the world's two most populated countries, China and

India, with the rural poor in the latter suffering the harshest deprivations. Although Indian economic growth in the 1990s had been impressive and by 1999 India exported considerable rice, the economic gains had benefited primarily upper and middle class people in the towns—about 3 of every 10 Indians lived in urban areas—and wealthier farmers. About four-fifths of the Indian poor were landless agricultural laborers or small farmers—most Indian farmers possessed less than one acre of land. In India as a whole about 300 million people (one-third of the population) still had an income of less than $1 a day, and almost half of India's children were malnourished.

The poverty of India's rural poor also stemmed from other causes including poor access to water, electricity, good roads, storage facilities, or modern agricultural machinery. In India there were only 6 tractors per 1000 agricultural workers compared to between 900 and 1800 per 1000 workers in most west European countries, Canada, and the USA. Adult illiteracy was also a problem with about 43 percent of all Indian adults being illiterate, 32 percent for males, 56 percent for females. In addition, the inefficiencies, bureaucratization, and corruption at various levels of government also kept many Indian peasants impoverished.

The massive global influx from the countryside to urban areas had begun already in the nineteenth century, speeding up as that century neared its end. From 1801 to 1891, England's urban population went from 17 percent to 54 percent, and the USA's from about 4 percent to about 28 percent in almost the same period. Some cities grew especially rapidly in the final decades of the century. Los Angeles, for example, went from about 5,000 to 100,000 and Minneapolis from 2,500 to 200,000 in the years from 1860 to 1900. Although the Russian Empire's percentage of urban population growth was much smaller—from about 10 to 18 percent between 1856 and 1910— St. Petersburg's population more than tripled and Moscow's more than quadrupled in those years.

Yet in 1900 less than one-sixth of the world's 1.6 billion people lived in urban areas.[12] By 1991, however, urban inhabitants had become a majority in most areas with a few notable exceptions such as China, India, and sub-Saharan Africa. Although about 6 of 10 people in Latin America had lived in rural areas in 1950, by 1991 only about 3 of 10 still did. By then in the United States and Europe only about 1 in 4 citizens still resided in rural areas. But of the 20 largest cities in the world, more than half were in Asia and none in Europe. And even though China was still more rural than urban, it added more urban residents in the 1980s than all of Europe had added in the entire nineteenth century. By 1999, with almost half of the world's

6 billion people living in urban areas, this was almost twice the number of people as lived in *all* areas, urban and rural, in 1900.

Even those continuing to live in rural areas came increasingly under urban influences due to such phenomena as urban sprawl and technological advances. By the end of the twentieth century, for example, a much smaller percentage of the world's farming was subsistence farming and much more was part of an international agro-business that, like urban businesses, relied heavily on the latest technology to greatly increase production. The difference between the productivity of such agro-businesses and that of subsistence farming increased dramatically during the second half of the century. Better transportation and media technology, such as radio and television, including transistor radios and satellite and cable television, meant that many rural people became less isolated and enjoyed some of the same entertainment as urban dwellers.

In some areas, such as Latin America, most of the rural land remained in the hands of upper-class landowners—as late as the 1980s, 10 percent of Latin American rural landowners owned 90 percent of the farmland. As rural populations increased, many poor peasants found themselves unable to adequately provide for their families. They therefore sought better opportunities in towns and cities, whether in their own country or abroad. Millions of immigrants to the USA in the decades before World War I fell into the latter category, and in the late twentieth century "a steady stream of workers, most of them from rural areas . . . [moved] north and west from the Third World into the rich First World."[13] By 1999, many of these First World cities contained such workers or their descendents— for example, Hispanics in the USA, North Africans in France, Turks in Germany, and Asian (primarily from India and Pakistan) and Caribbean peoples in Great Britain. But there was also considerable migration from one Third World country to another, for example from Bolivia and Paraguay to Argentina, or from Upper Volta (Burkina Faso from 1984) to the Ivory Coast.

Besides dreams of economic betterment towns and cities appealed to many people, especially the young, because they seemed to offer the possibility of more freedom and excitement than a more limited and confined rural existence. In 1886, the Russian novelist Leo Tolstoy wrote, "I have spoken hundreds of times about it with peasants living in the city, and it became clear to me, from my conversations with them and from my observations, that the crowding of the country population in the cities was partly necessary, because they cannot otherwise earn a livelihood, and partly voluntary, and that the temptations of the city attract them thither."[14]

A poor Russian who in 1895 left his native village at the age of 16 reinforced Tolstoy's perception. He wrote that "there was no way we could live off the land alone, for our allotments were very paltry . . . I wanted to rid myself of the monotony of village life . . . to free myself from my father's despotism . . . I remember what a stunning impression Moscow made on me . . . What struck me most was the abundance of stores and shops."[15]

The initial enthusiasm and excitement, however, sometimes gave way to more ambivalent feelings, as we again see described by the young Russian:

> Two feelings were struggling in my soul. I longed for the village, the meadows, the brook, the bright country sun, the free clear air of the fields, and for the people who were near and dear to me. Here, in the hostile world of Moscow, I felt lonely, abandoned, needed by no one . . . But there was another, more powerful feeling that provided me with courage and steadfastness: my awareness of my independence, my longing to make contact with people, to become independent and proud, to live in accordance with my own wishes.[16]

In numerous true-life and fictional accounts on various continents throughout the twentieth century, we can read of similar stories.[17] Although these sentiments could just as well have been stated by a young woman, who would have also faced additional problems, male migrants were more common than female ones, and not all of those that left the countryside did so permanently. In writing of India and Indonesia in the late twentieth century, one author noted that migration often began as a "temporary phenomenon," with it being more common for young men to come to the city and work for a while, sometimes leaving young wives back in a village.[18] This was also true, for example in Russia at the beginning of the century and in Africa, India, and many other parts of the world later in the century.

Nevertheless, already before 1900, many women also came from the countryside to the city to become domestic servants and work in factories. In 1885, one-fifth of Russian factory workers, mainly from rural backgrounds, were women; and by 1914, one-third. They not only received lower pay, but were often exploited in other ways. Rural parents were often reluctant to allow daughters to migrate to cities, fearing that they might be taken advantage of by unscrupulous men. Despite such fears, however, economic need often led parents to allow migration. Once in the city, many women, like many male migrants, were expected to send money back home.

The massive urbanization of the twentieth century also had numerous other causes, many of them connected with some of the technological developments already mentioned (see Chapter 2). For example, improvements in agricultural technology greatly reduced the number of farm hands needed, and transportation advances made it easier for people and goods to move between rural and urban areas.

Many governments also contributed to the urban influx by enacting policies that stimulated such movement. In Soviet Russia this was especially true. The Communist Party that came to power in 1917 was primarily urban based and inherited the Marxist negative and condescending attitude toward peasants—in his *The Class Struggles in France, 1848–50* Marx referred to the peasants as "the class that represents barbarism within civilization," and his collaborator Friedrich Engels later wrote that the abolition of the antithesis between urban and rural life "will be able to deliver the rural population from the isolation and stupor in which it has vegetated almost unchanged for thousands of years."[19]

Although the communists in Russia at first did expropriate upper-class landholdings and make more land available to peasant communes, in 1928–9 Joseph Stalin instituted policies opposed by most Soviet peasants. Distrusting them and believing that rapid industrialization was of the utmost importance to the USSR, he attempted to speed up industrialization and forcibly collectivize the peasants. From 1928 to mid-1936, the number of peasant households collectivized on collective or state farms went from less than 3 percent to 90 percent. (See Chapter 1 for more on Stalin's repression of the peasants.) In the years 1928–32, about 12 million people left the countryside, willingly or unwillingly. Between 1929 and 1939 about 2 million peasants came to just one city, Moscow. From 1926 to 1939, the urban population throughout the USSR increased from about 18 to 33 percent—by the time of Stalin's death in 1953, it was about 43 percent.

Throughout the remainder of the Soviet period, which ended in 1991, the people in rural areas continued to suffer from government actions and inactions, though under Stalin's successors there were some attempts to improve their lot. The percentage of rural dwellers continued to decline, and as compared to the urban population included more children and older people. As late as 1950, only about one-sixth of the country's collective farms possessed electricity. Within fifteen years, however, almost all farms had electricity, but as late as 1980 most rural households still had no indoor toilets, running water, central heating, or telephones, and few rural settlements yet possessed paved roads. Meanwhile, in actions that displeased many villagers, the Soviet government moved many of them from small villages to newly-built agro-towns or central villages, containing perhaps 1,500 to 2,000 people.

The collapse of the USSR in 1991 produced little improvement for Russian rural residents in the 1990s. By 2003, still less than 10 percent of Russia's farmland was owned by individual farmers, and many private farmers leased the land they farmed. Most of those who farmed, whether collectively or individually, faced grim realities. They made little money, and often had to make do with old farming equipment, insufficient fertilizers, poor rural roads, and inadequate storage facilities.

Many other communist countries also enacted policies harmful to rural areas. In China, Mao Zedong's Great Leap Forward beginning in 1958 had similar consequences to Stalin's policies from 1929 to 1933—forcing peasants into larger collective farming arrangements, driving others from the countryside into the city, and causing terrible famine (on the resulting deaths, see Chapter 1). In China, as in Russia earlier, and as in the century overall, most famine deaths were peasant ones. From 1957 to 1958 the Chinese farm labor force decreased from 192 million to 151 million, and from 1957 to 1960 the urban population increased from 100 million to 130 million. For the next two decades, the people in the countryside continued to suffer under the collectivized agricultural system, consuming less food at the end of the 1970s and in 1980 than they had in the few years before Mao's "Great Leap."[20]

Rural living standards did not noticeably improve until Mao's successor, Deng Xiaoping, decollectivized agriculture in the early 1980s and turned most lands over to families who leased them. Yet by 1999, farmers could still not own the lands they farmed. As cities expanded, they often annexed former farm lands pushing the farmers off the lands and compensating them poorly—the expansion of urban areas into former rural ones was another global trend of the century. During China's significant economic expansion of the 1980s and 1990s, urban incomes increased faster than rural ones, averaging well over twice that of rural inhabitants in 1999, who still comprised 68 percent of China's population.

In the late 1960s British economist Michael Lipton began using the term "urban bias" to popularize the concept that governments favored urban areas over rural ones, thus hastening urbanization. In his survey of the Third World, Paul Harrison agreed with him and cited the great gap in income and services between urban and rural areas in Latin America, Asia, and Africa. He added that "the unfair channeling of public investment into the cities reaches scandalous proportions in most developing countries."[21] As a result, as in Russia, young adults and the better educated migrated to the cities leaving a disproportionate number of older, less educated people in the countryside. Harrison thought the reasons for this bias were complex, but that in general urban masses were better organized, had more power, and, if angered, were a greater potential threat to stability than were the scattered rural folk. Thus, governments provided more for urbanites.[22]

Slums and Suburbs

Slums, Shantytowns, and Poor Urban Conditions

One criticism of the urban bias thesis was that it overlooked the extent of urban poverty, which increased as more people flocked to the cities. Such poverty, however, was far from new. Squatter settlements, sometimes referred to as shantytowns, existed throughout the century and even well before it; for example, "between 1868 and 1875 an estimated 500,000 lived in New York's slums—about half the city's population."[23]

Numerous portraits and statistics indicate how widespread the urban slums were throughout the twentieth century. In 1933 George Orwell's *Down and Out in Paris and London* appeared depicting slum life and his own experiences in these two major European cities. About Paris he wrote, "Paris is vulgar—half grandiosity and half slums."[24] Describing the rooms in which he stayed in the two cities, he wrote of dirt, bugs, noise, foul smells, uncomfortable beds, and sharing space in crowded rooms with sick, sometimes coughing people.

During the Great Depression, which began in the United States in 1929 and then spread to Europe and other areas, the type of conditions described by Orwell were common in numerous cities. In the mid-1990s, Frank McCourt's *Angela's Ashes* described his boyhood in the early 1930s after his family had moved to the Irish city of Limerick. In the family's first lodging they had one furnished room with a fireplace, a table, three chairs and a bed where all six family members slept. McCourt described one night as such:

> Dad and Mam lay at the head of the bed, Malachy and I at the bottom, the twins wherever they could find comfort . . . Then Eugene sat up, screaming, tearing at himself . . . Eugene went on crying and when Dad leaped from the bed and turned on the gaslight we saw the fleas, leaping, jumping, fastened

to our flesh. We slapped at them and slapped but they hopped from body to body, hopping, biting. We tore at the bites till they bled. We jumped from the bed, the twins crying, Mam moaning, Oh, Jesus, will we have no rest![25]

After the death of two of the children the family moved to new lodgings, which were better in some respects but more foul smelling due to the odors coming from the lavatory next door, where they and their neighbors dumped their wastes from their toilet buckets—indoor toilets were then a luxury unavailable to most slum families. McCourt's story of the family's poverty, his father's drinking, and his mother's suffering as she attempted to hold their family together was similar to many others dealing with urban poverty in various places throughout the century.

While capitalist cities suffered greatly during the Depression era, so too did Soviet Russian cities, but for their own unique reasons, having more to do with Russian history and Stalin than any economic effects of the global Depression.

With about 2 million peasants coming to Moscow to work between 1929 and 1939, many had to live in factory dormitories (sometimes sleeping on the floor) or on the capital's outskirts, where some of them constructed mud huts, underground dugouts, or makeshift shanties. Although worse off than the average Moscow apartment-dwellers, most of the latter were also living in poor conditions. Most families in the capital still lived in communal apartments, where they had to share kitchens, bath and toilet facilities, and sometimes even a single living and sleeping room with other families.

But if Moscow had its hardships, they paled in comparison to a city like Magnitogorsk, which in the course of a half decade (1929–34) went from a village to a town of about 200,000. The American John Scott, who worked there, estimated that in 1938 three-fourths of the population lived in mud huts, underground dugouts, barracks, or temporary wooden structures. If families in huts were fortunate enough to own a cow, pigs, or chickens, these animals also usually shared the family hut.

In another Soviet city at this time, Berezniki in the Ural Mountains region, future Russian President Boris Yeltsin's family (including a goat) lived for a decade, crowded into one drafty room in a communal barracks of twenty small rooms. The barracks had no "modern conveniences," such as indoor toilets or running water.

In the USSR, as in Germany, Japan, and some other regions, World War II destroyed much urban housing. In 1947 in the city of Novgorod, almost one-third of the people still resided in earth dugouts, basements, or temporary barracks.[26]

At mid-century, housing conditions had worsened even in some areas not suffering the direct effects of war. Oscar Lewis wrote in his *Five Families* "that the crowding and slum conditions in the large cities [of Mexico] are actually getting worse." In the 1950 census he noted that 60 percent of households reported living in only one room, and he estimated that in the late 1950s about half of Mexico City's population lived in slum conditions.[27]

As urbanization accelerated after World War II, many children, especially in poorer countries, were born into the type of slum conditions described by Mark Mathabane in his autobiographical account *Kaffir Boy* (1986). He grew up in the 1960s in the segregated South African ghetto of Alexandra, a little north of Johannesburg proper. Already by the mid-1950s this ghetto contained over 100,000 inhabitants "squeezed into a space of one square mile."[28] He grew up in dingy little shacks, the first of which collapsed one night. In it, he slept next to his little sister on a cardboard bed under the kitchen table, and they could hear rats in the cupboard. The shacks contained no electricity or indoor plumbing—instead outhouses and 1 water tap for 100 people. When his father had a job, working as a menial laborer for a white company some distance away, he left home sometimes at 5 AM, sometimes at 3 AM, and returned at 8 or 9 PM. When he lost his job, he was arrested—"his crime, unemployment, was one of the worst a black man could commit." [29] During the time he was imprisoned (almost a year), his family almost starved to death and resorted to such desperate measures as scavenging food from a dump.

In racist South Africa what made this slum especially horrific were the constant police raids complete with shots ringing out, shouts, barking police dogs, doors being knocked down, and people being led away in handcuffs. Mathabane recalled being spat upon, kicked, and hit on the head with a truncheon by police breaking into his family's shack while he was still a little boy.

Although the severe segregation of apartheid South Africa had ended by 1999, slum inhabitants were more numerous globally than ever. By then they comprised a little over three-fourths of the urban population of the least developed countries, about one-third of the overall global urban population, and almost one-sixth of the world's total population. No less than half of these slum dwellers were under age of 20. One source estimated that around the turn of the century in just five metropolitan areas in India, Pakistan, and Bangladesh there were about 15,000 distinct slums, totaling more than 20 million people. In Ethiopia, Chad, Afghanistan, and Nepal slum dwellers made up over 90 percent of all urban inhabitants.[30]

Slums existed both in decaying parts of inner cities and on the outskirts, often in various types of squatter settlements. In some cities such as Cairo some newcomers to the city settled on rooftops.

Perhaps the worst off slum conditions existed in Africa. One expert on slums declared that "the poorest urban populations, however, are probably in Maputo [Mozambique] and Kinshasa [Congo] where . . . two-thirds of residents earn less than the cost of their minimum required daily nutrition." And that "Lagos, moreover, is simply the biggest node in the shanty-town corridor of 70 million people that stretches [in West Africa] from Abidjan to Ibadan: probably the biggest continuous footprint of urban poverty on earth."[31]

In the 1990s the journalist Robert D. Kaplan reported on his observations of slums in this region of Africa. "The cities of West Africa at night are some of the unsafest places in the world. Streets are unlit; the police often lack gasoline for their vehicles; armed burglars, carjackers, and muggers proliferate." In Abidjan (the Ivory Coast's largest city), he noted a slum nicknamed "Chicago," which was "a checkerwork of corrugated zinc roofs and walls made of cardboard and black plastic wrap. It is . . . ravaged by flooding. Few residents have easy access to electricity, a sewage system, or a clean water supply. The crumbly red laterite earth crawls with foot-long lizards both inside and outside the shacks. Children defecate in a stream filled with garbage and pigs, droning with mosquitoes. In this stream women do the washing. Young unemployed men spend their time drinking beer, palm wine, and gin while gambling on pinball games constructed out of rotting wood and rusty nails. These are the same youths who rob houses in more prosperous Ivorian neighborhoods at night."[32] By the end of the century, a UN report estimated that slum dwellers comprised about one-fifth of Abidjan's population. The main reason most people remained in such conditions was that they did not believe they could afford better housing.[33]

Slums were also plentiful in other parts of West Africa. In Guinea, Kaplan observed that his drive from the airport to downtown Conakry was "through one never-ending shantytown: a nightmarish Dickensian spectacle."[34]

A quick look at century's end at a few other slums outside of Africa also reveals appalling conditions. In Calcutta (Kolkata) almost half of the city's population lived in slums without sewerage systems or drinkable water or were homeless.[35] In Mexico City and in South America's largest city, São Paulo, the slum statistics were just as appalling. Squatter settlements, along with inner-city slum tenements, housed a majority of the people. The settlements often arose on land that was environmentally unsound—more susceptible to such problems as flooding, pollution, sanitation deficiencies, and landslides. Added to the crowded conditions in these settlements, these environmental factors help explain the higher death rates found in them.[36]

Although richer Western nations had less slum dwellers, cities such as Paris and Los Angeles still each had hundreds of thousands of people living in slum conditions. In addition there were also numerous homeless people. In Paris and many other western European cities (including their suburbs), many of the most unfortunate were immigrants or their descendents from Africa, Asia, or the Caribbean, many of them Muslims. In Los Angeles, which also had many immigrants, legal and illegal and mainly Latino, a three-day count in January 2006 discovered 83,347 homeless people in the greater Los Angeles area. As in most slums, the main cause of such conditions was poverty. The 2000 U.S. Census indicated that 22 percent of the people in Los Angeles were below the federal line determining poverty, with many of them being part of female-headed households.[37]

After notable income improvements in some areas such as Latin America between 1950 and 1980, the 1980s and 1990s were not so good. According to UN estimates, the percentage of impoverished families in urban Latin America increased from 25 to 32 percent between 1970 and 1985, and because of the much larger number of people in the cities by 1990 the total number of urban poor more than doubled in 20 years.

The blame for the growing number of global slum dwellers has been attributed to many causes. Leftist critics often faulted the United States and other major powers, plus international bodies that they dominated like the International Monetary Fund (IMF) and World Bank. Taking advantage of Third-World debt and the desire of heavily indebted countries to restructure it, the major economic powers, critics charged, pushed through so-called "neoliberal" policies that insisted that indebted nations cut government spending and open up their markets to greater foreign trade, investment, and competition.

In the *New Left Review*, Mike Davis cited a UN-Habitat Report conclusion that some of these policies "were 'deliberately anti-urban in nature' and designed to reverse any 'urban bias' that previously existed . . . [and] that the 'main single cause of increases in poverty and inequality during the 1980s and 1990s was the retreat of the state.'" But Davis argued that these policies also created greater economic inequalities, both within states and between rich and poor countries, and "at the same time . . . devastated rural smallholders by eliminating subsidies and pushing them out, 'sink or swim,' into global commodity markets dominated by First World agribusiness."

Many of these former rural inhabitants then made their way into the cities of the Third World, contributing to the mushrooming of slums. Davis again quoted the UN-Habitat report: "Instead of being a focus for growth and prosperity, the cities have become a dumping ground for a surplus population working in unskilled, unprotected and low-wage informal service industries and trade." [38]

Right-wing critics, on the other hand, tended to blame the continuation and growth of slums on such factors as the decline of morality, family disintegration, and government programs like welfare. The historian Gertrude Himmelfarb, part of a family of leading U.S. conservatives, asked "when we describe the 'cycle of welfare dependency,' or the 'culture of poverty,' or the 'demoralization of the underclass,' are we not defining that class and that culture in moral terms, and finding them wanting in those terms?" Her chief answer to dealing with many social problems including poverty was for societies to place more emphasis on the type of virtues emphasized by the Victorians, including an emphasis on self-help.[39]

Suburbs

Suburbs are areas outside of city limits, but many cities annexed areas that were previously suburbs. And suburbs varied greatly in various parts of the world. In Paris in the 1930s, for example, suburbs "referred chiefly to the dreary industrial districts that ringed the city like a sooty pall."[40] And by the 1990s, many of the poor housing settlements peopled by foreign workers and their descendents were in the Paris suburbs. In Latin America, some former shantytowns or squatter settlements became in the words of one author "proper suburbs," as residents improved their housing and gradually obtained electricity, water, and proper sewerage services, as well as paved roads, bus services, and neighborhood schools.[41]

Although improvements in public transport contributed to the development of suburbs, the latter were not just a twentieth century phenomenon. One scholar wrote, "Clearly, from the beginning of modern urban history, and contrary to much accepted wisdom, suburban development was very diverse and catered to all kinds of people and activities."[42]

Witold Rybczynski dated the first American suburbs to the early nineteenth century. Brooklyn was then a New York suburb, and in 1814 a ferry service began to bring Brooklyn commuters to Manhattan. In most other U.S. cities, it was trains or horse-drawn streetcars or omnibuses, and later electric streetcars, which enabled people to move beyond city limits and still commute to work in the city. In the USA by 1900, many people had already moved out of inner cities to detached suburban homes. By the mid-1930s, about one-sixth of U.S. inhabitants lived in suburbs; by 1960, one-third did. The greater number of automobiles in the United States as compared to other countries facilitated this growth, as did cheap gasoline and ever-expanding highways. With expanded suburbs, shopping plazas and malls eventually appeared that further separated those in the suburbs from those in towns and cities and contributed to the economic erosion of some inner cities.

Suburbs also expanded in other parts of the world. In Latin America by the 1950s, many people had moved to suburbs, but as one scholar put it "the rich moved one way, the poor another."[43] Thus, in Latin America, as in the USA, residential segregation according to economic status was quite common. (In the USA, for much of the early twentieth century, it was also often based on racial grounds— although racial zoning was outlawed by the Supreme Court in 1917, race-restrictive language continued being attached to some housing deeds, especially in newly constructed suburbs.) By 1999 the majority of people in European metropolitan areas resided in suburbs, and, as in the USA, lived more in houses, as opposed to apartments, and relied more on automobiles and suburban shopping centers than they had several decades earlier.

Pollution and Other Environmental Problems

One of the major problems associated with cities was pollution. One scholar estimated that air pollution alone killed 20–30 million people from 1950 to 1997, most of them in urban areas. Other more recent studies indicated that many chemicals in urban air, as well as in consumer products, caused cancer in animal tests. [44] Although not until the 1960s did many people express concern about "the environment" in general, urban pollution had been a problem for many years. The famous English novelist Charles Dickens immortalized some of the pollution problems of English industrial cities in his portrayal of Coketown in his 1854 novel *Hard Times*.

> It was a town of red brick, or of brick that would have been red if the smoke and ashes had allowed it; but as matters stood, it was a town of unnatural red and black like the painted face of a savage. It was a town of machinery and tall chimneys, out of which interminable serpents of smoke trailed themselves for ever and ever, and never got uncoiled. It had a black canal in it, and a river that ran purple with ill-smelling dye.[45]

Coal Burning and Pollution

As the name of the fictional Coketown suggests, a main culprit in many cities was the heavy use of coal. It was not just industry's use of coal that was the problem, for the smoke coming from household chimneys also often came from burning coal. London's use of coal, its vast population (over 6 million people in 1900), and its climate caused many respiratory illnesses. Overall, a much larger percentage of deaths from air pollution occurred in Victorian England than occurred globally in the 1990s.[46] Only after the Clean Air Act of 1956 went into effect, regulating the use of domestic coal, did London air become noticeably less polluted.

In other industrialized cities outside Britain, air pollution was also a major problem before 1900. Pittsburgh was notorious for its noxious air, and not far away in some northern West Virginia cities the air was also often foul. The main culprit again was chimney smoke, coming in this region primarily from coal-burning iron and steel plants. Like London, Pittsburgh also eventually took steps to reduce its coal use, both in industry and homes, and by 1953 it was less polluted than in the late 1890s. Later in the century, for a variety of economic reasons, numerous Pittsburgh steel and other manufacturing plants closed, also helping to reduce pollution. For a long time, however, coal-burning industries and homes continued to pollute various parts of the world in a major way. By the 1930s, besides Great Britain and the USA, Germany was also a major user of coal. And Osaka, Japan's heavy use of it made it one of the world's most polluted cities—by the early 1990s, however, Osaka and Tokyo had followed the example of London and Pittsburgh and considerably decreased their air pollution.

Gradually as the Western industrialized countries and Japan began relying more on oil and natural gas for energy, and became more concerned with pollution in the second half of the century, their percentage of non-vehicle-caused global air pollution declined. In fact, in the USA the emission of six principal air pollutants, nitrogen dioxide (NO_2), ozone (O_3), sulfur dioxide (SO_2), particulate matter (PM), carbon monoxide (CO), and lead (Pb), dropped by almost half between 1970 and 2000.[47] Unfortunately, however, U.S. carbon dioxide (CO_2) emissions, primarily from motor vehicles, increased during this period (see below)—in contrast, the UK was able to reduce overall CO_2 emissions.

During the 1930s, as part of the Soviet industrialization drive, coal use in the USSR shot up dramatically, mainly to fuel the rapidly expanding Soviet metallurgical industry. After World War II, Soviet control over eastern Europe led to expanded coal burning and more pollution in Soviet satellite states such as East Germany, Poland, Czechoslovakia, and Hungary. Unhindered by the type of public pressures increasingly brought to bear in the Western democracies, Soviet Bloc industrial smokestacks continued to spew forth pollution. Even before Soviet control of the region, air pollution caused mainly by coal containing high amounts of sulfur had been a problem in the "sulfuric triangle" bounded by Krakow, Prague, and Dresden. During the 1950s and 1960s, however, the pollution grew much worse and continued to worsen until the collapse of communist regimes in eastern Europe and the USSR between 1989 and 1991.

One of the most polluted cities in the USSR was Magnitogorsk, whose Magnitogorsk Works at the end of this period were still producing almost as much steel as being turned out in all of Great Britain. The health effects of its pollutants, in the form of green, blue, yellow, and grey smoke belching from the mills, were such that 34 percent of the adults and 67 percent of children younger than 15 suffered from respiratory ailments. A coroner in the city estimated that at least nine-tenths of the children born in the city suffered from "pollution-related illnesses: chronic bronchitis, asthma, allergies, even cancers."[48]

By the end of the century, the latest rapidly industrializing major powers were China and India, and they repeated the earlier experiences of other such countries as being heavy polluters, except the pollution was made worse by the fact that the two countries together contained over 2 billion people. And heavy industrial and domestic use of coal was again one of the major contributors to pollution. A visitor to China in 1996 observed that "after 15 more years of coal-powered economic development, there was so much coal dust in the air over cities like Bejing and X'ian that the midafternoon sky looked as dark as dusk. At that time, China boasted five of the world's ten most air-polluted cities (the ratio would increase to nine of ten by 1998), [and] two million Chinese were dying every year from air and water pollution."[49]

A report on Indian air pollution soon after the end of the twentieth century declared:

Industrialization and urbanization have resulted in a profound deterioration of India's air quality. India has more than 20 cities with populations of at least 1 million, and some of them—including New Delhi, Mumbai, Chennai, and Kolkata [Calcutta]—are among the world's most polluted. Urban air quality ranks among the world's worst. Of the 3 million premature deaths in the world that occur each year due to outdoor and indoor air pollution, the highest number are assessed to occur in India. Sources of air pollution, India's most severe environmental problem, come in several forms, including vehicular emissions and untreated industrial smoke. Continued urbanization has exacerbated the problem of rapid industrialization, as more and more people are adversely affected and cities are unable to implement adequate pollution control mechanisms.[50]

Another source noted that during the last quarter of the twentieth century, breathing Calcutta's air was like daily smoking a pack of domestic cigarettes and that in the 1980s air pollution caused lung ailments among almost two-thirds of the city's inhabitants.[51]

The Automobile and other Motor Vehicles

The air quality in Magnitogorsk or in Chinese and Indian cities would have been much worse if these cities had had anywhere near the number of automobiles per capita that existed in advanced Western countries. In the world overall by the 1990s, automobiles and other vehicles were contributing more to air pollution than any other single source.

At the start of the twentieth century, of course, cars were not yet a major source of air pollution. Horse manure on city streets was more of a concern—around 1900 New York had some 150,000 horses, the healthiest ones discharging 20–5 pounds of manure a day.[52] By 1955, however, there were more than 100 million motor vehicles in existence globally; and by 1995, almost 800 million, with people in the United States still driving more than those in any other country. (See Chapter 2 for figures on automobile production.)

As early as the 1940s, Los Angeles (LA) enacted measures to reduce its infamous pollution-caused smog. Despite such actions, however, the city's smog problem continued, and in 1976 the air quality was considered unhealthy three-fourths of the year. Two decades later, LA's air pollution was still very bad, worse than that of any other U.S. city. Although the city's bowl-like shape and its surrounding mountains, along with plenty of sunshine, contributed to the smog, the greatest cause of its air pollution was the automobile. Even though by 1992 the average new car in California spewed forth only one-tenth the amount of pollutants as a 1970 car, the city continued sprawling and the population and number of vehicles increasing.

Mexico City and Athens were two other cities that shared some of LA's geographic characteristics, such as surrounding mountains that contributed to stagnant air, polluted primarily by motor vehicle exhaust. Both cities also eventually took various steps to contain the problem, but it remained a serious one, killing thousands of people each year, into the twenty-first century. Air pollution also damaged historic monuments such as Athens' Acropolis. In the case of Mexico City, even more so than LA, the vast number of people in the city's metropolitan area (roughly 20 million by the last few years of the century) and the presence of many older vehicles exacerbated the problem.

By the 1990s, automobile pollution was also a major problem in many big cities outside of the Americas and Europe. One example was Bangkok. One visitor to the city in 1992 recalled that the traffic from the international airport to the city at 1 AM on a weekday morning was "like Los Angeles during Friday afternoon rush hour." He also commented that "the pollution of Bangkok's air had been so extreme . . . you felt you could scoop up a handful of the stuff and splatter it against the wall like a dirty snowball." He also complained of the "foul chemical odor" that gave him a headache "within two minutes of stepping onto the sidewalk."[53]

By the end of the century the continued negative effects of the world's motor vehicles on people's health and the environment were becoming more worrisome than ever. One 1995 study concluded that 30,000 Americans per year died as a result of respiratory ailments connected to automobile emissions—motor vehicle accidents took even more lives, a little over 43,000 U.S. lives in 1995; estimates for global deaths from auto accidents in the years 1993–5 were around 885,000–888,000 deaths per year.[54]

Global Warming

One of the greatest negative effects of vehicle emissions was the impact they had on global warming.[55] As a result of the CO_2 spewed into the air by these emissions, more heat was prevented from escaping into space, creating a "greenhouse effect." Although CO_2 was not the only greenhouse gas—methane, ozone, and nitrous oxide were a few of the others—and motor vehicles were not the only contributors to this heat increase, they were by century's end one of the biggest single causes. For about ten thousand years the concentration of CO_2 in the atmosphere had hovered around 260 to 280 parts per million (ppm). Largely as a result of increased coal burning in the nineteenth century the rate increased to about 295 ppm by 1900, and then as the effect of automobile and other motor vehicle exhaust became greater, it jumped to 320 ppm by 1965, 360 ppm by 1995, and 379 ppm by 2005.[56]

Another major cause of increased global warming was the increase in meat production mentioned earlier in this chapter. An article posted on a UN site in 2006 proclaimed "Rearing Cattle Produces More Greenhouse Gases than Driving Cars, UN Report Warns." The report itself stated that "the livestock sector is a major player, responsible for 18 percent of greenhouse gas emissions measured in CO_2 equivalent. This is a higher share than transport." These increased emissions of CO_2 and other greenhouse gases, like methane and nitrous oxide, came from such sources as deforestation (in order to create more land for pastures and feedcrops) and manure.[57]

The percentage of CO_2 emissions, as compared to that of all the non-CO_2 gasses, was much larger in countries with many cars and trucks like the United States than in those with a smaller number of such vehicles. In the year 2000, for example, the percentage of carbon-equivalent greenhouse emissions coming from CO_2 was 83 percent in the USA, but only 36 percent in Brazil.[58] As a result of increased emissions from all sources, by the end of 2002 it was possible to conclude that the 16 warmest years in over 120 years occurred after 1980.[59] Ironically, even though the richer, mainly northern, countries of the world were most responsible for global warming, it was the poorer, mainly southern countries, that were most adversely affected by it.

For decades prior to 2000 various individuals, especially scientists, had expressed concern about global warming. Among others, Al Gore in the U.S. Congress from the late 1970s and later as U.S. vice-president called attention to the problem.[60] But energy lobbyists and others downplayed the issue or denied it was caused by human activity. By the late 1990s, however, the alarm among scientists grew greater and continued to grow into the twenty-first century. In 1995, the UN's Intergovernmental Panel on Climate Change (IPCC) relying on more than 2,000 scientists from around the world concluded that evidence did indeed suggest that human actions were heating up the planet.

In 2001, that same panel issued a new report, *Climate Change 2001: The Scientific Basis*, in which the panel revised higher their earlier estimate of global warming and the dangers presented by it. The report stated: "Analyses for the last 1,000 years over the Northern Hemisphere indicate that the magnitude of 20th century warming is likely to have been the largest of any century during this period. In addition, the 1990s are likely to have been the warmest decade of the millennium. New analyses indicate that the global ocean has warmed significantly since the late 1940s."[61] (A 2007 report by the panel was even direr about future climate consequences.[62])

In 2001 British researchers concluded that temperatures would heat up much faster than previously thought, and the following year researchers in the journal *Science* warned of a "catastrophic buildup of atmospheric CO_2" unless a massive transition was undertaken to using more non-carbon energy sources such as wind and solar power and hydrogen fuel.[63] By 2007 more evidence, cited by the IPCC and others, was available regarding global temperature increases and the effects they were having—the melting of glaciers; rising waters threatening islands, coastlands, and flood-prone cities; vanishing species but an increase in microbes, plants, and insects that make humans sick; and more unstable weather, including hurricanes and tornadoes.[64] The connection of global warming, if any, to the deadly tsunami that arose in the Indian Ocean and killed more than 200,000 people in late 2004 was less clear.

During the twentieth century, there was little concerted effort to reduce global warming. It was not until 1997 that most of the world's nations agreed to the Kyoto Protocol that called for a reduction in the use of carbon dioxide and other gases responsible for global warming. The major users of fossil fuels such as the United States and Japan were to cut their usage of greenhouse gases the most—the USA by 2008–12 was supposed to use 7 percent less than it had in 1990. Although the USA, which emitted more greenhouse gasses than any other country (about one-fifth of the world's total), signed the treaty in 1998, the U.S. Senate never ratified it. By the time enough other nations finally approved it so that it went into effect in 2005, the United States was the only major power still not to assent to it. U.S. President George W. Bush declared, "I will not commit our nation to an unsound international treaty that will throw millions of our citizens out of work."[65]

President Bush's comment indicated one reason why more was not done about global warming despite the danger many scientists and others believed it posed. The subtitle of Ross Gelbspan's book *Boiling Point: How Politicians, Big Oil and Coal, Journalists, and Activists Are Fueling the Climate Crisis—and What We Can Do to Avert Disaster* tells another part of the story. Since cutbacks in the use of coal and oil would have hurt the industries that produced them, "Big Oil and Coal" companies organized and financed a major campaign to cast serious doubts upon global-warming claims. And this campaign and the lobbying groups it financed helped to reduce criticism by the media (much of it controlled by large conglomerates) and prevent many U.S. politicians from doing more. Despite the global-warming concerns of many scientists and prestigious scientific bodies, including the national academies of science of the major countries of the world (those of the G8 countries, Brazil, China, and India), companies like ExxonMobil, according to Gelbspan, confused people about the seriousness of the issue, and led many to believe that global warming was a theory, not a fact. [66] One of the tactics used was similar to that used in debates about evolution—that is to find some scientists, whether experts on the subject in question or not, to express doubts about the beliefs of the overwhelming majority of scientists in the field and then say "the scientific community is split on the question."[67]

Another reason global warming was not taken more seriously is that it was indeed a complex question and not perceived by many uninformed people as that significant or as that immediate a threat. After all, even those most worried about the issue only claimed that the average global surface temperature had increased by about 1 degree Fahrenheit in the entire twentieth century. Even if it increased several more degrees, or even by as much as 5 degrees in the twenty-first century, to some people that did not seem that alarming. It became scarier, however, if one realized that temperatures continuing to rise at the rate of 1980s and 1990s would confront a newborn infant of the twenty-first century with the likelihood of eventually living on a warmer planet than humans had *ever* experienced—with all the uncertainties that implied. And it became even scarier yet when one looked at the probable effects such a warming would have on weather, water, crops, diseases, animals, and people, and when one realized that because of the actions of past decades some degree of global warming would continue to occur even if effective steps were taken to stop increasing greenhouse gas emissions. Most carbon dioxide emitted in the twentieth-century would still be there, for example, more than a century later. By the end of the twentieth century, one did not have to be an alarmist to be concerned about global warming, only humane enough to care about the fate of future generations.

Acid Rain and Ozone Depletion

Coal burning, vehicle exhaust, and livestock also contributed to acid rain, which came primarily from the emission of sulfur, ammonia, and nitrogen oxides. Winds carried the pollutants across national borders, where they came to earth with rains that polluted lakes, rivers, trees, and soil. Because of prevailing westerly winds, British, U.S., and Chinese emissions caused high concentrations of acid rain respectively in Scandinavian countries, Canada, and, to a lesser extent, Japan, leading to complaints from the governments of the affected nations. During the last quarter of the century, European and U.S.–Canadian agreements finally reduced sulfur emissions by about one-fifth, but less was done to reduce nitrogen emissions, which came primarily from motor vehicles. And Japan was less successful than downwind countries in the Western world in getting its polluting neighbor (China) to reduce any emissions, sulfur dioxide being the main problem.

Another environmental problem was the heavy emissions of chlorofluorocarbons (CFCs), which depleted atmospheric ozone and consequently increased solar radiation, certain health problems such as skin cancer, and damage to food crops. The first CFC was Freon, created by a General Motors chemist in 1930. Freon eventually came to be widely used in refrigerators and air conditioners; and by 1970, about 37.5 times as many CFCs were being emitted as in 1950.[68] In the late 1970s some countries banned CFCs in aerosol sprays, but CFC use globally continued to climb. At Montreal in 1987, 46 nations agreed to reduce chlorofluorocarbon emissions 50 percent by 1999. Subsequent meetings led to further reduction agreements among many of the major nations.

Although adequate substitutes for CFCs were often discovered, some countries increased CFC emissions as they manufactured more refrigerators and air conditioners—Thailand, for example, doubled its use of CFCs from 1986 to 1989.[69] Nevertheless, on a global basis CFC use fell by about 80 percent between 1986 and 1994. By the end of the later year, estimates of skin cancer from ozone depletion were in the 1–2 million case range.[70] Because CFCs remained for long periods in the atmosphere and continued to deplete ozone into the twenty-first century, additional depletion-caused deaths would continue for decades to come.

Water Pollution

In 1962 Rachel Carson's *Silent Spring* was published. She selected her title to suggest that if humans did not change their ways, a spring might arrive when no more birds would sing. In this book that helped to launch the environmental movement of the late twentieth century, she wrote that "the pollution entering our waterways comes from many sources: radioactive wastes from reactors, laboratories, and hospitals; fallout from nuclear explosions; domestic wastes from cities and towns; chemical wastes from factories. To these is added a new kind of fallout—the chemical sprays applied to croplands and gardens, forests and fields."[71] Like air pollution, water pollution had been around for a long time, but the rapid growth of population, urbanization, industrialization, and new chemical compounds in the decades before Carson's influential book appeared exacerbated the problem. So too did the increase of nitrogen and phosphorus from urban sewage and chemical fertilizers that made their way into waterways, especially lakes.

In her chapter "Rivers of Death" Carson documented the terrible consequences for fish life of the man-made compound DDT and other pesticides that found their way into U.S. rivers. "Our waters," she wrote, "have become almost universally contaminated with insecticides."[72] In 1969, pollution in Cleveland's Cuyahoga River was so bad that the river caught fire. Finally, in 1972, thanks in good part to Carson's book and the environmental movement it helped spur, the USA enacted a Clean Water Act and banned DDT. That same year a U.S.–Canadian Great Lakes Water Quality Agreement was signed. Subsequently, many U.S. rivers and lakes became less polluted. Man-made compounds such as polychlorinated biphenyl (PCB), however, continued to pollute many U.S. waterways. One toxicologist concerned about the water quality of Lake Michigan's Green Bay warned in 2001 that "approximately 40,000 individuals in the Fox River and Green Bay region are faced with PCB cancer risks similar to smoking two to three packs of cigarettes a day."[73]

Among other Western industrialized countries, the pattern was similar—increased water pollution until the environmental movements of the latter decades of the twentieth century finally helped lead to some improvements, but certainly not an end to the problem. England's Thames River, for example, was much cleaner in the last few decades of the century than in the 1950s. But Europe's most famous example of improving the quality of a badly polluted river was the heavily-trafficked Rhine River. Until about the mid-1970s the pollution kept getting worse as many of the sources Carson cited for U.S. water pollution also increased Rhine River levels of DDT, PCB, cadmium, chromium, copper, mercury, nickel, nitrogen, phosphorus, and zinc. Many fish could no longer survive or were too polluted for humans to eat. By the 1990s, however, conditions improved and more fish such as salmon could once again survive in the river, though salmon counts were far below late nineteenth-century numbers.[74]

In the communist countries of the Soviet Bloc, oppressive governments insured that the impact of environmental movements was weak, and rivers such as Poland's Vistula and Russia's Volga, the longest river in Europe, continued to increase their pollution levels. Into the Volga by the late 1980s, some 200 major industrial enterprises emptied their wastes, as did cities dumping untreated urban sewage. Whereas in 1989, the U.S. Environmental Protection Agency concluded that only 10 percent of U.S. bays, streams, and rivers were seriously polluted, in the USSR at about the same time almost 80 percent of samples from 200 rivers indicated "dangerous levels of bacterial and viral agents." Larger Soviet bodies of water also continued to be seriously polluted in the late 1980s. A 1992 book stated that "untreated, waterborne agricultural, industrial and human wastes together threaten to kill the Sea of Azov, the Black Sea and the Caspian."[75]

In much of Asia, larger increases in population and weaker environmental movements than in the West helped explain why less progress was made in curtailing river pollution. In India's Ganges River basin, one source estimated that the number of people dumping their wastes in that great river increased from about 10 million to 70 million between 1900 and 1990.[76] As a result of early industrialization, Japan experienced some of Asia's earliest major twentieth-century water pollution problems, but in the latter decades of the century it was an Asian leader in dealing with water pollution, as well as other environmental problems.

In general water pollution was more of a problem in rivers and lakes than in seas and oceans, partly because the larger amounts of water in the latter categories helped dilute the pollution. Among seas in the 1980s, the Baltic and Black seas and the Sea of Japan were more polluted than the Mediterranean, the earth's largest inland sea. But despite a pact among Mediterranean nations that became operative in the late 1970s and helped lessen the increasing rate of pollution, the Mediterranean was still more polluted in the late 1990s than it had been two decades earlier.[77]

Sea and ocean pollution came from many of the same sources that polluted rivers and lakes. In the latter decades of the century, however, oil spills and leaks and an increasing amount of plastics, made from petrochemicals, were especially apparent in these larger bodies of water. In the late 1970s estimates suggest that somewhere in the range of 500,000–800,000 tons of oil per year leaked into the Mediterranean. When Thor Heyerdahl crossed the Atlantic Ocean in 1969 he observed oil slicks on more than two-thirds of his 57 days on the ocean. Some of the oil in the ocean came from oil tanker spills. A tanker accident in the English Channel in 1967 resulted in a spill of 120,000 tons of oil. Another tanker, the *Exxon Valdez*, in 1989 spilled 34,000 tons of oil into Prince William Sound on Alaska's Pacific Ocean coast. Such accidents resulting in spills of tens of thousands of tons of oil, plus routine oil dumping and other oil polluting activities remained commonplace in the 1990s.[78]

Nuclear Pollution

Beginning with nuclear testing during World War II, soon followed by the dropping of atomic bombs (A-bombs) on Hiroshima and Nagasaki in August 1945, human beings were confronted with a new source of pollution. Exposure to the radioactivity emitted by the bombs in Japan killed many people (see Chapter 1), some soon after exposure, and others only many years later as sort of a delayed reaction, often in the form of cancers. Heavy exposure also caused many genetic defects in offspring. After the war nuclear tests, primarily by the USA and USSR, continued to pollute, but the process was slowed down when over 100 nations signed the Nuclear Test Ban Treaty in 1963. It prohibited testing in the atmosphere and underwater. Among major nations, France and the People's Republic of China did not sign and did some testing after 1963. By this time nuclear power plants for the civilian use of nuclear energy had also developed in countries such as the USA, the USSR, and the UK. By 1998, about 437 such plants in 29 countries existed. Occasionally, beginning in the 1950s, there were accidents in some of these plants, as well as in nuclear facilities being used for weapons' purposes.[79] There were also reports of secret dumping of nuclear wastes into various waters.

The worst offender in regard to trying to keep nuclear pollution secret was the Soviet Union, which also experienced in 1986 the greatest nuclear accident of the twentieth century. Even earlier in 1957 an unreported accident in the Ural Mountain region spewed forth tons of radioactive material, killing an unknown number of people and contaminating a large area, from which almost 11,000 people had to be evacuated. A reliable book on Soviet ecology reported that in the 1950s in that same Ural region great amounts of nuclear waste were dumped into a lake, and that in the years 1964–86, the nuclear waste of 11,000 containers was dropped into waters in the White Sea area of Murmansk.[80] But the 1986 accident at the Chernobyl Nuclear Power Station in the Soviet Ukrainian town of Pripiat could not so easily be covered up. A nuclear reactor exploded, spewing at least 50 tons of radioactive particles into the atmosphere, hundreds of times more than the A-bombs dropped on Japan. Winds then carried considerable contamination into other parts of the USSR and Europe. In the USSR, hundreds of thousands of people were eventually evacuated from affected areas, and millions of people in Ukraine, Belarus, and Russia alone (then republics of the USSR but now independent countries) were affected by the contamination. At times, the mental stress of knowing one had been exposed to the accident's radiation was more damaging than the actual physical exposure.

In subsequent years much was written about this disaster and the harm it caused. And well into the twenty-first century, its effects were still being debated. In 2006, a lengthy report by the environmental group Greenpeace, "Chernobyl Catastrophe: Consequences on Human Health" concluded that a 2005 International Atomic Energy Agency (IAEA) report had greatly underestimated the health impact of the Chernobyl accident. The Greenpeace report stated "the 2005 IAEA report predicted that 4,000 additional deaths would result from the Chernobyl accident. The most recently published figures indicate that in Belarus, Russia and the Ukraine alone the accident resulted in an estimated 200,000 additional deaths between 1990 and 2004."[81]

Because of Chernobyl and the long life of many radioactive elements (usually measured in "half-life" years) nuclear power continued to arouse concerns about other possible nuclear accidents, terrorism, or wars, as well as the disposal of nuclear wastes and weapons. And although the Chernobyl accident slowed the building of nuclear plants, it did not stop it, and debates about the use of nuclear energy continued into the twenty-first century.

Why Continuing Pollution?

Despite dire warnings about the dangers of global warming and other harm being done to our planet and ultimately to ourselves, and despite the growth of environmental movements in various parts of the world, the earth's people continued polluting on a vast scale. Why? One of the most valuable sections of J. R. McNeill's *Something New under the Sun: An Environmental History of the Twentieth-Century World* is his chapter "Ideas and Politics," which attempts to answer this question. The chapter suggests that the two biggest influences on environmental factors in the past century were (1) "the priority of economic growth," which McNeill labeled "easily the most important idea of the twentieth century," and (2) national security anxieties.[82]

Capitalist and communist countries alike used economic growth as an important test for success. Capitalist governments usually measured growth by increases in gross national product (GNP) or gross domestic product (GDP). Communist regimes placed great emphasis on increasing industrial production, usually by fulfilling the targets set out by Five Year Plans.

It was much more common in Soviet newspapers, as compared to Western capitalist ones, to see front-page articles devoted to stories about achieving economic-growth goals. Soviet newspapers and books frequently cited statistics, which were often unreliable. Soviet leader Nikita Khrushchev liked to predict that soon the USSR would produce more of some product or other than would the USA. For example, in 1957 he said that within several years Soviet meat and dairy production would surpass that of the USA; and in 1961, he said that by 1980 the USSR "will leave the United States far behind in industrial and agricultural output per head of the population." The slowing growth of Soviet production in the early 1960s helped lead to Khrushchev's removal from power in 1964, and an even slower growth rate in the late 1970s and early 1980s helped lead to Mikhail Gorbachev's attempts to try new methods to improve Soviet economic performance. In turn, the failure of these attempts helped lead to the collapse of the USSR itself in 1991, followed by a decade of poor economic performance in Russia.

Meanwhile, the other communist giant, China, was more successful in spurring economic growth in the 1980s and 1990s, and took great pride in the growth of its GDP. As the new century opened, it announced its goal of doubling its GDP by 2010—in May 2003, Russian leader Vladimir Putin announced a similar goal of doubling Russia's GDP within a decade.

The main problem with all this emphasis on economic growth and the increased consumption it often implied, at least from an environmental viewpoint, was that it tended to ignore environmental consequences. In regard to the USSR, a book on Soviet ecology insisted that "for the environment, the central planning system became Frankenstein's monster . . . The plan and its fulfillment became engines of destruction geared to consume, not to conserve, the natural wealth and human strength of the Soviet Union."[83] Capitalist systems were also unfavorable to the environment. In his 1992 book, *Earth in the Balance*, U.S. Senator Al Gore emphasized this point, writing that capitalism's "calculations often completely ignore the value of . . . fresh water, clean air, the beauty of the mountains, the rich diversity of life in the forest, just to name a few." He added that "for all practical purposes, GNP treats the rapid and reckless destruction of the environment as a good thing!" As one example of this he noted that the *Exxon Valdez* oil spill and its cleanup increased U.S. GNP. He faulted mainstream economists for ignoring the economic costs of poisoning water, polluting air, washing away topsoil, and destroying forests; and he urged them to follow the example of a small number of economists who were urging more environmentally conscious methods of calculating economic progress.[84]

The effect of national security anxieties on the environment was also readily apparent. These anxieties stimulated communist industrialization, wars, military spending, and the development of nuclear power, all of which had negative environmental consequences.

Compared to the priorities of economic growth and national security, most other considerations such as religious, moral, or even direct environmental concerns had less impact on environmental policies and actions. As McNeill stated, "Explicit, conscious environmental politics, while growing in impact after 1970, still operated in the shadow cast by conventional politics."[85]

Changing Mentalities——Time, Space, and the Impact of Technology

Up to this point, we have been dealing with twentieth-century changes to our *physical* environment, and in our next two chapters we shall be considering cultural changes, which are changes that affect the content of our *mental* environment. But a few words are appropriate here about how our mental world has changed in the twentieth century, not only in regard to content, but also as to the type and speed of images that pass through our minds.

In his novel *Immortality* (1990), Milan Kundera captured an important change in the twentieth-century mental environment when he wrote that "imagology is stronger than reality, which has anyway long ceased to be what it was for my grandmother, who lived in a Moravian village and still knew everything through her own experience: how bread is baked, how a house is built, how a pig is slaughtered and the meat smoked, what quilts are made of, what the priest and the schoolteacher think about the world; she met the whole village every day ... For contemporary man reality is a continent visited less and less often."[86]

By imagology Kundera means the pseudo reality created by image makers: "advertising agencies; political campaign managers; designers who devise the shape of everything from cars to gym equipment; fashion stylists; barbers; show-business stars dictating the norms of physical beauty that all branches of imagology obey."[87]

At the beginning of the century, when five-sixths of the global population still lived in rural areas, when many were still illiterate, and when few had seen a motion picture and people did not yet have radios or televisions, most of their experiences were similar to those of Kundera's Moravian grandmother or Chekhov's peasants mentioned earlier in this chapter. Most people back then were closer to nature and experienced life more directly.

Although the popular press and literature already offered some escape from reality, especially for literate urban residents, imagology was still in its infancy in this pre-Hollywood era. As the century advanced, first silent films and then "talkies" became increasingly popular, and the lines between manufactured images and reality became increasingly blurred, as in the mind of the Depression-era heroine of Woody Allen's *The Purple Rose of Cairo* (1985) who imagines her screen idol taking on a real existence in her life. The funeral in 1926 of silent-film heartthrob Rudolph Valentino indicated that some women had already merged reality and fantasy. Tens of thousands of them turned out for his funeral, some of them becoming hysterical and fainting, while others were injured in a mob scene at the funeral home where his body was laid out.

The historian Eric Hobsbawm has written that "from the 1960s on the images which accompanied human beings in the Western world—and increasingly in the urbanized Third World—from birth to death were those advertising or embodying consumption or dedicated to commercial mass entertainment."[88] By the 1970s the average person in the USA was watching about four hours of television per day. By 1981 in Mexico City the average elementary school child watched 1,460 hours of television a year while attending school for only 920 hours. By the mid-1990s, many of the 1 million ads the average U.S. person was exposed to by age 20 were television commercials. Some outdoor ads competed with nature, reminding one of Ogden Nash's poem:

> I think that I shall never see
> A billboard lovely as a tree.
> Perhaps, unless the billboards fall,
> I'll never see a tree at all.[89]

After the communists came to power in 1917 in Russia, they blurred the lines between reality and pseudo reality in different ways, mainly through state-sponsored propaganda. Both Lenin and Stalin had a keen realization of the power of films. Lenin declared in 1922 that "the cinema is the most important of all the arts," and Stalin personally approved new films before they were shown to the public and sometimes gave personal directions to film directors. But the communist attempt to create images and ideas in the minds of Soviet citizens made use of all media and education, not just films. A favorite propaganda slogan of the late 1930s, the years of greatest Soviet state terror, was "Life has become better, life has become merrier!"

After World War II, as communist governments came to power in eastern Europe, China, and elsewhere, Soviet propaganda techniques spread to other countries, including Kundera's Czechoslovakia. Some writers like him who lived under communist regimes acquired an attuned sensibility for the disconnection between propaganda and reality. But Kundera also came to appreciate the similarity of capitalist advertising to Soviet propaganda. ("Are you objecting that advertising and propaganda cannot be compared, because one serves commerce and the other ideology? You understand nothing.")[90]

Viktor Pelevin, a younger writer who grew up in the Soviet Union, shared a similar appreciation. In his early novel *Omon Ra* (1993), a cosmonaut in Brezhnev's Russia thinks that he has blasted off for the moon, but reality turns out differently thanks to Soviet fakery. In this and other works, Pelevin combined his metaphysical interests with a critical view of both the Soviet past and the post-Soviet present. He often satirized the new post-Soviet Russia bombarded by media, advertising, get-rich schemes, and crime, and he observed that "media . . . transfer an illusory reality created out of commercial and propagandist motives to the physical plane, displacing what really exists out of sight."[91]

By the end of the century, after the collapse of communist governments in Europe and the adoption of many capitalist methods in communist China, Western-style advertising was sweeping the globe. But government propaganda in China and other non-democratic states also continued. To a lesser extent, democratic governments also engaged in propaganda, attempting to influence public opinion through the media.

By 1999 some video and computer games, software programs, the Internet, expanded cable television (including MTV), and the means to watch media at times of our own choosing (VCRs, videos, DVDs, TiVo, etc.) had all helped increase exposure to simulated life. The increased presence in many people's lives of such pseudo or simulated reality seemed unhealthy to some. Perhaps, it reflected what the poet T. S. Eliot had observed already in 1943 in his poem *Burnt Norton*, "human kind cannot bear very much reality." In the mid-1980s an observer of American life wrote that "our politics, religion, news, athletics, education, and commerce have been transformed into congenial adjuncts of show business," and that Las Vegas had become "a metaphor of our national character and aspiration." He thought "we are a people on the verge of amusing ourselves to death."[92] In 2000, a philosopher defined virtual reality broadly to include not just computer simulations, but also other synthetic pseudo reality environments such as movies. And he added that "the present flight into virtual reality also distracts masses of people from more earthy realities and hence increases still further the component of unproductive fantasy in our society."[93]

The proliferation of media images was just one aspect of an increase in all types of data. The amount of information and entertainment available to someone in 1999 as compared to 1900 was mind boggling and changed people's mental environment in a major way. Words and phrases such as "information overload" and "multi-tasking" became common as a reflection of people's attempt to cope with data overload. In one sense people had more choices than ever before in regard to what information to access and what entertainment to enjoy. But as Eric Fromm, and before him Dostoevsky and others, had realized many choices can contribute to greater anxiety.

To cope with the increase in data and as a reflection of much else that technology produced in the twentieth century, people tried to do things faster. From the image of Charlie Chaplin coping with a sped-up assembly line in the film *Modern Times* to later phrases like "fast food" and "speed reading" humans were reminded of the emphasis modernity placed on doing things faster. As one cultural historian wrote and demonstrated by examining a wide spectrum of cultural works, "Modernity is about the acceleration of time."[94]

With more than ever available to do, more information than ever to access, more miles to travel to get to jobs, more money needed to buy expanding human wants, and more education required to keep up with accelerating technological changes, humans at the end of the twentieth century seemed "busier than ever." Surrounded by cell phones, televisions, laptop computers, and more people and urban noises than ever, it seemed harder for people in 1999 than 1900 to achieve any moments of quietness or oneness with nature. Minds seemed to be fuller of clutter and trivia, and to be more harried than ever.

One was reminded again of lines from Eliot's poem *Burnt Norton*, (1943), where he wrote of

> . . . strained time-ridden faces
> Distracted from distraction by distraction
> Filled with fancies and empty of meaning.

Just as people's perceptions of time changed so too did their sense of space. In 1903, it took 63 days to go from San Francisco to New York by automobile on the first coast-to-coast automobile trip. In 1969, U.S. astronauts went to the moon, 240,000 miles away, in only four days. Not only transportation, but communication developments such as satellite television shrunk distances. In 1900, many people in the world never traveled outside of the rural areas where they were born, or even saw images of distant places. By 1999, a much larger percentage of people traveled not only to different parts of their own country but also to foreign lands. On the other hand, as the century proceeded what people saw when they traveled abroad became more similar to what they saw at home. By 1999, for example, McDonald's franchises existed in over half of the world's countries, and billboards advertising Marlboro or other U.S. cigarettes appeared in cities around the world.

The very concepts of time and space became less distinct and more relative to each other. As Peter Conrad wrote toward the end of the twentieth century, "[Einstein's] relativity theory may have merged time with space, but it hardly cancelled them out; still we have gained a relative power over them, and learned new ways of manipulating them."[95]

7

Culture and Social Criticism

Many of the developments discussed in this book—violence, science and technology, capitalism and communism, imperialism, freedom, the environment—were intertwined with culture. In the broadest sense and in the way many anthropologists use the term, culture embraces the whole way of life of a group, including their physical and mental activities: thus, Chinese, French, or U.S. culture, or even more broadly Asian, Western, or African culture. Related to this definition are terms such as "youth culture" or "popular culture," both indicating an aspect or subculture of a larger culture. Subcultures can sometimes seem more significant than a larger culture. Being raised in a Jewish or Catholic subculture in the early twentieth century, for example, might have had a greater impact on a young person than being brought up in an English or U.S. culture.

The term culture has also often been used as a collective term for the arts, humanities, and higher knowledge generally. This is a more elitist definition, sometimes referred to as "high culture," and is related to what is meant by referring to someone as "a very cultured person." Usually the context in which the word is used makes clear whether the broader or more restrictive use is intended.

Cultural Criticism of Capitalist Society in the Early Twentieth Century

In England during the nineteenth century, the poet Matthew Arnold and others had thought of high culture as an alternative and corrective to the values and manners that the Industrial Revolution and *laissez-faire* capitalism had introduced into English society. Arnold thought of it as a process as well as a body of learning. In his *Culture and Anarchy* (1882) he wrote: "The whole scope of the essay [his book] is to recommend culture as the great help out of our present difficulties; culture being a pursuit of our total perfection by means of getting to know on all the matters which most concern us, the best which has been thought and said in the world."[1] The English thinker Raymond Williams later noted about British thought from 1780 to 1950 that "the development of the idea of culture has, throughout, been a criticism of what has been called the bourgeois idea of society."[2]

Many writers, philosophers, and artists in the twentieth century, and not only in Britain, continued to criticize the life that industrialism, capitalism, and bourgeois society had produced. They often feared the consequences of a Taylorized world too focused on efficiency (see Chapter 2 on Taylor's Scientific Management), and sometimes suggested, as Arnold had done, that culture offered a means to overcome at least some of the deficiencies of a bourgeois existence.

This criticism came from many angles and was intensified after the horrors and devastations of World War I. Some individuals like the writer D. H. Lawrence criticized their society for reducing beauty in the world. In 1929, remembering his own boyhood experience growing up in a mining village of about 3,000 people, he wrote:

> The real tragedy of England, as I see it, is the tragedy of ugliness. The country is so lovely: the man-made England is so vile . . .
>
> Now though perhaps nobody knew it, it was ugliness which betrayed the spirit of man, in the nineteenth century. The great crime which the moneyed classes and promoters of industry committed in the palmy Victorian days was the condemning of the workers to ugliness, ugliness, ugliness: meanness and formless and ugly surroundings, ugly ideals, ugly religion, ugly hope, ugly love, ugly clothes, ugly furniture, ugly houses, ugly relationship between workers and employers. The human soul needs actual beauty even more than bread . . .
>
> If the company, instead of building those sordid and hideous Squares, then, when they had that lovely site to play with, there on the hill top: if they had put a tall column in the middle of the small market-place, and run three parts of a circle of arcade round the pleasant space, where people could stroll or sit, and with the handsome houses behind! If they had made big, substantial houses, in apartments of five and six rooms, and with handsome entrances. If above all, they had encouraged song and dancing—for the miners still sang and danced—and provided handsome space for these. If only they had encouraged some form of beauty in dress, some form of beauty in interior life—furniture, decoration. If they had given prizes for the handsomest chair or table, the loveliest scarf, the most charming room that the men or women could make! If only they had done this, there would never have been an industrial problem. The industrial problem arises from the base forcing of all human energy into a competition of mere acquisition.[3]

In 1950 one of America's most prominent historians stated: "Who, in the half century from Cleveland to Franklin Roosevelt, celebrated business enterprise or the acquisitive society . . . ? Almost all the major writers were critical of those standards, or contemptuous of them . . . Most authors portrayed an economic system disorderly and ruthless, wasteful and inhuman, unjust alike to workingmen, investors, and consumers, politically corrupt and morally corrupting."[4]

These writers, especially the novelists, "exposed the inequities of business, romanticized labor, lamented the slums, and denounced corruption." The literature of the 1920s, reflected "aversion to Mammon, . . . distaste for the standards of the market place and the country club," and "hatred of vulgarity." Writings of the 1930s, after the Depression had struck, "pulsed with anger and pity—anger against an economy that wasted the resources, paralyzed the energies, and corrupted the spirits of the people, pity for the victims of that economy." Even in what remained of the first half century, even with victory in World War II, very few novelists revised "the judgment which had been passed on the acquisitive society . . . The novelists remained irreconcilable."[5]

At times, U.S. writers expressed anti-urban sentiments that were linked to their anti-bourgeois sentiments and, like D. H. Lawrence, criticized U.S. cities for their lack of concern with beauty. Sinclair Lewis grew up in Sauk Centre, Minnesota, and in his novel *Main Street* (1920) he based his fictional city of Gopher Prairie on it. His heroine walked down its main street, which resembled "ten thousand towns from Albany to San Diego." Lewis then added:

> In all the town not one building save the Ionic bank which gave pleasure to Carol's eyes; not a dozen buildings which suggested that, in the fifty years of Gopher Prairie's existence, the citizens had realized that it was either desirable or possible to make this, their common home, amusing or attractive.
>
> It was not only the unsparing unapologetic ugliness and the rigid straightness which overwhelmed her. It was the planlessness, the flimsy temporariness of the buildings, their faded unpleasant colors. The street was cluttered with electric-light poles, telephone poles, gasoline pumps for motor cars, boxes of goods. Each man had built with the most valiant disregard of all the others. Between a large new "block" of two-story brick shops on one side, and the fire-brick Overland garage on the other side, was a one-story cottage turned into a millinery shop. The white temple of the Farmers' Bank was elbowed back by a grocery of glaring yellow brick. One store-building had a patchy galvanized iron cornice; the building beside it was crowned with battlements and pyramids of brick capped with blocks of red sandstone.[6]

In Germany, "one characteristic that binds together numerous writers of various styles over the entire span of the years between

1871 and 1933 is an antibourgeois sentiment ... The widespread antibourgeois sentiment received heady intellectual sustenance from Nietzsche's attacks on the culture of the middle class and his call for a reevaluation of all values."[7]

Yet, whereas in England and the United States the social critics were attacking primarily their own dominant culture, in Germany and some other countries the criticism of bourgeois society was often connected with the criticism of foreign ways and influences. Before and during World War I, many Germans thought that Germany represented a true and superior *Kultur* (high culture) as opposed to the more bourgeois mentality of the British and French. The German economist and socialist Werner Sombart contrasted the nation of shopkeepers (the English) with that of heroes (the Germans) and told his fellow Germans: "Let us think of the inexhaustible wealth of Germanism which includes every real value that human culture can produce ... Germany is the last dike against the muddy flood of commercialism which threatens to cover all other people."[8] Even the great novelist Thomas Mann, who later regretted his wartime mentality, thought that Germany stood against "a rationalist, bourgeois, materialistic, superficial, optimistic civilization."[9]

Most German intellectuals during the era of the democratic Weimar Republic, which lasted until 1933 when Hitler brought it to an end, continued to criticize bourgeoisie society. Two examples were Oswald Spengler, whose *Decline of the West* (1918–22) was a best-seller (see Chapter 4), and the German philosopher Martin Heidegger. The latter supported the Nazis, but paradoxically also strongly influenced later thinkers of the left such as Jean Paul Sartre (see below) and Herbert Marcuse (see Chapter 5). The Bauhaus School of artists and architects begun by Walter Gropius was also critical of the bourgeoisie.[10]

Although Hitler received considerable support from German big business, his Nazi Party was officially the National Socialist German Workers' Party. The Nazi ideologue Alfred Baeumler wrote in 1937: "Nietzsche and National Socialism stand on the other side of the traditions of the German bourgeoisie ... When we call National Socialism a world view we mean that not only the bourgeois parties but also their ideologies have been annihilated."[11] Of course, Nietzsche, who died in 1900, also held many ideas that were contrary to the ideology later developed by Hitler, but the Nazis' contempt for many aspects of bourgeois society was certainly not new.

In Russia, many critics of Western bourgeois society also existed. After a trip to western Europe in 1862, Dostoevsky wrote a critical essay on the European bourgeoisie (as part of his *Winter Notes on*

Summer Impressions). Early in the twentieth century, Leo Tolstoy wrote of the Western bourgeoisie as "people who, being protected by violence, arrange for themselves easy and comfortable lives, free from hard work." He also denounced the "production of the most unnecessary, stupid, depraving products," among which he included automobiles and many other new consumer items.[12] In his later years, an increasingly moralistic Tolstoy criticized not only Western bourgeois society but also much of Western high culture.

Just as the Nazis *selectively* praised Nietzsche, so the Russian Marxists, including Lenin, *selectively* praised Tolstoy. Lenin admired his "unremitting accusations against capitalism" and "the calamities it inflicts on the masses"; but, of course, criticized Tolstoy's religious views and doctrine of non-violent resistance (for the latter, see Chapter 1).[13] Lenin was critical of the Western culture of his day partly because of the Marxist belief that culture was part of the "superstructure" of society and reflected the views of the dominant class under capitalism, the bourgeoisie. Although the new communist government that he headed attempted to control cultural life in Soviet Russia, some independent views, though not anti-communist ones, were still tolerated. Lenin's successor as Communist Party chief, Joseph Stalin, went much further in greatly tightening cultural controls. By the late 1930s, the Communist Party in the Soviet Union and the Nazi Party in Germany had become more successful in controlling cultural life for propaganda and other government-directed purposes than any regimes in history. And a major difference between the "bourgeois societies" that so many intellectuals had criticized and the two powerful dictatorships was that the former permitted criticism of itself and the latter did not.[14]

Outside of Russia, the Marxist who eventually exercised the most influence on cultural thinking was the Italian Antonio Gramsci (1891–1937). The editors of a collection of his writings on culture (from Harvard University Press) proclaimed that he was "the greatest Marxist writer on culture."[15] Much of his thought on culture was published in his *Prison Notebooks*, written while he was imprisoned under Mussolini, but not printed until after World War II. Although critical of bourgeois culture, Gramsci's approach to culture was more nuanced than that of Lenin or Stalin. He believed that the capitalists continued to dominate most Western societies not only by their economic strength, but also by a "cultural hegemony" that convinced many others in such societies to share bourgeois social, cultural, and moral values and even think of them as their own. To overthrow the capitalists, Gramsci believed that their hegemonic culture had to be challenged and overthrown by a new culture reflecting the broader interests of working-class people. Thus, unlike Lenin, Gramsci believed that a cultural revolution could *precede* an economic, social, and political revolution. His other ideas on culture are quite varied. He wrote of high culture and popular culture, and he realized that cultures are "always fluid and protean entities." He thought of himself, for example, as part of both an Italian culture and a proletarian culture.[16] In the latter part of the century, Gramsci's cultural ideas exercised considerable influence on postmodernist thought (see below, Chapter 8).

In other parts of the world, Marxist thinking also influenced various intellectuals' criticism of Western bourgeois existence, and among some Asian thinkers the criticisms of Western bourgeoisie life by Dostoevsky and Tolstoy were quite popular.[17] In Latin America, intellectuals often directed their criticism at North American culture. The Uruguayan José Enrique Rodó wrote in 1900 that "the North American has with his wealth achieved all the satisfaction and vanity that come with sumptuous magnificence—but good taste has eluded him. In such an atmosphere, true art can exist only in the form of individual rebellion." He also criticized rich North Americans who thought of art "as a trophy for their vanity." And he added, "If a word may some day characterize their taste in art, it will be a word that negates art itself: the grossness of affectation, the ignorance of all that is subtle and exquisite, the cult of false grandeur, the *sensationalism* that excludes the serenity that is irreconcilable with the pace of a feverish life." He also acknowledged North America's attempt to broaden education, but he then insisted that "the persistent North American war against ignorance has resulted in a universal *semi-culture*, accompanied by the diminution of high culture. To the same degree that basic ignorance has diminished in that gigantic democracy, wisdom and genius have correspondingly disappeared. This, then, is the reason that the trajectory of their intellectual activity is one of decreasing brilliance and originality ... The bourgeois leveling process, ever-swifter in its devastation, is tending to erase what little character remains of their precarious intellectualism."[18]

Popular, Mass, Consumer, and High Cultures in the Early Twentieth Century

The Masses and Popular Culture

In the late nineteenth century Nietzsche wrote contemptuously not only of bourgeois culture but also of democracy and the masses or herd. In the United States, one of Nietzsche's most ardent followers, H. L. Mencken, who was very popular in the 1920s, wrote critically of the mob or the "boobs." In 1930, in *The Revolt of the Masses*, the Spaniard José Ortega y Gasset wrote of the "radical defects" of the European culture of his day, defects he believed that stemmed from the fact that "the mass crushes beneath it everything that is different, everything that is excellent, individual, qualified, and select. Anybody who is not like everybody, who does not think like everybody, runs the risk of being eliminated." "We are living," he added "under the brutal empire of the masses." The result he believed was that "Europe has been left without a moral code." The problem, as he saw it, was not just in democratic governments, but also in non-democratic governments such as Soviet Russia and Fascist Italy. He blamed the "revolt of the masses" on several factors. One was their tremendous increase in number since the early nineteenth century. Other causes included the crumbling of social restraints, the rise of the specialist—"he is not learned, for he is formally ignorant of all that does not enter into his speciality"—and the self-satisfaction of the masses, their refusal to learn from those more cultured than they or from history.[19] For some other writers, however, the term "masses" was a more positive one. In the United States, two leftist magazines, *The Masses* (1911–17) and *The New Masses* (1926–48) used the term proudly.

Related to the "masses" is "mass culture," a term increasingly used in the second half of the twentieth century (see below). Because of greater government controls over media in Nazi Germany and Stalinist Russia, the use of the term might be more appropriate in these countries at an earlier date than in the capitalist West. And indeed one collection of popular cultural selections dealing with Russia from 1917 to 1953 is entitled *Mass Culture in Soviet Russia*.[20] Prior to mass culture, however, popular culture had long existed.

During the interwar years it was vibrant in the more advanced industrialized countries, partly because of increased leisure time. It was not so much concerned with what Arnold called "the best which has been thought and said in the world," but more transitory amusements. As they had done before 1914, people continued to visit one another; to talk; play music, sports, and games of chance; sing and dance; and go to films, sporting events, amusement parks, fairs, circuses, vaudeville shows, concert halls, and drinking establishments. But the development of the radio and the tremendous increase of popular reading materials, films, and automobiles helped change some of the characteristics of interwar popular culture, especially in the more technologically advanced countries. (See Chapter 2 for statistics on radios, automobiles, and movie theaters.)

In Britain during the interwar years national daily newspapers sales went from a combined 3 million copies to over 10 million per day. By the mid-1930s, an average of one morning paper per family was being sold. In the United States, magazines appealing to sexual and romantic interests, but with a careful eye on censorship, became very popular, as did movie magazines.

Although more than half of U.S. homes had radios by 1930, the percentage was not nearly as high in other industrialized countries such as Great Britain and Germany. Yet the number in each of the latter countries still reached into the millions. In Britain, as opposed to the United States, broadcasting was controlled by the late 1920s not by commercial interests but by a public corporation, the British Broadcasting Corporation (BBC). Unlike U.S. broadcasting, the BBC banned advertising. Largely because of the BBC, British radio offerings were also at a higher cultural level than those on U.S. radios. One was more likely to hear a classical concert or a play on British radio. Although symphony orchestras were also broadcast on U.S. radio, and boat races, cricket matches, and comedians were aired on British radio, sporting events and popular entertainment were much more common on U.S. radios. During and after World War II, the BBC introduced more light programing, which became very popular. The war increased the radio's popularity generally. Listening doubled to the BBC's plays and classical music, and Prime Minister Churchill's talks were enormously popular—other leaders such as Roosevelt, Hitler, and Brazil's Vargas also used the radio effectively both before and during the war.[21]

Well before that war the radio had also helped to increase the popularity of non-classical music. It helped, for example, spread the popularity of the samba from the shantytowns of Rio de Janeiro to it being eventually embraced and promoted by the Vargas government as Brazil's unique contribution to world music. Brazilian radio and film samba singer and dancer Carmen Miranda became in the 1940s one of Hollywood's highest-paid actresses.[22] The radio also helped spread the global popularity of U.S. jazz, but both the Nazis and Stalinist Russia criticized it as degenerate.[23] During World War II, after Soviet Russia and the United States became allies, Stalin relented somewhat and wartime enthusiasm for jazz was so great that Soviet pilots, cooks, and even the NKVD (secret police agency) formed jazz groups of their own. After the war, however, during the early Cold War, the government again turned against jazz and Western-influenced popular music. In 1949, the government declared jazz as a means of spreading U.S. imperialism, and banned the saxophone.

With the aid of newspapers and radios, sports in the United States began the ascent to the mass popularity that they achieved throughout the rest of the century. Large sections of U.S. newspapers were devoted to sports and some of the largest incomes in the country were eventually earned by sports stars. One analysis of the amount of newspaper space devoted to sports in Muncie, Indiana indicated that already in 1923 such coverage was taking up 13.2 percent of the papers (still small as compared to many papers by 1999) as compared to only 3.8 percent in 1890. Although interwar sports salaries were still small as compared to the millions earned each year by top professional players in the 1990s, they were still large for the time. In the late 1920s, boxer Gene Tunney received $1.74 million for three years of boxing, and in 1931 homerun-hitting slugger Babe Ruth earned more than the U.S. president. Tunney's bout with Jack Dempsey in 1927 was watched by 145,000 people and listened to by many more in their homes. And the results of such big fights were announced in big front-page newspaper headlines, even in the *New York Times*.

Films also became increasingly popular during the 1920s and continued to increase in popularity until television began offering increasing competition in the late 1940s and 1950s. U.S. films were especially popular. In the 1920s, they provided 95 percent of all films shown in Britain. Although U.S. films continued to dominate the British market throughout the first half of the century, British directors such as Alfred Hitchcock, David Lean, and Carol Reed did produce quality films. Even in Soviet Russia in 1924, U.S. films made up 57 percent of the total films shown.

Despite the presence of great European directors such as Fritz Lang in Germany and Sergei Eisenstein in Russia, U.S. films featuring Charlie Chaplin, Mary Pickford, and Douglas Fairbanks were often more popular in those countries. Sometimes a director such as Chaplin produced high-quality films that bridged the gap between popular and high culture. Both Soviet Russia and Nazi Germany, however, realized the importance of film for propagandist purposes—already in 1922, Lenin had stated that "the cinema is the most important of the arts."

After Stalin came to power in the late 1920s, and the Nazis in 1933, the percentage of U.S. films declined in both countries. When U.S. films such as John Ford's 1940 classic *Stagecoach* (retitled *The Journey Will Be Dangerous*) were shown in the USSR, government propaganda often attempted to present them in a way different than intended by their director. *Stagecoach*, for example, was depicted as a frontier battle of native Indians against white imperialists.

Stalin took a great interest in films, insisted on personally approving them before they were shown to Soviet audiences, and sometimes gave personal direction to directors. After Joseph Goebbels was appointed Nazi propaganda minister, he gathered prominent German filmmakers, told them the type of films he expected, and insisted that movie theaters show government-sponsored newsreels.

Outside of the United States and Europe, thriving film industries also existed in such cities as Tokyo, Shanghai, and Cairo. Latin American countries, especially Argentina, Brazil, and Chile, also produced their own films. In the interwar period, however, U.S. films dominated these latter markets and exercised considerable influence. On one occasion some Argentine businessmen complained that the U.S. film *It Happened One Night* (1934) was hurting their men's clothing businesses because in the film Clark Gable, by taking off his shirt, revealed that he wore no undershirt, influencing young Argentines to stop buying undershirts. The attire of Hollywood actors also influenced people in other parts of the world. In his autobiography, Nelson Mandela recounted how South African gangsters in the 1940s emulated "the well-tailored gangsters in American movies." [24]

The increase of automobiles, trucks, and airplanes changed popular culture by opening up new opportunities to go to more places. It also facilitated the delivery of various media to wider areas. Young people were able to use autos to avoid parental supervision, and one U.S. Midwestern judge complained of all the sex occurring in them.

At the beginning of their social history of Great Britain in these years, *The Long Week-End*, Robert Graves and Alan Hodge noted that news read in the newspapers and heard on the radio was soon forgotten. Another writer dealing with the United States, stated that one of the notable characteristics of the mid and late 1920s "was the unparalleled rapidity and unanimity with which millions of men and women turned their attention, their talk, and their emotional interest upon a series of tremendous trifles—a heavyweight boxing match, a murder trial, a new automobile model, a transatlantic flight."[25] The most celebrated such flight was that of Charles Lindbergh, who in 1927 became the first person to fly solo nonstop across the Atlantic, from New York to Paris. His tumultuous welcome back to the United States was unprecedented.

Radio, newspapers, films, and magazines also fueled public interest in other events and personalities from crime and criminals such as Chicago's Al Capone to the Scopes "Monkey Trial" of 1925. The latter featured a Tennessee biology teacher charged with teaching Darwinian evolution, his famous attorney Clarence Darrow, and

former Secretary of State William Jennings Bryan. When movie actor
Rudolph Valentino died in the late 1920s, crowds stretched out for
11 blocks to view his body. The modern-day fascination with
celebrities, celebrityitis one might call it, was already evident.

Consumer Culture

Increasingly related to popular culture was what some have labeled
"consumer culture." As William Leach has written:

> From the 1890s on, American corporate business, in league with key
> institutions, began the transformation of American society into a society
> preoccupied with consumption, with comfort and bodily well-being, with
> luxury, spending, and acquisition, with more goods this year than last, more
> next year than this. American consumer capitalism produced a culture almost
> violently hostile to the past and to tradition, a future-oriented culture of
> desire that confused the good life with goods. It was a culture that first
> appeared as an alternative culture ... and then unfolded to become the
> reigning culture in the United States.[26]

Already in 1902, philosopher William James wrote of "the worship of
material luxury and wealth, which constitutes so large a portion of the
'spirit' of our age."[27] In the mid-1920s the leading paper in Muncie
Indiana stated: "The American citizen's first importance to his country
is no longer that of a citizen but that of a consumer. Consumption is a
new necessity." "The way to make business boom is to buy."[28]

This early U.S. consumer culture was promoted not only by
capitalists and other business people, but also by educators (including
some prominent economics professors), museums, governmental
bodies, labor unions, and even by many religious leaders. Before
the 1890s, U.S. educational institutions paid almost no attention to
business subjects such as marketing, fashion, commercial art,
investment banking, or the credit system. But by 1920 more than 100
higher education institutions were teaching such subjects, including
Harvard's famed School of Business. Various U.S. government bodies,
from the municipal to the federal level, also assisted the development
of a consumer culture. Lobbied by such companies as the large mail-
order firms of Sears, Roebuck and Co. and Montgomery Ward, the
Federal Government assumed responsibility through the Postal
Service for rural-free and parcel-post deliveries, greatly facilitating the
mailing out of numerous consumer items throughout the country.
Even Big Bill Haywood, the radical leader of the Industrial Workers of
the World (IWW or "Wobblies"), despite his anti-capitalist feelings,
stressed the necessity of increased consumption for the workers.

The listing of many U.S. religious leaders as supporters of a consumer culture might at first seem surprising. For do not all of the great religions teach that happiness comes not from material possessions but from inner spiritual qualities? And indeed a few prominent U.S. religious figures such as the Baptist theologian Walter Rauschenbusch (1861–1918), one of the leaders of the Social Gospel Movement, and the Catholic theologian John Ryan were critical of the developing consumer culture. But many Protestant, Catholic, and Jewish leaders, as well as their followers, had no problem squaring their religious beliefs with the growing consumerism. In the 1920s Metropolitan Insurance put out a pamphlet, *Moses Persuader of Men*, extolling Moses as "one of the greatest salesmen and real-estate promoters that ever lived." Bruce Barton in *The Man Nobody Knows* stated that Jesus was a great business executive, "the founder of modern business," and that his parables were "the most powerful advertisements of all time."[29] In 1925–6 this book topped the non-fiction best-seller list (see Chapter 3 for more on Barton). The global depression of the 1930s, followed by World War II, slowed the growth of consumer culture, but by the 1950s it had begun again to accelerate rapidly, at first in the United States, then in western Europe, and eventually to other parts of the world.

High Culture

In the philosophy of Nietzsche, who died as the new century was beginning, we see many of the themes that influenced other thinkers, writers, and artists during the twentieth century. His ideas reflected not only his contempt for bourgeois society and "the herd," but also for much of Western culture. He believed that "God is dead," that Christianity was a curse enslaving the strong, and that those capable of it should go "beyond good and evil" and become new "supermen."

Some of his ideas dovetailed with those of another powerful nineteenth-century thinker, Charles Darwin (1809–82). Like Nietzsche's ideas, Darwin's belief in evolution that occurred through natural selection and led to the survival of the "fittest" seemed to challenge traditional religious beliefs and look favorably upon the "fittest" or strong. A third important nineteenth-century intellectual force on twentieth-century culture was the thinking of Karl Marx (1818–83). Like the ideas of Nietzsche and Darwin, those of Marx challenged traditional religious beliefs. Although more politically revolutionary than Darwin, he claimed that his socialist ideas were also "scientific."

Two other men of science, both born in the nineteenth century but doing their most important work in the early twentieth century, were Sigmund Freud and Albert Einstein. Freud believed that people were driven by unconscious desires such as sexuality, but that these desires often conflicted with social codes, leading to inner conflicts. To probe the unconscious mind, Freud used such methods as indicated by the title of his turn-of-the-century book, *The Interpretation of Dreams*. Einstein's Theory of Relativity challenged the earlier belief that the universe was three-dimensional. He thought that time was a fourth dimension and that it was not absolute but relative, interrelated to space. This meant that the time a phenomenon took to occur could actually be different if viewed from different locations.

Thus, even before World War I older beliefs regarding religion, science, rationality, and society were under siege. The French philosopher Henri Bergson downplayed rationality and emphasized intuition. Writers and artists such as symbolist poets in France and Russia, the painters Paul Cézanne, Vincent van Gogh, Paul Gauguin, Henri Matisse, Pablo Picasso, and Vasili Kandinsky, and the composers Arnold Schoenberg, Igor Stravinsky, and Alexander Scriabin attempted to depict higher truths or greater beauty than were rendered by their predecessors who had used older modes of artistic expression more dependent upon traditional religious, scientific, or social views. A revolt against a supposedly objective, rational, industrialized view of life, which standardized and demystified it, was evident and helped stimulate the type of criticism of bourgeois and industrial life typified by D. H. Lawrence and others.

In their search for alternate approaches to life many of the thinkers, writers, and artists of the period discovered or rediscovered other cultures, either in the past or in non-Western parts of the world. The U.S. historian Henry Adams wrote appreciatively of medieval cathedrals and the spirit they reflected. In England writers like John Ruskin, William Morris, Hilaire Belloc, and G. K. Chesterton contrasted various positive aspects of medieval life with the industrialized Western civilization of their day—Romantic writers of the early nineteenth century had been moved by a similar spirit to romanticize the medieval and primitive.

Outside of Europe, some intellectuals' criticisms of modern Western industrialization and standardization merged with romanticizing their own society's pre-colonial past (see Chapter 4's section on "Westernization and Its Opponents"). And thinkers such as Tagore in India and Rodó in Uruguay contrasted favorably their own culture's spirituality with the West's—or more specifically in Rodó's case, the USA's—emphasis on materialism. [30]

The new field of anthropology, pioneered by the Englishman Sir James Frazer and the German-American Franz Boas, broadened appreciation for other cultures and helped overcome the belief that outside of the Western world others had nothing to offer the "civilized" world. Frazer's *The Golden Bough* (1890) and Boas's *The Mind of Primitive Man* (1910) influenced many thinkers, writers, and artists and helped foster the popularity of primitivism.

By the beginning of World War I, psychoanalysts Freud and Carl Jung, artists such as Gauguin (who went to Tahiti in 1891), Matisse, Van Gogh, and Picasso, and composers such as Stravinsky and Claude Debussy reflected the influence of other cultures in their works. Many of the painters were influenced by the discovery of Japanese prints or African art. In 1912, the famous Irish poet William Butler Yeats drew attention to the poetic writings of the Indian poet and philosopher Rabindranath Tagore, who the following year would become the first non-European writer to win the Nobel Prize for Literature. In 1914, the German Expressionist painter Emil Nolde, some of whose paintings had already reflected the influence of other cultures, visited the South Pacific and contrasted primitive people, "the only real human beings left," with Europeans who seemed "malformed puppets, artificial and full of conceit."[31] In pre-war Spain, the Nicaraguan poet Rubén Darío (1867–1916) strongly influenced Spanish poetry. The Spanish poet Federico Lorca later stated about him that "as a Spanish [language] poet, he was a teacher in Spain to the older masters as well as to the children."[32]

Just as European cultures were influenced by other cultures, so too were non-European ways influenced by Europe's cultural practices. Although not an ideal way of increasing cross-cultural contacts, imperialism did facilitate these mutual influences. The Russian Empire, containing both European and Asian territories, contributed and radiated its own unique cultural mixing.

World War I accentuated the pre-war tendency of finding fault with Western civilization and culture. Spengler's *Decline of the West* has already been mentioned. The post-war paintings of the Germans George Grosz and Otto Dix depicted smug capitalists and wounded veterans with prosthesis. Grosz was associated for a while with a group called the Dadaists. They sprang up in Zurich, Switzerland during the war, and were especially indicative of the disillusionment with the Western tradition that they thought had helped produce "the slaughterhouses of the world war."[33] After the war, Paris and Berlin became Dadaist centers, where poets and artists of the movement demonstrated their contempt for traditional culture by acts and works that seemed nonsensical to many, but to the Dadaists themselves merely reflected the senselessness of life.

During the 1920s French poets began another cultural movement, Surrealism, later joined by some European artists and filmmakers. They were influenced by Freud and the Dadaists, and like the latter they enjoyed shocking the public. One of their originators, André Breton, had worked in a French wartime psychiatric center. Reflecting the post-Einstein world, Breton declared in 1921 that "the belief in an absolute time and space seems about to vanish."[34] The Surrealists believed that our unconscious minds, the world of our fantasies, dreams, and nightmares, gave us access to higher, more significant truths than did any rational, logical approach to reality. They thought that technology and the bourgeoisie had disenchanted the world, turning much of it into commodities and soulless objects. They wished through their works to reawaken people to a sense of the world's awe, mystery, and enchantment. Their most famous painter was the Spaniard Salvador Dali, and a leading filmmaker was his fellow Spaniard Luis Buñuel.

The most celebrated poet of the interwar years was the American-born T. S. Eliot, who lived in England after 1914. His most famous poem, *The Waste Land* (1922), reflected well the pessimism of the 1920s. Another work of that same year was the novel *Ulysses* (1922) by the Irishman James Joyce—a novel banned in the United States and Great Britain for decades for being obscene, but eventually recognized as one of the great novels of the twentieth century. Joyce made ample use of a stream-of-consciousness technique reflecting the subconscious life of his characters. Other writers of the 1920s such as the Frenchman Marcel Proust and the Englishwoman Virginia Woolf also used this technique which, as with Surrealism, reflected an increased awareness of the mental life described by Freud, Jung, and other psychoanalysts.

Although named after Homer's ancient Greek epic hero, Joyce's Ulysses (his character Leopold Bloom) is not heroic in the sense of Homer's protagonist. Like the novelist Ernest Hemingway, who has one of his disillusioned characters in *A Farewell to Arms* (1929) say that "abstract words such as glory, honor, courage or hallow were obscene," Joyce and many other writers believed that the age of old-fashioned heroes was past. They thought that too many young men had been sacrificed in World War I for noble-sounding abstractions. Instead, Joyce's Ulysses is an outwardly ordinary man living an ordinary day in 1904 Dublin. But he does enjoy life—food, drink, friendship, love, sex, and other pleasures.

Works like *The Wasteland* and *Ulysses* were complex and difficult to read. Eliot even furnished references and notes to help clarify his

great poem. In fact, much of the literature, music, and art of the
century's first three decades was perplexing to the average person,
who had a difficult time understanding paintings that were not as
representational as photographs, music that was as atonal as
some of Arnold Schoenberg's or as dissonant as Igor Stravinsky's, or
literature with as many references and complex language as *The
Wasteland* and *Ulysses*—Joyce's later novel *Finnegan's Wake* was even
more difficult to understand than was *Ulysses*.

The works of one of the leading philosophers of the century,
Ludwig Wittgenstein, were also difficult to understand. Born in
Austria, but later teaching at England's Cambridge University, his
major work *Tracatus Logico-Philosophicus* appeared in 1921. In it he
insisted on the limited ability of language to reflect reality and
maintained that words could not say anything meaningful about art,
metaphysics, or values. Like many post-war writers, artists, and
thinkers, he believed the world was in a period of decline. Already
before World War II, his analytic philosophy dominated the teaching
of philosophy in Great Britain; after the war it soon did likewise in
the USA and maintained that dominant position in both countries for
decades to come.

Following the onset of the Great Depression and coming to power
of Hitler in 1933, writers and artists in the West dealt more with
concrete economic, social, and political issues. Works such as George
Orwell's *Down and Out in Paris and London* (1933) and John Steinbeck's
The Grapes of Wrath (1939) reflected sympathy for the victims of
economic hard times. Chaplin's films such as *Modern Times* (1936) and
The Great Dictator (1940) satirized economic and political conditions
such as dehumanizing factory mechanization and the Hitlerite order.
The Depression also led some writers and artists to despair more than
ever of capitalism and place greater hopes in Marxism.

By the mid-1930s writers and artists sympathetic to Marxist views
included a number of significant personalities. Among them were the
German dramatist Bertold Brecht, the British poets W. H. Auden and
Stephen Spender, the U.S. novelist Richard Wright, the Chilean poet
Pablo Neruda, and the Mexican artist Diego Rivera. When civil war
broke out in Spain in 1936, writers and artists overwhelmingly
supported the leftist coalition fighting against the rightist forces of
General Franco. Many Western writers such as the Englishmen George
Orwell, the Frenchman André Malraux, and the American Ernest
Hemingway went to Spain to aid the anti-Franco forces. The Spaniard
Pablo Picasso painted *Guernica*, one of the greatest paintings of the
century, capturing the horror of the pro-Franco German bombing of
the market town and Basque religious center of Guernica.

In the Soviet Union during the 1920s many writers criticized Western capitalism. But at least several novelists also expressed fears about the fate of the individual, imagination, and spontaneity in any state (Western or Soviet) that placed a premium on science, technology, order, and efficiency. One example was Evgeni Zamiatin's *We* (first published abroad in 1924). It is an anti-utopian novel along the lines of *Brave New World* (Aldous Huxley's 1932 novel) and *1984* (George Orwell's 1949 novel). All three anti-utopian novels portray a future where scientific-technological developments and mechanization facilitate elite control over people whose freedoms have been reduced. *We*'s main character is D-503, who ultimately is forced to undergo an operation eliminating his imagination. Another Soviet writer, Boris Pilniak, in works such as *The Naked Year* and *Machines and Wolves*, suggested the superiority of spontaneous (and primitive) ways versus the rationalistic-technological approach of the new communist elite.

An appreciation of the primitive and spontaneous, as opposed to Western industrialism and capitalism, also continued to appeal to many Western thinkers, writers, and artists. The anthropologists Margaret Mead and Ruth Benedict, both students of Boas, continued in works such as *Coming of Age in Samoa* (1928) and *Patterns of Culture* (1935) to depict other cultures, though not without their own imperfections, from which Westerners could learn valuable lessons. One of the writers who believed this was so was the German Herman Hesse, who had been influenced by Freud and Jung, and even psychoanalyzed by the latter. In 1922, the same year as the publication of *The Waste Land* and Joyce's *Ulysses*, Hesse's *Siddhartha* was published. It was a retelling of the story of the young Gautama Buddha, the founder of Buddhism, with Hesse's hero discovering that happiness lies not in restless seeking, more typical of Western cultures than Eastern ones, but in achieving oneness with nature. In his novel *Steppenwolf,* Hesse has his protagonist criticize both capitalism and communism for reducing man to a "machine-made article."

An appreciation of non-Western cultures, especially that of Africa, also led some Europeans to praise American black culture. And indeed the Harlem Renaissance of the 1920s produced works by a diverse group of black writers, artists, social and political thinkers, musicians (especially of jazz), and actors. Among the major talents were the writers Langston Hughes, Claude McKay, Jean Toomer, and Countee Cullen, the political thinker Marcus Garvey, sociologist Charles Johnson, and the multi-talented actor-singer Paul Robeson. Some of these talents such as McKay and Garvey had come from Caribbean islands, but most of them had been born in the United States. In Paris, the American black dancer Josephine Baker performed her erotic "dance sauvage," and many European intellectuals thought that such dancing and black music generally (especially jazz) indicated that Americans blacks, like their African ancestors, were closer to the primitive, spontaneous roots of human nature than were Western whites who had become too dehumanized by the Western industrial order. European composers such as Debussy, Ravel, Stravinsky, and Milhaud incorporated jazz elements into their music.

Like Josephine Baker, many others from the Harlem Renaissance visited and sometimes lived in foreign lands. McKay was attracted to Russian communism for a while and traveled to Russia. Langston Hughes visited African countries and, like F. Scott Fitzgerald, Ernest Hemingway, and many other American writers, spent some time in Paris, as well as in other parts of Europe.

Interwar writers, artists, and composers in general moved around a great deal. Writers from other non-European countries also spent time in Europe. One was the African poet and future president of Senegal, Léopold Senghor, who lived in France during the 1930s and became a French citizen. Although strongly influenced by Western culture, Senghor was also influenced by Claude McKay and other Caribbean writers and helped to develop the idea of negritude, which he defined as "the sum total of the values of the African world." Senghor believed that African writers like him should not just mirror Western influences, but also reflect the "Africanness" of their native land and people. Another poet who spent part of his interwar years in Europe was the Chilean Pablo Neruda. Although European ideas exerted considerable influence on him, he believed, like Senghor, that a poet should reflect the culture of his native land. For Neruda this meant paying special attention to the Indian background of Chile. Two Caribbean writers who resided in interwar France and were influenced by surrealism were the West Indian Aimé Césaire and the Cuban Alejo Carpentier. Césaire, a friend of Senghor, co-developed the concept of negritude, wrote poems and plays that reflected that principle, and protested against colonialism. Eventually one of Cuba's most gifted prose writers, Carpentier later helped to develop the unique Latin American literary style referred to as "magic realism" (see below). Although their European experiences helped a small number of writers from poorer parts of the world, European imperialism in general harmed and disrupted native cultures.[35]

The communist revolution in Russia led many intellectuals to leave their homeland and settle in the West. Among the most prominent to leave, either temporarily or permanently, were the composer Stravinsky, the writers Vladimir Nabokov, Maxim Gorky, and Ivan Bunin, and the painters Kandinsky and Marc Chagall.

Nazi rule beginning in 1933 led to an even greater exodus of cultural figures, especially Jews, from Germany and later from Austria and other parts of Nazi-occupied Europe. Most of the Germans and Austrians made their way to the United States, but Paris, London, and Amsterdam also had communities of such *émigrés*. From the beginning of 1933 until the end of 1941, 7,622 academics and "another 1,500 artists, journalists specialising in cultural affairs, or other intellectuals" arrived in America.[36] One historian stated that "the migration to the United States of European intellectuals fleeing fascist [primarily Nazi] tyranny has finally become visible as the most important cultural event—or series of events—of the second quarter of the twentieth century."[37] Besides Albert Einstein, a few of the others who came to the United States in these years included composer Arnold Schoenberg, novelist Thomas Mann, playwright Bertold Brecht, and architect Walter Gropius.

Evaluations of Early Twentieth-Century Culture

In 1948, T. S. Eliot wrote: "We can assert with some confidence that our own period is one of decline; that the standards of culture are lower than they were fifty years ago; and that the evidences of this decline are visible in every department of human activity." Earlier, in 1939, he had written about "the steady influence which operates silently in any mass society organized for profit, for the depression of standards of art and culture. The increasing organization of advertisement and propaganda . . . is all against them. The economic system is against them."[38] In 1940 the English novelist E. M. Forster added another pessimistic note. After defining culture as "the various beautiful and interesting objects which men have made in the past, and handed down to us, and which some of us are hoping to hand on," he complained that the love of the beautiful was being replaced by radio broadcasting, the cinema, and crooners. He lamented the "hostility to cultural stuff" he discerned around him. If people were giving up appreciating Dante, for example, he believed "it is a sign that they are throwing culture overboard." "Cultivated people are a drop of ink in the ocean," he added.[39]

Opposing these pessimistic views was the more upbeat assessment of Frederick Lewis Allen. In his *The Big Change* (1952), a popular history of U.S. life in the first half of the century, he quoted some of Eliot's critical words cited above, and also commented on Eliot's lack of sympathy for the type of mass society coming into existence in the United States. Allen, on the other hand, believed that critics such as Eliot failed to give sufficient credit to the USA for raising the prosperity and cultural level of a higher percentage of the population than had any previous society. He believed it unfair to compare the cultural level of these people with a much smaller percentage of people in other countries who had traditionally supported high culture. Although admitting to some cultural failings—for example, "roadtown eyesores (garages, tourist courts, filling stations, billboards, second-hand auto salesrooms, junk dealers, and more billboards)," he cited U.S. figures indicating an increasing appreciation of high culture. Among such figures, he mentioned the large number of sales of books like George Orwell's *1984*, Norman Mailer's *The Naked and the Dead*, Tennessee Williams' play *A Streetcar Named Desire*, and a translation of Homer's *Odyssey*; the increasing number of art museums and sales of art supplies; and, most notably, the proliferation of symphony orchestras, music festivals, and classical record sales. Finally, Allen believed that part of the blame for the failure of even more people to appreciate high culture was the failure of writers and artists like Eliot and Joyce to make themselves intelligible to a wider audience, rather than viewing "difficulty itself . . . [as] a primary virtue."[40]

Culture and Criticism in the Late Twentieth Century

In 1963 anthropologist Jules Henry's *Culture Against Man* appeared. Henry had been a student of Franz Boas and Ruth Benedict, and his focus was on the U.S. culture of his day. He believed it was "a culture increasingly feeling the effects of almost 150 years of lopsided preoccupation with amassing wealth and raising its standard of living." One of the main contrasts he perceived between U.S. culture and primitive cultures was "between primitive culture's assumption of a fixed bundle of wants and our culture's assumption of infinite wants."[41] He believed that the two main "commandments" of U.S. culture were "Create more Desire" and "Thou Shalt Consume," and that these two commandments contributed to planned obsolescence, instability, "technological drivenness," and to making any religious or moral restraint on wants outmoded. These effects, in turn, led to others including massive job dissatisfaction. As might be expected, given these conclusions, Henry included material on advertising—a 55 page chapter entitled "Advertising as a Philosophical System."

One of his conclusions was that advertising is generally so blatantly contrary to truth that "people must learn to be fuzzy-minded and impulsive" or they would not spend as the system requires."[42] (See above, Chapter 3, for more on consumption, advertising, and marketing.) Although primarily concerned with U.S. culture, Henry recognized that much of what he stated also applied to other contemporary non-communist industrial countries.

Although Henry saw the U.S. economic system as the main determinant of U.S. culture, he also acknowledged other influences on it, most noticeably fear of the Soviet Union—he completed his work only months after the Cold War had led to the construction of the Berlin Wall in 1961.

Henry's further examination of American culture focused mainly on families and especially on the children within them. In his summation of U.S. schoolrooms, he stated, "education became the instrument for narrowing the perceptual sphere . . . of learning to be stupid; of learning to alienate one's Self from inner promptings."[43] A chapter on U.S. society's treatment of sick and frail people at the other end of the age spectrum, "Human Obsolescence," is no more cheerful. In general, he concluded that in his society, old people were less likely to be valued than in primitive cultures.

At the end of the 1970s, after the "youth revolts" of the 1960s (see Chapter 5) had petered out and elements of them had been co-opted by the dominant consumer culture, historian Christopher Lasch followed up with another study of American life, *The Culture of Narcissism*. He believed that in the face of defeat in Vietnam, stagflation, the depletion of natural resources, a lack of confidence in political leaders, and malaise in political and historical thinking (and in the humanities generally), the United States, as well as other capitalist countries, was undergoing a "crisis of confidence." And he added that "bourgeois society seems everywhere to have used up its store of constructive ideas." Instead, he thought, a "culture of narcissism," "the final product of bourgeois individualism" had arisen, stressing such goals as self-awareness. This new culture, he believed, meshed with an expanding culture of mass consumption in which advertising goaded "the masses into an unappeasable appetite not only for goods but for new experiences and personal fulfillment."[44]

But Lasch's pessimism did not resonate with most of his fellow citizens, at least not after the perpetually optimistic Ronald Reagan became U.S. president for most of the 1980s. And the collapse of communist regimes in eastern Europe, followed by the collapse of the Soviet Union in 1991, and then the booming U.S. stock market in the 1990s, fueled a U.S. triumphalism for the remainder of the century. Some U.S. thinkers such as Francis Fukuyama and Michael Mandelbaum believed that U.S.-like economic and political institutions would increasingly spread around the world.

Mass and Consumer Cultures

During the 1950s, the term "mass culture" became increasingly popular. In 1957 an anthology containing about 50 selections appeared entitled *Mass Culture: The Popular Arts in America*. In his *Culture and Society, 1780-1950*, the English thinker Raymond Williams also discussed the phenomenon. Although Williams, the U.S. sociologist Daniel Bell, and some of the contributors to *Mass Culture* criticized many intellectuals for being fuzzy or overly negative toward mass culture, the majority of contributors were certainly critical and sometimes contemptuous.

The post-war development of television was certainly a leading factor in bringing about the full flowering of mass culture. From 1949 to 1960 the percentage of U.S. homes possessing at least one television jumped from 6 to almost 90 percent, and by 1988 more than half of U.S. homes had more than one TV set. Although the United States led the rest of the world in owning televisions, owning about two-thirds of all TV sets in the world by 1959, western Europe and then other parts of the world also eventually experienced the TV revolution. In the early 1960s Great Britain followed by West Germany and then France and Italy significantly increased their TV viewership. By 1969 about 90 percent of British households had at least one set.

During the 1970s, TV sets also made their way into the overwhelming majority of homes in the Soviet Union. As in most other countries, attendance at movie houses and sporting events declined; leisure became more privatized, and an increasing amount of indoor free time was devoted to TV watching. In the very popular 1980 Soviet film *Moscow Does Not Believe in Tears*, one of the characters complains that "people have forgotten how to communicate; they sit in their apartments watching television and don't even know their neighbors." In 1981 the average primary school child in Mexico city averaged watching television about four hours per day. U.S. children and adult television watchers averaged at least that, more according to some estimates. In 1969 about one-fourth of all the leisure time of the English and Welsh was spent watching TV. From 1980 to 1996, the number of TV sets available globally almost tripled, reaching 1.4 billion, with the increase in Asia being the greatest. By 1996, for every thousand people there was the following number of television receivers per country:

USA	805
Japan	684
Germany	564
United Kingdom	516
Kuwait	510
Russia	405
China	319
Brazil	223
Egypt	119
South Africa	116
Iran	64
India	61

The area with the least televisions was sub-Saharan Africa, where only about 3 percent of the population owned a TV by century's end. But these figures only partially reflect the number of individuals who had access to TVs. In China, for example, it was estimated that the number of TV watchers increased from about 18 million in 1975 to 1 billion in 1995 (about five-sixths of the population). In India, by the end of the century only about half of the population had access to TVs, with someone in an urban area being twice as likely to have access as someone in a rural area.

Television played such a large role in mass culture because it soon enabled millions of people to view the same program or event. After the development of commercial satellite television in the early 1960s, many millions in different countries watched live coverage of such events as the funeral of U.S. President John Kennedy in 1963 and the first moon walk in 1969, which was viewed simultaneously by over a half a billion viewers worldwide. International sporting events such as the 1974 World Cup soccer playoff (reaching 600 million people) and Olympic Games were also beamed to numerous countries via satellite.

In the last few decades of the century, viewers in many countries watched U.S. programs such as *Baywatch*, *Dallas*, *Miami Vice*, and *Columbo*. After the development of cable stations like CNN (aired in about 150 countries by 1990), MTV, and ESPN, millions more around the world viewed their programing. Although by century's end the United States still produced the most programs seen abroad, other countries also exported programs, including Qatar, from where the Al-Jazeera news channel beamed signals to many other Arab countries.

The choice of programing in various countries was usually determined by factors other than a concern with cultural quality, although entities such as the BBC and PBS in the United States did concern themselves more with quality than did most networks and cable stations. In communist countries such as the Soviet Union, government propaganda was more important. In the United States advertisers' concerns about reaching potential consumers not only interrupted programs with frequent commercials, but also led TV executives to shy away from any programing that might appeal only to appreciators of "high culture" and to alter content in keeping with advertisers' concerns—in one case a cigarette advertiser of a crime program instructed writers not to have "bad guys" smoking. By the 1990s more minutes of networking programs than ever were devoted to ads, and costs kept escalating. The annual Super Bowl became not only the most important U.S. football game of the year, but also (because of its mass audience) the most important advertising event of the year (see Chapter 3 for more on advertising).

Outside the United States and communist countries, the mix of commercialism and government control varied. In Britain the BBC monopoly over TV content ended by law in 1954, and the first programing dependent on advertising appeared the following year. Commercial TV was not, however, completely deregulated because a new Independent Television Authority (ITV) oversaw it, including its advertising. Although satellite TV later broadened commercial opportunities in Britain, the BBC continued to be a major television force. In many other countries, especially ex-communist ones in the 1990s, the trend was toward greater commercialization of TV, meaning less government control, more soap operas, commercials, and concern with ratings. Although it was true that some of the new cable choices (such as HBO) could be watched free of commercials, many people could not afford the luxury.

The quality of television programing was debated extensively. In the early days of TV, a BBC executive stated that in the United States competition "has driven advertisers to play down to what they believe is the majority taste for crime, cheap sex, appeals to avarice and worse."[45] In 1961, the Chairman of the U.S Federal Communication Commission (FCC), Newton Minow addressed the National Association of Broadcasters, and in a speech most remembered for his "vast wasteland" reference he told them:

> But when television is bad, nothing is worse. I invite you to sit down in front of your television set when your station goes on the air and stay there without a book, magazine, newspaper, profit-and-loss sheet or rating book to distract you—and keep your eyes glued to that set until the station signs off. I can assure you that you will observe a vast wasteland.
>
> You will see a procession of game shows, violence, audience participation shows, formula comedies about totally unbelievable families, blood and

thunder, mayhem, violence, sadism, murder, western bad men, western good men, private eyes, gangsters, more violence and cartoons. And, endlessly, commercials—many screaming, cajoling and offending. And most of all, boredom.[46]

In another speech 30 years later, while acknowledging some positive developments, he still believed that U.S. television had in general not served the public interest well. He declared that most people learned more from television than any other source, including formal education, but he deplored what they often learned. He cited one source that stated by age 18, a U.S. child would have seen 25,000 murders on TV, and he quoted Bob Keeshan, TV's Captain Kangaroo, as saying that in the USA "television is not a tool for nurturing. It is a tool for selling."[47] Minow further believed that some other countries did a better job using television to help nurture children. In his scathing criticism of U.S. culture in the early 1990s, critic Robert Hughes wrote that television was "a medium now more debased in America than ever before."[48]

In *Mass Culture: The Popular Arts in America* (1957) and frequently thereafter, however, articles with titles such as "In Defense of Television" rejected such criticism. What did seem inarguable was that watching television was a more passive form of culture than many other forms such as reading a book, that it became increasingly prevalent globally, and that it had a significant global effect on culture.

Besides television, other significant developments that contributed to mass culture were the increase of leisure time and increased income to purchase the products of consumer cultures that became increasingly intertwined with mass cultures. As one expert on U.S. popular culture stated, "the commercialization of culture accelerated rapidly after World War II . . . [and the 1950s] marked the true beginning of mass consumption."[49] Mass-market paperbacks had already appeared by the 1950s, and by 1953 paperbacks sales were three times higher than in 1946. Nation-wide standardization and production also accelerated, as did the use of credit cards, still in their infancy in the early 1950s. In that same decade shopping malls, McDonald's, Disneyland, and Elvis Presley's first nation-wide TV appearance (on *The Ed Sullivan Show*) all occurred.

The popularity of Presley among teenagers awakened many potential sellers of mass culture to the importance of a youth subculture. As one historian claimed: "'Youth culture,' like 'teenagers,' was in part a concept created by the consumer society in order to increase sales."[50] Because of the appearance of long-playing records (LPs) in 1948 and transistor radios in the early 1950s, youth could conveniently experience Presley through various commercial media: radio, records, TV, and films. After his death in 1977, his Memphis Palace, Graceland, became one of the most popular U.S. tourist attractions.

Despite its early opposition to "the system," the youth of the late 1960s and early 1970s, or at least much of it, was also soon absorbed by the growing consumer culture that sold mass entertainment (including music by folk and rock musicians, films, and books) to young people.[51] The appearance of cassette tapes and players in the late 1960s further helped boost the sales of music by such groups as the Beatles and Rolling Stones. Whether it was music, clothes, books, or some other goods, U.S. youth continued being major consumers. In 1987, over 90 percent of U.S. teenage girls listed shopping as their favorite leisure activity. Advertisers also increasingly targeted younger children.[52]

Although the United States led the way in developing a consumer culture, western Europe and then later much of the rest of the world followed its example. In his survey of twentieth-century British history, Peter Clarke started off his chapter on the years 1955–63 with a section entitled "A Consumer Culture," and he noted that consumers spent 45 percent more (adjusting for inflation) in 1964 than in 1952.[53] The year 1964 was, coincidently, the year of the Beatles' triumphant tour of the United States. Like Elvis Presley eight years earlier, they appeared on *The Ed Sullivan Show,* and this time one-third of the U.S. population watched them.

Although their records were most popular in the United States and Britain, they also sold well in other markets—sales of "I Want to Hold Your Hand," for example, were a combined 4.5 million in the USA and Britain, and a combined 5 million in other areas. Although their songs could not be legally purchased in countries such as the Soviet Union during the 1960s and 1970s, Soviet and east European youth listened to them (when government jamming was relaxed or overcome) on Radio Free Europe, Voice of America, the BBC, and cassette tapes. A man who later became Soviet leader Gorbachev's English interpreter recalled the Beatles' influence on him and his friends in the 1960s: "We 'knew' their songs by heart ... To the Beatles ... I owe my accent ... The Beatles were our quiet way of rejecting 'the system' while conforming to most of its demands."[54] Overall, the appeal of the West's consumer culture, including its music, films, and other consumer items, must be numbered as one of the reasons for the collapse of communist governments in eastern Europe and the USSR.

The spread of a consumer culture of music, television programing, video games, shopping malls, advertising, fast food chains, and

Disneylands to various parts of the world did not mean that national cultural differences disappeared. But they did lessen, especially in urban areas. (See Chapter 4's section on "Westernization and Its Opponents" for some examples of the spread of Western TV and rock music to countries such as Thailand, Mongolia, Ghana, and Iran, but also for opposition to Westernization.) India's films and television shows were a good example of media that displayed both Western and native influences. Many of its "Bollywood" films reflected Hollywood techniques, but the films of the great Indian film director Satyajit Ray (1921–92) and some of its TV programing also reflected national uniqueness. A good example was the beaming of 91 episodes of an adaptation of the ancient Hindu epic *Mahabharata* during 1988–90 to nine-tenths of India's television owners.

In the last few decades of the century several new developments occurred that both brought the world closer together, thus contributing to a greater global mass culture, but at the same time opened the door to a more individualistic approach to culture. Perhaps the most significant was the development and spread of personal computers (PCs) and the Internet (see Chapter 2's section on "Transportation, Communication, and Consumer Products"). The Internet greatly broadened the cultural choices of individuals, who by the end of the century could download onto their computers literature, paintings, and music of many of the world's greatest writers, artists, and composers, especially of earlier centuries or those no longer covered by copyright protections. PC owners could then enjoy such works privately at times of their own choosing. In the 1980s video recorders (VCRs), and later video CDs and systems such as TiVo (developed in the 1990s), also gave viewers more flexibility in deciding when to watch their favorite TV programs and movies. These systems also broadened the choices available to cultural consumers.

High Culture?

Many leading historians, including Jacques Barzun, Norman Cantor, Robert Conquest, and Eric Hobsbawm, have written of the decline of high culture in the late twentieth century. Barzun wrote that in "the second half of the century ... it was hard to find a figure of the intellectual world to put side by side with those signaled out earlier."[55] Hobsbawn made a similar point in comparing artists, composers, and novelists in the two halves of the century and wrote of "the decline of the classical genres of high art and literature." He believed they were undermined by "the universal triumph of the society of mass consumption," and added that compared to the mass entertainment it helped produce, "the impact of the 'high arts' . . . was occasional at best."[56]

One problem for high culture was that some artistic talents took up newer forms of expression such as directing or writing film and television scripts, creating film music or animation, or even advertisements. Milan Kundera had one of his fictional characters ask, if living in the latter part of the twentieth century "would Shakespeare write scripts for Hollywood? Would Picasso produce cartoon shows?"[57] The historian Michael Kammen declared that by the late 1960s most Americans thought that advertising was an art, and "because it has become virtually impossible to avoid it or escape it, advertising has emerged as the most common kind of art in our culture."[58]

Already by the 1960s, artists such as Andy Warhol (1928–87) had so blurred the lines between art, advertising, and consumption that it became increasingly difficult to distinguish between high culture and a mass consumer culture. He was part of a "pop art" phenomenon that began in England in the 1950s and soon spread to the United States and beyond. Pop artists reacted against the art of abstract expressionists such as the American Jackson Pollack (1912–56), which had more to do with expressing the artists' unconscious mind than any outside reality. Like the Surrealists, many of these expressionists were fascinated with psychoanalysis, particularly the Jungian approach. Pop artists, on the contrary, embraced the material images of everyday urban reality and of mass culture—those of advertising, television, billboards, celebrities, comic strips, household furnishings, and junk. Sometimes their medium was the collage, consisting of assembled materials from various sources like magazines and junk yards.

Warhol himself had been a successful commercial illustrator and worked in advertising before museums like New York's Museum of Modern Art began displaying his works. Among the many quotes attributed to him were: "Buying is much more American than thinking"; "in the future, everyone will be world famous for 15 minutes"; "when you think about it, department stores are kind of like museums"; and "making money is art, and working is art and good business is the best art." He eventually produced works of many types including paintings, drawings, silkscreen prints, posters, sculptures, and films. And "produced" is the most accurate term, for beginning in 1962 he and his artistic workers started producing prints, posters, and often bizarre films in a place he called the Factory. Among the many images he portrayed were money, dollar signs, himself, male nudes (Warhol was openly gay), and newspaper clippings; consumer goods like Campbell Soup cans, Coke bottles, Brillo Boxes, and women's shoes; and celebrities such as Elvis Presley, Marilyn Monroe, Elizabeth Taylor, Jacqueline Kennedy, Brigitte Bardot, Mick Jagger, and Michael Jackson.

Pop art was just one of the signs that high culture and mass culture were becoming increasingly intertwined. Insisting that one piece of work was a reflection of "high culture" and another of "mass culture" seemed too arbitrary to many; and to some, too elitist and non-democratic. Could not a good novel, film, or other work of art be both? Who was to judge? As the century moved on, people relied less on the judgments of scholars or professional art or literary critics and more on popularity ratings, sales, and mass media lists. In the United States by the end of the century, many more people, especially members of her book club, bought books based on the recommendations of talk-show host Oprah Winfrey than on those of any literary critic—within two weeks of her recommending Tolstoy's nineteenth-century novel *Anna Karenina* (in the early twenty-first century), it shot up to the top of *New York Times* best-seller list.

To some the marriage in 1956 of Hollywood actress Marilyn Monroe and playwright Arthur Miller personified the blurring of high and mass culture. Miller's plays also contributed to this merging, especially his *Death of a Salesman* (1949), which in the last half of the century became one of the most performed plays in the world and the basis of several film or TV versions.

The popularity of colorful individuals like Picasso, composer Leonard Bernstein (1918–90), and opera singers Luciano Pavarotti and the Three Tenors also helped blend mass and high culture. Technological developments also played a part, as artistic reproductions and music could now be reproduced in more numerous forms, including in the latter case LPs, cassette tapes, and CDs. Already by 1952, for example, more than 300 LP sides of Beethoven's music were available. Bernstein became familiar to many people not only because he composed symphonies and other classical music, but also a great variety of other music including that for the jazz ballet *Fancy Free* (1944), the musical *West Side Story* (1957), and the film score for *On the Waterfront* (1954). He also lectured on TV in the 1950s about music in a manner that was intelligible to many.

Besides Warhol other cultural figures increasingly thought of their work as commodities necessary to sell. The U.S. writer Norman Mailer, though critical of capitalism, realized the link between publicity, of which he garnered a great deal, and sales. He entitled a 1959 book of essays *Advertisements for Myself*. In 1982 the actress Liz

Taylor said, "I am my own industry"; "I am my own commodity."[59] By the end of the century, authors and other cultural figures, if popular enough, often helped sell their works by appearing at book signings or on talk shows.

The popularity of a post-war French group of writers lumped together as existentialists by the press also helped blur the lines between high and mass culture. Most notable among them were Jean Paul Sartre, Simone de Beauvoir, and Albert Camus, who for a while in post-war France spent many hours together in the same French cafes and other establishments.

In a 1957 survey of young French adults, they listed Sartre as the writer who most influenced their generation. About him British writer Paul Johnson (no admirer of Sartre) wrote: "Certainly no philosopher this century has had so direct an impact on the minds and attitudes of so many human beings, especially young people, all over the world. Existentialism was the popular philosophy of the late 1940s and 1950s. His plays were hits. His books sold in enormous quantities, some of them over two million copies in France alone."[60] His books included novels, essays, biographies, and his lengthy philosophical work *Being and Nothingness* (1943). He also gave public lectures and edited a leading literary and political journal. Proclaimed the winner of the Nobel Prize for Literature (NPL) in 1964, he refused the honor.[61]

Beauvoir, Sartre's long-time companion, was a major thinker and writer herself. She won France's highest literary prize for her novel *The Mandarins* (1954) and later wrote four volumes of memoirs and an historical examination of the perceptions of old age among various writers and cultures. But her chief fame globally came with the publication and translations of her classic feminist work, *Le Deuxième Sexe* (1949, translated into English as *The Second Sex*). The English language translation alone sold over 1 million copies.

Like Sartre, Camus, who died in an accident in 1960 at age 46, also wrote novels, plays, essays, and longer prose works of non-fiction, for example *L'Homme Révolté* (1951, translated as *The Rebel*). The latter was his artistic, historical, and metaphysical study of rebellion in which he criticized "Absolutist" philosophies such as Marxism, but also bourgeois societies. He grew up in Algeria and also worked at various times as a journalist, newspaper editor, and in the theater in various capacities, not only as a playwright but also as an actor, director, and translator. His novel *La Peste* (1947, translated as *The Plague*) became one of the best-selling books in France's post-war decade. In 1957 he was awarded the NPL (see also Chapter 5 for Camus on freedom).

Although all three writers were labeled existentialists, Camus rejected being so tagged. Nevertheless, he did share certain basic convictions with Sartre and Beauvoir. All three believed that no God existed, that the world was "absurd," that concepts such as "human nature" were to be regarded with suspicion, and that it was people's actions that determined their essence. Existentialists were suspicious of academic philosophies and of systems such as that of the philosopher Hegel (1770–1831) that placed too much dependence on abstract ideas such as Spirit or Reason or seemed deterministic, thereby reducing individual choices. Because Soviet Marxism was willing to sacrifice the lives of present-day people in the name of a utopian future, Camus thought it was incompatible with the existentialism professed by Sartre. By 1952, however, Sartre had come to prefer Soviet communism to Western capitalism and democracy, and the two men polemicized in Sartre's journal, leading to a definitive break between them.

Besides these three French writers, many other thinkers came to be labeled existentialists in the 1950s and 1960s, including the nineteenth-century philosophers Kierkegaard and Nietzsche, as well as Martin Heidegger (see above), whose ideas had had a major influence on the young Sartre. As the case of Kierkegaard indicates, not all of these thinkers were atheists; it was enough to share the other chief existentialist ideas.

Bearing some similarities to existentialism with its emphasis on the absurdness of life was a new type of drama (called the Theater of the Absurd) that appeared in Paris at about the same time as the heyday of Sartre, Beauvoir, and Camus. Its chief playwrights were Irish-born Samuel Beckett, Romanian-born Eugene Ionesco, and the former French convict (about whom Sartre wrote a biography) Jean Genet. The first two would be especially influential on later dramatists like the American Edward Albee and the British Harold Pinter.

While existentialism was the dominant post-war cultural movement in France, in the United States and Britain two groups known respectively as The Beats and Angry Young Men emerged. Like Sartre, Beauvoir, and Camus, their writers were critical of the capitalist societies in which they lived, and most shared Camus's distrust of all "isms" including communism. A paperback anthology of their writings published in 1959 was entitled *The Beat Generation and the Angry Young Men*. Its introduction mentioned their common "existentialism," their realization of the anxiety of modern life, their belief that "long-term goals have lost their relevance," and that in the atomic age it was necessary to live in the "moment."[62] Among the works excerpted from the American Beats, the two most notable were

Allen Ginsberg's poem *Howl*, and Jack Kerouac's *On the Road*. Among the Angry Young Men's writings was an excerpt from Colin Wilson's book *The Outsider*, which included favorable mention of Sartre, and excerpts from Kingsley Amis's popular novel *Lucky Jim* and his book *Socialism and the Intellectuals*, which reflected dissatisfaction with British politics generally, whether of the right or left.[63]

In the communist world, some of the best writers of the quarter century between 1950 and 1975, such as NPL winners Boris Pasternak and Alexander Solzhenitsyn, also expressed unhappiness with their political system. Pasternak's great novel *Doctor Zhivago*, prohibited from being published in his native USSR, was published abroad in 1957. Dealing mainly with the communist revolution and civil war, its hero, a doctor and a poet, symbolized a desire for spontaneity and freedom in a political system that denied both. For almost three decades after Pasternak's death in 1960, the novel remained unpublished in the USSR. Although Alexander Solzhenitsyn's short novel *One Day in the Life of Ivan Denisovich* was published in the USSR in 1962, later novels such as *The First Circle, Cancer Ward*, and *August 1914* had to be smuggled out of the country and published abroad, as was the first volume of his non-fictional *The Gulag Archipelago*. Having been imprisoned and in the Soviet forced labor camps himself, his works reflected the nightmarish world of those caught up in the Stalinist prison system. Accused of treason and deported from the USSR in 1974, Solzhenitsyn remained abroad, primarily in the United States, until returning to Russia in 1994, after the collapse of the USSR.

Once in the United States, Solzhenitsyn made it clear that not only was he opposed to communism, but that he also had little use for modern Western civilization. This became especially clear in 1978 when he gave a commencement address at Harvard. In it he criticized the whole Western secular tradition since the Renaissance with its emphasis on Reason and commercial gain. He also criticized the twentieth century's mass conformism and prejudices, its overemphasis on legality and personal freedoms, and its neglect of morality and matters of the spirit.

A third Russian NPL winner (1987), Joseph Brodsky, although usually writing non-political, complex, philosophic poetry, was also displeased with the Soviet system. He was arrested in 1964 and exiled to an Artic region. After being pressured to leave the USSR in 1972, he settled in the United States and served for a while as its poet laureate. Although certainly freer in the United States, he never experienced the popular acclaim that some young poets had achieved under Khrushchev (1953–64), when poetry readings on some occasions attracted audiences the size of which only sporting events or popular entertainers could attract in the West.[64]

The phenomena of leading writers arising from countries other than those of the industrialized West became increasingly common after World War II. After producing no NPL recipients before 1945, Latin America had five writers who received the award from 1945 to 1990. Some of them, such as Gabriel García Márquez (Colombia), had a strong global influence. His *One Hundred Years of Solitude* appeared in 1967 and was translated into 32 languages by 1981. Its style, sometimes referred to as "magic realism," soon had many imitators. Besides NPL winners, other first-class writers like Jorge Luis Borges (Argentina), Mario Vagras Llosa (Peru), and Carlos Fuentes (Mexico) also achieved international status. Excellent writers also appeared on the Caribbean islands, two of the most notable being V. S. Naipaul (Trinidad) and Derek Walcott (St. Lucia), both eventually became NPL recipients. Writers of international repute from India included R. K. Naryan, Salman Rushdie, and Anita Desai.

Africa and Japan also produced world-class writers including Chinua Achebe, Wole Soyinka (NPL, 1986), and Ben Okri, all of Nigerian origin; Nadine Gordimer (NPL, 1991) and J. M Coetzee (NPL, 2003), both from South Africa; Nagib Mahfouz from Egypt (NPL, 1988); and Yasunari Kawabata (NPL, 1968), Yukio Mishima, and Kenzaburo Oe (NPL, 1994), all from Japan. Like many writers earlier, some of these later non-European writers, including Naipaul, Rushdie, Desai, Okri, and Coetzee, later moved to other countries than the one in which they grew up. Taken together, all of these non-European writers made important stylistic contributions such as the magic realism of Márquez, which influenced many writers including Rushdie and Okri. They also provided significant insights into the lives and cultures of their homelands and of the mixing and clashing of cultures. Achebe's *Things Fall Apart* (1958), for example, deals with the disintegration of an African village and the tragedy of one of its strongest men when confronted with British imperialism around the end of the nineteenth century.

Several outstanding non-Western film directors also appeared in the post-war period. The case of India's Satyajit Ray has already been mentioned, but the best known non-Western director was Akira Kurosawa of Japan. Films such as *Rashomon* (1950), *Living* (1952) *The Seven Samurai* (1954), *The Hidden Fortress* (1958), *Throne of Blood* (1957), *Yojimbo* (1961), and *Derzu Uzala* (1975) demonstrated his wide familiarity not only with Japanese culture and traditions but also with foreign culture, including Shakespeare's plays. He became a strong influence on foreign directors—the U.S. western *The Magnificent Seven*, for example, was an adaptation of his *The Seven Samurai*.

As earlier in the century, anthropologists also continued to broaden the understanding of culture. Claude Lévi-Strauss was born in Belgium, brought up in France, did field work in Brazil, and, like many other famous European Jews, spent most of World War II in the United States. In the 1950s he lived in Paris and, unlike the writings of the Parisian existentialists, his influential culture theory of structuralism emphasized the social system rather than the alienated individual.

Influenced by Freud, Marx, and linguistic studies, Lévi-Strauss believed that an objective but unconscious code or structure existed in all societies shaping peoples' language, beliefs, and myths. All peoples' minds, he thought, worked in a similar way, creating more or less sophisticated myths to understand and explain reality. Unlike his predecessors Boas, Mead, and Benedict, he emphasized the similarity, not the differences, of basic mental processes. But he agreed with them that "The Savage Mind," (also the translated title of one of his most influential works) was not inferior. He even suggested its superiority to the West's mentality because it was less repressed, confused, and conflicted. He was a severe critic of Western imperialism; and, like many others who had earlier stressed the nobility of primitive peoples and criticized industrial civilization, he greatly admired many of the ideas of the eighteenth-century thinker Jean-Jacques Rousseau.

In the 1970s Lévi-Strauss's influence, already great in France, spread rapidly abroad in such fields as psychoanalysis, literature, and cultural and religious studies. His emphasis on an objective, though masked, reality and on structure and system fit in well with such developments as the discovery of DNA and the emergence of computers and software programs.

In regard to art and music, the judgment of the Marxist Hobsbawm in regard to its late twentieth-century decline (see above) was echoed by others on the Cultural Right, for example Roger Kimball, one of the editors of the journal *New Criterion*. In 1997, he wrote of the art of the preceding few decades: "The spectacle that the contemporary art world presents is distinctly unappetizing. Whatever merits individual artists here and there may exhibit, most of the established art of our time is pretentiously banal when it is not downright pathological . . . In our day, the art world and the world of culture generally have changed, changed dramatically, and they have changed for the worse."[65]

During the 1970s most of the last of the greatest artistic and musical talents of the early part of the century died out, including Stravinsky

(1971), Picasso (1973), and Dmitri Shostakovich (1975)—the painter Chagall, however, survived until 1985. Certainly there was a great deal of experimentation, foreign borrowing, and trying of new techniques, including the production of electronic sounds, by composers such as Pierre Boulez, Karlheinz Stockhausen, and John Cage. But few music critics put them in the same category as the major composers of the nineteenth and early twentieth centuries. Kundera in *Immortality* (see above) had one of his characters visit New York's Museum of Modern Art and make a harsh judgment, but one shared by at least some cultural critics. After admiring the paintings of Matisse, Picasso, and others who earned their reputations in the first half of the century, he went to the next floor, "reserved for contemporary paintings, [and] he found himself in a desert."[66]

This perceived decline that so many leading critics observed was also due, in the words of Hobsbawm, to "the death of 'modernism.'" He believed that this earlier *avant-garde* cultural movement had rejected "nineteenth-century bourgeois liberal conventions in both society and art" and that "innovation had been its core."[67] He noted a significant reaction against modernism by the late 1960s and that by the 1980s this reaction had sprouted into a movement often labeled postmodernism (see Chapter 8 for more on this late twentieth-century trend). In Kundera's *Immortality*, he captures this transition when he notes that from medieval painters up through Picasso "they all knew that they were blazing a trail into the unknown, a common goal united them all. And then suddenly the road disappeared," replaced by artistic chaos and decline.[68] As the century neared its end, such pessimism about the fate of "high culture" was increasingly prominent.

8

Values and Virtues

Postmodernism, Culture, and Science

The Columbia Encyclopedia, 6th ed. (2000), defines postmodernism as follows:

> Term used to designate a multitude of trends—in the arts, philosophy, religion, technology, and many other areas—that come after and deviate from the many 20th-cent. movements that constituted modernism. The term has become ubiquitous in contemporary discourse and has been employed as a catchall for various aspects of society, theory, and art ... In general, the postmodern view is cool, ironic, and accepting of the fragmentation of contemporary existence. It tends to concentrate on surfaces rather than depths, to blur the distinctions between high and low culture, and as a whole to challenge a wide variety of traditional cultural values.

Postmodernists rejected any absolute or objective truths, whether scientific, political, religious, or cultural, thus tending to an extreme relativism. Instead, they stressed conflicting viewpoints and the blurring of distinctions between images and reality. By the late 1980s this viewpoint was even evident in the Soviet Union under the more permissive Mikhail Gorbachev. Victor Erofeyev, a Russian writer, described the new movement in literature, "The new Russian literature has called absolutely everything into question: love, children, faith, the Church, culture, beauty, nobility of character, motherhood, and even the wisdom of the common people."[1]

Postmodernism spread not only to different parts of the globe, but to different fields such as literary criticism, the social sciences, and humanities. One of its most significant manifestations was deconstructionism. This "ism" developed after Lévi-Strauss's structuralism (see Chapter 7) had been the main trend in French thought, and it had both similarities and differences with the earlier movement. One of the main differences was that it was a more radical challenge to Western society and traditions. The two most influential deconstructionists were the French academics Michel Foucault and Jacques Derrida. As one scholar observed, "The overwhelming elite of the younger generation of literary critics or scholars who received their doctoral degrees in a field of literature in the United States in the 1980s and 1990s were deconstructionists." Furthermore, "by 1990 Derrida and Foucault had become established figures in the graduate schools of the humanities throughout the Western world."[2] Some psychologists, social scientists, scientists, law professors, artists, and architects also fell under deconstructionist influences.

Foucault wrote historical books dealing with mental illness, clinics, prisons, and sexuality, but he was more interested in the structures of knowledge and power in past societies than in presenting any chronological succession of events. Influenced by thinkers such as Marx, Nietzsche, and the Italian Marxist Gramsci, he thought that any society's determination of mental illness, criminality, deviance (including sexual deviance), manners, morality, and education (including the norms of academic disciplines) was based upon power. The ruling elites defined, for example, insanity and crime to protect their own positions, while rebels against established practices like feminists and gays (Foucault was openly gay and died of AIDS in 1985) battled ruling elites partly to strengthen their own powers. Unlike some earlier historians, Foucault did not see history as a march toward "progress" or increased "rationality" but rather as a continuing struggle for power. Like Lévi-Strauss, Derrida thought that "meaning resides in the structure of language itself," but that the human use of language was far too inconsistent to ever come close to capturing reality. "Truth is plural," he said, and he believed "there is no fixed meaning, canon, or tradition."[3]

As was almost inevitable a strong reaction to postmodernism, especially to deconstructionism, developed before the end of the century. In his best-selling The Closing of the American Mind (1987), Allan Bloom wrote, "Deconstructionism ... is the last, predictable, stage in the suppression of reason and the denial of the possibility of truth in the name of philosophy ... This fad will pass."[4] In the early 1990s, U.S. conservative columnist George Will frequently criticized postmodernism. Its central tenet he thought was, as he quoted Nietzsche, "there are not facts, but only interpretations." He called such ideas "profoundly dangerous" and believed "they subvert our civilization."[5]

The best example of the hostility to deconstructionist postmodernism, however, was evidenced by the publicity given to a paper submitted, accepted, and printed in 1996 in the U.S. journal *Social Text*. Its author was Alan Sokal, a professor of physics at New York University, and his article was entitled "Transgressing the Boundaries: Towards a Transformative Hermeneutics of Quantum Gravity." It contained far more references and notes than the text itself. But the article was a hoax and viewed by its self-proclaimed "Old Leftist" author as a parody on postmodern deconstructionist thought and use of jargon. Unfortunately for the journal editors, they failed to realize the bogus nature of the paper. After Sokal revealed his hoax in the journal *Lingua Franca*, newspaper editors, columnists, and letter writers relished the opportunity to comment on it. Four years later the editors of that journal published some of those pieces, sympathetic and unsympathetic to the hoax, in a book entitled *The Sokal Hoax: The Sham That Shook the Academy*.

Because deconstructionists often used a jargon that was only intelligible to those familiar with it, it was easy to make fun of them. A website of an emeritus professor of anthropology at the University of California-San Diego, for example, furnished this parody of a deconstructionist sentence, "Naming in principle constitutes an act of violence, which valorizes constructed spaces of colonial hegemony across boundaries appropriated by didactic official discourse implicated by scientifico-disciplinary mechanisms of cultural production and alters the native imaginary."[6] Another website, Postmodernism Generator, randomly generated bogus essays in deconstructionist jargon.[7]

One historian, referring specifically to the USA, wrote of the "growing discordance ... between the media and academic cultures in the last quarter of the twentieth century."[8] And the media reaction to the Sokal hoax certainly revealed the gap. Part of the responsibility for this lay with academics, particularly the deconstructionists, who often did a poor job communicating their insights to a general public. When academic historians, for example, wrote prose laden with jargon—an increasing phenomenon in the 1990s—they could hardly be surprised when non-academic historians such as David McCullough, author of best-selling histories and frequent host or narrator of U.S. public television programs, appealed much more than they did to general readers interested in history.

Yet, as George Will's earlier criticisms made clear, it was not just the jargon, but the postmodernist ideas themselves that bothered some people. Unfortunately for the postmodernists, however, they had no one in the United States who had the media reach of Will to defend their ideas.

In addition, academic intellectuals and high culture had always been suspect to many Americans. In the early 1940s, Walt Disney noted that for many people the term culture had an "un-American connotation" and seemed "snobbish and affected."[9] In his Pulitzer-Prize-winning historical work of 1963, *Anti-Intellectualism in American Life*, historian Richard Hofstadter referred to the lack of sympathy of non-intellectuals for "intellectuality." Regarding the 1950's presidential candidate Adlai Stevenson, the historian wrote: "for a substantial segment of the public this quality was indeed a liability."[10] Stevenson was perceived by many as an "egghead," which one right-wing novelist defined as "a person of spurious intellectual pretensions, often a professor or the protégé of a professor. Fundamentally superficial. Over-emotional and feminine in reactions to any problem."[11] Anyone living in the USA for very long could point to other examples of anti-intellectualism in later decades, especially in regard to politics. Although some other countries esteemed intellectuals more, the advance of mass media globally worked in favor of brief sound bites and shorter print articles, not of longer articles dealing with complex, difficult ideas such as deconstructionism. [12]

As easy as it was to make fun of deconstructionist jargon and some of their more extreme ideas, some of the major points they made were certainly worthy of serious consideration. Long before them, the influential philosopher Wittgenstein (and others before him) had emphasized the limitations of language in reflecting reality. And was it really so outlandish to state, as Foucault did, that elites have more power to determine social conventions, including acceptable manners, morality, and education, than those with little power?

The difficulty that deconstructionists experienced in gaining wider general popularity was both similar and different than that faced by scientists earlier in the century. We have already seen that the influence of scientists such as Darwin, Freud, and Einstein was great on twentieth century culture. Yet the ideas of such men were often misinterpreted. In 1959 British scientist and novelist Sir Charles Snow delivered his famous lecture "The Two Cultures." In it he bemoaned the lack of communication and understanding between scientific culture and literary/humanistic culture. As he put it, many of his literary colleagues failed to communicate with scientists "as though the scientists spoke nothing but Tibetan." As he made clear later, he saw this as part of a larger problem, namely that "in our society (that is, advanced western society) we have lost even the pretense of a common culture."[13] As with the later deconstructionists and other postmodernists, the lack of adequate communication of scientists with others was due to both the complexity of their ideas and their technical language.

But a main difference between science and postmodernist ideas was that the public generally had great respect for the former, even if they did not understand theories like those of Einstein very well. One reason for this respect was the close connection between science and technology; scientific discoveries helped lead to the production of things that people valued, not only consumer products and weapons but also medical advances. As the response to the Sokal hoax indicated, there was no such respect for deconstructionists. George Will's comment about the latter and the journal that accepted Sokal's bogus essay was typical of the disdain expressed: "Deconstructionists read things like *Social Text*, which will never again be called a 'learned journal.'"[14]

The Sokal Hoax also revealed that scientists felt threatened by postmodernist ideas, and this brings us back to Snow's views of two cultures. Snow argued that scientists had contributed much to what we have called "high culture." (See above, Chapter 7.) He also argued that applied science was the great hope of mankind. "Applied science," he wrote, "has made it possible to remove unnecessary suffering from a billion individual human lives." And he added: "The scientific revolution is the only method by which most people can gain the primal things (years of life, freedom from hunger, and survival for children)."[15]

At the end of the twentieth century, the BBC featured a debate entitled "The Two Cultures 40 Years On." Another British writer, Peter Watson, had just about completed a book in which he, like Snow, argued strongly for the value of science in relation to culture. In his *The Modern Mind: An Intellectual History of the 20th Century* (2001), he maintained that science was one of the "three great intellectual forces" of the century—free-market economics and the mass media were his other two choices. He noted that in 1900 the humanities could still plausibly be thought "a form of knowledge superior to science," but that by the end of the century science "was taking over from the arts, humanities, and religion as the main form of knowledge."[16] Watson thought that science was superseding other forces as the "engine of social development." Several of science's aspects that appealed to him, as opposed to some other fields, was that it had "no real agenda" but was open, tolerant, and objective, and its results were cumulative, one discovery building upon others.[17]

Although quite critical of the impact of Freud and Jung (and also Marx), Watson was especially impressed with Darwinian advances. In various fields including genetics (see Chapter 2) he thought that sciences were coming together to reinforce and expand upon evolution, which Watson seemed to agree was "the best idea, ever." He concluded "we are now [in 2000] in the era of 'universal Darwinism.'" He ended his book suggesting that the arts and humanities can also become part of the evolutionary "story." "Evolution," he concluded, "enables us to place the world of culture within the world of nature with as comfortable a fit as possible."[18]

Watson was also hopeful that science could help bridge the gap between high culture, of which it was a part, and mass culture, noting that by the end of the century science books were selling well.

The main point at issue between many scientists and postmodernist critics was the latter's charge that science was not as objective, rational, or trustworthy as many scientists thought. The dispute continued until the end of the century and beyond. The prominent Oxford Darwinist Richard Dawkins asserted in 1998 that many postmodernists were "not harmless eccentrics at third-rate state colleges. Many of them have tenured professorships at some of the best universities in the United States. Men of this kind sit on appointment committees, wielding power over young academics who might secretly aspire to an honest academic career in literary studies or, say, anthropology. I know—because many of them have told me—that there are sincere scholars out there who would speak out if they dared, but who are intimidated into silence."[19]

Education and the Disciplines

Much of the controversy about postmodernism centered on its place in colleges and universities, especially in the social science and humanities disciplines. It is therefore appropriate to examine here some important trends in twentieth-century education.

Two important developments were the great increases in literacy and in formal schooling that occurred throughout the world, first in the more industrialized nations and then in other areas. A few statistics will illustrate this growth. In the USA in 1899–1900, the median educational attainment was only 5.5 years of schooling, and only about 62,000 people graduated from high school; in 1969–70 over 2.5 million graduated. In the USA in 1900 there were about 300,000 students enrolled in higher education; in 1970 the figure was

8.6 million (or about one-third of the world's total); and in 1999 about 15 million. In Britain, Germany, and France combined before World War II, there were at most 150,000 university students; by 1990 each of those countries had over 1 million such students. In Russia between 1917 and 1937, literacy rates rose from less than half to over three-fourths of those between ages 9 to 49. In Indonesia, with the world's largest Muslim population, the literacy rate went from 39 to 77 percent in the years from 1960 to 1990. At the beginning of the twenty-first century China and India, partly because of their large populations, were each graduating more higher education students than was the United States.

As education spread and became less elitist, curriculums broadened; and as democracy and individualism increased, what people studied became more a matter of individual choice. Perhaps the most influential educational theorist of the twentieth century was the American John Dewey (1859–1952). A philosopher who emphasized the pragmatic idea that truth is determined by what is practically useful, by what works, Dewey emphasized more individual choice, "learning by doing," and problem solving. He criticized older methods of education that stressed mass conformity and rote learning. Some cultural conservatives, such as Allan Bloom (see above), later blamed him for ignoring moral virtues and contributing to cultural relativism.[20] Although Dewey's ideas were most influential in the USA, his educational theories also had an impact in areas such as Europe, Latin America, Japan, and even communist Russia in the early 1920s. A few other thinkers whose educational ideas are worthy of note include the Italian Maria Montessori, and the Indians Gandhi and Tagore, both men mentioned frequently in previous chapters. Montessori stressed allowing the education of a child to proceed based on his/her own interests, and the latter two men emphasized the importance of integrating book learning with life, work, and one's social obligations.[21]

What was studied varied considerably from one era to another and from country to country. In keeping with more individual choices, from the 1950s to the 1990s U.S. universities greatly reduced the specific courses required for graduation and in the 1960s had fewer students preparing for business careers than in subsequent less radical decades. In Europe university students generally had fewer course choices than in the USA. In communist countries such as the USSR and China technical fields like engineering attracted a larger percentage of students than was the case in the United States. And many countries required more foreign language competency than did the USA. Great discrepancies also existed in the length of time spent in school. Japanese school children, for example spent many more days of a year in school in the 1990s than did U.S. students.

The democratization of education had significant implications for culture. On the one hand, it meant that a much larger percentage of the world in 1999 than in 1900 was capable of reading, including the world's best literature. On the other hand, the likelihood of a college or university student in 1999 willingly reading much of such literature was probably less than it was for his predecessor in 1900, who was part of a small elite group. In addition to having greater access to alternate mass media, the 1999 student, living in a more relativist and less elitist, age, was less likely than his 1900 counterpart to agree on what was "best."

In arguing that late twentieth century culture was in a state of decadence Jacques Barzun, thinking mainly of the USA, regarded "the course offering of the large colleges and universities [as] a smorgasbord and not a balanced meal. And large parts of it were hardly nourishing ... The liberal arts were subdivided by SPECIALISM into bits and pieces of scholarly interest, but of little benefit to young minds that lacked previous knowledge of the larger field."[22] Barzun's concern with "specialism" was one echoed by other social critics, one of the most prominent being R. Buckminster Fuller (1895–1983), an innovative and global-minded thinker. In his *Operating Manual for Spaceship Earth* (1969), he described some of the chief global problems of his day, especially poverty. He then added:

> Of course, our failures are a consequence of many factors, but possibly one of the most important is the fact that society operates on the theory that specialization is the key to success, not realizing that specialization precludes comprehensive thinking. This means that the potentially-integratable-techno-economic advantages accruing to society from the myriad specializations are not comprehended integratively and therefore are not realized, or they are realized only in negative ways, in new weaponry or the industrial support only of warfaring.
>
> All universities have been progressively organized for ever finer specialization. Society assumes that specialization is natural, inevitable, and desirable.[23]

In a later work, Fuller wrote:

> We are in an age that assumes the narrowing trends of specialization to be logical, natural, and desirable. Consequently, society expects all earnestly responsible communication to be crisply brief. Advancing science has now discovered that all the known cases of biological extinction have been caused by overspecialization, whose concentration of only selected genes sacrifices general adaptability. Thus the specialist's brief for pinpointing brevity is dubious. In the meantime, humanity has been deprived of comprehensive

understanding. Specialization has bred feelings of isolation, futility, and confusion in individuals. It has also resulted in the individual's leaving responsibility for thinking and social action to others. Specialization breeds biases that ultimately aggregate as international and ideological discord, which, in turn, leads to war.[24]

Part of the ire of cultural conservatives directed at postmodernists was that their relativism was undermining respect for the great classics of the past. In the early 1990s, George Will bemoaned the idea "that there should not be in this [U.S.] pluralistic society any core culture passed on from generation to generation." He believed that "transmitting the best of the West—the culture of our civilization—"was one of the main jobs of a university, and one that should not be sacrificed because of a fear that stressing that task would "'underrepresent' certain groups—racial, sexual, ethnic or class-based groups."[25]

Before and during the period of being influenced by deconstructionism and other postmodern ideas, the academic disciplines continued to make valuable contributions to culture. We have already touched on them in such fields as philosophy, science, and anthropology. To take one more example, twentieth-century historians greatly broadened their field by dealing more with economic and social history and with other parts of the world besides the West.

During the nineteenth century some isolated voices had called on historians to write more about the common people. In Russia, the great novelist Tolstoy chided them for not paying more attention to those who "made the brocades, broadcloth, clothes, and damask cloth which the tsars and nobles flaunted, who trapped the black foxes and sables that were given to ambassadors, who mined the gold and iron, who raised the horses, cattle, and sheep, who constructed the houses, palaces, and churches, and who transported goods."

Until the twentieth century, however, most historians continued to concentrate on political history. In 1929 two French historians, Lucien Febvre and Marc Bloch, began a journal, *Annales d'histoire économique et sociale*, "that in the next decade was to become the single most important forum for the revitalization of historical studies in the Western world."[26] Following the lead of this journal, historians began paying more attention to economic and social history. Marxism also led some in this direction. But change was slow, and in the United States during the 1950s, political history was still dominant. Comparing a typical text on U.S. history written in the 1950s with one written in the 1990s, one notes that the latter devotes much more space to economic and social developments, to the common people, to women and minorities, and to popular culture. Although cultural conservatives like George Will might have thought that fear of underrepresenting "certain groups—racial, sexual, ethnic or class-based groups"—was harming academic disciplines,[27] there is little doubt that historians' treatment of the past of such groups broadened historical understanding.

As the century advanced, Western and non-Western historians gradually began to pay more attention to non-Western parts of the world. The British historian Basil Davidson, for example, not only wrote such important works as *Old Africa Rediscovered* (1959) but also narrated a popular six-part television series, *Africa: The Story of a Continent*. And for many decades before Gorbachev came to power in the USSR, Western historians, including Russian *émigrés* to the West, wrote some of the best historical works dealing with Russia and the Soviet Union.

Religion

Just as leading scientific ideas were part of high culture, so too were religious ones. For most of recorded history, as Europe's medieval art and architecture or the Golden Age of Islam illustrate, religion was a dominant influence on culture. One expert on culture writing of pre-modern times noted that "in no genuinely religious epoch is the high culture separate from the religious rite," and "the core of common culture is religion."[28]

During the eighteenth-century European Enlightenment, however, significant opposition to traditional religious ideas emerged. One prominent historian, Peter Gay, subtitled his study of the Enlightenment as "The Rise of Modern Paganism." Among the most prominent of the thinkers of this period was the Scotchman David Hume, who, while not denying God, rejected traditional religious teachings regarding miracles. As he saw it, belief in them was necessary for belief in Christianity—"The Christian Religion not only was at first attended with miracles, but even at this day cannot be believed by any reasonable person without one."[29] In 1997, the Pew Research Foundation found that 61 percent of those surveyed in the USA still believed in miracles.

During the nineteenth-century, belief in rationalism, science, and culture moved into the vacuum brought about by a declining belief in traditional religions. In the early 1840s the German Ludwig Feuerbach proclaimed that God was merely a human projection.

His fellow countryman David Strauss argued that much of the Bible was not factual but based on legends. In France several decades later, Ernest Renan's *The Life of Jesus* (1863) furthered the tendency toward the "higher criticism" of the Bible, refusing to accept it as literally true in many of its details. By the end of the century, Nietzsche was contending that "God is dead" and Christianity a "great curse" and an attempt by the weak to curtail the strong. Freud declared religion a collective fantasy.

Most of these thinkers, like Renan, believed they were furthering the cause of science. Following the publication of Darwin's *Origin of Species* in 1859, enthusiasm for Darwinism and scientific explanations permeated the Western world. During the 1860s and beyond, enthusiasm for science, though not always Darwinism, was strong among the Russian intelligentsia, many of whom renounced the Orthodox religious beliefs of most of their fellow Russians. The German Karl Marx, who spent most of his latter life in England, admired Darwin's work and thought of his own interpretation of history as being scientific.

Although many Christians eventually reconciled themselves to the idea of Darwinian evolution and to interpreting at least some portions of the Bible in a non-literal fashion, others rejected both Darwinism and the "higher criticism" of the Bible that had begun in Germany. This was especially true of those conservative evangelical Christians who by the 1920s were referred to in the USA as "fundamentalists." Their rejection of such modernist ideas was clearly evident in the famous Scopes "Monkey Trial" of 1925. In it a Tennessee biology teacher was found guilty of teaching evolution rather than the biblical account of creation as favored by the fundamentalists. Between 1907 and 1910 the Catholic pope, Pius X, also frequently criticized modernist trends threatening papal authority. Although a later pope, John XXIII, called together the Second Vatican Council in 1962 and demonstrated more openness to modern science and scholarship, many Protestant fundamentalists continued to reject Darwinian teachings. This was especially true in the United States, where Gallup Poll surveys in the 1990s indicated that, as opposed to almost all scientists, almost half of U.S. citizens believed that God created the first human within the last 10,000 years.[30] And in some U.S. states in the final decades of the century fundamentalists waged campaigns to allow the teaching of "creation science" as a counterbalance wherever evolutionary theory was taught in public schools—by the early twenty-first century, many fundamentalists were advocating a somewhat modified form of creationism know as "intelligent design."[31]

Just as religious believers were split over reconciling themselves to scientific findings, so scientists disagreed about religion. They spanned the spectrum from being atheists to belonging to a religious denomination. Einstein, the most famous scientist of the century, wrote (probably in 1927): "I cannot conceive of a personal God who would directly influence the actions of individuals, or would directly sit in judgment on creatures of his own creation . . . My religiosity consists in a humble admiration of the infinitely superior spirit that reveals itself in the little that we, with our weak and transitory understanding, can comprehend of reality."[32] Near the end of the century, Oxford's Richard Dawkins declared: "There is no reason for believing that any sort of gods exist and quite good reason for believing that they do not exist and never have. It has all been a gigantic waste of time and a waste of life. It would be a joke of cosmic proportions if it weren't so tragic."[33] At about the same time, however, the British physicist and Anglican priest John Polkinghorne wrote several books arguing that a personal God did exist and that it was reasonable to believe in the resurrection of Jesus Christ.[34]

As trust in religious authority declined, whether in the Bible, the pope, or other religious leaders, high culture offered to some a replacement. In the nineteenth century Matthew Arnold was criticized for making a "religion of culture"; and although he valued religion, he valued high culture more.[35] In 1911 the Russian painter Vasili Kandinsky wrote: "When religion, science and morality are shaken, the two last by the strong hand of Nietzsche, and when the outer supports threaten to fall, man turns his gaze from externals in on to himself. Literature, music and art are the first and most sensitive spheres in which this spiritual revolution makes itself felt . . . They turn away from the soulless life of the present towards those substances and ideas which give free scope to the non-material strivings of the soul."[36]

In *The Case Against College* (1975), feminist writer Caroline Bird accused the most passionate proponents of liberal arts of making a religion out of them. At the end of the century, the British philosopher Roger Scruton wrote that "there should attach to the products of a high culture the same sense of profound mystery and ineffable meaning that is the daily diet of religion" and that after the Enlightenment "art [including the masterpieces of literature and music] became a redeeming enterprise, and the artist stepped into the place vacated by the prophet and the priest." But Scruton saw high culture going further than religion in some ways, opening "itself to human possibilities other than those contained in its religious root" and venturing "into spiritual territory that has no place on the Christian map."[37]

Although some of the staunchest defenders of high culture, such as T. S. Eliot, were also defenders of traditional religions, many other writers, thinkers, artists, and composers valued art and culture more. Early in the century, James Joyce portrayed his young hero in *A Portrait of the Artist as a Young Man* rebelling against his Irish Catholic schooling by the Jesuits, who were so assured in their teachings about sin, heaven, hell, and the workings of God. Such rebellions against the faith of their parents occurred often among artistic types of people and intellectuals (including some scientists) in the remaining decades of the century.

At century's end sociologist Peter L. Berger observed that an influential and international strand of intellectuals "with Western-style higher education, especially in the humanities and social sciences" tended to be more secular, less religious in any traditional sense, than the general populations among whom they lived.[38] It certainly seemed to be the case with many professors in the Western world, who generally valued high culture more than did the general population.

For a long time during the twentieth century, it seemed that as science and technology advanced and the world became more urban, people generally became more secular and less religious. Under communist governments and in other areas such as Mexico (after 1917) and interwar Turkey, governments took deliberate secularization steps. In 1947 the new state of India was established on a secular basis, favoring no particular religion despite its overwhelming Hindu majority.

By the late 1970s, however, there were increasing signs of fundamentalists of various religions challenging secularist beliefs. Gabriel A. Almond, a scholar who studied different types of religious fundamentalism and realized that considerable differences existed among them, nevertheless thought they all were "reactions against the modern secular world and its twin engines of modernization—technology and science."[39]

Beginning with the fall of the shah of Iran in 1979, fundamentalists started to reverse secularist trends in a number of Muslim countries. And by the end of the century Muslim political forces were exerting increasing pressure upon the Turkish secular government, as well as other secular governments in Muslim lands. In India a resurgence of Hindu fundamentalism was displayed by the success of the Hindu nationalist Bharatiya Janata Party (BJP). By the mid-1990s it had become the largest party in the Indian parliament, and in 1998 it formed a coalition government.

Among U.S. Protestants, after a more liberal predominance in the middle of the century, fundamentalists also displayed renewed vigor

in the final decades of the century. In 1979 Jerry Falwell founded the
Moral Majority, a conservative political lobbying movement, which
the next year supported the presidential candidacy of Ronald
Reagan. Thereafter, it and other conservative Christians remained a
potent force in U.S. politics. Falwell's views were summed up well in
a July 2004 speech, formerly on his website:

> During the past 35 years or so, we have expelled prayer from our schools and
> legalized abortion on demand. Our divorce rate has soared to 50%. There are
> one million teen pregnancies each year. We have a drug epidemic. We are
> considering legalizing same sex marriage and trying hard to normalize the
> gay and lesbian lifestyle. School violence has burst upon the scene. Our
> culture is collapsing. Hollywood, television, video games, internet
> pornography and other influences are destroying our children and our
> values. America is in serious jeopardy of self-destroying.[40]

In these same decades, Reform, Conservative, and even Orthodox
Judaism were increasingly being challenged by a form of Judaism
one textbook referred to as "ultra-Orthodoxy." Perceiving it as
another form of the fundamentalism that was resurging "around the
globe since the mid-1970s," this text stated that the ultra-Orthodox
"rejected a life portioned between two worlds (secular and religious)
and sought, instead, one whole life in total segregation from the
modern world and modernist forms of Judaism, in communities of
distinctive dress, occupation, and self-governance."[41]

By the end of the century, many scholars believed, as Peter L.
Berger stated, that "the world, with some notable exceptions [such as
Europe] . . . is as religious as it ever has been, and in some places is
more religious than ever."[42] Although some distinctions regarding
religiosity will be made later when we consider virtues and values,
statistics from the late 1990s offer some support for Berger's position.

At the end of the century, over 80 percent of the world's population
thought of themselves as belonging to some religion or another. Less
than 20 percent, slightly over 1 billion people, did not adhere to any
particular faith, but about half of them believed in some sort of a
supreme being or beings. Slightly more than half of the world's
population considered themselves Christians (a little over 2 billion) or
Muslims (about 1.3 billion); Hindus, overwhelmingly living in
India, were the third largest religious group (over 800 million); and
Buddhism, the fourth (about 350 million). Sikhism, Judaism,
Baha'ism, Confucianism, Jainism, and Shintoism followed in that
order with a combined total of about 55 million adherents. There were
also numerous other religious believers in smaller groups or in ones
difficult to classify. One source estimated that if one combined

believers in Chinese traditional religion, African traditional and diasporic religion, and the primal-indigenous religions of other peoples, the total would be about 800 million people.[43] In China, Africa, and to a lesser extent in other places many people combined teachings of different religions, for example Chinese traditional religious beliefs with Confucianism and/or Taoism.

The government of China, like other communist governments such as that of the Soviet Union up until the mid-1980s, selectively persecuted religious believers. Marxism had taught that religion was unscientific and superstitious, the "opium of the people." Years of such persecution and propaganda, including that taught in the schools, did reduce the percentage of religious believers in countries such as the Soviet Union and China. By 1937, for example, after the Soviet government had reduced by persecution the number of priests and religious ministers to less than half of its 1926 total, slightly less three-fifths of Soviet adults still considered themselves religious believers. At the beginning of the century, when Russian Orthodoxy was closely connected to the tsarist government, the number of Orthodox and other believers was still well over 90 percent of the population of the Russian Empire. Despite the return of some people to religious belief after the collapse of the Soviet Union, especially in the economically troubled 1990s, a survey by the Pew Research Center in the early twenty-first century found that only 14 percent of the Russian people interviewed said that religion was important to them. (In this same survey the percentage in the United States was 59 percent; Great Britain, 33 percent; Japan, 12 percent; and France 11 percent.)[44]

During approximately seven decades of communist religious persecution in Russia, many Orthodox priests cooperated with the government. The same could be said for many German Lutheran and Catholic clergy under the less directly anti-religious Nazis.[45] The reasons for the cooperation of clergy with governments were often complex, as were the political stances of religious leaders. Should more clergy, for example, have condemned their country's participation in World War I? Very few did. Throughout the century, should more religious people have followed the example of Tolstoy, Gandhi, and Martin Luther King Jr. and preached non-violence? Among religious followers, there was little consensus.

Throughout the century in most religions important divisions continued to exist. We have already mentioned the division between fundamentalists and liberal Protestants. Within the Catholic Church the emergence in Latin America in the late 1960s of Liberation Theology and later papal criticism of it was an important development.

Faced by the grinding poverty suffered by many Latin Americans, the theologians who advocated this new approach emphasized the importance of Christianity being grounded in a concern for the poor and in helping them to overcome the many social injustices they faced. One of the leaders of the movement, the Peruvian theologian Gustavo Gutiérrez, wrote of the necessity "of a commitment of solidarity with the poor, with those who suffer misery and injustice ... It is not a question of idealizing poverty, but rather of taking it on as it is—an evil—to protest against it and to struggle to abolish it."[46]

In 1978, however, a Polish cardinal was elected Pope John Paul II. He was convinced that the communist rule he had experienced in Poland was evil and that liberation theology reflected too much Marxian influence. In the years that followed, he weakened the liberationists' sway. To aid him in this and other efforts to insure the purity of Catholic doctrine, in 1981 he appointed Joseph Ratzinger, archbishop of Munich, to head the Congregation for the Doctrine of the Faith, earlier known as the Holy Office, and further back as the Holy Inquisition. In the mid-1980s, Ratzinger authored two criticisms of liberation theology, *Instruction on Certain Aspects of the "Theology of Liberation"* and *Instruction on Christian Freedom and Liberation*. In some preliminary notes in 1984, he acknowledged that there were different types of liberation theology but that his criticism was directed at "those theologies which, in one way or another, have embraced the marxist fundamental option" and that "an analysis of the phenomenon of liberation theology reveals that it constitutes a fundamental threat to the faith of the Church."[47] He believed that liberation from sin, rather than liberation from poverty, should be the primary Christian emphasis. For the remainder of the century and beyond, Cardinal (as he had become) Ratzinger helped weaken the influence of liberationists, as well as other Catholic dissenters who strayed too far from what John Paul II and he thought of as proper Catholic doctrine.[48] Upon the death of John Paul in 2005, Cardinal Ratzinger was selected as Pope Benedict XVI.

Although weakened in many ways by the end of the century, liberation theology still exercised considerable influence in the poorer countries of the world. Considering that more Catholics lived in Latin America than in Europe and North America combined and that Africa had many more Catholics than all of North America, this continuing influence was especially significant.

From an organizational perspective, the three main Christian divisions in order of adherents in the 1990s were Catholics, Protestants, and Orthodox, with Protestants having numerous sub-divisions such as Baptists, Methodists, and Lutherans. In Islam the major division was between Sunnis and Shia, with the former outnumbering the latter by about a 7 to 1 ratio in the 1990s. At various times in their long histories, there have been serious conflicts leading to bloodshed between branches of the same faith, for example, between Catholics and Protestants, and between Sunni and Shia. In the twentieth century, this phenomenon still occurred sporadically, usually interrelated to ethnic conflicts. Catholics and Protestants fought, for example, in Northern Ireland and Catholics and Orthodox (as well as Muslims) clashed in a disintegrating Yugoslavia in the early 1990s. But conflict between people of different religions (as opposed to different branches of the same faith) took even more lives in the century, especially those of large numbers of Hindus and Muslims in the area of what had once been British India, today's India, Pakistan, and Bangladesh. (See Chapter 1 for more on religion and violence.)

Counterbalancing such divisions were ecumenical trends that attempted to bring religions closer together. In 1948 the World Council of Churches was established, and for the remainder of the century helped foster cooperation between Protestants, Catholics, and Orthodox. The ecumenical spirit of the Catholic Vatican II has already been mentioned, and some Christian leaders also made attempts to overcome a legacy of antisemitism.

As opposed as some religious leaders were to the spirit of postmodernism, with its rejection of absolute or objective truths, some scholars saw postmodernist influences as an opportunity for religion. One religious text states: "With the relativizing of scientific knowledge in the postmodern period, religious knowledge no longer suffers from the disadvantage that had allowed modern critics to dismiss its validity. Now both science and religion come to be seen as equal, if only because, from a postmodern perspective, they are equally relative."[49] This same text looks upon the postmodern condition, and a globalization that brings various believers more into contact with each other, as an opportunity for people to become more tolerant of each other's beliefs and leave behind the idea that only their religion possesses ultimate truth.

Virtues and Values

Underlying much of the discussion about culture, science, education, and religion is the question of virtues and values. In her book *The De-Moralization of Society* (1994), historian Gertrude Himmelfarb argued that "it was not until the present century that morality became so thoroughly relativized and subjectified that virtues ceased to be 'virtues' and became 'values.' This transmutation is the great philosophical revolution of modernity."[50] For this change, she specifically blamed Nietzsche and Max Weber, one of the fathers of modern sociology. And "blamed" is the correct word, for she thought that when Victorians thought of virtues they thought of such traits as honesty, integrity, chastity, fidelity, respectability, politeness, courage, generosity, prudence, sobriety, thrift, cleanliness, and self-reliance, in short qualities to which Victorians, and later Himmelfarb herself, thought people should aspire. The problem she has with "values" as they are generally defined is that they are too subjective and carry too little moral weight—"they can be beliefs, opinions, attitudes, feelings, habits, conventions, preferences, prejudices, even idiosyncrasies." And about others' values modern society often tells us to be non-judgmental, while Victorians felt more comfortable judging the presence or absence of virtues.[51]

Like Himmelfarb, other conservatives also liked to speak of virtues. Himmelfarb mentioned favorably the British Conservative Party prime minister of the 1980s, Margaret Thatcher, who praised both Victorian virtues and conservatives who wrote of virtues such as the American Michael Novak. In Thatcher's memoirs she mentions being impressed by his emphasis on democratic capitalism as a system that "encouraged a range of virtues."[52] Former Secretary of Education under President Reagan, William Bennet, edited *The Book of Virtues: A Treasury of Great Moral Stories* (1993) illustrating such virtues as self-discipline, compassion, responsibility, courage, perseverance, honesty, loyalty, and faith.

Like many conservatives, Himmelfarb believed that people in the Western world in the final decades of the twentieth century were less moral (despite the efforts of Thatcher and Reagan) than the Victorians of a century earlier. Thus, the title of her book *The De-Moralization of Society*. Among the contemporary moral conditions and "social pathologies" that alarmed her in the USA and Great Britain were "crime, drugs, violence, illegitimacy, promiscuity, [and] pornography." Like Thatcher, she believed government welfare policies had helped create a culture of dependency. She also faulted political and cultural leaders, fearful of seeming to make moral judgments, for failing to champion virtues that would strengthen society.[53]

Himmelfarb's book on de-moralization provided ammunition for the conservative side of what some in the USA termed the "cultural war." This conflict over values clearly emerged by the end of the 1980s and continued through the remainder of the century and beyond. Art critic Robert Hughes, in his book *The Culture of Complaint: The Fraying of America* (1993), dates its start in the visual arts to 1989 when a U.S. senator on the Senate floor tore up in disgust a copy of a photograph entitled "Piss Christ," and insisted that taxpayer money should not be used to support such "trash." In other areas, however, the cultural war began even earlier.

An early prelude to this conflict was the debate over the book *Situation Ethics* (1966) written by the Anglican theologian Joseph Fletcher. Basically, Fletcher argued that an ethics based on unbending moral laws with no exceptions was too rigid. He gave the specific example of abortion, rejecting the moral position that it was always wrong regardless of the situation or circumstances, for example even in case conception was due to rape. In place of a system of absolute "dos" and "don'ts," he advocated acting in the most loving way possible in any particular situation. For the remainder of the century, conservative Christians argued against such thinking. One Christian writer was appalled when most of the people in a Bible class agreed that in some cases it might be appropriate to lie, for example "if a robber breaks into your house and seems to be interested in doing harm to your wife and children, and asks you if they are in the house." The writer argued that it was not permissible to lie even in such a case.[54]

In the year 2000, the editor of the conservative *Christian Courier* wrote an article "Did Jesus Endorse Situation Ethics?" In it he wrote:

> Situation ethics is the notion that there are no absolute rules governing "right" and "wrong." Rather, all human activity is determined by the situation of the moment—supposedly guided by "love" alone . . . This philosophy of situation ethics is bereft of merit . . . Subjectivity can never be the standard for human conduct . . . If "situation ethics" is valid, there is no act under heaven that cannot be justified! . . . Situation ethics is a voguish belief in a world of immoral rebels who are determined to cast off divine restraints and "play God."[55]

Besides the ethics debate, the 1960s in the West also featured the countercultural critique of the dominant culture. Thus, cultural conflict was nothing new in the 1990s, but the "cultural war" of that decade had its unique features. On one side of this "war" were conservatives who believed that some sort of eternal, unchangeable, external moral authority existed that enabled them to determine what was right and wrong. For most of them the ultimate such authority was God, but their church, scripture, or some other source or combination of sources aided them in determining God's will. On the other side were those whom the scholar James Davison Hunter in his book *Culture Wars* (1991) called progressives. They relied more on reason, their inner selves, and contemporary conditions in deciding right from wrong. These divisions cut across many religious lines, with different Catholics, Protestants, and Jews, for example, being on both sides of the line.

In his book Hunter referred to Gramsci's view that "during periods of societal transformation ... a significant cleavage forms among intellectuals and other cultural elites." After elaborating further on Gramsci's ideas, Hunter added, "these ideas are immensely relevant to understanding the contemporary American situation."[56] Some conservatives also thought that Gramsci's thinking was pertinent to the cultural war. U.S. talk-show host Rush Limbaugh wrote in his book *See, I Told You So* that "leftist think tanks worship at Gramsci's altar," and that "Gramsci succeeded in defining a strategy for waging cultural warfare—a tactic that has been adopted by the modern left, and which remains the last great hope for chronic America-bashers." According to Limbaugh, the left was following the advice of the "obscure Italian communist" Gramsci to capture the leading cultural institutions and subvert belief in God and "divinely inspired moral absolutes."[57]

In addition to Limbaugh, at least several other conservatives identified Gramsci as a chief influence on their opponents in the cultural war, perhaps even overemphasizing his influence because he was a communist. One conservative wrote that "beneath the surface of American politics an intense ideological struggle is being waged between two competing worldviews," one of which he labeled "Gramscian." He described Gramsci's position as "'absolute historicism,' meaning that morals, values, truths, standards and human nature itself are products of different historical epochs. There are no absolute moral standards that are universally true for all human beings outside of a particular historical context; rather, morality is 'socially constructed.'" The author was troubled by what he saw as "the slow but steady advance of Gramscian and Hegelian-Marxist ideas through the major institutions of American democracy, including the Congress, courts, and executive branch," and he also lamented that these "ideas are also prominent in three other major sectors of American civil society: foundations, universities, and corporations."[58]

In his book *Values Matter Most* (1995), Ben J. Wattenberg agreed "that the values situation in America has deteriorated" and recommended books by Himmelfarb and Novak, but concentrated on values' interrelationship with politics and policy. Among the 44 value issues he listed were abortion, pornography, illegitimacy, infidelity, homosexuality, movies and television, and various issues related to what occurred in public schools, for example, sex education, dispensing condoms, and prayer.[59] About curriculum issues like teaching evolution or having students read books that some parents found offensive, he has little to say, but these were also school issues contested in the cultural war.

Cultural conflict also existed in Europe. George Weigel, the author of *Witness to Hope: The Biography of John Paul II* (1999), wrote that "John Paul argued for the priority of culture over politics and economics as the engine of historical change; and at the heart of culture, he proposed, is cult, or religion."[60] Weigel also believed that culture lay at the center of a crisis facing Europe by the end of the twentieth century. Looking back at the century, he blamed many of Europe's earlier problems on "atheistic humanism." During the 1990s, European culture was no longer "bedeviled by atheistic humanism in its most raw forms"; but, Weigel believed, it was "profoundly shaped . . . by a kinder, gentler cousin . . . 'exclusive humanism': a set of ideas that, in the name of democracy, human rights, tolerance, and civility, demands that all transcendent religious or spiritual reference points must be kept out of European public life."[61]

During the early twenty-first century, Weigel addressed more thoroughly Europe's cultural conflict in a book, *The Cube and the Cathedral* (2005), and in an article, "Europe's Two Culture Wars" (2006).

In his article he stated: "The first of these wars [is] . . . a war between the postmodern forces of moral relativism and the defenders of traditional moral conviction. The second . . . is the struggle to define the nature of civil society, the meaning of tolerance and pluralism, and the limits of multiculturalism in an aging Europe whose below-replacement-level fertility rates have opened the door to rapidly growing and assertive Muslim populations." He thought that "the aggressors" in the first war were "radical secularists, motivated by . . . 'Christophobia,'" wishing "to eliminate the vestiges of Europe's Judeo-Christian culture from a post-Christian European Union by demanding same-sex marriage in the name of equality, by restricting free speech in the name of civility, and by abrogating core aspects of religious freedom in the name of tolerance." In the second war, Weigel identified "the aggressors" as "radical and jihadist Muslims who detest the West, who are determined to impose Islamic taboos on Western societies by violent protest and other forms of coercion if necessary, and who see such operations as the first stage toward the Islamification of Europe."[62]

In other parts of the world, cultural conflicts also existed, again often pitting traditional religious views against more secularist ones. A good overview of global value changes in the last two decades of the twentieth century is presented in the *World Values Surveys* (WVS), conducted in 1981, 1990–1, 1995–6 and 1999–2001.[63] One of the major findings of the surveys was that technological and economic development had a great impact on values. In general, the poorer and less technologically developed countries were more likely to have values that were traditionally religious, not secular and rationalistic. Such societies also tended to emphasize absolute standards, traditional family values, and respect for authority, while repudiating divorce, abortion, suicide, and euthanasia. Such societies also tended to be more nationalistic than those espousing more secular-rational values.

By the end of the twentieth century, based on data from the WVS, Latin American, African, and Middle Eastern countries such as El Salvador, Puerto Rico, Columbia, Morocco, Nigeria, Algeria, Tanzania, and Jordan held the most traditional values. But the Muslim countries surveyed, including Indonesia with the world's largest number of Muslims, were no more traditional on average than the Catholic Latin American countries.

The most secular-rationalist countries were Japan and Sweden, while the rest of "Protestant Europe" and most "ex-communist" countries (as well as communist-led China) also scored high on secular-rationalist values. One point that needs to be noted, however, is that while established religious institutions grew weaker (measured, for example, by attendance at religious services) in such countries, an increasing interest in personal spiritual matters (measured, for example, by an increase in thinking about the meaning of life) was also often evident.

The countries of "Catholic Europe" and the English-speaking world generally scored lower in secular-rationalist values than those of "Protestant Europe," with Ireland and Portugal scoring the lowest. Thus, as important as technological and economic development was in influencing values, other factors such as religious and cultural traditions also had their effects. The more technologically and economically developed Ireland, for example, with its strong Catholic tradition, espoused less secular-rationalist values than the ex-communist Bulgaria, whose per capita income in 1999 was only about one-fifteenth of that of Ireland.

Among other countries surveyed, secular-rationalist values in the USA were less widespread than the rest of the English-speaking countries or Europe with the clear exceptions of Portugal and Ireland. The USA score on a secular-rationalist/traditional-religious WVS map was closest to Poland and India.

In the 1990s within surveyed countries with more than one significant religious group, Protestants tended to be more secular-rationalist than Catholics; but Catholics and Hindus more so than Muslims. Yet one's national culture seemed to have a greater impact than one's religion. Thus, although U.S. Protestants were more secular-rationalist than U.S. Catholics, they were less so than West German or Swiss Catholics. Similarly, the Nigerian Christians were more secular-rationalist than Nigerian Muslims, but were less so than Indian Muslims.

Another interesting finding of the WVS was that as countries modernized, became wealthier, and switched more of their economies from manufacturing to service and knowledge sectors, their populations tended to worry less about economic security and became more concerned with values such as self-expression, individual freedom, subjective well-being, and the quality of life, including environmental quality. Such people also tended to be more tolerant of diverse groups including foreigners, gays and lesbians, and they tended to offer greater support to gender equality.

The regions that received the highest scores for their concern for such values were Protestant Europe and the English-speaking countries, with Catholic Europe, Japan, and Latin America next, and the ex-communist countries, South Asia, and Africa lagging further behind. Islamic countries were much less tolerant of homosexuality, divorce, abortion, and gender equality than were industrialized Western countries, but much more supportive of strong religious leaders.

Most of the ex-communist countries underwent a wrenching economic experience in the1990s as they attempted to convert their economies from the old government-planned economies to more free market systems. Thus, their people's emphasis on survivor (economic security) versus self-expression values is hardly surprising, nor is the emphasis on such values among poor Africans like those in Zimbabwe or South Asians like those in Bangladesh, both countries with a per capita yearly income in 1999 of less than $600.

Since economic development generally spurred both secular and self-expression values, they were usually higher in the late 1990s than during earlier *World Values Surveys*. But the difficult times that many ex-communist countries underwent in the 1990s moved them in the opposite direction. Those countries that suffered the most showed the greatest tendency to retreat to traditional religious and survivor values. As might be expected, young people in wealthier and ex-communist countries tended to be less traditional in their values than older people. This was much less true, however, in poorer countries.

Conclusion

The *World Values Surveys* provide considerable global perspective not only on virtues and values, but also on cultural wars, postmodernism, and other topics treated in this chapter. They indicate that religious beliefs and attitudes towards virtues and values are strongly influenced by economic, social, and cultural conditions. The fact that Indian Muslims scored higher on the secular-rationalist chart than Nigerian Christians, or that Russians' support for traditional-religious views increased in the economically troubled 1990s, reinforces the point that national culture and economic environment greatly influence the way people think. Such a realization might lead to more tolerance of others' views and greater humility concerning the righteousness of one's own views. The U.S. culture wars were especially marked by the frequent absence of humility and tolerance and the presence on both sides of feelings of moral superiority. This was ironic considering the emphasis that Christian tradition has often placed on humility and secular-rational thinking on tolerance.

The surveys also provide perspective on feelings of national superiority. Because about 50 percent of those surveyed in the USA in the mid and late 1990s, as compared to less than 10 percent of those in Sweden or Japan, responded that God was of the highest significance in their lives, did that make the USA morally superior to Sweden or Japan? If so, then did it make Brazil and Nigeria, where almost 90 percent of respondents gave God's place in their lives the highest significance, superior to the USA?

One of the questions in the surveys was "How often, if at all, do you think about the meaning and purpose of life?" From 1981 into the late 1990s, the percentage of people globally who responded "often" increased, especially in advanced industrial democracies. Thus, despite increasing economic prosperity, consumerism, and cultural movements such as postmodernism, people increasingly looked for deeper meaning in their lives. Even the often inspiring wonders of science did not seem enough for many people, and when setbacks or hard times occurred, people often sought meaning or solace in religion or other areas that spoke to the spirit such as poetry, philosophy, or music.

The findings of the *World Values Surveys* call to mind the experience of Robert Kennedy after the assassination of his brother, U.S. President John Kennedy. He turned for consolation to both his Catholic faith and to the wisdom of Greek dramatists and the writings of Emerson, Camus, and other thinkers.

9

An Age of Progress?

In the 1860s the Russian novelist Leo Tolstoy accused historians of muddled thinking when they wrote of progress. Emphasizing the dazzling array of new technologies—in print, transportation, communication (railroads, steam engines, telegraphs, and the like)—historians seemed to assume that such developments necessarily contributed to improvements in the overall welfare of individuals and nations. But Tolstoy was convinced that "progress on one side is always paid back by retrogression on the other side of human life." For him the growth of cities and newspapers, gas-lighting, railways, and sewing machines, all were either regressive developments or not worth the cost of destroying forests and people's sense of simplicity and moderation.[1] Whether Tolstoy was right or wrong about the effects of such developments is less important than the questions his criticism prompts. What is progress? How is it to be measured? Tolstoy himself equated it with an overall improvement of well-being, which is perhaps as good a definition as any. Thus, the task at hand is to summarize the changing nature of global well-being over the course of the twentieth century, as well as changing perceptions about it.

A key figure in developing the nineteenth-century view of progress, criticized by Tolstoy, was the eighteenth century Scotch economist Adam Smith. He believed that economic progress depended upon the division of labor, free trade, and people pursuing their own economic self-interest. But he also thought that a benevolent God, by use of an "invisible hand" and the free-market system, coordinated this individual self-seeking to advance the public good and keep "in continual motion the industry of mankind." In his study of the history of progress, Christopher Lasch wrote that "compared to

Smith's incisive analysis of the social implications of desire, various tributes to the power of reason and to the progress of the arts and sciences . . . contributed very little to a plausible theory of progress."[2]

Early Twentieth-Century Views of Progress

More than a century after Smith's death his belief that an "invisible hand" was guiding individual acquisitive desires toward the overall improvement of mankind was still strong. In a previous chapter, we have seen how the rise of a consumer culture in the United States before and after World War I helped produce "a future-oriented culture of desire that confused the good life with goods."[3]

Of course, early twentieth century views of progress were not limited to measuring it solely by human's ability to buy more, but technological and economic developments that increased this possibility certainly remained important. In his memoir the Austrian Jewish writer Stefan Zweig (1881–1942) captured well the more comprehensive view of progress shared by many people. He wrote:

> In its liberal idealism, the nineteenth century was honestly convinced that it was on the straight and unfailing path towards being the best of all worlds. Earlier eras, with their wars, famines, and revolts, were deprecated as times when mankind was still immature and unenlightened. But now it was merely a matter of decades until the last vestige of evil and violence would finally be conquered, and this faith in an uninterrupted and irresistible "progress" truly had the force of a religion for that generation. One began to believe more in this "progress" than in the Bible, and its gospel appeared ultimate because of the daily new wonders of science and technology.[4]

Zweig went on to mention the turn-of-the-century wonders of electric lights, telephones, horseless carriages, indoor plumbing, improved sanitation and medical treatment, expanded justice and human rights, including the right to vote, and added "even the problem of problems, the poverty of the great masses, no longer seemed insurmountable." And people "honestly believed that the divergences and the boundaries between nations and sects would gradually melt away into a common humanity and that peace and security, the highest of treasures, would be shared by all mankind."[5]

By 1910, after he had traveled to various parts of Europe, India, Africa, and America, he still believed that "there was progress everywhere."[6] Three decades later however, writing his memoirs while living abroad during World War II, he acknowledged the mistake many of his generation had made in believing that moral progress was accompanying "technical progress." He wrote of how the bestial developments of more recent decades had made him and others skeptical about the chances of mankind's moral improvement.[7] In 1942 he and his second wife committed suicide while residing in Brazil.

Even before World War I not everyone was as optimistic as young Zweig had been. Historian Barbara Tuchman later acknowledged the progress that existed and the optimism that many had, but insisted that "our misconception lies in assuming that doubt and fear, ferment, protest, violence and hate were not equally present."[8] In chapters dealing with such topics as anarchism, militarism, and imperialism, she clearly indicated the less positive developments of the time. In a chapter on German culture ("Neroism Is in the Air"), she asserted that besides the "dominant mood of self-confident power and pugnacity," there was a weaker trend that suggested "disaster, of a city ripe for burning, of Neroism in the Air."[9] In his study of Russian culture, *The Icon and the Ax*, historian James Billington discerned a similar mood of apocalypticism during this same period. He thought it was one of the three chief Russian cultural trends of the era, along with sensualism and Prometheanism, the more optimistic belief that humans could heroically transform earthly existence.

Another problem, and one that helped lead to World War I, was the skewed view of progress held by some who interpreted (or misinterpreted) the ideas of Charles Darwin to argue that progress required conflict and war. Take, for example, the German General Bernhardi, who wrote a few years before the outbreak of the war:

> War is a biological necessity of the first importance, a regulative element in the life of mankind which cannot be dispensed with, since without it an unhealthy development will follow, which excludes every advancement of the race, and therefore all real civilization . . .
> . . . It is clear that those intellectual and moral factors which insure superiority in war are also those which render possible a general progressive development. They confer victory because the elements of progress are latent in them. Without war, inferior or decaying races would easily choke the growth of healthy budding elements, and a universal decadence would follow.[10]

Such thinking did not go unopposed. For example, the Englishman Norman Angell in his popular pre-war book *The Great Illusion* argued that "war has no longer the justification that it makes for the survival of the fittest; it involves the survival of the less fit. The idea that the struggle between nations is a part of the evolutionary law of man's advance involves a profound misreading of the biological analogy."[11] Yet, it took the horrific experiences of World War I to convince many people, especially in Europe, that war retarded rather than stimulated progress.

Scientific, Technological, Economic Progress, and Greater Freedom

Although few people still believed as Bernhardi had by the end of the twentieth century, many individuals continued to be affected by Smith's view of progress, believing that the ever-expanding products of industry contributed greatly to the overall improvement of human well-being. And like the young Zweig, some people were also heartened by "the daily new wonders of science and technology."

Before detailing and analyzing the violence of the bloodiest century ever—and helping thereby dispel any rosy view of the twentieth century—historian Niall Ferguson wrote that "the hundred years after 1900 were a time of unparalleled progress." He noted that from 1870 to 1998, per capita global domestic product increased by more than six and a half times and that "by the end of the twentieth century, thanks to myriad technological advances and improvements in knowledge, human beings on average lived longer and better lives than at any time in history."[12] And there was indeed little doubt that by 1999 people possessed more goods than they had in 1900, and most of them worked at their jobs far fewer hours than their ancestors had. U.S. factory workers, for example, averaged 53 hours per week in 1900 as compared to 42 hours in 2000. Many western European workers reduced their workweek even more.

Despite setbacks and much economic misery during the century, and despite continuing great disparities between the world's rich and poor, figures from the World Bank and the Asian Development Bank indicate that the percentage of the world's population living in extreme poverty also declined in the final decades of the twentieth century. In China, for example, the poverty rate fell from 28 percent in 1978 to 9 percent in 1998; in India, it dropped from 51 percent in 1977–8 to 26 percent in 1999–2000.[13]

Along with better economic conditions, the expansion of freedom has also often been considered a hallmark of progress (see above, Chapter 5, for more on the relationship of economic well-being and freedom). In his *History of the Idea of Progress* (1980), Robert Nisbet devoted a whole chapter to eighteenth and nineteenth century thinkers who thought "the very purpose, the ultimate objective, of progress would be the steady and evermore encompassing advance of individual freedom in the world."[14] Freedom House, which has been calculating the percentage of free and unfree countries in the world since the early 1970s, estimated that in 1973, 1990, and 2000 the respective percentage of unfree nations declined from 43 to 37 to 25 percent. At the beginning of the twentieth century, with imperialism still in its heyday, the percentage of unfree countries was certainly much higher than even the 43 percent indicated in 1973. One reason for the increased political freedom from 1973 to 2000 was that by the latter date the former communist countries of Europe were freer than they had been under communist domination. And despite its continuing communist government, the Chinese people were certainly freer by century's end than they had been before Mao Zedong's death in 1976.

Despite the legitimate concerns about technology's negative impact on freedom expressed by individuals from Aldous Huxley to the Unabomber, Theodore Kaczinski, there was also greater overall freedom and recognition of human rights at the end of the twentieth century than at the beginning. The experience of women illustrates the point. Although there were significant regional deviations and exceptions—for example, the restrictions on women imposed by the Taliban in Afghanistan during the century's final decade, one has only to compare the situation of the world's women in 1900 and 1999 to see that overall their freedoms expanded during the century (see Chapter 5).

Environmental, Moral, and Cultural Progress?

Although significant scientific, technological, and economic progress, as well as expanded freedoms cannot be denied, in other fields the measurement of twentieth century progress (or well-being) was more complicated. We have already noted that two forces that greatly contributed to twentieth century progress—scientific/technological developments and economic growth—also had detrimental environmental effects (see Chapter 6). There was little doubt that by 1999 Planet Earth was in worse shape overall than in 1900, with global warming having become an especially troubling problem.[15]

Part of twentieth-century environmental history was the tremendous growth of urbanization, with the percentage of people living in urban areas jumping from less than one-sixth's of the earth's population to almost one-half from 1900 to 1999. Well before the twentieth century began and all during it, people debated the extent to which urbanization contributed to, or detracted from, people's welfare.

From the beginning of the Industrial Revolution in England in the eighteenth century, there had been voices raised against the new urban industrial centers, and the Romantic Age of literature in the early nineteenth century, featuring such poets as William Wordsworth, expanded criticisms of urban life. In the United States, Thomas Jefferson once wrote: "I view great cities as pestilential to the morals, the health, and the liberties of man."[16] In his *Notes of Virginia* (1784) he had also expressed anti-urban sentiments; but later developments, including the War of 1812, softened such sentiments as he became more convinced of the necessity of U.S. manufacturing self-reliance. Later American writers such as Ralph Waldo Emerson, Henry David Thoreau, Herman Melville, Nathaniel Hawthorne, Edgar Allen Poe, Henry Adams, Henry James, William Dean Howells, Frank Norris, Theodore Dreiser, and Willa Cather also expressed anti-urban sentiments to varying degrees, many of the latter writers being especially critical of New York.

The sentiments of Howells were influenced by England's William Morris and John Ruskin and Russia's Leo Tolstoy. Tolstoy was an especially severe critic of urban life, which he thought was a corrupting influence. To him agricultural work was honorable and most urban work was done by workers exploited by a parasitical bourgeoisie devoted to the "production of pleasing trifles" and "the most unnecessary, stupid, depraving products" (see above, Chapter 7).

Tolstoy's anti-urbanism also influenced Mahatma Gandhi. He established a rural commune in South Africa which he called the Tolstoy Farm and corresponded with Tolstoy before the latter's death in 1910. A year earlier, Gandhi sounded very Tolstoyan in praising his Indian ancestors who "reasoned that large cities were a snare and a useless encumbrance and that people would not be happy in them, that there would be gangs of thieves and robbers, prostitution and vice flourishing in them and that poor men would be robbed by rich men. They [modern India's ancestors] were, therefore, satisfied with small villages."[17]

In other parts of the world, other writers also often criticized city life. Many African writers, for example, wrote of the corrupting effects of it. Passages like the following taken from Cyprian Ekwensi's novel *People of the City* (1954) are not unusual: "Lajide had lived too long in the city [a fictional city resembling Lagos] to care about right or wrong, so long as the end was achieved. And that end was so often money."[18]

From time to time later in the century, for example in the USA in the 1960s, some people, disenchanted with city life, abandoned it and established rural communes—such communes were in keeping with an older utopian tradition stretching back to the nineteenth century.

In the 1960s, a move to the countryside was sometimes motivated by a nostalgic and rosy vision of what rural life was like. As one author writing of the USA in the decades after the Civil War observed: "It is difficult to think of country life without illusion. We are always tempted to invest it with virtues that appear to have been corrupted in urban culture . . . Country living presents visions of nostalgia to soothe city nerves." He then added, however, that "these visions are grossly inaccurate especially when applied to the good old days. Country life in the post-Civil War era was an unremitting hardship."[19] The temptation to idealize a past rural existence was widespread. To take just the example of Russia, the nostalgic village poetry of Sergei Esenin (1895–1925) appealed to many newly urbanized Soviet citizens whose roots remained in the countryside. And from the 1960s into the 1980s, "village prose" was perhaps the most significant fictional genre. It was characterized by its sympathy with village life and people and concerned with the preservation of village values, nature, and Russian traditions. And it reflected a distrust of modern "progress" and technology.[20]

While Tolstoy, Gandhi, and many other critics faulted urban life mainly for ethical reasons, others did so more from an aesthetic viewpoint. Although there is no denying the beauty existing in some of the architecture, parks, street life, and cultural institutions like art galleries, urban life also had its uglier side. Raymond Unwin, the chief planner of London's Hampstead Garden Suburb, wrote in 1909, "We have become so used to living among surroundings in which beauty has little or no place that we do not realise what a remarkable and unique feature the ugliness of modern life is." He attributed it primarily to the consequences of industrial development.[21]

More modern critics such as the architect Witold Rybczynski also commented on the paucity of concern with beauty in most U.S. cities. Although acknowledging some interest in "city beautification," especially early in the century, he thought that city planners became much more "concerned with engineering, economic efficiency, and social reform, not with aesthetics." He contrasted this situation with Paris, which, "unlike almost all North American cities, shows evidence of having been planned according to an aesthetic vision."[22]

Also entering into the question of urbanization's impact on human welfare was the growth of slums. Since by 1999 they comprised a little over three-fourths of the urban population of the least developed countries and about one-third of the global urban population (see Chapter 6), it was difficult to be very positive about the extent to which urbanization had contributed to overall global well-being. In 1990, U.S. theologian Harvey Cox wrote that in the preceding quarter century "much has happened to the cities of the world, including American cities, and most of it has not been good. Instead of contributing to the liberative process, many cities have become sprawling concentrations of human misery, wracked with racial, religious and class animosity. The names Beirut, Calcutta [Kolkata], South Bronx and Belfast conjure images of violence, neglect and death."[23]

Cox's comments came 25 years after the publication of his controversial book *The Secular City*, which eventually sold more than 1 million copies and was translated into more than a dozen languages. In that book Cox argued that "the rise of urban civilization and the collapse of traditional religion are the two main hallmarks of our era and are closely related movements."[24] At that time, however, Cox looked positively upon large secular cities and the opportunities they presented for theological and other types of liberation, including from rural and small town conventions and provincialism. Although 25 years later he was less optimistic about city life, and also willing to recognize the resurgence of traditional religions, Cox's thinking, revolving around such questions as urbanization, modernization, and secularism, continued to touch on the question of moral progress.

One means of appraising such progress would be the level of killing that occurred. During World War II, before Stefan Zweig committed suicide in 1942, it is understandable why he doubted any moral progress had occurred since 1914. In the second half of the century, no global wars took place to match the two world wars of the first half. But many smaller wars occurred that still killed millions, and "27 major armed conflicts" remained at century's end (see Chapter 1 for details). The repressive policies of Mao Zedong and Cambodia's Pol Pot killed many additional millions, as did global poverty. We have already quoted the observation of the World Health Organization (WHO) in the mid-1990s that poverty "wields its destructive influence at every stage of human life, from the moment of conception to the grave." And although poverty rates seemed to be dropping at century's end, ever-faster population increases insured that poverty remained "the world's greatest killer."[25]

Like many writers on progress that will be considered in this section, Robert Nisbet included moral considerations in his assessment of it. Believing that humanity could only advance morally if people continued to believe in progress, he was dismayed in 1980 about the decline of belief in progress that he witnessed in the West. He commented that "there is a great deal more conviction of the reality of progress in some of the unfree nations of the world, beginning with the Soviet Union, than there is the free Western nations," and "there are no prophets of hope and progress, and least of all in the United States." His greatest hope for progress was in a religious renewal, which he already saw signs of in 1980. He ended his *History of the Idea of Progress* stating his belief that it was "in the context of a true culture in which the core is a deep and wide sense of the *sacred*" that we are "likely to regain the vital conditions of progress itself and of faith in progress—past, present, and future."[26]

The end of the Cold War, the collapse of communist governments in the Soviet Bloc from 1989 to 1991, and the less repressive methods used by Mao's successors in China led to renewed Western optimism about global moral progress. The failure of communism, following the earlier collapses of Nazism and Italian Fascism, also led some thinkers to believe that people had progressed by demonstrating that they had become less susceptible to the unrealistic promises of utopian and totalitarian ideologies. People in Russia and some of the other former parts of the former Soviet Bloc, however, were less optimistic in the 1990s, especially where the proclaimed transition to a new order created great insecurities and inequities.

Francis Fukuyama and Michael Mandelbaum maintained that by the end of the century market economies and democratic political systems had gained almost universal recognition as the best means for organizing economic and social life.[27] Mandelbaum added a third element that he believed had become globally accepted, at least in theory, the idea that peaceful means were the proper basis for international relations. Because of the global recognition of these three models, he suggested that moral progress had been made, that "the world was a better, happier place after the end of the Cold War than before." [28]

Another thinker who has seen signs of moral progress in recent decades is the historian Bruce Mazlish. He has argued that globalization and the rise of a global culture has contributed to a "higher level of morality," evidenced by more global regard for others and more concern with global human rights and humanity in general. He also believed that the spread of scientific ideas was helping to overcome local and regional differences. He thought that "the most important aspect of globalization, at least in long-range terms, is the change in consciousness that the process represents," the "bringing into being of a global consciousness." Despite his realization of failures and obstacles to further enlightened globalization and a "higher morality," he has remained hopeful that human efforts can further both goals.[29]

Like Mazlish, Thomas L. Friedman has viewed globalization as a sign of progress. But his thinking has been closer to that of Fukuyama and Mandelbaum in stressing the importance of capitalist "free markets." In 1999, he quoted approvingly the following Merrill Lynch brokerage ad:

> It's no surprise that the world's youngest economy—the global economy—is still finding its bearings. The intricate checks and balances that stabilize economies are only incorporated with time. Many world markets are only recently freed, governed for the first time by the emotions of the people rather than the fists of the state. From where we sit, none of this diminishes the promise offered a decade ago by the demise of the walled-off world . . . The spread of free markets and democracy around the world is permitting more people everywhere to turn their aspirations into achievements. And technology, properly harnessed and liberally distributed, has the power to erase not just geographical borders but also human ones. It seems to us that . . . the world continues to hold great promise.[30]

Many other free-market enthusiasts shared the hopes expressed in these last three sentences and saw them in moral terms. For many years, for example, Michael Novak reiterated thoughts like the following: *"Business is a noble Christian vocation, a work of social justice, and the single greatest institutional hope of the poor of the world. If the poor are to move out of poverty, no other institution can help them as much as business, especially small business." "The best route to liberate the poor is grassroots capitalist development."* "The encouragement of tens of millions of small entrepreneurs in the poorest regions of the globe is the number-one priority of social justice in our time."[31]

As an example of encouraging small entrepreneurs in a poor country like Bangladesh, Novak cited the case of several women who were helped by small loans to expand their businesses. One woman bought small tools, fertilizer, and seedlings to help her begin a flower business, and another used a loan to buy a cell phone that enabled her to check various markets so she could obtain the best price for rice. Starting in 1976, when he loaned $27 to 42 villagers, a Bangladeshi economist, Muhammad Yunus, through the Grameen Bank that he founded, made similar micro-loans. By the time, he and his bank won the Nobel Peace Prize in 2006, his bank had made millions of such small loans, mainly to poor women. The money went to people such as beggars, farm laborers, sweepers, and rickshaw drivers. The bank encouraged those that begged from house to house to take items like cookies or candy with them to sell, and many of the beggars, starting with loans that typically were less than $20, were gradually transformed from beggars to door-to-door salespeople. In awarding the prize the Nobel committee stressed the importance of micro-credit for lessening global poverty and noted the influence that the bank had on other institutions, thousands of which were influenced by the Grameen example in many of the world's poor countries.[32]

Another example of the ability of market principles to alleviate global suffering was the example of the Danish company Vestergaard Frandsen. Originally a weaving company, in the 1980s and 1990s it gradually concentrated its focus to producing relief-aid products and disease control textiles including blankets, tents, tarpaulins, and nylon filter cloths used in Guinea Worm Eradication campaigns in Africa. Early in the new century, it began producing inexpensive mosquito nets coated with insecticide. By 2007 it was selling about 4 million of them every month, and the World Health Organization estimated that such nets were reducing childhood deaths by about one-fourth in sub-Saharan Africa. That same year the company was developing LifeStraw, a $3 portable water filter that offered great hope that it could help lead to a major reduction of the large number of deaths caused by drinking impure water (see Chapter 2 for more on malaria and impure water).

LifeStraw was just one item displayed or spoken of at a 2007 New York exhibit that showcased inventions of greatest use to poor people. Among other items was a water drum that could hold 20 gallons and be rolled along by a child and human-powered water pumps that could help poor farmers irrigate their crops. The building where LifeStraw was exhibited was Andrew Carnegie's former mansion on Fifth Avenue, and it reminds us of the widespread philanthropic legacy of a man once regarded by many as a cut-throat capitalist or "robber barron."[33] John D. Rockefeller, another "robber barron," was also a prominent U.S. philanthropist. Toward the end of the twentieth century, the philanthropy of other capitalists was also aiding progress. Much of the humanitarian work done by Dr. Paul Farmer (see Chapter 1) was funded by the owner of a Boston construction firm. And in 2000 an organization begun by Farmer, Partners in Health, was one of a number of groups that received a $45 million grant to help eliminate multi-drug resistant TB in Peru. The donor was the Bill and Melinda Gates Foundation, which was able to dispense such large sums thanks largely to the fortune made by the world's richest capitalist and head of Microsoft.

Individuals such as Michael Novak and Thomas Friedman also argued that capitalism offered the greatest hope of solving environmental problems. Friedman stated that "the only way we are going to get innovations that drive energy costs down . . . is by mobilizing free-market capitalism . . . Clean-tech is going to be the next great global industry."[34] Despite Al Gore's criticism of capitalism's "abject failure . . . to even take note [in GNP or GDP calculations] of the poisoning of our water, the fouling of our air," he also maintained that market principles had an important role to play in solving environmental problems. He believed, however, that these principles had to be adjusted so that environmental costs and benefits were included in economic calculations such as GNP and measurements of productivity.[35] Thus, despite the reluctance of many industries and politicians to deal with environmental problems because they thought it would harm profits and national economies, other voices expressed the belief that businesses and market economies in general could adjust and even prosper by pursuing "green" practices.

Overall, there was little doubt that entrepreneurs, private businesses, and capitalists could and did contribute to real progress in major ways, but thinkers like Novak tended to accentuate only the positives of capitalist actions, while deemphasizing the importance of positive government actions, and downplaying some of the negative effects of capitalists' activities. To take just one recent example, Benjamin R. Barber wrote in *Consumed: How Markets Corrupt Children, Infantilize Adults, and Swallow Citizens Whole* (New York, 2007) the following: "Once upon a time, capitalism was allied with virtues that also contributed at least marginally to democracy, responsibility, and citizenship. Today it is allied with vices which— although they serve consumerism—undermine democracy, responsibility, and citizenship." The quote is taken from a review of two books, Barber's and another by Eric Clark, *The Real Toy Story: Inside the Ruthless Battle for America's Youngest Consumers* (New York, 2007). The two works together indicate a less positive side of capitalism—the constant attempt to create new "needs," even among children as young as the age of two (see also above, Chapter 3's section on "Capitalism, Consumption, and Marketing").[36]

Critics of capitalism's negative influences were not the only ones tending to be pessimistic about progress. Other observers also viewed the post-Cold War 1990s negetively. Two writers who did so were Samuel P. Huntington of Harvard University and journalist Robert Kaplan, who witnessed and wrote about some of the 1990s horrors in the Balkans. In Huntington's 1996 book, *The Clash of Civilizations and the Remaking of World Order,* he predicted that clashes between various civilizations would be the major conflicts of the future. Among these civilizations he numbered among others Western, Slavic-Orthodox, and Islamic civilizations, and he later believed that the NATO–Serbian conflict over Kosovo in 1999 was an example of Western versus Slavic-Orthodox conflict. In Kaplan's book completed in 1999, *The Coming Anarchy* (2000), his title indicates the pessimism reflected in his account, where he predicted increasing environmental pressures (see Chapter 6) and class and ethnic conflicts.

Although Mandelbaum also recognized many of the conflicts of the 1990s, he still believed the world was becoming more peaceful. He noted that many of the armed interventions of that decade were carried out for noble, humanitarian reasons. In an Epilogue to a 2004 edition of his book *The Ideas that Conquered the World*, Mandelbaum noted that the U.S.-British invasion of Iraq in 2003 was carried out in the name of the three great liberal ideas of democracy, free markets, and peace. But to what extent this invasion of Iraq reflected "progress" is debatable.

As at the beginning of the century so at the end of it, one's view of progress was strongly affected by the degree of one's confidence in human nature. Around 1900 Russia's de facto minister of religious affairs (Procurator of the Holy Synod), Constantine Pobedonostsev, had a gloomy view of humans, most of whom "were born for submission, and together constitute a herd." He thought that "the actual life of all and each of us is an uninterrupted history of failure and duality, a melancholy discord between thought and work, between faith and life," and that the belief in secular progress and the "false idea of human perfectibility" had caused human beings much misery.[37] Only religion and the afterlife provided much hope. During the twentieth century, similar religious views also disposed others to believe that secular progress was a fool's dream.

Other religious thinkers, however, were great believers in progress, though also believing that a divine force, along with humans, helped propel it. One such thinker was the French Jesuit priest, geologist, and paleontologist, Pierre Teilhard de Chardin (1881–1955). In early 1941, he stated, "I am convinced that finally it is upon the idea of progress, and faith in progress, that Mankind, today so divided, must rely and can reshape itself." In his most significant work, *The Phenomenon of Man*, he wrote: "Is evolution a theory, a system or a hypothesis? It is much more: it is a general condition to which all theories, all hypotheses, all systems must bow and which they must satisfy henceforth if they are to be thinkable and true. Evolution is a light illuminating all facts, a curve that all lines must follow." And he added, "Between these two alternatives of absolute optimism or absolute pessimism, there is no middle way because by its very nature progress is all or nothing."[38]

Whether human nature should lead to optimism or pessimism remained an open question, but there seemed little doubt that progress in cultural and moral development was less evident during the century than that in science and technology. It was true that significant gains occurred in broadening literacy and formal education. And major cultural and moral figures produced works of great merit. Nevertheless, whereas there was little doubt that twentieth century scientific knowledge was far advanced as compared to that of Isaac Newton's day, the same could not so easily be said in regard to twentieth century literature as compared to that of Shakespeare's era or that of Dickens, Melville, Dostoevsky, Turgenev, and Tolstoy. Thinkers as different as Jacques Barzun, Norman Cantor, Robert Conquest, Eric Hobsbawm, and Robert Nisbet, all wrote of the decline of high culture during all or part of the late twentieth century.[39] Whereas it had earlier reflected considerable criticism of society, by century's end its significance was increasingly undermined by mass consumer cultures and specialization.

As we have seen, many conservatives such as Gertrude Himmelfarb believed that morality had declined in the Western world in the final decades of the twentieth century (see Chapter 8). In 1999 Fukuyama, despite the optimism of his *The End of History and the Last Man* (see above), wrote that the period from "roughly the mid-1960s to the early 1990s . . . was also marked by seriously deteriorating social conditions in most of the industrialized world." He then elaborated:

> Crime and social disorder began to rise, making inner-city areas of the wealthiest societies on earth almost uninhabitable. The decline of kinship as a social institution, which has been going on for more than 200 years, accelerated sharply in the second half of the twentieth century. Marriages and births declined and divorce soared; and one out of every three children in the United States and more than half of all children in Scandinavia were born out of wedlock. Finally, trust and confidence in institutions went into a forty-year decline . . .
>
> . . . Although William J. Bennett and other conservatives are often attacked for harping on the theme of moral decline, they are essentially correct: the perceived breakdown of social order is not a matter of nostalgia, poor memory, or ignorance about the hypocrisies of earlier ages. The decline is readily measurable in statistics on crime, fatherless children, broken trust, reduced opportunities for and outcomes from education, and the like.[40]

On the general question of values, the *World Values Surveys* of the last two decades of the twentieth century indicate, as we have seen (see Chapter 8), that as countries became more technologically and economically developed they tended to become more secular and rationalistic and less traditionally religious. There were, however, many other factors that affected values, and generalizations about countries sometimes masked the great differences among people in any particular country—many of the U.S. citizens who rejected evolution, for example, did not seem especially "secular and rationalistic." And whether this twentieth century trend toward secularism and rationalism, partly subdued by a late century resurgence of traditional religious beliefs, was a sign of real progress or not, whether it was "good" or "bad," was hotly contested by conservatives, liberals, and radicals.

One of the central problems faced by many people during the century was that technological progress greatly outpaced people's ability to deal with technological change in a wise and prudent fashion. In 1970, Alvin Toffler popularized the term "Future Shock" in a best-selling book of the same name. In it he wrote that accelerating technological change was propelling more rapid social change, which in turn was producing "increasing malaise, mass neurosis, irrationality, and free-floating violence." He predicted that for the remainder of the twentieth century, many people in the most advanced technological countries would "find it increasingly painful to keep up with the incessant demand for change."[41] In 1999, as we have seen earlier (see Chapter 4), Thomas Friedman noted how economic globalization contributed to an unsettling pace of change.

By the end of the century, it was indeed evident how difficult it was for people's prudence, wisdom, and morality to keep pace with technological change. In traditional societies where technology had changed slowly, the moral ideas of older generations had more relevance for younger people. The world that children grew up in was more similar to that in which their mothers and fathers had been raised. As the twentieth century advanced and the rate of technological change accelerated, many younger people believed that their parents and older people generally had little of moral and cultural value to pass on to them. In the 1960s one of the heroes of the young, Bob Dylan, in his song "The Times They Are A-Changin," told parents that their "old road" was rapidly aging and that their children were beyond their command. He advised them to make way for their sons and daughters and not to criticize what they could not understand.

In the final decades of the century, the values of teenage children in the advanced industrialized countries were increasingly shaped less by parents and more by an ever-expanding media and by peers influenced by that media. Many social critics placed much of the blame on television, especially criticizing its impact on young people. According to his friend Thomas Langan, the famous media observer Marshall McLuhan once said about televisions, "If you want to save a single shred of Hebrew-Hellenistic-Roman-Christian humanist civilization, take an axe and smash those infernal machines."[42] U.S. humorist Dave Barry once said: "Another possible source of guidance for teenagers is television, but television's message has always been that the need for truth, wisdom and world peace pales by comparison with the need for a toothpaste that offers whiter teeth and fresher breath."[43] And Zbigniew Brzezinski, former National Security Adviser to U.S. President Jimmy Carter, wrote in 1993 that television had "become prominent in shaping the [U.S.] national culture and its basic beliefs," that it "had a particularly important effect in disrupting generational continuity in the transfer of traditions and values," and that it helped produce "a mass culture, driven by profiteers who exploit the hunger for vulgarity, pornography, and even barbarism."[44]

In such an atmosphere old people and their life experiences were little valued by youth-centric popular cultures; and wisdom, whether from older people or·other sources, was an undervalued virtue. *The Oxford English Dictionary* (2d ed., 1989) defines wisdom as "the capacity for judging rightly in matters relating to life and conduct; soundness of judgment in the choice of means and ends," and the seventeenth-century Dutch philosopher Spinoza indicated that wisdom implied viewing life *sub specie eternitatis*, that is, from the perspective of eternity.

As early as the 1930's the poet T. S. Eliot had written:

Where is the wisdom we have lost in knowledge?
Where is the knowledge we have lost in information?
(from "The Rock", Chorus 1).

During the same decade a distinguished Dutch historian, Jan Huizinga, wrote about the tremendous scientific and technological progress of the early twentieth century, and commented that "the masses are fed with a hitherto undreamt-of quantity of knowledge of all sorts." But he added that there was "something wrong with its assimilation," and that "undigested knowledge hampers judgment and stands in the way of wisdom."[45] In general, Huizinga thought that his era reflected the deterioration of culture, moral standards, and judgment. General Omar Bradley later expressed a similar sentiment when he said: "Ours is a world of nuclear giants and ethical infants. If we continue to develop our technology without wisdom or prudence, our servant may prove to be our executioner."[46]

In his 1973 collection of essays, *Small Is Beautiful*, the German-born English economist E. F. Schumacher suggested that twentieth-century science, technology, and economics had gone astray by failing to be employed in a wise fashion. He wrote:

The exclusion of wisdom from economics, science, and technology was something which we could perhaps get away with for a little while, as long as we were relatively unsuccessful; but now that we have become very successful, the problem of spiritual and moral truth moves into the central position. . .

The cultivation and expansion of needs is the antithesis of wisdom. It is also the antithesis of freedom and peace. Every increase of needs tends to increase one's dependence on outside forces over which one cannot have control . . . Only by a reduction of needs can one promote a genuine reduction in those tensions which are the ultimate causes of strife and war . . .

... Ever-bigger machines, entailing ever-bigger concentrations of economic power and exerting ever-greater violence against the environment, do not represent progress: they are a denial of wisdom. Wisdom demands a new orientation of science and technology towards the organic, the gentle, the nonviolent, the elegant and beautiful.[47]

By the end of the twentieth century, however, it was clear that Schumacher's ideas were having little impact on the global economy. Fed by expanded advertising and globalization, "needs" had continued expanding, contributing to worsening environmental conditions. At the same time, increased freedoms and choices had made it more crucial than ever for governments and people to possess the wisdom to make correct choices. This could most readily be seen in regard to environmental policies and leisure time. Cable and satellite television, the World Wide Web, and cell phones, to take just a few examples, had greatly expanded people's choices of how to spend their free time. Sports viewers, for example, could spend weekends on their couches watching one sporting event after another.

Although there were notable exceptions like South Africa's Nelson Mandela, who indicated his appreciation of wisdom in his autobiography, in general it became less valued as the twentieth century advanced.[48] Nevertheless, this virtue had once been highly appreciated. One scholar, writing mainly of the West, noted that "wisdom was a virtue highly and consistently prized in antiquity, the Middle Ages, and the Renaissance."[49] Many non-Western religions also emphasized the importance of wisdom. The ancient Hindu book *The Bhagavad-Gita* tells us "there is no purifier in this world like wisdom ... The man who is full of faith obtaineth wisdom, and he also who hath mastery over his senses; and having obtained wisdom, he goeth swiftly to the supreme peace." Buddhist scriptures also praised wisdom and declared that obtaining perfect wisdom was the key to achieving blissful Nirvana, that state where suffering and individual craving and dissatisfaction ceased to exist. Into the twentieth century, some of Asia's most prominent thinkers such as Tagore and Gandhi, continued being influenced by the Asian religious respect for wisdom. For example, Tagore wrote:

When the heat and motion of blind impulses and passions distract it on all sides, we can neither give nor receive anything truly. But when we find our centre in our soul by the power of self-restraint, by the force that harmonises all warring elements and unifies those that are apart, then all our isolated impressions reduce themselves to wisdom, and all our momentary impulses of heart find their completion in love; then all the petty details of our life reveal an infinite purpose, and all our thoughts and deeds unite themselves inseparably in an internal harmony.[50]

At various times during the twentieth century, some Western individuals sought wisdom by turning to Eastern religious traditions or gurus. In general, however, from the seventeenth century onwards, technology gradually gained momentum in influencing Western people's perspectives on life. Just as gradually, respect for wisdom declined, as the modern world with all of its technological wonders and explosion of information came into being. And if respect for wisdom was in decline, could there be much moral progress?

Thus, in summing up the twentieth century, progress is clearly evident in many areas—science, technology, economic betterment, increased freedoms, expanded literacy—but much less so in other areas, especially in regard to environmental, moral, and cultural matters. At the end of his long historical study *The True and Only Heaven: Progress and Its Critics* (1991), Christopher Lasch called for greater global equality, which "implies a more modest standard of living for all." He noted that globally extending the living standards of the rich to the poor would place "an unbearable burden of the earth's natural resources." (What if, for example, all the people in the poorer countries used up as much energy as the average U.S. citizen?) Instead, he advocated recognizing the necessity "of limits, both moral and material," and criticized the advocates of "endless economic expansion," whether on the left or right, for failing to realize the need for such limits.[51]

In 1980, Nisbet included a section entitled "The Attack on Economic Growth," in his *History of the Idea of Progress*. He believed such an attack was symptomatic of a decreasing belief in progress. But by the early twenty-first century, there was increasing evidence to suggest that placing less emphasis on economic growth as traditionally measured by increases in GNP or GDP might not be anti-progressive, but rather help to increase global welfare. Besides the obvious fact that continued global warming and other environmental deterioration, partly resulting from past economic expansion, would certainly decrease global well-being, various studies indicated that people in the world's most prosperous countries increasingly measured their own well-being by values other than material ones.

The *World Values Surveys* (see Chapter 8) discovered that the type of values increasingly found in the most industrialized and prosperous countries of the world "give priority to environmental protection and cultural issues, even when these goals conflict with maximizing economic growth."[52] And a 2002 study used by the British government found that although people in faster growing economies were generally happier than those in more stagnant ones, "the relationship between economic growth and changes in life satisfaction appears weak—and certainly much weaker than would have been expected on the basis of cross-national association between GDP per capita and average life satisfaction." That same study concluded that people "tend to overestimate the pleasure that they will derive from a given purchase ... Similarly, evidence indicates that people tend to overestimate the importance of income for their wellbeing." An annex to this work refers to various alternate well-being indices, many of them reflecting an attempt to consider environmental and other factors often ignored in measuring GNP or GDP. These indices indicate two important points: 1) measuring economic growth by such measures as increases in GDP is by itself an inadequate tool to measure overall progress, and 2) when factoring in environmental and other changes, some countries that displayed considerable GDP growth actually regressed in overall well-being.[53]

Thus, we end this chapter as we began it, noting that judgments about progress depend largely on how it is defined. Writing about the twentieth century almost a decade into our new century also affects our view of twentieth-century progress. After the attack on New York's World Trade Center on 9/11/2001 and amidst the turmoil continuing in Iraq in 2007, it is more difficult to share the optimism that some writers displayed earlier after the collapse of communist governments in eastern and central Europe.

We should not forget, however, that when the twentieth century ended, various possibilities were available that no longer are. To take just one significant example, if Vice President Al Gore would have been elected U.S. president in 2000, rather than George W. Bush, it is probable that the United States and Great Britain would not have become involved in Iraq in the way they did, and it is likely that the United States would have started off the new century dealing more forcefully with global warming and other environmental problems.

Yet, it is still appropriate that our judgments about twentieth-century progress in regard to attitudes towards war and violence are and will be affected by what happens in the twenty-first century. If a nuclear war occurs between some of the expanding number of countries acquiring nuclear weapons or if terrorists set off nuclear devices or release biological agents that kill hundreds of thousands or even millions of people, historians will probably look back to the twentieth century, note people's increasing vulnerability to nuclear, biological, and chemical weapons, and point to failures that helped bring about such a horrendous occurrence. And if a truly catastrophic nuclear holocaust occurs, any future historians who remain alive will probably emphasize not all the positive twentieth-century developments, but those failings that contributed to making such a holocaust possible.[54]

The future will also help historians to determine how much, or little, progress humans made during the twentieth century regarding environmental questions. If environmental developments such as global warming create catastrophic conditions, historians will no doubt emphasize the twentieth-century's failures to prevent the worsening of warming conditions. If, on the other hand, a powerful twenty-first century global environmental movement drastically alters past destructive environmental practices, historians might emphasize the progress of twentieth-century environmentalism that helped bring about such a movement.

The state of the world in the 1990s and beyond can be viewed from the pessimistic perspective of books such as Huntington's *The Clash of Civilizations and the Remaking of World Order* and Kaplan's *The Coming Anarchy* or from the more optimistic viewpoint of someone like Nelson Mandela. In the midst of his 27 years in prison, he gave the name Zaziwe, meaning "Hope" to one of his granddaughters, and continued to believe that "man's goodness is a flame that can be hidden but never extinguished."[55] His hopeful dynamism and wise leadership helped create a nonracial democratic system in South Africa without resorting to a bloody revolution or civil war.

Regardless of pessimistic or optimistic outlooks, many major challenges faced people in the early twenty-first century. They included effectively controlling and using wisely the tremendous technological forces available; bringing the global economy more into balance with environmental and moral principles; overcoming prejudices and discrimination and increasing global tolerance; and changing the distribution of power at various institutional levels so that humans' best instincts and ideas can be more fully implemented.

In regard to these concerns, as well as others, various possibilities still remain open, and it is impossible to foretell which will emerge most successfully in the years ahead. Numberless forces, positive and negative, exist that could come forward or weaken in the future. Just as violence, hatred, intolerance, close-minded provincialism, laziness, ignorance, and greed have continued to manifest themselves on a global scale, so too have desires and efforts for peace, for the alleviation of global poverty and suffering, and for maintaining a more sustainable environment.[56] Not only our futures, but also our judgments regarding twentieth-century progress will continue to be affected by the interaction of all these forces.

Notes

Preface

1. Peter Watson, *The Modern Mind: An Intellectual History of the 20th Century* (New York, 2001), 761–62. Steven G. Marks offers some good insights on Russian global influences in his *How Russia Shaped the Modern World: From Art to Anti-Semitism, Ballet to Bolshevism* (Princeton, 2003).

Chapter 1

1. Ian McEwan, *Black Dogs*, Picador ed. (London, 1993), 165.
2. From a letter published in *Philadelphia Ledger*, November 11, 1901, as quoted in "Secretary Root's Record: 'Marked Severities' in Philippine Warfare: An Explanation by Private Soldiers," found on the *Humanities Web*, http://www.humanitiesweb.org/human.php?s=s&p=l&a=c&ID=1110&=(accessed August 1, 2006).
3. All three soldiers' letters originally printed in Soldier's Letters, pamphlet (Anti-Imperialist League, 1899), reprinted in "American Soldiers in the Philippines Write Home about the War," available at http://historymatters.gmu.edu/d/58/ (accessed July 15, 2007).
4. Eric D. Weitz, in his *Century of Genocide: Utopias of Race and Nation*, (Princeton, 2003), 240, refers to the murder of the Herero as "probably the first genocide of the twentieth century." It is also the first of more than one dozen twentieth-century genocides treated in Samuel Totten, William S. Parsons, and Israel W. Charny, eds., *Century of Genocide: Critical Essays and Eyewitness Accounts*, 2d. ed. (New York and London, 2004).
5. On the difficulty of defining terrorism, see Bruce Hoffman, *Inside Terrorism*, 2d rev. ed. (New York, 2006), Ch. 1; the first edition of this chapter is available at http://www.nytimes.com/books/first/h/hoffman-terrorism.html (accessed July 17, 2007). For a historical treatment of terrorism from 1881 into the twenty-first century, see Matthew Carr, *The Infernal Machine: A History of Terrorism* (New York, 2007). On pp. 4–6 Carr also deals with the difficulty of defining the word and points out how governments often misuse it for self-serving purposes.

6. Anna Geifman, *Thou Shalt Kill: Revolutionary Terrorism in Russia, 1894–1917* (Princeton, 1993), 21, 46, 90–6. Simon Sebag Montefiore's *Young Stalin* (London and New York, 2007) is especially detailed in recounting many of the young Stalin's "terrorist" activities, especially in the Caucasus, in the early years of the century.

7. "The Constitution of the Ujedinjenje ili Smrt-*Unification or Death*," http://www.lib.byu.edu/~rdh/World War I/1914m/blk-cons.html (accessed August 1, 2006).

8. Quoted in my *Russia in the Age of Alexander II, Tolstoy, and Dostoevsky* (London, 2002), 248.

9. Like some other prominent female pacifists, Addams believed that as nurturers and protectors of human life, women had a special pacifist role to play. On Addams visit to Tolstoy's estate in Russia and his influence on her, see her *Twenty Years at Hull-House* (New York, 1910), 259–80, http://www2.pfeiffer.edu/~lridener/DSS/Addams/2hh12.html (accessed August 5, 2006).

10. Nelson Mandela, *Long Walk to Freedom: The Autobiography of Nelson Mandela* (Boston, 1994), 144, 246–7, 451, 453. For an interesting history of successful uses of non-violent approaches during the twentieth century, see Peter Ackerman and Jack DuVall, *A Force More Powerful: A Century of Nonviolent Conflict* (New York, 2000). For a few recent books reflecting non-violent approaches to different types of violence, see Ronald J. Glossop, *Confronting War: An Examination of Humanity's Most Pressing Problem*, 4th ed. (Jefferson, NC, 2001), and Tom H. Hastings, *Nonviolent Response to Terrorism* (Jefferson, NC, 2004).

11. *Theodore Roosevelt (1858–1919): An Autobiography* (1913), http://www.bartleby.com/55/8.html (accessed August 1, 2006).

12. Barbara Tuchman, *The Proud Tower: A Portrait of the World before the War, 1890–1914*, Bantam Books ed. (New York, 1967), 125–6, 179, 319, 326.

13. Ibid., Ch. 5, "The Steady Drummer," presents an overview of both conferences and the attitude of various governments toward them. See p. 336 for Roosevelt's disgust; Tolstoy's "Letter on the [1st] Peace Conference" can be found at http://www.lewrockwell.com/orig7/tolstoy3.html (accessed December 24, 2006). Among Tolstoy's many Russian critics was the philosopher and poet Vladimir Soloviev (1853–1900). See, e.g., his *War, Progress, and the End of History, Including a Short Story of the Anti-Christ* (London, 1915).

14. For links to various Hague and Geneva conventions and other agreements, see http://www.yale.edu/lawweb/avalon/lawofwar/lawwar.htm (accessed May 2, 2007).

15. Niall Ferguson, *The War of the World: Twentieth-Century Conflict and the Descent of the West* (New York, 2006), xli.

16. "20th Century Democide," http://www.hawaii.edu/powerkills/20TH.HTM. See also the excellent work of Milton Leitenberg, *Deaths in Wars and Conflicts in the 20th Century*, http://www.clingendael.nl/publications/2006/20060800_cdsp_occ_leitenberg.pdf (accessed December 15, 2006), which estimates the total number of deaths at 231 million. On the difficulty of estimating the toll of twentieth-century violence and for Ferguson's considerably lower total estimate, see Ferguson, 647–54.

17. See, for example, http://www.armenian-genocide.org/genocidefaq.html (accessed July 14, 2007). Most scholars agree that the term "genocide" is appropriate for the Armenian killings. On the controversial nature of the term itself, see Weitz, 8–10.

18. Estimates, however, vary widely. For two recent estimates, see Richard Overy, *Russia's War*, Penguin ed. (New York, 1998), 287–9, and Ferguson, 649–50.

Although Wikipedia must be used with caution, its entry on World War II casualties is well-documented. See http://en.wikipedia.org/wiki/World_War_II_casualties (accessed December 2, 2006).

19. Deb Riechmann, "Nixon Discussed Nuclear Strike in Vietnam," *Boston Globe*, March 1, 2002, A2.

20. Ferguson, xxxiv.

21. http://editors.sipri.se/pubs/yb00/ch1.html (accessed May 12, 2007).

22. Martin Gilbert, *History of the Twentieth Century*, Concise ed. (New York, 2001), 645; Ferguson, 630.

23. Ferguson, 617. See also below, Ch. 5's section on "The Cold War and Human Rights" for more on U.S. policy in Latin America.

24. http://editors.sipri.se/pubs/yb00/ch7.html (accessed May 12, 2007).

25. Nelson Mandela in his *Long Walk to Freedom: The Autobiography of Nelson Mandela* (Boston, 1994), mentions favorably many South African communist freedom fighters and even states (p. 163) that "communism and Christianity, at least in Africa, were not mutually exclusive."

26. Quoted in Nicholas Werth, "The Iron Fist of the Dictatorship of the Proletariat," in *The Black Book of Communism: Crimes, Terror, Repression* (hereafter BBC), ed. Stephane Courtois et al., trans. Mark Kramer and Jonathan Murphy (Cambridge, MA, 1999), 58.

27. "Hanging Order," U.S. Library of Congress site at www.loc.gov/exhibits/archives/ad2kulak.html (accessed August 1, 2006).

28. Quoted in Stephane Courtois, "Conclusion: Why?" in BBC, 749.

29. Quoted in Nicholas Werth, "From Tambov to the Great Famine," in BBC, 115.

30. Quoted in my *A History of Russia*, vol. 2, *Since 1855*, 2d. ed. (London, 2005), 358. More detail on much of the material found in this and succeeding chapters that deals with Russia can be found in this later volume.

31. *The Gulag Archipelago: 1918–1956*, vol. 1 (New York, 1974), 60.

32. Cited in Mikhail Heller and Aleksandr M. Nekrich, *Utopia in Power: The History of The Soviet Union from 1917 to the Present* (New York, 1986), 220.

33. See my *A History . . .*, 250, on the scholarly dispute regarding the famine and Stalin's intentions.

34. Jean-Louis Margolin, "China: A Long March into Night," in BBC, 498.

35. Ibid., 464.

36. Quoted in Jonathan Glover, *Humanity: A Moral History of the Twentieth Century* (New Haven, 2000), 291.

37. Quoted in David Reynolds, *One World Divisible: A Global History since 1945* (New York, 2000), 254.

38. Glover, 307.

39. Gao Xingjian, *One Man's Bible* (New York, 2002), 212.

40. Glover, 339.

41. Ibid., 342.

42. Ibid., 344, 354.

43. http://www.cfr.org/publication/9240/; http://cain.ulst.ac.uk/sutton/tables/Organisation_Responsible.html (both sites accessed December 27, 2006).

44. Walter Laqueur, *The New Terrorism: Fanaticism and the Arms of Mass Destruction* (New York and Oxford, 1999), 21.

45. *The Minimanual of the Urban Guerrilla* is available at http://www.baader-meinhof.com/students/resources/print/minimanual/manualtext.html (accessed July 17, 2007).

46. Jonathan R. White, *Terrorism: An Introduction*, 3d ed. (Belmont, CA, 2002), 136.
47. Laqueur, 186.
48. See Karl A. Seger, *Left-Wing Extremism: The Current Threat*. Prepared for the U.S. Department of Energy (Washington, DC, 2001), www.fas.org/irp/world/para/left.pdf (accessed August 1, 2006).
49. Laqueur, 12.
50. The complete manifesto is available at http://www.thecourier.com/manifest.htm (accessed August 1, 2006).
51. On the Internet at http://www.pbs.org/newshour/terrorism/international/fatwa_1996.html (accessed August 1, 2006).
52. Paul R. Pillar, "The Dimensions of Terrorism and Counterterrorism," in *Terrorism and Counterterrorism: Understanding the New Security Environment, Readings and Interpretations*, 2d ed., ed. Russell D. Howard and Reid L. Sawyer, (Dubuque, 2006), 28.
53. Laqueur, 4.
54. Robert Gilman, "Structural Violence. Can We Find Genuine Peace in a World with Inequitable Distribution of Wealth among Nations?" Available at www.context.org/ICLIB/IC04/Gilman1.htm (accessed May 1, 2007). The author also provides estimates on how the number of deaths from structural violence compare with other types of violent deaths.
55. Paul Farmer, *Pathologies of Power* (Berkeley, 2003), 50. Ch. 1 of this book, which includes these quotes, deals with structural violence and is available at http://www.ucpress.edu/books/pages/9875/9875.ch01.html (accessed May 1, 2007). The WHO report, *The World Health Report 1995—Bridging the Gaps*, as well as reports for subsequent years through 2005, is available at http://www.who.int/whr/previous/en/ (accessed July 9, 2007). See also Tracy Kidder, *Mountains Beyond Mountains* (New York, 2004), which details the medical and other humanitarian work of Farmer.
56. Amartya Sen, in his *Identity and Violence: The Illusion of Destiny* (New York, 2006), 142–6, provides some further reflections on the relationship of poverty, violence, and injustice.
57. After examining closely the causes of seven twentieth-century wars John Stoessinger, in *Why Nations Go to War*, 5th ed. (New York, 1990), 209, stated that *"with regard to the problem of the outbreak of war, the case studies indicate the crucial importance of the personalities of leaders . . .* [which] have often been decisive."
58. Sen, xv. Daniel Chirot and Clark McCauley, in *Why Not Kill Them All? The Logic and Prevention of Mass Political Murder* (Princeton, 2006), 81–7, deal with how labeling or "essentializing" others according to various ethnic, national, and religious categories can make genocidal killing easier.
59. See Glover, 84, for a brief summary of Just War Theory. See also Michael Walzer, *Just and Unjust Wars* (Harmondsworth, 1988).
60. For a good, recent overview of the decisions to undertake such bombings and a consideration of whether they were morally justified, see Glover, 69–112.
61. Gwynne Dyer, *War* (New York, 1985), 14.
62. Ibid., 110. See also Glover, 51, on a Soviet soldier serving in Afghanistan during the 1980s who was told that he should become "a bloody-minded brute with an iron fist and no conscience!"; John Mueller, in *Retreat from Doomsday: The Obsolescence of Major War* (New York, 1989), 41–2, comments on the perception before World War I that war was manly.

63. Philip Caputo, *A Rumor of War: With a Twentieth Anniversary Postscript by the Author* (New York, 1996), 6.

64. Ibid., 228.

65. Quoted in Michael Evans, "The Serpent's Eye: The Cinema of 20th-Century Combat," *Military Review* (November–December 2002): 87, http://usacac.army. mil/cac/milreview/download/ English/NovDec02/bob.pdf (accessed August 1, 2006).

66. Ferguson, 477.

67. Cited in Glover, 176.

68. Glover, 50, quoting Robert J. Lifton, *Home from the War: Vietnam Veterans, Neither Victims Nor Executioners* (New York, 1985), 202.

69. Quoted in Stephane Courtois, "Conclusion: Why?" in BBC, 750.

70. *Forever Flowing* (New York, 1972), 142–4.

71. Glover, 355.

72. Ibid., 405. Some religious thinkers like Michael Novak believes that religion contributes to respect for human rights and that if you "take away the immortality of the soul . . . it is difficult to establish the dignity of man any higher than that of any other animal." See his *The Universal Hunger for Liberty* (New York, 2004), 145. See also below, Ch. 8, for more on religion.

73. Glover, 406.

74. Farmer, available at http://www.ucpress.edu/books/pages/9875/9875. ch01.html (accessed May 1, 2007).

Chapter 2

1. Amartya Sen, in his *Identity and Violence: The Illusion of Destiny* (New York, 2006), 56–7, 68–70, 90–2, reminds us, however, that many earlier important scientific contributions came from other parts of the world.

2. Caroline F. Ware, K. M. Panikkar, and J. M. Romein, eds. *History of Mankind: Cultural and Scientific Development*, vol. 6, *The Twentieth Century* (New York, 1966), 471.

3. *Nancy F. Koehn*, "Henry Heinz and Brand Creation in the Late Nineteenth Century: Making Markets for Processed Food," *Business History Review* 73 (Autumn 1999), 348–92, excerpt available at http://hbswk.hbs.edu/item/ 0788.html (accessed July 18, 2007).

4. For a good overview of the impact of electricity on the USA, see David E. Nye, *Electrifying America: Social Meanings of a New Technology, 1880–1940* (Cambridge, MA, 1990).

5. *Inside the Third World: The Anatomy of Poverty*, 2d ed., with a revised overview (London, 1987), 147.

6. http://news.bbc.co.uk/2/hi/health/6275001.stm;   http://www.bmj.com/ cgi/content/extract/334/7585/111-a (both accessed May 3, 2007).

7. For an interesting article comparing health in the late nineteenth century with health in the early twenty-first century, see Gina Kolata, "So Big and Healthy Grandpa Wouldn't Even Know You," *New York Times*, July 30, 2006, http://www.nytimes.com/2006/07/30/health/30age.html?ex = 1184558400 &en = ca6ba2b120bf4efe&ei = 5070 (accessed July 20, 2007).

8. For a recent overview of AIDS in Africa, see Sharon LaFraniere, "New AIDS in Africa Outpace Gains," *New York Times*, June 6, 2007, http://www. nytimes.com/2007/06/06/health/06aids.html?_r = 1&hp&oref = slogin (accessed July 20, 2007).

9. For a detailed listing of infant mortality rates by country at century's end, see *State of the World's Mothers, 2000,* at http://www.savethechildren.org/publications/mothers/2000/sowm2000.pdf (accessed May 8, 2007).

10. Robert D. Kaplan, *The Ends of the Earth: A Journey at the Dawn of the 21st Century* (New York, 1996), 9, 16–17. For an illuminating examination of how Italy eventually overcame the scourge of malaria, see Frank Snowden, *The Conquest of Malaria: Italy, 1900–1962* (New Haven, 2006).

11. UNICEF/WHO Report, *Pneumonia: The Forgotten Killer of Children, 2006,* http://www.unicef.org/publications/files/Pneumonia_The_Forgotten_Killer_of_Children.pdf (accessed May 11, 2007).

12. http://unesdoc.unesco.org/images/0012/001295/129556e.pdf; see also www.worldwater.org (both accessed May 3, 2007).

13. John Barber and Mark Harrison, *The Soviet Home Front, 1941–1945: A Social and Economic History of the USSR in World War II* (London, 1991), 180.

14. *Vietnam: A History* (New York, 1983), 436–7.

15. Numerous books have dealt with the Gulf War and the media. See, for example, Robert E. Denton, Jr., ed., *The Media and the Persian Gulf War* (Westport, CN, 1993).

16. See, for example, Richard Stites, *Revolutionary Dreams: Utopian Vision and Experimental Life in the Russian Revolution* (New York, 1989), 146–9.

17. For more examples, see George Ritzer, *The McDonaldization of Society* (Newbury Park, CA, 1993).

18. Christopher Freeman, "Technology and Invention," in *The Columbia History of the 20th Century*, ed. Richard W. Bulliet (New York, 1998), 315.

Chapter 3

1. Joseph Schumpeter, *Capitalism, Socialism and Democracy*, Harper Colophon ed. (New York, 1975), 83.

2. Robert W. Strayer, *Communist Experiment: Revolution, Socialism, and Global Conflict in the Twentieth Century* (Boston, 2007), 7. A more detailed treatment of the history of communism, including a chapter on Marx and Engels, is Robert Service's *Comrades! A History of World Communism,* (Cambridge, MA, 2007).

3. Strayer, 7.

4. http://usinfo.state.gov/products/pubs/oecon/chap2.htm (accessed May 15, 2007).

5. Nikita Khrushchev, *Socialism and Communism: Selected Passages, 1956–1963* (Moscow, 1963), 15–16.

6. Sergei Khrushchev, *Khrushchev on Khrushchev: An Inside Account of the Man and His Era* (Boston, 1990), 19.

7. Nikita Khrushchev, *Khrushchev Remembers: The Last Testament* (Boston, 1976), 164.

8. For a good account of changes in French consumption patterns during the late nineteenth century, see Rosalind H. Williams, *Dream Worlds: Mass Consumption in Late Nineteenth-Century France* (Berkeley, 1982).

9. William E. Leuchtenburg, *The Perils of Prosperity, 1914–32* (Chicago, 1958), 200.

10. Quoted in Vance Packard, *The Waste Makers* (New York, 1963), 21.

11. Reprinted at http://www.acmi.net.au/AIC/RADIO_ESSAYS.html (accessed November 12, 2006).

12. Quoted in Leuchtenburg, 242.

13. Bradley R. Schiller, *The Economy Today*, 5th ed. (New York, 1991), 481–2.

14. http://www.avoncompany.com (accessed July 21, 2007).

15. Quoted in Alan Thein Durning, "Can't Live Without It," in *Essays from Contemporary Culture*, 2d ed., ed. Katherine Anne Achley (Fort Worth, 1995), 63.

16. Quoted in Richard H. Robbins, *Global Problems and the Culture of Capitalism* (Boston, 1999), 25.

17. Paperback edition (New York, 1978), 71–2.

18. Thomas K. McGraw, ed., *Creating Modern Capitalism: How Entrepreneurs, Companies, and Countries Triumphed in Three Industrial Revolutions* (Cambridge, MA, 1997), v.

19. *Communist Manifesto*, at http://www.anu.edu.au/polsci/marx/classics/manifesto.html (accessed October 29, 2006).

20. For a few different approaches see, for example, John B. Judis, "Value-free: How Capitalism Redefines Morality," *The New Republic* (April 26 and May 3, 1999), 53–6.

21. Milton Friedman, "The Social Responsibility of Business Is to Increase Its Profits," *New York Times Magazine*, September 13, 1970.

22. Niall Ferguson, *The War of the World: Twentieth-Century Conflict and the Descent of the West* (New York, 2006), 332.

23. On the Internet at http://www.marxists.org/archive/marx/works/1867-c1/ch10.htm (accessed October 29, 2006).

24. Estimates are provided at http://www.bbc.co.uk/history/british/victorians/famine_01.shtml (accessed May 15, 2007).

25. Amartya Sen, *Identity and Violence: The Illusion of Destiny* (New York, 2006), 143.

26. Daniel T. Rodgers, *Atlantic Crossings: Social Politics in a Progressive Age* (Cambridge, MA, 1998), 210.

27. Quoted in D. C. Somervell, *English Thought in the Nineteenth Century* (London, 1929), 201.

28. Rodgers, 201.

29. Quotes cited in Thomas C. Cochran and William Miller, *The Age of Enterprise: A Social History of Industrial America*, rev. ed. (New York, 1961), 176, 180.

30. Thomas E. Skidmore and Peter H. Smith, *Modern Latin America*, 3d ed. (New York and Oxford, 1992), 49.

31. See Eric Hobsbawm, *The Age of Extremes: A History of the World, 1914–1991*, Vintage ed. (New York, 1996), 128, where he refers to Nazism as "a non-liberal capitalist economy."

32. Gary Teeple, *Globalization and the Decline of Social Reform* (Toronto, 1995), 15.

33. *The Downing Street Years, 1979–1990* (New York, 1993), 7.

34. Ibid., 6.

35. Ibid., 687.

36. "Britain: Gordon's Theorem," *The Economist* (March 13, 1999), 66–7.

37. Quoted in Matthew Josephson, *The Robber Barons: The Great American Capitalists, 1961–1901* (New York, 1962), 359.

38. William Greider, *Who Will Tell the People: The Betrayal of American Democracy* (New York, 1992), 331.

39. Paul Kennedy, *Preparing for the Twenty-First Century* (New York, 1993), 55.

40. Joshua Karliner, *The Corporate Planet: Ecology and Politics in the Age of Globalization* (San Francisco, 1997), 2.

41. Richard J. Barnet and John Cavanagh, *Global Dreams: Imperial Corporations and the New World Order* (New York, 1994), 427.

42. In his book *Creating the Corporate Soul: The Rise of Public Relations and Corporate Imagery in American Big Business* (Berkeley, 1998), Ronald Marchand provides an overview of the rise and effectiveness of corporate public relations.

43. *Time* (November 16, 1998), 80, 88–9.

44. Greider, 349–52.

Chapter 4

1. Michael Doyle, for example, in *Empires* (Ithaca, 1986), 45, wrote: "Empire is a relationship, formal or informal, in which one state controls the effective political sovereignty of another political society. It can be achieved by force, by political collaboration, by economic, political or cultural dependence. Imperialism is simply the process or policy of establishing, or maintaining an empire." Edward Said in *Culture and Imperialism*, Vintage ed. (New York, 1994), 9, quotes approvingly Doyle's definitions of empire and imperialism.

2. Eric Hobsbawm, in his *Age of Empire, 1875–1914*, Vintage ed. (New York, 1989), 60, goes so far as to say that in the late nineteenth century imperialism "was a novel term devised to describe a novel phenomenon." Hobsbawm, although criticized by some for a "Marxist bias," also provides a useful overview of the imperialism of the period. For a different point of view, see Robert Conquest, *Reflections on a Ravaged Century* (New York, 2000), Ch. 13.

3. Quoted in Timothy Burke, "Colonialism, Cleanliness, and Civilization in Colonial Rhodesia,"in *European Imperialism 1830–1930*, ed. Alice L. Conklin and Ian Christopher Fletcher (Boston, 1999), 91.

4. Quoted in Julius W. Pratt, *Expansionists of 1898* (Chicago, 1964), 228.

5. General James Rusling, "Interview with President William McKinley," *The Christian Advocate* 22 (January 1903), http://historymatters.gmu.edu/black board/mckinley.html (accessed May 30, 2007).

6. Quoted in Burke, 92, 93.

7. See his essay "Autocracy and War—1905," available at http://etext.library. adelaide.edu.au/c/conrad/joseph/c75nl/part15.html (accessed November 16, 2006).

8. Leo Tolstoy, *The Russian Revolution*, trans. Louise and Aylmer Maude (Christchurch, Eng., 1906), 16–17.

9. M. K. Gandhi, "The Disease of Civilization," in *European Imperialism, 1830–1930*, 23.

10. For the complete poem, see the website edited by Jim Zwick, *Anti-Imperialism in the United States, 1898–1935*. The link for the poem is http://www. boondocksnet.com/ai/kipling/kipling.html (accessed November 16, 2006).

11. On Roosevelt's views, see above, Ch. 1. For differences in the United States on the U.S. suppression of the Filipino independence, see Barbara Tuchman's Ch. 3, "End of a Dream," in *The Proud Tower* (New York, 1967), and Jim Zwick, "'The White Man's Burden' and Its Critics," at http://www.boondocksnet. com/ai/kipling/ (accessed November 16, 2006).

12. For a good overview of how the Soviet empire compared with others, see Mark R. Beissinger, "Rethinking Empire in the Wake of Soviet Collapse," in *Ethnic Politics after Communism*, ed. Zoltan Barany and Robert Moser (Ithaca, 2005), 14–45; also available at http://www.princeton.edu/~mbeissin/ beissinger.rethinking.empire.pdf (accessed May 19, 2007). Unlike many scholars, however, Beissinger argues (p. 17) that the Soviet Union should not be thought of as the "last empire," but rather "as one of the first of a new form of empire." On the Soviet post-World War II empire and Soviet imperialism, see also John Lewis Gaddis, *We Now Know: Rethinking the Cold War*, Oxford paperback (Oxford, 1998), 32.

13. http://www.aaanet.org/stmts/racepp.htm (accessed May 22, 2007). Along these same lines, see Stephen Jay Gould, *The Mismeasure of Man* (New York, 1981).

14. See http://www.aaanet.org/committees/commissions/aec/teach_race.htm, which links to the essay by Carol Mukhopadhyay and Rosemary C. Henze, "How Real Is Race? Using Anthropology to Make Sense of Human Diversity," at http://www.pdkintl.org/kappan/k0305muk.htm (both sites accessed May 22, 2007). For an interesting study of ideas about race, see Richard Graham, ed., *The Idea of Race in Latin America, 1870–1940* (Austin, 1990).

15. Quotes are in Paul F. Boiler, Jr., *American Thought in Transition: The Impact of Evolutionary Naturalism, 1865–1900* (Chicago, 1969), 219, also available at http://www.mtholyoke.edu/acad/intrel/ajb72.htm (accessed July 24, 2007).

16. Thomas Schoonover, *Uncle Sam's War of 1898 and the Origins of Globalization* (Lexington, 2003), 99.

17. Quoted in Tuchman, 176.

18. Sutan Sjahrir, *Out of Exile* (New York, 1969), 22.

19. Quoted in John Grenville, *A History of the World in the Twentieth Century*, vol. 2, *Conflict and Liberation, 1945–1996* (Cambridge, MA, 1997), 410.

20. Quoted in Arthur S. Link, *Woodrow Wilson and the Progressive Era, 1910–1917* (New York, 1963), 65.

21. *See Pogroms: Anti-Jewish Violence in Modern Russian History*, ed. John Klier and Shlomo Lambroza (New York, 1992); the "Conclusion and Overview" essay by Hans Roger is especially useful in that it compares Russian antisemitism with other types of bigotry and racism in other countries.

22. See above, Ch. 1's section on "Hitler and Right-Wing Authoritarian Movements."

23. Nelson Mandela, *Long Walk to Freedom: The Autobiography of Nelson Mandela* (Boston, 1994), 106, 497.

24. Amartya Sen, *Identity and Violence: The Illusion of Destiny* (New York, 2006), 7 and Ch. 2.

25. *The Random House Dictionary of the English Language*, College ed. (New York, 1968), 886.

26. Isaiah Berlin, "The Bent Twig: A Note on Nationalism," in *A Foreign Affairs Reader: Editor's Choice* (New York, 1995), 17.

27. Eric Hobsbawm and Terence Ranger, *Invented Tradition* (Cambridge, Eng., 1983). Also useful are Benedict Anderson, *Imagined Communities: Reflections on the Origins and Spread of Nationalism* (London, 1983), Miroslav Hroch, *Social Preconditions of National Revival in Europe* (Cambridge, Eng.,1985), and Geoff Eley and Ronald Grigor Suny, eds., *Becoming National: A Reader* (New York, 1996). For interesting reflections on the meaning of nation and nationalism in Africa, see Nigerian writer Wole Soyinka's *Open Sore of a Continent: A Personal Narrative of the Nigerian Crisis* (New York, 1966), 18–25.

28. See, for example, Eugene Weber, *Peasants into Frenchmen: The Modernization of Rural France, 1870–1914* (Stanford, 1976).

29. A fuller treatment of post-World War I self-determination is given in Walter Moss, Janice Terry, and Jiu-Hwa Upshur, *The Twentieth Century: Readings in Global History*, (Boston, 1999), Ch. 6.

30. *The Memoirs of Counte Witte*, trans. and ed. Sidney Harcave (Armonk, NY, 1990), 126–7. In his U.S. Senate campaign in 2006, Senator George Allen of Virginia used a variation of the "macacques" term in referring to a young man of Indian origin. The reference was perceived to be a racial slur and helped lead to Allen's defeat.

31. Quoted in Daniel Patrick Moynihan, *Pandaemonium: Ethnicity in International Politics* (Oxford, 1994), 10.

32. Scholarly differences on the causes of the Cold War have long existed. For an example of these differences see Gaddis, 32–9, who maintains that it emerged primarily as a result of Western opposition to Soviet expansion, and the more leftist position by Noam Chomsky and others as indicated at http://www. redpepper.org.uk/cularch/xalmeida.htm, a website of *Red Pepper*, "an independent magazine of news, debate and culture for the left" (accessed May 23, 2007). Chomsky insists that the Cold War resulted not only from Soviet attempts to control portions of eastern Europe, but also from U.S. domestic considerations and its desire to exploit various parts of the world for economic gain. Although U.S. economic interests played some role in the Cold War, Gaddis's view seems closer to the truth, as I have indicated in my *A History of Russia*, vol. 2, *Since 1855*, 2d ed. (London, 2005), 321–30.

33. *The Moor's Last Sigh* (New York, 1997), 350.

34. Sen, 49–50 and in his Ch. 5, "West and Anti-West," makes a number of similar points and is generally quite good at pointing out the many complexities of any West versus anti-West positions. See also Pankaj Mishra, *Temptations of the West: How to Be Modern in India, Pakistan and Beyond* (New York, 2006).

35. As I indicated in my "Vladimir Soloviev and the Russophiles," (Ph.D. diss., Georgetown University, 1968), Ch. 7, the Russian philosopher Vladimir Soloviev (1853–1900) was quite critical of Danilevsky's ideas and made some cogent points regarding Russia and the West. See also Sen, 10–11, 40–3, 46–50. Sen is very critical of Huntington's book for placing people in a "unique set of rigid boxes" (p. 11).

36. Tolstoy, 20–1.

37. Theodore Von Laue, *The World Revolution of Westernization: The Twentieth Century in Global Perspective* (New York, 1987), 61.

38. For two end-of-the-century perspectives on Russia and the West, see the Richard Pipes book review, "East is East" (a review of Martin Malia's *Russia under Western Eyes*), *The New Republic*, April 26 and May 3, 1999, 100–08.

39. *Inside the Third World: The Anatomy of Poverty*, 2d ed. (London and New York, 1987), 48.

40. Robert D. Kaplan, *The Ends of the Earth: A Journey at the Dawn of the 21st Century* (New York, 1997), 374.

41. See, for example, Paul Theroux, *The Happy Isles of Oceania: Paddling the Pacific* (New York, 1992); Frank Viviano, *Dispatches from the Pacific Century* (Reading, MA, 1993); and David Remnick, *Resurrection: The Struggle for a New Russia* (New York, 1997).

42. Said, 218.

43. *The Penguin Gandhi Reader*, ed. Rudrangshu Mukherjee (New York, 1996), 37.

44. Martin Green, *Gandhi: Voice of a New Age Revolution* (New York, 1993), 384.

45. For a good fictional depiction of such conflict in Turkey in the 1990s, see Nobel Prize winner Orhan Pamukh's novel *Snow* (New York, 2005).

46. See also below, Ch. 7, n. 30, for Frantz Fanon comment's on the psychological need to discover an alternative to Western culture. For some examples from Asia, see Nathan P. Gardels, ed., *At Century's End: Great Minds Reflect on Our Times* (La Jolla, CA, 1995), 189, 191–2, 197 247–8; George Bernard de Huszar, ed., *The Intellectuals: A Controversial Portrait* (Glencoe, IL, 1960), 431, 435, 438; and Rabindranath Tagore, *Sadhana: The Realization of Life* (Tucson, 1972). 4–14.

47. For a recent example of Fuentes's thought, see his "A Need for the Best of Europe: Continental Drift," *Le Monde diplomatique*, November 2003, available at http://www.hartford-hwp.com/archives/60/061.html (accessed May 24, 2007).

48. Kaplan, 185.
49. Niall Ferguson, *The War of the World: Twentieth-Century Conflict and the Descent of the West* (New York, 2006), lxix, 636–46.
50. For a convenient bibliography on globalization, see http://www.ilr.cornell.edu/globalPortal/documents/GlobalizationHistoryBibliography.html. Also see Anthem Studies in Development and Globalization, a series of books available from Anthem Press at http://www.anthempress.com/serieses.php?cPath = 122 (both sites accessed July 29, 2007). For a recent overview of globalization from a historical viewpoint, see Bruce Mazlish, *The New Global History* (New York, 2006). For the perspective of someone who made a major contribution to scholarly thinking about globalization but by 1999 viewed much of the discourse about it as a "gigantic misreading of current reality," see Immanuel Wallerstein, "Globalization or The Age of Transition? A Long-Term View of the Trajectory of the World-System," http://fbc.binghamton.edu/iwtrajws.htm (accessed May 26, 2007).
51. Based on IMF figures found at http://www.imf.org/external/np/speeches/2000/041300.htm (accessed July 25, 2007).
52. From his 1999 State of the Union speech as found at http://www.cnn.com/ALLPOLITICS/stories/1999/01/19/sotu.transcript/ (accessed November 19, 2006).
53. Nicholas D. Kristof, with Edward Whatt, "Who Sank, or Swam, in Choppy Currents of a World Cash Ocean," *New York Times*, February 15, 1999, available at http://www.hartford-hwp.com/archives/25/094.html (accessed July 25, 2007).
54. Sen, 126; see also his Harvard commencement address, June 8, 2000, available at http://www.commencement.harvard.edu/2000/sen.html (accessed May 26, 2007).
55. Sen, *Identity and Violence*, 123–4.
56. Friedman, *The Lexus and the Olive Tree*. (New York, 1999), xvi.
57. Ibid., xvi, 7–8, 10, 294.
58. "What I Learned at the World Economic Crisis," available at www2.gsb.columbia.edu/faculty/jstiglitz/download/opeds/What_I_Learned_at_the_World_Economic_Crisiis.htm (accessed November 23, 2006). For a website with links to many articles by Stiglitz, as well as other materials on global perspectives, see http://www.project-syndicate.org/series/11/description. For links to many additional publications of Stiglitz, see http://www2.gsb.columbia.edu/ faculty/jstiglitz/press.cfm (both accessed May 25, 2007).
59. The report is available at http://hdr.undp.org/reports/global/1999/en/ (accessed November 19, 2006). For a brief consideration of these statistics and a look at a different set of statistics that indicate that globalization has had more positive effects, see http://www.globalisationguide.org/03.html (accessed November 23, 2006). See also Benjamin M. Friedman, "Globalization: Stiglitz's Case," *New York Review of Books*, August 15, 2002, available at http://www.arlindo-correia.com/globalization_stiglitzs_case.html (accessed November 23, 2006).
60. See his interview with Sophie Boukhari, January 10, 2002, in *The New Courier*, at http://assistive.usablenet.com/tt/portal.unesco.org/en/ev.php-URL_ID = 6609and URL_DO = DO_TOPIC and URL_SECTION = 201.html (accessed November 23, 2006).
61. Ibid. Stiglitz was not only critical of the IMF, but also of U.S. policies, including those of the Clinton administration in which he served.

62. "Globalization and Poverty," *Resurgence*, September/October 2000, available at http://www.resurgence.org/resurgence/issues/shiva202.htm (accessed May 25, 2007). Sharing the viewpoint of Shiva and other critics of neoliberal globalization is the World Social Forum, which came into existence in 2001. See its India branch's website at http://www.wsfindia.org (accessed May 26, 2007).

63. Friedman, *Lexus*, xviii, 9–10.

Chapter 5

1. Quoted in Ralph Barton Perry, *The Thought and Character of William James* (Cambridge, MA, 1948), 246. See below, the section "The Cold War and Freedom" for further thoughts on later U.S. foreign policies as they related to freedom.

2. For an excellent recent biography of Roosevelt, see Jean Edward Smith, *FDR* (New York, 2007).

3. http://www.freedomhouse.org/template.cfm?page = 2 (accessed May 30, 2007). Non-governmental organizations (NGOs) such as Freedom House played an important part in furthering freedom and human rights, especially in the latter part of the twentieth century.

4. For an example of the stress on freedom among Africans seeking independence in the 1950s, see the reading on "The Kenyan Independence Movement," in Walter Moss, Janice Terry, and Jiu-Hwa Upshur, *The Twentieth Century: Readings in Global History* (Boston, 1999), 256–60.

5. For the experiences of other former eastern European countries in the post-communist period, see Padraic Kenney, *The Burdens of Freedom: Eastern Europe since 1989* (London, 2006).

6. See "Freedom in the World Country Rankings, 1972–2006," http://www.freedomhouse.org/uploads/fiw/FIWAllScores.xls (accessed December 30, 2006).

7. Rabindranath Tagore, *Gitanjali (Song Offerings): A Collection of Prose Translations Made by the Author from the Original Bengali*, with an Introduction by W. B. Yeats (New York, 1971), 44; also available at http://www.sacred-texts.com/hin/tagore/gitnjali.htm (accessed December 28, 2006).

8. Rabindranath Tagore, *Sadhana: The Realization of Life* (Tucson, 1972), 32, 84, 85, 120.

9. Cited in Alastair Bonnett, *The Idea of the West: Culture, Politics and History* (Houndmills, 2004), 86.

10. Quoted in Amartya Sen, "Tagore and His India," available at http://www.countercurrents.org/culture-sen281003.htm (accessed December 28, 2006).

11. Nikolai Berdyaev, *Slavery and Freedom (New York, 1944)*, 119, 183–4, 209, 215, 221.

12. Jacques Ellul, *The Technological Society*,Vintage ed. (New York, 1967), 21, 72–3, 78–9, 97, 138.

13. Ibid., xxx.

14. *One-Dimensional Man: Studies in the Ideology of Advanced Industrial Society* (Boston, 1969), 1; also available at http://www.marcuse.org/herbert/pubs/64onedim/odm1.html (accessed December 28, 2006).

15. Ibid., 50.

16. Herbert Marcuse, *An Essay on Liberation* (Boston, 1969), 91.

17. Ibid., 12.

18. Ibid., 90.

19. *The Making of a Counter Culture: Reflections*, Anchor Books ed. (Garden City, NY, 1969), 84. Brown's most influential book was his *Life Against Death: The Psychoanalytic Meaning of History* (New York, 1959).

20. Marcuse, *Essay*, 56.
21. Charles A. Reich, *The Greening of America*, Bantam ed. (New York, 1971), 2, 5–6.
22. Ibid., 379.
23. *Europe since Hitler: The Rebirth of Europe*, rev. ed., (Harmondsworth, 1982), 448–9.
24. *The Year of the Young Rebels*, Vintage ed. (New York, 1969), 64.
25. Cited in "Privacy & Human Rights 1999," available at http://pi.gn.apc.org/survey/Overview.html (accessed December 29, 2006).
26. David Brin, *The Transparent Society: Will Technology Force Us to Choose Between Privacy and Freedom?* (New York, 1998), 5.
27. Norton Critical ed., ed. Ralph E. Matlaw (New York, 1976), 232–3.
28. Erich Fromm, *Escape from Freedom*, Avon Books ed. (New York, 1965), xii.
29. Clinton Rossiter, *Conservatism in America: The Thankless Persuasion*, 2d Vintage ed. (New York, 1962), 24.
30. Richard Pipes, *Property and Freedom*, Vintage ed. (New York, 2000), 283.
31. Vol. 2, Vintage ed. (New York, 1954), 12.
32. Eric F. Goldman, *Rendezvous with Destiny: A History of Modern American Reform*, rev. and abr. Vintage ed. (New York, 1958), 33, 41, 42.
33. Quoted in Cass R. Sunstein, *The Second Bill of Rights: FDR'S Unfinished Revolution and Why We Need It More than Ever* (New York, 2004), 242–3.
34. Isaiah Berlin, *Four Essays on Liberty* (New York and Oxford, 1969), 125.
35. Ibid., 31.
36. G. A. Cohen, "Freedom and Money," http://www.pem.cam.ac.uk/international-programmes/Cohen.pdf (accessed December 30, 2006). Cohen also argues here, as opposed to his friend Berlin, that "lack of money, poverty, carries with it lack of freedom."
37. *The Crosswinds of Freedom: From Roosevelt to Reagan—America in the Last Half Century*, Vintage ed. (New York, 1990), 276.
38. Zbigniew Brzezinski, *Out of Control: Global Turmoil on the Eve of the Twenty-first Century* (New York, 1993), 69–70.
39. From an interview of February 10, 1999, available at http://www.hoover.org/publications/uk/3411401.html (accessed June 2, 2007).
40. For two very different assessments of Friedman's significance, as seen by the year of his death in 2006, see Michael Strong, "Milton Friedman, A Modern Galileo," http://www.realclearpolitics.com/articles/2006/11/milton_friedman_a_modern_galil.html, and Greg Grandin, "The Road from Serfdom: Milton Friedman and the Economics of Empire," http://www.counterpunch.org/grandin11172006.html (both accessed May 30, 2007).
41. Pipes, 284.
42. *Resistance, Rebellion, and Death*, trans. Justin O'Brien, Vintage ed. (New York, 1974), 90, 248.
43. (New York, 1966), ix.
44. John Rawls in his *A Theory of Justice* (Cambridge, MA, 1971) and other writings attempted to outline what he believed was the proper balance between liberty and justice, and Sen has been influenced by his ideas, though he has gone further than Rawls in emphasizing what he calls "substantive freedom." In a later work, *Identity and Violence: The Illusion of Destiny* (New York, 2006), Chs. 8 and 9, Sen expounded some significant ideas about the relationship between identity and freedom and how individuals' multiple identities could contribute to freedom.
45. *Women and Human Development: The Capabilities Approach* (Cambridge, MA, 2000), 54. See also Cécile Fabre and David Miller, "Justice and Culture", Rawls,

Sen, Nussbaum and O'Neill, *Political Studies Review* 1, no. 1 (2003), 4–17. For a variation of the argument that economic conditions help determine freedom, see Brink Lindsey, *The Age of Abundance: How Prosperity Transformed America's Politics and Culture* (New York, 2007), where the author argues that U.S. capitalist prosperity greatly expanded citizens' freedoms.

46. The complete Universal Declaration can be found at http://www.unhchr.ch/udhr/lang/eng.htm (accessed December 30, 2006).

47. Mandela's speech, "No Easy Walk to Freedom," can be found at http://thirdworldtraveler.com/Human%20Rights%20Documents/Mandela_NoEasyWalk.html (accessed December 30, 2006).

48. The speech can be found at http://www.southafrica-newyork.net/consulate/speeches/address.htm (accessed December 30, 2006).

49. Peter Reddaway, ed. and trans., *Uncensored Russia: Protest and Dissent in the Soviet Union: the Unofficial Moscow Journal, A Chronicle of Current Events* (New York, 1972), 24.

50. See http://www.gwu.edu/~nsarchiv/NSAEBB/NSAEBB191/index.htm for some documents related to the Helsinki Watch groups. For Charter 77, a 1977 proclamation of prominent Czech intellectuals proposing that their government live up to the UN and Helsinki human rights conventions that they had signed, see http://www.cnn.com/SPECIALS/cold.war/episodes/19/documents/ charter.77, and http://www.gwu.edu/~nsarchiv/NSAEBB/NSAEBB213/index.htm (all three site accessed May 31, 2007).

51. Although the film *Missing* (1982) exercised some artistic license and was criticized on a number of points by the U.S. State Department, it conveys fairly well the repressive nature of the Pinochet consolidation of power.

52. Quoted in Richard Stites, *The Women's Liberation Movement in Russia: Feminism, Nihilism, and Bolshevism, 1860–1930* (Princeton, 1978), 6–7.

53. David Reynolds, *One World Divisible: A Global History since 1945* (New York, 2000), 314–15.

54. Nelson Mandela, *Long Walk to Freedom: The Autobiography of Nelson Mandela* (Boston, 1994), 144.

55. http://usinfo.state.gov/journals/itdhr/1098/ijde/perspect.htm (accessed December 30, 2006).

56. For a global breakdown of women in politics as of March 2000, see http://www.ipu.org/pdf/publications/wmnmap00_en.pdf (accessed December 31, 2006).

57. For a good overview of women's global situation at the turn of the century, see the annual surveys of "Women's Human Rights" covering the years 1999 and 2000 at the Human Rights Watch sites http://www.hrw.org/wr2k/Wrd.htm#TopOfPage, and http://hrw.org/wr2k1/women/index.html (both accessed June 1, 2007).

58. An excellent book on the subject is Alan M. Ball, *And Now My Soul Is Hardened: Abandoned Children in Soviet Russia, 1918–1930* (Berkeley, 1993).

59. *Promises Broken: An Assessment of Children's Rights on the 10th Anniversary of the Convention on the Rights of the Child*, http://www.hrw.org/press/1999/nov/children.htm (accessed August 3, 2007).

60. Various copies of the speech are available on the Internet; see, for example, http://www.usconstitution.net/dream.html (accessed December 31, 2006).

61. http://www.hrw.org/reports/1999/india/India994-02.htm#P350_19723 (accessed December 31, 2006).

62. For a valuable guide to the UN and minority rights, see the United Nations Guide for Minorities (2001), available at http://www.ohchr.org/english/issues/minorities/guide.htm (accessed December 31, 2006).

63. Caroline Ware, K. M. Panikkar, and J. M. Romein, *History of Mankind, Cultural and Scientific Development*, vol. 6, *The Twentieth Century* (New York, 1966), 1124.

64. www.ilo.org/dyn/declaris/DECLARATIONWEB.DOWNLOAD_BLOB? Var_DocumentID = 1581 (accessed December 31, 2006).

Chapter 6

1. J. R. McNeill, *Something New under the Sun: An Environmental History of the Twentieth-Century World* (New York, 2001), 4. An earlier work that dealt with the environment and history over a much longer period of time was Clive Ponting's *A Green History of the World: The Environment and the Collapse of Great Civilizations* (New York, 1992).

2. Robert D. Kaplan, *The Ends of the Earth: A Journey at the Dawn of the 21st Century* (New York, 1996), 19–20. In 2007 the U.S. Center for Naval Analyses, a government-financed research group, issued a report acknowledging that global warming posed a serious threat to national security. This report, written by a group of retired generals and admirals called the Military Advisory Board, is available at http://www.globalpolicy.org/empire/intervention/2007/0416climatethreat.pdf (accessed June 9, 2007).

3. For more on the relationship of increasing consumption and the environment, see Alan Durning, "Asking How Much Is Enough," *State of the World, 1991*, ed. Lester R. Brown et al. (New York, 1991), 153–65; an abridged version is reprinted in Walter Moss, Janice Terry, and Jiu-Hwa Upshur, *The Twentieth Century: Readings in Global History*, (Boston, 1999), 180–8.

4. William H. McNeill, "Demography and Urbanization," in *The Oxford History of the Twentieth Century*, ed. Michael Howard and Roger Louis (Oxford, 1998), 10.

5. J. R. McNeill, 360–1.

6. For two UN reports on global water problems, see http://www.unesco.org/water/wwap/wwdr1/table_contents/index.shtml, and http://www.unesco.org/water/wwap/wwdr2/index.shtml (both accessed June 5, 2007).

7. J. R. McNeill, 246. For a convenient statistical summary of the twentieth century's environmental impact, see his table on pp. 360–1. For an assessment of fish availability as of 2006, see also Richard Black, "'Only 50 Years Left' for Sea Fish," http://news.bbc.co.uk/2/hi/science/nature/6108414.stm (accessed June 5, 2007).

8. http://www.worldwatch.org/node/1626 (accessed June 7, 2007). A chart on this site shows the average person in the United States eating about one-third more meat than the average German or Italian and about two-thirds more than the average Japanese. For more on livestock water usage, see Alex Kirby, "Hungry World 'Must Eat Less Meat'," BBC News, August 16, 2004, http://news.bbc.co.uk/go/pr/fr/-/2/hi/science/nature/3559542.stm (accessed June 8, 2007).

9. H. Steinfeld et al., *Livestock's Long Shadow: Environmental Issues and Options* (Rome, 2006). Quotes are from the summary at http://www.virtualcentre.org/en/library/key_pub/longshad/A0701E00.htm#sum; full report is available at http://www.virtualcentre.org/en/library/key_pub/longshad/a0701e/A0701E00.pdf (both accessed June 7, 2007).

10. The story can be found at http://www.online-literature.com/anton_chekhov/ 1285/ (accessed January 7, 2007).

11. Oscar Lewis, *Five Families: Mexican Case Studies in the Culture of Poverty*, Mentor ed. (New York, 1965), 35–45.

12. No universally accepted standard for distinguishing urban from rural areas yet exists and census counts are often inexact, so many figures are only close approximations at best, but the general trends are indisputable.

13. Paul Harrison, *Inside the Third World: The Anatomy of Poverty*, 2d ed., with a Revised Overview (London, 1987), 141.

14. *What Then Shall We Do*, trans. Leo Wiener (New York, 1904), 71. For the anti-urbanism of Tolstoy and others, see below, Ch. 9.

15. Semën Ivanovich Kanatchikov, *A Radical Worker in Tsarist Russia: The Autobiography of Semën Ivanovich Kanatchikov*, ed. and trans. Reginald E. Zelnik (Stanford, 1986), 2, 6–7.

16. Ibid., 8.

17. See, for example, Nelson Mandela's *Long Walk to Freedom: The Autobiography of Nelson Mandela* (Boston, 1994), 51, 139, where he describes his first impressions of Johannesburg in the early 1940s and states "it all seemed tremendously glamorous" and "the possibilities seemed infinite," but that "he remained a country boy at heart."

18. Harrison, 140.

19. http://www.marxists.org/archive/marx/works/1850/class-struggles-france/ch02.htm; http://www.marxists.org/archive/marx/works/subject/hist-mat/hous-qst/ch03b.htm (both sites accessed January 7, 2007).

20. David Reynolds, *One World Divisible: A Global History since 1945* (New York, 2000), 251–2, 438.

21. Harrison, 147.

22. Ibid., 148. For a recent and a somewhat revised statement of Lipton's position, see M. Lipton, "Urban Bias," in *Encyclopedia of International Development*, ed. T. Forsyth (London, 2005), 724–6; for a recent critique of the "urban bias" thesis, see Stuart Corbridge and Gareth A. Jones, "The Continuing Debate About Urban Bias: The Thesis, Its Critics, Its Influence, and Implications for Poverty Reduction," http://www.lse.ac.uk/collections/geographyAnd Environment/research/Researchpapers/99%20corbridge%20jones.pdf (accessed January 7, 2007).

23. Otto Bettmann, *The Good Old Days—They Were Terrible!* (New York, 1974), 43.

24. http://www.george-orwell.org/Down_and_Out_in_Paris_and_London/ 23.html (accessed January 7, 2007).

25. *Angela's Ashes: A Memoir* (New York, 1996), 59.

26. More information on Soviet urban conditions can be found in my *A History of Russia, vol. 2, Since 1855*, 2d. ed. (London, 2005), 336–40, 487–91.

27. Lewis, 23.

28. *Kaffir Boy: The True Story of a Black Youth's Coming of Age in Apartheid South Africa* (New York, 1987), 5.

29. Ibid., 35. For a similar account of slum poverty in Sao Paulo, Brazil, including scavenging for food in a dump, see Carolina Maria de Jesus, *Child of the Dark: The Diary of Carolina Maria de Jesus*, trans. David St. Clair (New York, 1962), 40–1; another valuable account of impoverished living, but in a northeastern Brazilian shantytown, is Nancy Scheper-Hughes's, *Death Without Weeping: The Violence of Everyday Life in Brazil* (Berkeley, 1992).

30. Mike Davis, "Planet of Slums" *New Left Review* 26 (March–April 2004), 13–14; Davis took many of his figures from UN and other official reports, but noted that in such reports slum dwellers were often undercounted.

31. Ibid., 13, 15.

32. Kaplan, 4, 10–11.

33. http://www.ucl.ac.uk/dpu-projects/Global_Report/cities/abidjan.htm. See http://www.ucl.ac.uk/dpu-projects/Global_Report/a-z.htm for links to good brief summaries of slum conditions in many other cities of the world (both accessed January 8, 2007).

34. Kaplan, 17.

35. http://www.soesju.org/arsenic/kolkata_pollution1.htm; Reynolds, 680.

36. For a good overview of the problems in such big Latin American cities, see Alan Gilbert, ed., *The Mega-City in Latin America*, (Tokyo, 1996) hereafter Gilbert, Mega-City, also available at http://www.unu.edu/unupress/unupbooks/uu23me/uu23me00.htm#Contents (accessed January 8, 2007).

37. http://shininglight.us/archives/2005/06/homelessness_is_epidemic.php; Neal Richman and Bill Pitkin, "The Case of Los Angeles. U.S.A.," http://www.ucl.ac.uk/dpu-projects/Global_Report/pdfs/LA.pdf; http://www.unhabitat.org/documents/media_centre/sowcr2006/SOWCR%2015.pdf (all three sites accessed January 8, 2007).

38. Davis, 18–19, 21–3. See also Joseph E. Stiglitz and Andrew Charlton, *Fair Trade for All: How Trade Can Promote Development* (Oxford, 2006). Although Stiglitz was the chief economist at the World Bank for a few years in the late 1990s, he agrees that many of the previous World Bank policies had created greater economic inequalities and that some of the neoliberal policies it advocated were unwise.

39. *The De-Moralization of Society: From Victorian Virtues to Modern Values* (New York, 1995), 251. For more on Himmelfarb's view, see below, Ch. 8's section on "Virtues and Values."

40. Witold Rybczynski, *City Life* (New York, 1996), 173.

41. Alan Gilbert, "Land, Housing, and Infrastructure in Latin America's Major Cities," in Gilbert, *Mega-City*, 78.

42. Witold Rybczynski, "Suburban Despair: Is Urban Sprawl Really an American Menace?" *Slate*, November 7, 2005, http://www.slate.com/id/2129636/ (accessed January 8, 2007), quoting Robert Bruegmann's *Sprawl: A Compact History* (Chicago, 2005).

43. Gilbert, "Land," 91.

44. J. R. McNeill, 103; Marla Cone, "Breast Cancer Linked to Chemicals," *Baltimore Sun*, May 14, 2007, available at http://www.baltimoresun.com/news/health/bal-te.cancer14may14,0,1594768.story?coll = bal-nationworld-headlines (accessed May 15, 2007).

45. This novel is available at ftp://metalab.unc.edu/pub/docs/books/gutenberg/etext97/hardt10.txt (accessed January 15, 2007).

46. J. R. McNeill, 58.

47. http://www.epa.gov/air/airtrends/aqtrnd03/pdfs/chap1_execsumm.pdf (accessed January 15, 2007).

48. Stephen Kotkin, Steeltown, *USSR: Soviet Society in the Gorbachev Era* (Berkeley, 1991), 135–6; Murray Feshbach and Alfred Friendly, *Ecocide in the USSR: Health and Nature under Siege* (New York, 1992), 92–3, quoted material from p. 93.

49. Mark Hertsgaard, *Earth Odyssey: Around the World in Search of Our Environmental Future* (New York, 1999), vi.

50. http://www.eia.doe.gov/emeu/cabs/indiaenv.html (accessed January 15, 2007).
51. J. R. McNeill, 80.
52. Bettmann, 3.
53. Hertsgaard, 84–5.
54. Ibid., 95–6; *The World Almanac and Book of Facts, 2001* (Mahwah, NJ, 2001), 878; J. R. McNeill, 103.
55. For a variety of reasons, including sharp regional variations in climate changes, some scholars prefer to address the issue dealt with here under the heading of "global climate change" or "climate crisis"; the central problem, however, remains the earth's warming.
56. J. R. McNeill, 109; http://www.ipcc.ch/SPM040507.pdf (accessed June 11, 2007).
57. The UN article is available at http://www.un.org/apps/news/story.asp? NewsID = 20772&Cr = global&Cr1 = environment#; the report and its summary by H. Steinfeld, et al. are as indicated above in n. 9. For a more scathing criticism of "cattle culture," see Jeremy Rifkin, *Beyond Beef: The Rise and Fall of the Cattle Culture* (New York, 1992).
58. John M. Reilly, Henry D. Jacoby, and Ronald G. Prinn, *Multi-Gas Contributors to Global Climate Change: Climate Impacts and Mitigation Costs of Non-CO$_2$ Gases*, prepared for the Pew Center on Global Climate Change, February 2003, available at http://www.pewclimate.org/document.cfm?documentID = 211. For a table of greenhouse gases emitted by country, see http://www. carbonplanet.com/home/climate_emissions.php (both sites accessed June 9, 2007).
59. Lester R. Brown, "Deflating the World's Bubble Economy," in *Global Issues, 06–07*, ed. Robert M. Jackson (Dubuque, 2007), 46.
60. Al Gore, *Earth in the Balance: Ecology and the Human Spirit* (Boston, 1992), 5–7, 29, 39–40, 89–98. The concern was evident enough already in the early 1980s for a textbook to note that "another fear expressed in the 1970s was that the increased burning of fossil fuels might cause an increase in global temperatures, thereby possibly melting the polar ice caps, and flooding low-lying parts of the world." Richard Goff et al., *The Twentieth Century: A Brief Global History* (New York, 1983), 259.
61. http://www.grida.no/climate/ipcc_tar/wg1/049.htm (accessed January 15, 2007).
62. See http://www.ipcc.ch/ for the panel's website and latest findings (accessed June 8, 2007).
63. Ross Gelbspan discusses some of these findings and others in Ch. 1 of his *Boiling Point: How Politicians, Big Oil and Coal, Journalists, and Activists Are Fueling the Climate Crisis—and What We Can Do to Avert Disaster* (New York, 2004).
64. During 2006 the film *An Inconvenient Truth*, which featured Al Gore presenting a slide lecture on the dangers of global warming, further increased worldwide awareness of global warming. A summary of the 2007 IPCC Report is available at http://www.ipcc.ch/SPM040507.pdf. Another valuable source on global warming is the Pew Center on Global Climate Change at www.pewclimate.org (both sites accessed June 5, 2007). See also Elizabeth Kolbert, "Butterfly Lessons: Insects and Toads Respond to Global Warming," *The New Yorker*, January 9, 2006, 33–4.
65. Quoted at http://www.commondreams.org/headlines02/0215-01.htm (accessed January 15, 2007).
66. Gelbspan, Ch. 1. See also articles by Gelbspan and others in "As the World Burns," a special issue of *Mother Jones*, May–June 2005, available at http://www.motherjones.com/news/featurex/2005/05/world_burns.html; see also http://www.motherjones.com/search/category_environment.html

for links to more *Mother Jones* articles on the environmental crisis (both sites accessed June 6, 2007).

67. For a recent popular article that attempts to "go inside the denial machine" of oil lobbyists and others, see Sharon Begley, "The Truth about Denial," *Newsweek*, August 13, 2007, 20–9.

68. J. R. McNeill, 113.

69. Hertsgaard, 87.

70. J. R. McNeill, 114.

71. Rachel Carson, *Silent Spring*, Fawcett Crest Book ed. (Greenwich, CN, 1964), 44. Carson's book continues to the present to be influential and controversial. See, for example, Peter Matthiessen, ed., *Courage for the Earth: Writers, Scientists, and Activists Celebrate the Life and Writing of Rachel Carson* (Boston, 2007), and John Tierney, "To Spray or Not to Spray," *New York Times*, June 4, 2007. Tierney suggested that Carson "hyped" the danger of DDT and that more pesticides should be used to prevent the spread of diseases; the online version of this article, available at http://tierneylab.blogs.nytimes.com/2007/06/04/to-spray-or-not-to-spray/, was accompanied by 100 responses within a week (accessed June 11, 2007).

72. Carson, 46.

73. http://www.foxriverwatch.com/foran/index.html (accessed January 19, 2007).

74. J. R. McNeill, 132–3.

75. Feshbach and Friendly, 3, 114, 120.

76. J. R. McNeill, 129.

77. Ibid., 140–7.

78. Ibid., 141, 146, 304–5.

79. Ibid., 312.

80. Feshbach and Friendly, 174–5.

81. www.greenpeace.org/chernobylhealthconsequncesreport; for a summary of the IAEA Report, see http://www.iaea.org/NewsCenter/Focus/Chernobyl/pdfs/pr.pdf (both sites accessed January 19, 2007).

82. J. R. McNeill, 334–6, 341–4.

83. Feshbach and Friendly, 40.

84. Gore, 183–90. By 2007, however, partly due to the efforts of Gore and others more corporations and economists were beginning to heed environmental concerns. See below, Ch. 9.

85. J. R. McNeill, 341.

86. Milan Kundera, *Immortality*, trans. Peter Kussi (New York, 1992), 114–15.

87. Ibid., 114.

88. *The Age of Extremes: A History of the World, 1914–1991*, Vintage ed. (New York, 1996), 513.

89. In 2006 the U.S. state of Florida enacted a law prohibiting local governments from planting trees that would block the view of billboards, of which there were almost 21,000 in Florida.

90. Kundera, 113.

91. Viktor Pelevin, "Intel Inside," *Autodafe*, no. 3–4 (Spring 2003), online at http://www.autodafe.org/autodafe/autodafe_03/art_15.htm (accessed February 25, 2006).

92. Neil Postman, *Amusing Ourselves to Death: Public Discourse in the Age of Show Business*, new ed. (New York, 2006), 3–4.

93. Thomas Langan, *Surviving the Age of Virtual Reality* (Columbia, MO, 2000), 13, n. 2, 122–5.

94. Peter Conrad, *Modern Times, Modern Places* (New York, 1998), 9.
95. Ibid., 713.

Chapter 7

1. http://www.library.utoronto.ca/utel/nonfiction_u/arnoldm_ca/ca_ch-1.html (accessed January 27, 2007).
2. Raymond Williams, *Culture and Society, 1780–1950*, Harper Torchbooks ed. (New York, 1966), 328.
3. D. H. Lawrence, "Nottingham and the Mining Country," *Selected Essays*, Penguin ed. (Harmondsworth, Eng., 1950), 119–20. For an example of Lawrence's poetry critical of the bourgeois, see "How Beastly the Bourgeois Is," http://poetry.poetryx.com/poems/5768/ (accessed June 21, 2007).
4. Henry Steele Commager, *The American Mind: An Interpretation of American Thought and Character since the 1880s* (New Haven, 1950), 247.
5. Ibid., 248–50.
6. http://etext.library.adelaide.edu.au/l/lewis/sinclair/main/chapter4.html (accessed January 27, 2007).
7. Francis M. Sharp, "Literature in Germany, 1871–1933," in *Contemporary Germany: Politics and Culture*, ed. Charles Burdick, Hans-Adolf Jacobsen, and Winfried Kudzus (Boulder, 1984), 244.
8. Hans Kohn, *The Mind of Modern Germany: The Education of a Nation*, Harper Torchbook ed. (New York, 1965), 300.
9. Peter Gay, *Weimar Culture: The Outsider as Insider*, Harper Torchbook ed. (New York, 1970), 74. This German line of criticism of "civilization," directed primarily at the English and French, was apparent already at the beginning of the nineteenth century, partly stimulated by the reaction to Napoleon's conquests. Influenced by German thinkers such as Johann Gottfried Herder (1744–1803), the Russian Slavophiles, and after them anti-Westerners in other countries, applied similar criticism to "Western Civilization" in general (see above, Ch. 4's section on "Westernization and Its Opponents,") as well as Tolstoy and Gandhi's criticisms of the Western concept of civilization found at the beginning of that chapter.
10. For the importance of anti-bourgeois sentiments at the Bauhaus and its architectural influence in Europe and the United States, see Tom Wolfe's amusing *From Bauhaus to Our House* (New York, 1981).
11. From a selection of Baeumler quoted in George L. Mosse, *Nazi Culture: Intellectual, Cultural, and Social Life in the Third Reich* (New York, 1968), 97.
12. Leo Tolstoy, *The Russian Revolution*, trans. Louise and Aylmer Maude (Christchurch, Eng., 1906), 11, 15.
13. http://www.marxists.org/archive/lenin/works/1910/nov/16d.htm (accessed January 27, 2007).
14. Of course, some Russian and German writers left their countries and criticized these regimes from abroad or, despite government prohibitions, found other ways to voice their criticisms.
15. Antonio Gramsci, *Selections from Cultural Writings*, ed. David Forgacs and Geoffrey Nowell-Smith, trans. William Boelhower (Cambridge, MA, 1985), 14.
16. Kate Crehan, *Gramsci, Culture and Anthropology* (London, 2002), 208. Amartya Sen, in his *Identity and Violence: The Illusion of Destiny* (New York, 2006), 112–13, makes a similar point about the fluidity and heterogeneity of culture.

17. On the popularity of Dostoevsky and Tolstoy in the non-Western world, see Steven G. Marks, *How Russia Shaped the Modern World: From Art to Anti-Semitism, Ballet to Bolshevism* (Princeton, 2003), 95–101, 123–30.

18. José Enrique Rodó *Ariel*, trans. Margaret Sayers Peden (Austin, 1988); quotes are from excerpt available at http://www.utexas.edu/utpress/excerpts/exrodari.html (accessed June 12, 2007). On Rodó and other critics of the "West," including those in Russia, see above, Ch. 4's section on "Westernization and Its Opponents."

19. (New York, 1957), 18, 19, 91–2, 112–13, 187, 190.

20. James von Geldern and Richard Stites, eds., *Mass Culture in Soviet Russia: Tales, Poems, Songs, Movies, Plays, and Folklore, 1917–1953* (Bloomington, 1995).

21. For more on Vargas and the radio, as well as information on other aspects of Brazilian popular culture, see Daryle Williams. *Culture Wars in Brazil: The First Vargas Regime, 1930–1945* (Durham, NC, 2001).

22. For an interesting look at the relationship between popular music (especially the samba), radio, the government, and Brazilian national identity from 1930 to 1955, see Bryan McCann, Hello, *Hello Brazil: Popular Music and the Making of Modern Brazil* (Durham, NC, 2004).

23. For a work on jazz by a leading British historian, see Eric Hobsbawm, *The Jazz Scene* (New York, 1993); his *Uncommon People: Resistance, Rebellion, and Jazz* (New York, 1998) also contains some essays on jazz. See also Michael H. Kater, *Different Drummers: Jazz in the Culture of Nazi Germany* (Oxford, 2003), and Frederick S. Starr, *Red and Hot: The Fate of Jazz in the Soviet Union, 1917–1980* (New York,1983).

24. John King, *Magical Reels: A History of Cinema in Latin America*, 2d ed. (London, 2000), 32; Nelson Mandela, *Long Walk to Freedom: The Autobiography of Nelson Mandela* (Boston, 1994), 67–8. King's book also provides an excellent overview of Latin American cinema throughout the twentieth century. See also Anne T. Doremus, *Culture, Politics, and National Identity in Mexican Literature and Film, 1929–1952* (New York, 2001), and Roy Armes, *Third World Film Making and the West* (Berkeley, 1987).

25. Frederick Lewis Allen, *Only Yesterday: An Informal History of the 1920s* (New York, 1964), 155.

26. William R. Leach, *Land of Desire: Merchants, Power, and the Rise of a New American Culture* (New York, 1993), xiii.

27. *The Varieties of Religious Experience: A Study in Human Nature*, Mentor ed. (New York, 1958), 282.

28. Quoted in Robert S. Lynd and Helen Merrell Lynd, *Middletown: A Study in American Cultural Conflicts*, Harvest ed. (New York, 1956), 88.

29. Quotes are found in Allen, 149.

30. Frantz Fanon in his *The Wretched of the Earth*, paperback ed. (New York, 1968), 209, noted that the "passionate search for a national culture which existed before the colonial era finds its legitimate reason in the anxiety shared by native intellectuals to shrink away from that Western culture in which they all risk being swamped." Mandela, *Long Walk to Freedom: The Autobiography of Nelson Mandela*, 12 refers to his early schooling in South Africa as "a British education, in which British ideas, British culture, and British institutions were automatically assumed to be superior. There was no such thing [in the eyes of his teachers] as African culture." See also above, Ch. 5, for Tagore's thoughts on freedom and the West, and Alastair Bonnett, Ch. 4: "Soulless Occident/ Spiritual Asia: Tagore's West," in Alastair Bonnett, *The Idea of the West: Culture,*

Politics and History (Houndmills, 2004), Ch. 4, which deals with Tagore's views on the West.

31. Quoted in Peter Conrad, *Modern Times, Modern Places* (New York, 1999), 346.
32. Quoted in Pablo Neruda, *Memoirs*, trans. Hardie St. Martin, Penguin ed. (Harmondsworth, Eng., 1978), 113. As Neruda noted, both he and Lorca were great admirers of Darío's writings.
33. The words are those of one of the Dadaists Hans Arp, as quoted in Peter Watson, *The Modern Mind: An Intellectual History of the 20th Century* (New York, 2001), 161.
34. Quoted in Conrad, 78.
35. For a sampling of the negative impact of imperialism on non-Western cultures, see Fanon's chapter "On National Culture," in his *The Wretched of the Earth*, Grove paperback ed. (New York, 1968), 206–48, Ali A. Mazrui's chapter "A Clash of Cultures," in his *The African Condition: A Political Diagnosis* (London, 1980), 46–69; and Aimé Césaire's work written more than a half century ago, *Discourse on Colonialism*, trans. Joan Pinkham, new ed. (New York, 2000). Edward Said in such works as *Culture and Imperialism*, Vintage ed. (New York, 1994) also has much to say about imperialism's relationship to culture and cultures.
36. Watson, 350.
37. H. Stuart Hughes, *The Sea Change: The Migration of Social Thought, 1930–1965* (New York, 1975), 1.
38. T.S. Eliot, *Selected Prose*, ed. John Hayward (Harmondsworth, Eng., 1958), 241, 248.
39. E. M. Forster, "What I Believe," *Ten Contemporary Thinkers*, ed. Victor. E. Amend and Leo T. Hendrick (New York, 1964), 106–07, 108, 109.
40. *The Big Change: America Transforms Itself, 1900–1950* (New York, 1961), 236–43. The last quote is from Allen, 236, quoting Van Wyck Brooks.
41. Jules Henry, *Culture Against Man*, Vintage ed. (New York, 1963), 4–5, 9.
42. Ibid., 48.
43. Ibid., 320.
44. *Culture of Narcissism: American Life in an Age of Diminishing Expectations*, Warner ed. (New York, 1979),17–18, 22, 137.
45. Quoted in David Reynolds, *One World Divisible: A Global History since 1945* (New York, 2000), 291–2.
46. Newton N. Minow and Craig L. LaMay, *Abandoned in the Wasteland: Children, Television, and the First Amendment* (New York, 1996), 188.
47. Ibid., 201–02.
48. *Culture of Complaint: A Passionate Look into the Ailing Heart of America*, Warner reprint ed. (New York, 1994), 5.
49. Michael Kammen, *American Culture, American Tastes: Social Change and the Twentieth Century* (New York, 1999), 58.
50. Reynolds, 300.
51. One of the books praising the counterculture, Charles A. Reich's *The Greening of America*, Bantam ed. (New York, 1971), 7, proclaimed, "Our culture has been reduced to the grossly commercial; all cultural values are for sale."
52. For two recent books on the subject, see Benjamin R. Barber, *Consumed: How Markets Corrupt Children, Infantilize Adults, and Swallow Citizens Whole* (New York, 2007), and Eric Clark, *The Real Toy Story: Inside the Ruthless Battle for America's Youngest Consumers* (New York, 2007).
53. *Hope and Glory: Britain, 1900–1990* (London, 1997), 248–55.

54. Pavel Palazchenko, *My Years with Gorbachev and Shevardnadze: The Memoirs of a Soviet Interpreter* (University Park, Pa., 1997), 3.

55. Jacques Barzun, *From Dawn to Decadence: 500 Years of Cultural Life, 1500 to the Present* (New York, 2000), 797.

56. *The Age of Extremes: A History of the World, 1914–1991*, 512–13.

57. Milan Kundera, *Immortality*, trans. Peter Kussi (New York, 1992), 290.

58. Kammen, 192–3.

59. Quoted in Greil Marcus, *Lipstick Traces: A Secret History of the Twentieth Century* (Cambridge, MA, 1989), 106.

60. *Intellectuals* (New York, 1988), 225.

61. For more on NPL winners, see http://nobelprize.org/nobel_prizes/literature (accessed February 18, 2007).

62. Gene Feldman and Max Gartenberg, eds. *The Beat Generation and the Angry Young Men* (New York, 1959), 11–13.

63. Later in life, Amis became increasingly conservative.

64. For a useful collection of essays on post-Soviet culture, see Rita Lipson, ed., *Culture in Transition: A Search for Identity through the Arts in Post-Soviet Russia* (Moscow, 2006), http://www.websher.net/yale/rl/cultureintransition (accessed August 12, 2007).

65. "Art without Beauty," *Public Interest*, 127 (Spring, 1997), 1, http://findarticles.com/p/articles/mi_m0377/is_n127/ai_19416356/pg_1 (accessed February 18, 2007).

66. Kundera, 290.

67. Hobsbawm, 514–15.

68. Kundera, 289.

Chapter 8

1. Victor Erofeyev and Andrew Reynolds, eds., *The Penguin Book of New Russian Writing* (London, 1995), xiv.

2. Norman F. Cantor, *The American Century: Varieties of Culture in Modern Times*, Picture Essays by Mindy Cantor (New York, 1997), 451, 465.

3. Peter Watson, *The Modern Mind: An Intellectual History of the 20th Century* (New York, 2001), 632; Cantor, 457.

4. Allan Bloom, *The Closing of the American Mind*, Touchstone ed. (New York, 1988), 379.

5. George F. Will, *Leveling Wind: Politics, Culture, and Other News, 1990–1994*, Penguin ed. (New York, 1995), 134–5.

6. http://weber.ucsd.edu/~dkjordan/scriptorium/gibber/gibberpomo.html (accessed February 23, 2007).

7. http://www.elsewhere.org/pomo (accessed February 23, 2007).

8. Cantor, 432.

9. Quoted in Michael Kammen, *American Culture, American Tastes: Social Change and the Twentieth Century* (New York, 1999), 114–15.

10. Vintage ed. (New York, 1963), 224.

11. Ibid., 9, quoting from an article by Louis Bromfield.

12. For a fair overview of press coverage of deconstructionism, see Mitchell Stephens, "Deconstruction and the Get-Real Press," *Columbia Journalism Review* (September/October 1991), available at http://archives.cjr.org/year/91/5/deconstruction.asp (accessed February 23, 2007).

13. C. P. Snow, *The Two Cultures, and a Second Look: An Expanded Version of the Two Cultures and the Scientific Revolution*, Mentor ed. (New York, 1963), 10, 59.

14. From "Smitten with Gibberish," *Washington Post*, May 30, 1966, as reprinted in *The Sokal Hoax: The Sham That Shook the Academy*, ed. by the editors of *Lingua Franca* (Lincoln, NE, 2000), 91.

15. Snow, 73–4.

16. Watson, 752, 757.

17. Ibid., 4–5

18. Ibid., 3, 7, 752, 757, 770–1, Ch. 39.

19. "Postmodernism Disrobed," *Nature*, 394 (July 9, 1998), 141–3, http://www.physics.nyu.edu/faculty/sokal/dawkins.html (accessed February 23, 2007). For a useful collection on the "science wars," see also Jay A. Labinger and Harry Collins, eds., *The One Culture? A Conversation about Science* (Chicago and London, 2001).

20. Bloom, 29–30. See also James Davison Hunter, *Culture Wars: The Struggle to Define America* (New York, 1991), 24, and http://www.christianparents.com/jdewey.htm, a website run by the Christian Parents Information Network and critical of Dewey's influence on U.S. education (accessed June 23, 2007).

21. For a general overview of early twentieth-century education and the contributions of Dewey, Montessori, Gandhi, Tagore, and others, see Caroline Ware, K. M. Panikkar and J. M. Romein, *History of Mankind, Cultural and Scientific Development*, vol. 6, *The Twentieth Century* (New York, 1966), 897–949. For more on Tagore's educational ideas, see http://globalsolidarity.transcend.org/articles/nonformal.html, and for Gandhi's educational thinking, see http://www.ncte-in.org/pub/gandhi/gandhi_0.htm (both sites accessed June 23, 2007).

22. Jacques Barzun, *From Dawn to Decadence: 500 Years of Cultural Life, 1500 to the Present* (New York, 2000), 784–5.

23. http://reactor-core.org/operating-manual-for-spaceship-earth.html (accessed June 23, 2007).

24. http://www.rwgrayprojects.com/synergetics/intro/well.html (accessed June 23, 2007).

25. Will, 127–8.

26. H. Stuart Hughes, *The Obstructed Path: French Social Thought in the Years of Desperation, 1930–1960*, Harper Torchbook ed. (New York, 1969), 19.

27. Will, 128.

28. Roger Scruton, *An Intelligent Person's Guide to Modern Culture* (South Bend, 2000), 5, 18.

29. Quoted by Peter Gay, *The Enlightenment, An Interpretation: The Rise of Modern Paganism*, Vintage ed. (New York, 1968), 406.

30. See the summation of poll results at http://www.religioustolerance.org/ev_publi.htm (accessed June 27, 2007).

31. For a good overview, see Michael Ruse, *The Evolution-Creation Struggle* (Cambridge, MA, 2005). One of the most respected critics of creationism was the evolutionary biologist and historian of science Stephen Jay Gould; for his criticism, see "Evolution as Fact and Theory," *Discover* 2 (May 1981), 34–7, http://www.stephenjaygould.org/library/gould_fact-and-theory.html (accessed June 27, 2007).

32. *Albert Einstein, The Human Side*, ed. Helen Dukas and Banesh Hoffman (Princeton, 1979), 66. This excerpt is on the Internet at http://www.sacred-texts.com/aor/einstein/einprayr.htm (accessed March 18, 2007).

33. "The Improbability of God," *Free Inquiry*, 18, no. 3.(1998); on website http://www.positiveatheism.org/writ/dawkins3.htm#IMPROB (accessed March 18, 2007).

34. Polkinghorne has written many books; see, for example, his *Belief in God in an Age of Science* (New Haven and London, 1998).

35. See the online version of Ch. 2 of his *Culture and Anarchy* (1882) available at http://www.library.utoronto.ca/utel/nonfiction_u/arnoldm_ca/ca_ch-2. html (accessed March 19, 2007).

36. From Kandinsky's *Concerning the Spiritual in Art*, online at http://www. mnstate.edu/gracyk/courses/phil%20of%20art/kandinskytext2.htm#3 (accessed March 19, 2007).

37. Scruton, 40, 150.

38. Peter L. Berger, "Secularization and De-Secularization," in *Religions in the Modern World*, ed. Linda Woodhead et al. (London, 2002), 293–4.

39. The quote is taken from a Stanford University June 1, 1993 news release entitled "Common Passions Fuel Religious Fundamentalism," http://news-service. stanford.edu/pr/93/930601Arc3236.html, which featured an interview with Almond (accessed June 24, 2007). For many years Almond was involved in the Fundamentalism Project, which studied fundamentalism within seven world religions. One fruit of this project was the book he co-authored with R. Scott Appleby and Emmanuel Sivan, *Strong Religion: The Rise of Fundamentalisms around the World* (Chicago, 2002).

40. Quoted in Mary Pat Fisher, *Living Religions*, 6th ed. (Upper Saddle River, NJ, 2005), 479.

41. John L. Esposito, Darrell J. Fasching, and Todd Lewis, *World Religions Today* (New York and Oxford, 2002), 118–19.

42. Berger, 292.

43. http://adherents.com/Religions_By_Adherents.html (accessed March 19, 2007).

44. The results are available at http://people-press.org/reports/display. php3?ReportID=167 (accessed March 19, 2007).

45. On the German clergy, see Robert P. Ericksen, *Theologians under Hitler* (New Haven, 1985).

46. Quoted in Fisher, 353.

47. http://www.christendom-awake.org/pages/ratzinger/liberationtheol.htm (accessed March 18, 2007).

48. For an assessment of Cardinal Ratzinger's polarizing position among Catholic thinkers by 1999, see John L. Allen Jr., "The Vatican's Enforcer," *National Catholic Reporter*, April 16, 1999, available at http://www.natcath.com/ NCR_Online/archives/041699/041699a.htm (accessed March 18, 2007).

49. Esposito, Fasching, and Lewis, 32.

50. Gertrude Himmelfarb, *The De-Moralization of Society: From Victorian Virtues to Modern Values.* (New York, 1994), 9.

51. Ibid., 11–12.

52. *The Downing Street Years, 1979–1990* (New York, 1993), 627. See also Novak's *Universal Hunger for Liberty: Why the Clash of Civilizations Is Not Inevitable* (New York, 2004), 30–44, 176, 221–3, where he writes of virtues and makes a similar distinction as that of Himmelfarb between virtues and values.

53. Himmelfarb, 240–3. 251.

54. http://www.oldpaths.com/Archive/Brown/T/Pierce/1923/ethics.html (accessed March 24, 2007).

55. www.christiancourier.com/archives/jesusEthics.htm (accessed March 24, 2007).
56. James Davison Hunter, *Culture Wars: The Struggle to Define America* (New York, 1991), 40–1.
57. *See, I Told You So* (New York, 1993), 87.
58. John Fonte, "Why There Is a Culture War," *Policy Review* 104 (December 2000 and January 2001), http://www.hoover.org/publications/policyreview/3484376.html (accessed June 18, 2007).
59. *Values Matter Most: How Republicans, or Democrats, or a Third Party Can Win and Renew the American Way of Life* (New York, 1995), 10, 16, 177.
60. "John Paul II and the Priority of Culture," *First Things* 80 (February 1998), 19–25, http://www.firstthings.com/article.php3?id_article = 3470 (accessed June 18, 2007).
61. George Weigel, "Is Europe Dying? Notes on a Crisis of Civilizational Morale," *Watch on the West, A Newsletter of FPRI's Center for the Study of America and the West* 6 (June 2005), http://www.fpri.org/ww/0602.200506.weigel.europedying.html (accessed June 18, 2007).
62. George Weigel, "Europe's Two Culture Wars," *Commentary* 121 (May 2006), 29–36, www.discovery.org/scripts/viewDB/filesDB-download.php?command = download&id = 798 (accessed June 18, 2007).
63. See the WVS site at http://www.worldvaluessurvey.org, especially the Inglehart-Welzel Cultural Map of the World available at that site (accessed March 24, 2007).

Chapter 9

1. For more on Tolstoy's view of progress, see my *Russia in the Age of Alexander II, Tolstoy and Dostoevsky* (London, 2002), 118.
2. Christopher Lasch, *The True and Only Heaven: Progress and Its Critic* (New York, 1991), 54, 55.
3. See above, Ch. 7, and William R. Leach, *Land of Desire: Merchants, Power, and the Rise of a New American Culture* (New York, 1993), xiii.
4. Stefan Zweig, *The World of Yesterday: An Autobiography* (Lincoln, NE, 1964), 3. See also Robert Nisbet, *History of the Idea of Progress* (New York, 1980), 171, where he declares that progress had become the dominant idea in the West by 1900.
5. Zweig, 3–4.
6. Ibid., 193.
7. Ibid., 4.
8. Barbara Tuchman, *The Proud Tower: A Portrait of the World before the War, 1890–1914*, Bantam ed. (New York, 1967), xv.
9. Ibid., 378.
10. Friedrich von Bernhardi, *Germany and the Next War* (New York, 1914), http://h-net.org/~german/gtext/kaiserreich/bernhardi.html (accessed April 8, 2007).
11. http://net.lib.byu.edu/~rdh7/wwi/1914m/illusion.html (accessed July 6, 2007).
12. Niall Ferguson, *The War of the World: Twentieth-Century Conflict and the Descent of the West* (New York, 2006), xxxv.
13. Angus Deaton, "Is World Poverty Falling?" *Finance & Development* 39, no. 2 (2002), https://www.imf.org/external/pubs/ft/fandd/2002/06/deaton.htm (accessed April 6, 2007); Jagdish Bhagwati, *In Defense of Globalization* (Oxford,

2005), 65. For a less positive view see the 1999 UN Development Report referred to in Ch. 4, n. 60.

14. Nisbet, 179.

15. For a more upbeat assessment of the state of the Earth by 1999, see Michael Novak, *Universal Hunger for Liberty: Why the Clash of Civilizations Is Not Inevitable* (New York, 2004), 116–19.

16. Quoted in Morton and Lucia White, *The Intellectual Versus the City: From Thomas Jefferson to Frank Lloyd Wright*, Mentor ed. (New York, 1964), 28.

17. Rudrangshu Mukherjee ed. *The Penguin Gandhi Reader* (New York, 1996), 35.

18. Fawcett ed. (Greenwich, CT, 1969), 103.

19. Otto Bettmann, *The Good Old Day—They Were Terrible!* (New York, 1974), 47.

20. For more on Esenin and "village prose," see my *A History of Russia, vol. 2, Since 1855*, 2d ed. (London, 2005), 378–9, 523–5.

21. Cited in Witold Rybczynski, *City Life* (New York, 1995), 193. See also the quotes from D. H. Lawrence and Sinclair Lewis above, in Ch. 7, criticizing the bourgeois spirit and urban life for their aesthetic failings. For a visual demonstration of similar failings, see the film *Chain* (2005).

22. Rybczynski, 24, 136, 148.

23. "The Secular City 25 Years Later," *The Christian Century* (November 7, 1990): 1025–9, http://www.religion-online.org/showarticle.asp?title = 206 (accessed April 8, 2007).

24. *The Secular City: Secularization and Urbanization in Theological Perspective*, paperback ed. (New York, 1966), 1; see also Daniel Callahan, ed., *The Secular City Debate*, paperback ed. (New York, 1966).

25. See above, Chapter 1's section "Structural Violence" and n. 55 of that chapter which quotes from Paul Farmer's *Pathologies of Power* (Berkeley, 2003), 50. Ch. 1 of that book is available at http://www.ucpress.edu/books/pages/9875/9875.ch01.html (accessed May 1, 2007). The WHO report, as well as reports for subsequent years through 2005, is available at http://www.who.int/whr/previous/en/ (accessed July 9, 2007).

26. Nisbet, 8–9, 318, 333, 357. In a later work, first published in 1988, Nisbet seemed somewhat discouraged about certain U.S. religious developments during the Reagan years and expressed displeasure with the "extreme politicization" of the "religious message" by many U.S. evangelical leaders. See his *The Present Age: Progress and Anarchy in Modern America*, reprint ed. (Indianapolis, 2003), available at http://oll.libertyfund.org/title/876/77069 (accessed August 10, 2007).

27. Francis Fukuyama, *The End of History and the Last Man* (New York, 1991, and 2006 ed. with a new Afterword, and Michael Mandelbaum, *The Ideas that Conquered the World: Peace, Democracy, and Free Markets in the Twenty-First Century* (New York, 2002). In an Afterword to the 2006 paperback edition of his book (p. 343), Fukuyama maintained the optimistic view he had expressed years earlier. He stated: "I think that there is an overall logic to historical evolution that explains why there should be increasing democracy around the world."

28. Mandelbaum (2002), 400–02.

29. Bruce Mazlish, *The New Global History* (New York, 2006), 80, 90–1, 93, 102, 111.

30. *The Lexus and the Olive Tree* (New York, 1999), xiii–xiv. In a later work, *The World Is Flat: A Brief History of the Twenty-First Century* (New York, 2005), Friedman maintained his view that globalization was a progressive force.

31. Novak, 51, 108, 110. The italics are Novak's and he cites a few of his own earlier works.

32. Novak, 109; Celia W. Dugger, "Peace Prize to Pioneer of Loans to Poor No Bank Would Touch," *New York Times*, October 14, 2006, http://www. nytimes.com/2006/10/14/world/asia/14nobel.html? (accessed July 7, 2007).

33. The term was popularized by Matthew Josephson in his 1934 book, *The Robber Barons: The Great American Capitalists, 1861–1901*; chapters of the book are available online, see, for example, http://www.yamaguchy.netfirms.com/ josephson/baron_01.html (accessed July 7, 2007).

34. Novak, 129–33; Thomas Friedman, "The Power of Green," *The New York Times Magazine*, April 15, 2007, http://www.iht.com/articles/2007/04/15/opinion/ web-0415edgreen-full.php (accessed July 7, 2007).

35. Al Gore, *Earth in the Balance: Ecology and the Human Spirit* (Boston, 1992), 185, 277, 346.

36. Barry Schwartz, "Buyer Beware: Are we training our kids to be consumers rather than citizens?" *The Washington Post*, April 8, 2007, http://www. washingtonpost.com/wp-dyn/content/article/2007/04/06/AR2007040600049. html (accessed July 1, 2007).

37. Konstantin P. Pobedonostsev, *Reflections of a Russian Statesman* (Ann Arbor, 1965), 3, 42, 44.

38. Teilhard de Chardin's first quote is from *The Future of Mankind* (New York, 1959), Ch. 4, available online at http://www.religion-online.org/show chapter.asp?title=2287&C=2165; links to all chapters are available at http://www.religion-online.org/showbook.asp?title = 2287 (both accessed July 10, 2007); the quotes from *The Phenomenon of Man* are from the Harper Torchbooks ed. of his book (New York, 1961), 218, 232. The Russian religious thinker and philosopher Vladimir Soloviev (1853–1900), who was quite critical of Pobedonostsev, held some evolutionary ideas similar to those later adopted by Teilhard, but his final work, *War, Progress, and the End of History, Including a Short Story of the Anti-Christ* (London, 1915) is less optimistic about progress.

39. For all but Nisbet, see above, Ch. 7; for Nisbet, writing earlier (in 1980), see his work on progress cited above in n. 4, 343–9.

40. Quoted from http://crab.rutgers.edu/~goertzel/fukuyama1.htm (accessed July 10, 2007), which is an electronic version of the first part of Fukuyama's "The Great Disruption," *The Atlantic Monthly* 283 (May 1999), 55–80. The essay was later published in a slightly different form in Fukuyama's *The Great Disruption: Human Nature and the Reconstitution of Social Order* (New York, 1999).

41. Bantam ed. (New York, 1971), 2, 11.

42. Thomas Langan, *Surviving the Age of Virtual Reality* (Columbia, MO, 2000), 131, n. 10.

43. http://www.comedy-zone.net/quotes/Comedians/barry-dave.htm (accessed April 9, 2007).

44. Zbigniew Brzezinski, *Out of Control: Global Turmoil on the Eve of the 21st Century* (New York, 1993), 112.

45. *In the Shadow of Tomorrow*, Norton reprint ed. (New York, 1964), 78.

46. http://www.quoteworld.org/category/wisdom/author/general_omar_ nelson_bradley (accessed April 9, 2007).

47. *Small Is Beautiful: Economics as if People Mattered*, Perennial Library ed. (New York, 1975), 33–4.

48. On Mandela's appreciation of wisdom see, for example, his *Long Walk to Freedom: The Autobiography of Nelson Mandela* (Boston, 1994), 18, 88, 397, 466, 499, 542.

49. Eugene F. Rice, Jr., *The Renaissance Idea of Wisdom* (Cambridge, MA, 1958), 1.

50. Rabindranath Tagore, *Sadhana: The Realization of Life* (Tucson, 1972), 35.

51. Lasch, 532.

52. Ronald Inglehart, "Globalization and Postmodern Values," *The Washington Quarterly* 23 (Winter 2000), 223, www.twq.com/winter00/231Inglehart.pdf (accessed July 3, 2007).

53. Nick Donovan and David Halpern, with Richard Sargeant, "Life Satisfaction: The State of Knowledge and Implications for Government," 17, 35, 43–59, available at http://www.cabinetoffice.gov.uk/strategy/downloads/seminars/ls/paper.pdf (accessed July 3, 2007). For a recent work that argues that progress should not be equated with increased consumption, see Bill McKibben, *Deep Economy: The Wealth of Communities and the Durable Future* (New York, 2007). For an interesting treatment of a concept closely related to well-being, see Darrin M. McMahon, *Happiness: A History* (New York, 2007), see also http://www.cato-unbound.org/2007/04/08/darrin-m-mcmahon/the-pursuit-of-happiness-in-perspective/ (accessed July 11, 2007).

54. For a recent account of proliferation, see William Langewiesche, *The Atomic Bazaar: The Rise of the Nuclear Poor* (New York, 2007).

55. Mandela, 431, 542.

56. Among these efforts, the scholarly works of those who have written on subjects such as mass killings and ways to reduce them are of some significance. See, for example, Daniel Chirot and Clark McCauley, *Why Not Kill Them All?: The Logic and Prevention of Mass Political Murder* (Princeton, 2006); John K. Roth, ed., *Genocide and Human Rights: A Philosophical Guide* (Houndmills, Eng., 2005).

Glossary

Capitalism An economic system in which means of production such as land, labor, and machinery are privately owned by individuals and businesses that produce and exchange goods and services primarily to earn a profit.

Cold War The ideological and political struggle between the USA and the USSR, along with both sides' allies, from the mid-1940s to the late 1980s.

Collectivization The process begun in the USSR in 1929 of forcing peasants onto collective farms. Collectivization was also later implemented in other countries after communist governments came to power, for example in China in the 1950s.

Command economy A term frequently used to describe the centrally planned economy that began developing in the USSR with the introduction of the First Five Year Plan in 1928. Under it, the state determined the types, amounts, and prices of almost all goods produced, including most agricultural produce.

Communism Refers primarily to the economic, social, and political systems established by communist parties beginning in Russia in 1917. However, in Marxist theory it is the final stage of development, an egalitarian stateless society, envisioned by Marx but not yet achieved by Marxist governments. See **Socialism** below.

Communist Primarily a Marxist belonging to a communist party.

Consumer culture   A culture that places a great deal of emphasis on the consumption of goods and services. An extreme example of such an approach is this statement made by a U.S. marketing consultant of the mid-1950s: "Our enormously productive economy . . . demands that we make consumption our way of life, that we convert the buying and use of goods into rituals, that we seek our spiritual satisfactions, our ego satisfactions, in consumption . . . We need things consumed, burned up, worn out, replaced, and discarded at an ever increasing rate." See Chapter 3, Endnote 10.

Culture   Most commonly refers to whole way of life of a group, including their physical and mental activities, e.g. French culture, or used as a collective term for the arts, humanities, and higher knowledge generally. The latter is sometimes referred to as "high culture." See the beginning of Chapter 7.

Cultural wars   A term that became popular in the USA by the early 1990s to describe the conflict over values that pitted conservatives against progressives or liberals. The conservatives believed that some sort of eternal, unchangeable, external moral authority existed that enabled them to determine right and wrong, while their opponents relied more on reason, their inner selves, and contemporary conditions in deciding right from wrong.

Dalits   Sometimes referred to as untouchables. The Dalits of India, numbering about 160 million people in 1999, were often discriminated against because of India's caste system.

Deconstructionism   A type of postmodernism (see below), popularized by the French academics Michel Foucault and Jacques Derrida, that in the 1980s exercised considerable cultural influence on the humanities and to a lesser extent on psychology, the social sciences, law, and the arts.

Democide   As defined by the scholar R. J. Rummel, it is "the murder of any person or people by a government, including genocide, politicide, and mass murder."

Democratic socialism   A form of socialism that advocates democratic, reformist means of obtaining power and aims at greater economic equality than in capitalism, primarily by means of greater government ownership of at least some key areas of production and greater control and regulation of the economy. See **Socialism** below.

Existentialists   A term applied to a post-war French group of writers, most notably Jean Paul Sartre, Simone de Beauvoir, and Albert Camus. All three believed that the world was "absurd," that concepts such as "human nature" were to be regarded with suspicion, and that it was people's actions that determined their essence. Existentialists were suspicious of academic philosophies and of systems that placed too much dependence on abstract ideas such as Spirit or Reason or seemed deterministic, thereby reducing individual choices. Other thinkers who came to be labeled existentialists included the German Martin Heidegger and the nineteenth-century philosophers Kierkegaard and Nietzsche.

Freedom   See Chapter 6's section "Debates on Freedom."

Globalization   The process of increasing economic and other types of interconnectedness between the world's peoples and their societies that accelerated rapidly in the final decades of the twentieth century.

Global warming   The warming of the earth that became especially pronounced by the end of the twentieth century, making the 1990s (in the words of one scientific report) probably "the warmest decade of the millennium."

Harlem Renaissance of the 1920s   A New York cultural movement that produced a rich array of works by a diverse group of black writers, artists, social and political thinkers, and musicians (especially of jazz) and actors.

High culture   See **Culture** above.

Imperialism   A country's extension of rule or authority by force or the threat of its use over a foreign territory.

Laissez faire   A doctrine opposed to any significant government regulation of business or private property, especially any that would curtail employers' rights.

Left (left-wing)   A political term used to characterize ideologies including liberalism, socialism, and communism that are more favorable than the Right to government involvement and state aid to assist the lower classes and regulate business. See also **Right (right-wing)** below.

Liberation Theology   A religious belief that arose in Latin America in the 1960s stressing that Christianity needed to reflect a commitment to the poor and to helping them overcome the many social injustices they faced.

Market (or free-market) economy   As opposed to a Soviet-style command economy (see above), in a market economy the production of goods and services are determined primarily by private enterprise and consumer demand.

Mass culture   A term popularized in the late-twentieth century as mass media increasingly shaped the culture of the masses.

Nation   "1. A body of people, associated with a particular territory, that is sufficiently conscious of its unity to seek or possess a government peculiarly its own. 2. the territory or country itself" (Random House Dictionary definition; see Chapter 4's section "Nations and Nationalism").

Nationalism   An emotional loyalty toward one's nation; "an inflamed condition of national consciousness" (see Chapter 4's section "Nations and Nationalism").

Popular culture   As opposed to "high culture," the culture of "ordinary people," especially as reflected in their leisure pastimes and amusements.

Postmodernism   A cultural movement whose exact meaning is often disputed (See Chapter 8), but which generally challenges traditional cultural values and any absolute or objective truths, whether scientific, political, religious, or cultural, thus tending to an extreme relativism.

Progress   An overall improvement of human well-being.

Progressivism   A reform movement in the USA from about 1890 to 1914 that shared many characteristics of western European reforming efforts to limit the socially harmful effects of nineteenth-century capitalism, industrialization, and urbanization.

Right (right-wing)   A political term used to characterize ideologies including conservatism, fascism, and Nazism that are less sympathetic than the Left (see above) to using governmental powers to help the lower classes. See also Left, left-wing.

Self-determination   A principle popularized by U.S. President Woodrow Wilson that suggested that each nationality should have the right to live under a government of its own choice and that boundaries should reflect this principle. Although not applied beyond eastern Europe at the Paris Peace Conference, in the remainder of the 20th century leaders of nationalities wishing to achieve independence often insisted on the right to self-determination, and the United Nations Charter (1945) called for "respect for the principle of equal rights and self-determination of peoples."

Socialism   The term had different meanings in communist and non-communist countries. In communist countries it was perceived as the transitional stage they were in while preparing for a future communist society. Although communist governments such as in the USSR thought they were still in a socialist, not yet communist, stage of development, their systems were usually referred to as communism (see **Communism** above). In western Europe socialism often meant "democratic socialism" (see above).

Snow's "Two Cultures"   A scientific culture and a literary/humanistic culture. Snow bemoaned the lack of communication and understanding between these two cultures.

Sokal Hoax   A hoax perpetrated by Alan Sokal, a New York University physics professor, when he submitted an article to the U.S. journal *Social Text* that was accepted as genuine and printed in 1996, but in reality it was a parody on postmodern deconstructionist thought and use of jargon.

Structuralism   A theory advocated by anthropologist Claude Lévi-Strauss that stated that an objective but unconscious code or structure existed in all societies shaping peoples' language, beliefs, and myths and helping them to understand and explain reality.

Structural violence   The "physical and psychological harm that results from exploitive and unjust social, political and economic systems." See Chapter 1's section "Structural Violence."

Terrorism   The non-governmental use of violence, or threat of its use, for political purposes, but on a lesser scale than a revolution or warfare, whether guerrilla or conventional, civil war or war between nations. See Chapter 1's section "Terrorism before World War I."

Third World Originally a term used to characterize countries not part of the two Cold-War blocs led by the USA and USSR, it later came to mean primarily the less industrially developed nations of Asia, Africa, and Latin America.

Universal Declaration of Human Rights A UN declaration of 1948 that became the basis for numerous future international, regional, and national declarations, conventions, and other agreements. It contained 30 articles which stipulated that people should enjoy not only basic civil and political rights, but also economic, social, and cultural rights.

Welfare state A non-communist state where the government establishes a wide variety of policies, programs, and regulations to assist its population, especially in times of need such as when sick or unemployed. The term was increasingly used after 1946, when Great Britain legislated that its citizens would be eligible for free medical services.

Westernization The adoption of Western techniques, ideas, or customs by non-Western nations or peoples. See Chapter 4's section "Westernization and Its Opponents."

Index

Walter G. Moss obtained his Ph.D. from
Georgetown University and is a professor of
history in the Department of History and
Philosophy, Eastern Michigan University.
He is the author of three Anthem Press volumes:
the second editions of his two-volume *A History
of Russia* (2003–05) and his *Russia in the Age of
Alexander II, Tolstoy and Dostoevsky* (2002).
He has long taught 20th century global history
and has been a co-author of a pioneering
textbook on the subject, which first appeared
in 1983. It is now in its 7th edition under the
slightly revised title *The Twentieth Century and
Beyond: A Global History* (McGraw-Hill, 2007). He
is also a co-author, along with Janice Terry and
Jiu-Hwa Upshur, of *The Twentieth Century: Readings
in Global History* (McGraw-Hill,1998).